Sop.

The Social Democratic Dilemma

To my mother, father and brother

The Social Democratic Dilemma

Ideology, Governance and Globalization

Stuart Thomson

Public Affairs Consultant
DLA Upstream
and
Honorary Research Fellow
University of Aberdeen

First published in Great Britain 2000 by
MACMILLAN PRESS LTD
Houndmills, Basingstoke, Hampshire RG21 6XS and London
Companies and representatives throughout the world

A catalogue record for this book is available from the British Library.

ISBN 0–333–77674–7

First published in the United States of America 2000 by
ST. MARTIN'S PRESS, INC.,
Scholarly and Reference Division,
175 Fifth Avenue, New York, N.Y. 10010

ISBN 0–312–22786–8

Library of Congress Cataloging-in-Publication Data
Thomson, Stuart, 1972–
The social democratic dilemma : ideology, governance, and globalization / Stuart
Thomson.
  p.   cm.
Includes bibliographical references and index.
ISBN 0–312–22786–8 (cloth)
1. Socialist parties—Europe, Western. 2. Socialism—Europe, Western. 3.
Liberalism—Europe, Western. I. Title.
JN94.A979 T46   2000
324.2'172'094—dc21
                                            99–052522

This book is printed on paper suitable for recycling and made from fully managed and sustained
forest sources.

10   9   8   7   6   5   4   3   2   1
09   08   07   06   05   04   03   02   01   00

Printed and bound in Great Britain by
Antony Rowe Ltd, Chippenham, Wiltshire

Contents

List of Tables

List of Figures

Preface

As I find the actions of political parties and politicians interesting and exciting, I expect others to do likewise. Hopefully some of my enthusiasm comes across in this work. The nature of such a piece of comparative analysis means that it develops as boundaries and attitudes constantly shift. There has to be a stage where a line is drawn and the writing becomes 'complete'. For me that was August 1998. The work, I believe, will stand the test of time and can explain how the social democratic parties of Western Europe have developed and will develop.

The work involved constant contact with many of the parties around Europe. Although I was able to claim credit for translating the PS material from its native French, when it came to the PSOE material I must thank my aunt, Sheila Reyes, and cousins Helen and Jayne Reyes for assistance in its translation.

Acknowledgement is due to Cambridge University Press for their permission to use diagrams from H. Kitshelt, *The Transformation of European Social Democracy*, copyright © Cambridge University Press, 1994, and to Oxford University Press for their permission to use diagrams from A. Ware, *Political Parties and Party Systems*, copyright © Oxford University Press, 1996.

This work has been four years in the writing and it has seen me draw on help and support from many people. Financially, the Tenterden Town Council (my home town in Kent) awarded me some funds for my field trip to the 1995 French presidential elections; the Carnegie Trust for the Universities of Scotland made a small award which took me to London; and the Sir Richard Stapley Educational trust made an award which provided me with the means to survive.

Academically, I have benefited from being surrounded by a supportive department and the help of Professor Grant Jordan has been of particular use, but that is not to negate the advice given by others (such as Lynne Bennie, Roland Axtmann and Alasdair McLean). I must also acknowledge the constant support of my supervisor, Byron Criddle.

Personally, the encouragement, support and advice (not always taken) given to me by my mother, father and brother has been invaluable. Others have been there for me along the way, although not all have remained. Thanks to Katrina Bull, Elizabeth Byrne, Helen Stevenson, Jamie Patterson, Marie Patterson, Rob Grant; friends from home – Ed Ross, Ruan Courtney, Jeannette Head, Mark Bains, Julian Abbott; and all at Bruce Miller's, especially Scott Johnston, Arthur Deans and Gordon Ironside.

Subsequently, those at The Rowland Company have helped both myself and my career to develop – especially Jonathan Hopkins, Joe Brice, Tom Franklin, Charlotte Barraclough, Jackie Nixon and Kevin Craig.

List of Abbreviations

ACTU	Australian Council of Trade Unions
AES	Alternative Economic Strategy
ALP	Australian Labor Party
AP	Alianza Popular
APO	Ausserparlamentarische Opposition (extra-parliamentary opposition, Germany)
ATP	National Supplementary Pensions Scheme (Sweden)
CBI	Confederation of British Industry (UK)
CDS	Centro Democrático Social (Portugal)
CDU	Christlich Demokratische Union (German Christian Democratic Party)
CERES	Centre de Recherches et d'Etudes Socialistes (France)
CFDT	Confédération Française Démocratique du Travail
CFTC	Confédération Française des Travailleurs Chrétiens
CGT	Confédération Générale du Travail (French trade union federation)
CGTP	Communist-led trade union federation, Portugal
CNPF	Conseil National du Patronat Français (French employers confederation)
CSU	Christlich-Soziale Union (Christian-Social Union, Bavaria)
DGB	Deutscher Gewerkschatfsbund (German trade union federation)
DLC	Democratic Leadership Council (USA)
DNA	Det Norske Arbeiderparti (Norwegian Labour Party)
EC	European Community
EDA	Enaiaia Dimokratiki Aristera (United Democratic Left, Greece)
EEC	European Economic Community
EFTA	European Free Trade Agreement
ERM	European Exchange Rate Mechanism
EU	European Union
FDI	Foreign direct investment
FDP	Freie Demokratische Partei (German Free Democratic Party)
FEN	Fédération de l'Education Nationale (French teaching union)

FGDS	Fédération de la Gauche Démocratique et Socialiste (France)
FO	Force Ouvrière (French trade union)
GATT	General Agreement on Tariffs and Trade
GDP	Gross Domestic Product
GIS	Group of left-wing intellectuals in the PSP, Portugal
GMC	General Management Committee (British Labour Party)
GNP	Gross National Product
GSEE	Trade union confederation, Greece
KKE	Kommounistiko Komma Elladas (Greek Communist Party)
KKE-es	Kommounistiko Komma Elladas-esoterikou (Communist Party of Greece-Interior)
LO	Landorganisationen (Swedish trade union confederation) Norwegian trade union confederation Danish trade union confederation
MFA	Movimento das Forças Armadas (Armed Forces Movement, Portugal)
MNC	Multinational corporation
MRP	Mouvement Républicain Populaire (France)
NAF	Employers' Association (Norway)
NATO	North Atlantic Treaty Organization
NEC	National Executive Committee (British Labour Party)
ND	Nea Dimokratia (New Democracy, Greece)
NZLP	New Zealand Labour Party
OPEC	Organization of Petroleum Exporting Countries
PASOK	Panellinio Sosialistiko Kinima (Pan-Hellenic Socialist Movement)
PC	Parti Communiste Français (originally Parti Communiste de France)
PCE	Communist Party (Spain)
PCP	Partido Comunista Português (Portugal)
PDS	Partei des Demokratiscen Socialismus (Democratic Socialist Party, Germany)
PDS-DS	Party of the Democratic Left (former Communist Party) (Italy)
PLP	Parliamentary Labour Party (UK)
PP	Partido Popular (reformed right-wing party, Spain)
PPD	Popular Democratic Party (Portugal)
PPI	Progressive Policy Institute (USA)
PS	Parti Socialiste (France)

PSD	Social Democratic Party (right-wing party formerly the PPD, Portugal)
	Partido Social Democrata (Portugal)
PSOE	Partido Socialista Obrero Español (Spain)
PSP	Partido Socialista Português (Portugal)
PSU	Parti Socialiste Unifié (France)
RPR	Rassemblement pour la République (France)
RV	Radical-Liberal Party (Denmark)
SACO	Managerial trade union federation (Sweden)
SAF	Svenska Arbertsgivareföreningen (Swedish Employers' Association)
SAP	Socialdemokratiska Arbetarepartiet (Swedish Social Democratic Party)
SD	(Danish Social Democratic Party)
SF	Socialist People's Party (Denmark)
SF	Socialist People's Party (Norway)
SFIO	Section Française de l'Internationale Ouvrière (France)
SPD	Sozialdemokratische Partei Deutschlands (German Social Democratic Party)
SV	Socialistisk Ventreparti (Socialist Left Party, Norway)
TNC	Transnational Corporation
TUC	Trades Union Congress (UK)
UC	Enosis Kentrou (Union of the Centre, Greece)
UCD	Unión Centro Democrático (Spain)
UDF	Union pour la Démocratie Française (France)
UGT	Unión General de Trabajadores (trade union federation, Spain)
UGT	Trade union federation, Portugal

Introduction

Introduction

For parties on the Left the last twenty years have been particularly difficult. Although some retained their positions of power in national government, they have seen their distinctive views of society and how it operates come under attack. For many these ideas were finally consigned to history by the collapse of the Soviet Union. This is a highly simplistic notion as the social democrats of Western Europe had very little in common with the 'actually existing' socialism of the Eastern bloc. For the democratic Left in Western Europe, the 1980s appeared to be their nadir; only a few of their number were in office and those that were elected carried out governmental programmes that went against the traditional social democratic means and ends. They have been unable to form a coherent intellectual argument against attacks that ensued from the mid-1970s on the central tenets of their belief system. The role played by the welfare state, economic intervention and taxation in the political and economic armoury of social democrats came to be questioned.

The social democratic dilemma in a post-Fordist economy lies in the ability to achieve a more equitable society within capitalism and liberal democracy, without impinging upon consumer choice or entrepreneurial initiative. Advanced capitalism is leading to the breakdown of the institutions necessary to implement a social democratic agenda. Without alternative policies and with a value system being undermined, social democratic parties face an uncertain future.

Electoral performance

As far as popular support is concerned, however, on first examination, the electoral statistics do not seem to indicate any real problem for social democrats in Western Europe (see Figure 0.1 for graphical representations of the parties' electoral results). The parties have been able to maintain their share of the vote or have only declined relative to the strength of their political competitors. Wolfgang Merkl (1992) takes this view as he claims 'there has been no general decline of Social Democracy since the early 1970s',[1] i.e. since the so-called crisis of social democracy began.

What is noticeable, however, is the degree of volatility in the vote of the social democrats in Western Europe, but this again is common to most of the established parties and is not confined to those of the Left. If we examine the level of electoral support obtained by the parties that form this study, it can be noted that those now entering government are doing so on a lower percentage of the vote than they have historically achieved. The British Labour Party at 43 per cent, forming the largest majority it has ever enjoyed in the House of Commons, did so on a lower percentage of the vote than it achieved when it was unable to form a government in the 1950s, and on a lower total vote than the Conservative government achieved in 1992. In France, the PS became the leader of a coalition government in 1997, but on the first ballot gained less of the vote than in 1981 and 1988 when it formed governments. In Greece, PASOK has grown from when it was formed in 1974, but has seen its vote fall from the early 1980s. The Danish and Norwegian Labour parties have both seen their vote fall, as has the SPD in Germany (with a slight recovery in 1994), and the Swedish SAP has recovered slightly after its historically low vote in 1991. In Spain, PSOE's vote continued to decline over the entire period it was in office during the 1980s, so that only in Portugal and Britain has the vote of the social democrats seen a slight recovery, but still at historically low levels. So whereas over a period of time the election results look more favourable, in recent times the social democrats have been on a generally downward spiral and have seen their vote open to large fluctuations. The causes of such volatility are numerous – economic conditions, political scandal, the tactics and policies of opposition parties, length of time spent in office – this does not necessarily confirm a decline of social democracy *per se*.

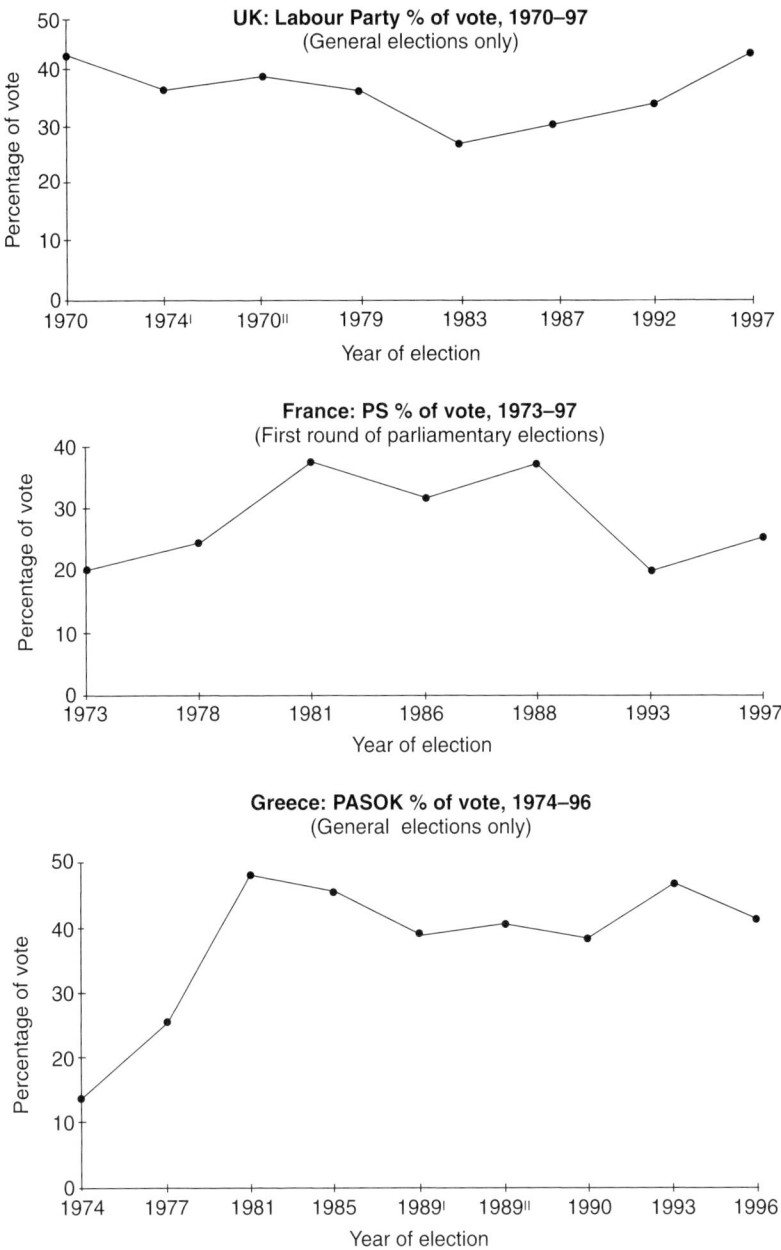

UK: Labour Party % of vote, 1970–97
(General elections only)

France: PS % of vote, 1973–97
(First round of parliamentary elections)

Greece: PASOK % of vote, 1974–96
(General elections only)

Figure 0.1   Electoral statistics of social democratic parties

Portugal PSP % of vote, 1975–95
(General elections only)

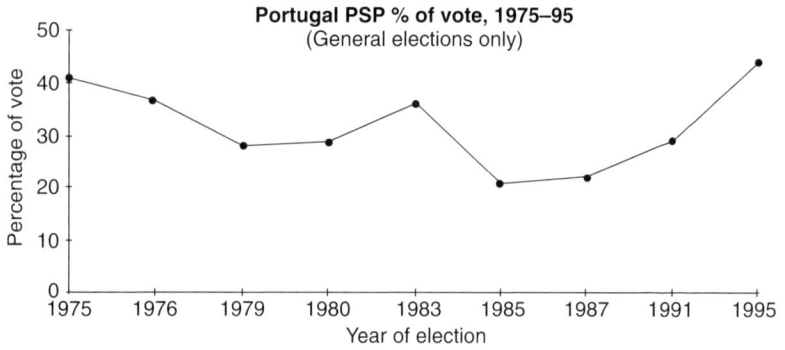

Percentage of vote

Year of election

Spain: PSOE % of vote, 1977–97
(General elections only)

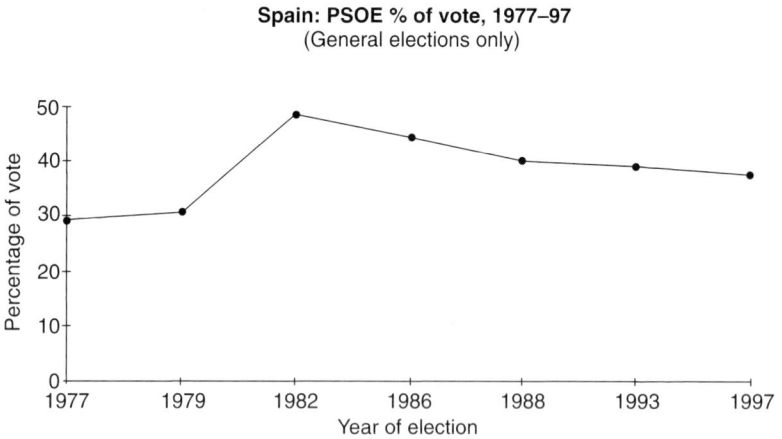

Percentage of vote

Year of election

Germany: SPD % of vote, 1976–98
(General elections only)

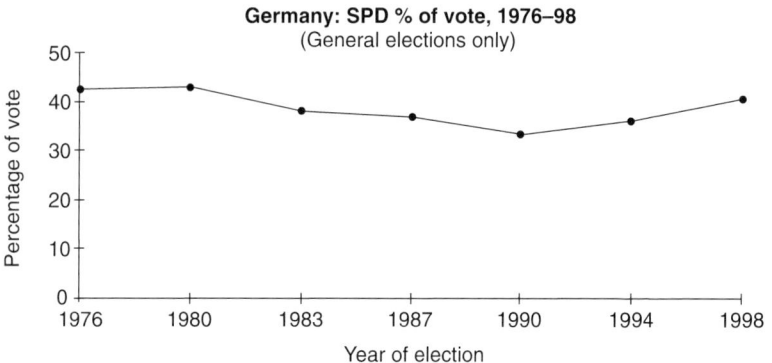

Percentage of vote

Year of election

Figure 0.1   (continued)

Sweden: SAP % of vote, 1976–98
(General elections only)

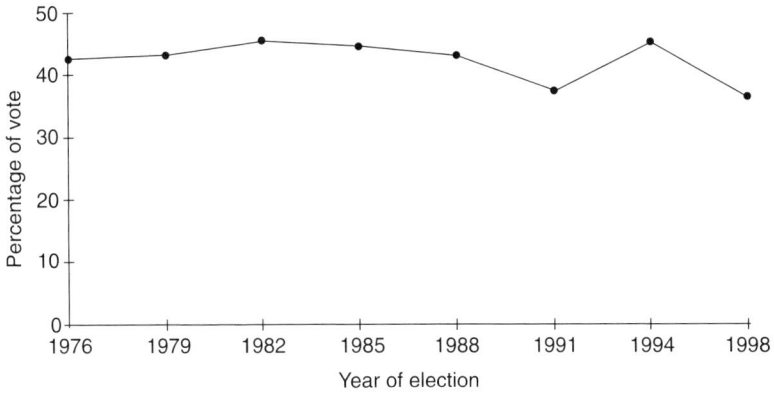

Norway: DNA % of vote, 1973–97
(General elections only)

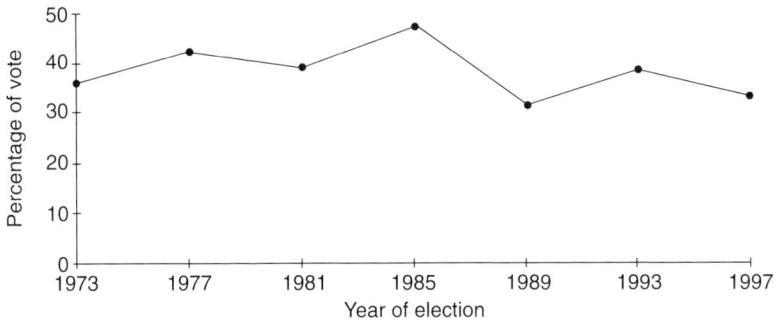

Denmark: SD % of vote, 1973–98
(General elections only)

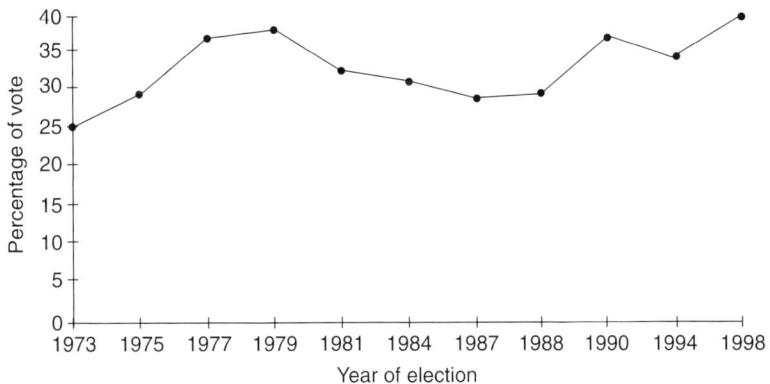

Figure 0.1   (*continued*)

Australia: Labor % of vote,1975–98
(General elections only)

New Zealand: NZLP % of vote,1972–96
(General elections only)

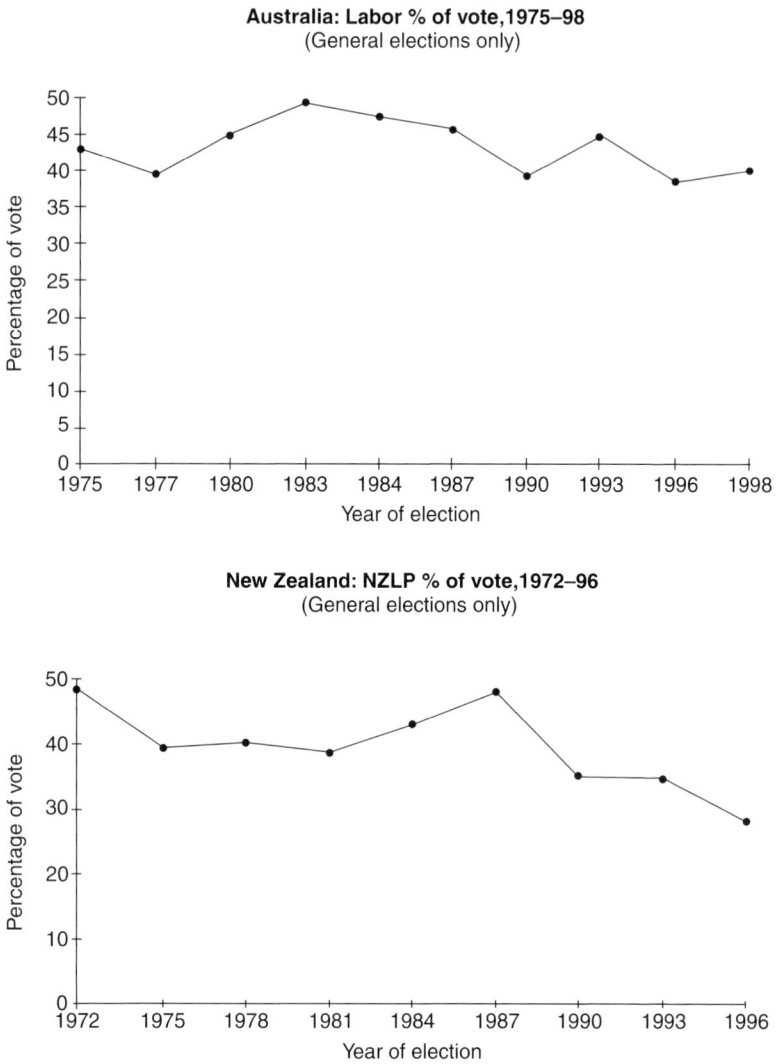

Figure 0.1   (continued)
Source: Adapted from various issues of *Electoral Studies*.

In terms of their positions in government their circumstances have improved since the 1980s, as they formed 13 out of 15 European governments (either on their own or in coalition) by 1998. Most social democratic parties alternate in government with right of centre or 'bourgeois' competitors. For the SAP in Sweden, the breakdown in the former social democratic hegemony is demonstrated by this very alternation.

The aims of this work are twofold:

1 to demonstrate that the major social democratic parties in office in 1998 (13 out of 15 European countries) have undergone a process of change since the mid-1970s and have now become increasingly more neoliberal than social democratic in character (even though they still appear to offer the electorate the benefits of social democracy);

2 to explain why the changes occurred, by reference to the economic and social difficulties the parties encountered.

The work will end by arguing that the changes in the parties have not ultimately been to their advantage, and that they must return to social democratic policies if they are to survive.

The parties have deemed it necessary that they accept the existing economic system, with its labour market flexibility and macroeconomic stability, so as to gain the appearance of competence. Some parties, such as the French PS, maintain a rhetorical commitment to radicalism but this is required by the party system in which they operate. There is also a failure to tackle those concerns that should play an important role, if the parties claim to remain social democratic.

The accepted definition of 'classic' social democracy is ill-suited to the situation in which social democratic parties now find themselves. Yet it was always the case that such a sweeping definition failed to adequately cover differences and nuances between the various parties. It is, therefore, more accurate to consider two varieties of social democracy, Southern and Northern European versions. These idealized types take account of differences in the structures of the countries, the electoral bases of the parties and the types of policies pursued by each set of parties. It becomes apparent that the two types of social democracy differed on such matters as the role of the state, the structures of the parties themselves, and the roles that outside groups played in maintaining the parties and their presence in society.

The 'classic' definition is useful in providing us with an overall framework within which to place these parties, so that we are able to contend that we are considering parties of the same 'type'.

There are a series of authors who have outlined definitions of social democracy but the definition which appears to best summarize 'classic' social democracy is provided by Mark Kessleman:[2]

1 an acceptance of a capitalist economy coupled with state intervention to counteract uneven development;
2 Keynesian economics to achieve full employment;
3 state policies to redistribute economic surpluses progressively;
4 the working class organized in a majority-bent social democratic party closely linked to a powerful, centralized, disciplined trade union movement.

Eric Shaw (1993) provides a checklist of the key features of the 'classic' social democratic model which he employs in relation to the British Labour Party. He defines social democracy firstly mainly in terms of its values, typified by a commitment to equality, as well as social justice and social welfare; secondly, as involving a large role for the public sector, not as an all-powerful commander but more as an overarching body, a saviour of industries; and thirdly, a commitment to state intervention as necessary to prompt the market into behaving in a desired manner, so protecting weaker elements in society and promoting economic growth. Normally redistribution, to give rise to a greater level of wealth equality, would be employed. Fourthly, it involves – usually as top priority – full employment and sustained economic growth; fifthly, the welfare state is seen as crucial to protect and aid those who find it impossible to help themselves (a force for equalization in society based upon need not wealth); and sixthly, as a response to growing problems in the economic sphere, social democratic governments have increasingly employed corporatism – the linking of state, employers and trade unions in a form of social contract.[3]

David Marquand (1993) saw socialism as having five dimensions. Firstly, it involved an ethic which could be summarized in terms of cooperation, commonwealth and fellowship. Secondly, socialism was an economic theory, social ownership being deemed more efficient than the market in which companies would pursue the public interest instead of merely maximizing the returns for shareholders. Thirdly, socialism was a science of society, a movement toward a socialist utopia through a natural evolutionary process; any socialist government was merely aiding the process making the lives of workers more bearable along the way. Fourthly, socialism was a vehicle of social interest 'the instrument, inspiration and mentor of the labour move-ment'.[4] Finally, socialism was a secular religion with its own language, symbols and scripture.

Goodwin's (1989) definition again is of socialism, as opposed to social democracy, but it helps to provide a broad outline for what makes the Left distinct from the Right – its concern with poverty, its class analysis of society, egalitarianism, command ownership of the means of production, popular sovereignty, a belief in human creativity and sociability, cooperation, the idealization of work as unalienated labour, internationalization and the subordination of the individual to society. However, social democracy has a more market-orientated approach, which is willing to work within the confines of the capitalist system, whilst rejecting the morals of the market. It may be the only form of socialism compatible with capitalism.

John Gray (1996) believes that social democracy has come to an end because of economic, social and political changes. He states that its central objectives and policies were:

- the pursuit of greater equality of income and wealth through redistributive tax and welfare policies;
- the promotion of full employment through economic growth;
- a 'cradle-to-grave' welfare state defended as the social embodiment of citizen rights;
- support for and cooperation with a strong labour movement as the principal protector of workers' interests.[5]

Gray also recognizes that variation in the application of social democracy occurred between countries and over time. But its ideal was always 'a form of society-wide egalitarian community of which the workplace com-munity was conceived to be the germ'.[6] All social democratic parties looked to reduce income and wealth inequalities.

What unites social democrats is their value system of equality through social justice and social welfare based around cooperation and community with a form of government that employs collective action. While the policies may vary, these two elements must remain con-stant. The idea implicitly put forward by the above is that there is one definition of social democracy, though this would be to ignore the distinct variations between countries such as the Scandinavian model's success because of the nature of the coalition built in the 1930s around the workers and the peasants, and the British Labour Party's organic link to the trade union movement. Likewise, the French Socialist Party has a set of beliefs which combine to make it an unusual case. John Gaffney (1990) suggests that the PS retains a strong commitment to state intervention and centralized control, along with a belief in strong national defences and a 'romantic relationship to the history of republicanism'. This is also reflected in the party's reference to the 'rhetoric and mythology of liberation'.[7] There was thus a high degree of ideological diversity between each country, and many country-specific factors such as their institutional arrangements.

A series of examples of how social democratic parties, of both the Northern and Southern models have developed illustrates how the traditional model of social democracy became out of date and how a new model has come forward out of the problems that all the countries face. These problems are both internal and external in nature. The internal problems comprise social, economic and political institutions and the constraints which they impose upon the social democratic parties. The internal constraints can also come from political competitors; other political, social and economic actors; the country's institutions; the internal dynamics of the political party; and the personalities involved. External problems mainly concern the economic environment and wider movements on which the parties have little direct influence. These external problems are common between the two models and in many ways are shaping the nature and scope of the internal debate. The shift to a post-Fordist system and neoliberal policies ensures the dominance of external considerations. It must be emphasized that the two sets of problems are not mutually exclusive and there is often overlap between them.

Such external problems as the failure of existing economic policies and the rise of inflation, the onset of globalization, a backlash against taxation and redistributive policies and the growing importance of 'post-materialist' concerns have all contributed to the change in direction for social democracy. Essentially, social democrats have been unwilling to accept arguments which may damage their image of competence and, therefore, their chances of winning power. As a result of these internal and external problems the operation of the 'classic' model of social democracy has ceased to be effective.

European models of social democracy

As a result of the internal and external problems a single 'new' model of social democracy is emerging, on which both the Northern and Southern models are converging. It is an idealized model and represents the direction in which social democracy in Western Europe is moving. Not all the parties are proceeding towards 'new' social democracy at the same speed or are at the same position; the internal constraints for each party play an important role. 'New' social democracy is different from the previous version because it accepts neoliberal economics which run counter to its historic aims of greater equality, the public provision of welfare services and social enhancement. The central tenets of the neoliberal settlement are that 'markets should rule under the guidance of entrepreneurs, with minimal intervention from government; taxes and public spending, and in particular the redistributive effect of direct taxation, should be kept down; and trade unions should have as marginal a role as possible'.[8] It emphasizes the individual at the expense of the collective, rejecting the supreme state power. Less emphasis is given to social considerations and social democracy, therefore, abandons its reforming role, its use of collective goods and prefers instead to concentrate upon provision centred around the individual. The most successful social democratic parties, i.e. those of Scandinavia, have always looked to strengthen capitalism, i.e. to achieve economic growth and company profits, but with an emphasis on social considerations. This has led 'new' social democracy to abandon the tests of 'classic' social democracy – jobs for all, reducing inequality and increasing democratic control over the economy. Country variations still exist, but this does not halt the evolution of the model to a more market-friendly, individualist and less statist approach.

The parties examined in this thesis are all members of the 'Socialist International' and represent a selection from the Northern and Southern models of social democracy. All of the parties have exerted an influence over the shape of social democracy, either through their historical importance or through time spent in governmental office during the 1980s. The parties of the smaller, less influential West European countries have been excluded because of space, and because they share the characteristics of other countries and can, therefore, be placed within one of the two models.

The parties of Sweden, Norway, Denmark, Germany and Britain are the examples employed in the case of the Northern model of social democracy, while Spain, France, Greece and Portugal are taken as examples of the Southern model.

The northern model parties

For the purposes of this thesis Sweden, Norway and Denmark are deemed the most important of the Scandinavian countries. The Scandinavian model has often been highlighted as the most enlightened and advanced of any social democratic movement.

Esping-Andersen (1985) gives a number of shared constitutional characteristics that go towards making up a Scandinavian model including the smooth process of political democratization, the upholding of constitutional rules and parliamentary procedures allowing for an alliance of peasants, farmers and workers, an electoral system based on proportional representation, and the unusually strong linkage between class divisions and the party system.[9]

The peasantry were, as Esping-Andersen claims, the decisive factor in the social democratic breakthrough, and the Nordic outcome 'must be explained by a combination of late industrialization in a somewhat democratic political setting, an independent peasantry capable of allying workers, and benevolent historical circumstances'.[10]

But Norway and Sweden remain slightly different from Denmark and this goes some way to explaining the dominance of the social democrats in those countries. Unlike their Nordic neighbours they have been unable to reformulate their electoral appeal, a move necessary to remain a potential party of government.

All three countries retain distinctive attributes. Although there is a Scandinavian model within Northern social democracy it varies considerably, and in the Danish case has not led to social democratic dominance. More recent economic developments have made consideration of the Scandinavian model less relevant as the traditional linchpins of the model, i.e. centralized wage bargaining structures, come under threat.

The Labour Party in Britain has enjoyed close links with the trade unions making it an important case and slightly different from other parties. The move to New Labour has increased the significance of the party still further.

The German SPD has for many years been viewed as one of the more right-wing social democratic parties in Europe. Its historical significance was ensured in 1959 at the Bad Godesberg party congress when it became one of the first left-wing parties to explicitly reject Marxism and embrace the market. But for the past twenty years the party has been unable to decide upon a consistent electoral strategy.

The southern model parties

The French Socialist Party had historically been very poor at winning elections, especially with the creation of the Fifth Republic. A disparate Left in France with both a Socialist and Communist party fighting elections along with a two-ballot election system and separate presidential elections every seven years meant that neither could hope to conquer. The adoption of François Mitterrand as leader of the reconstituted PS in 1971 proved to be an object lesson in political strategy as he led the party to both presidential and parliamentary victories in the 1980s.

The Spanish PSOE followed a right-wing government into power in the early 1980s, after a long period of dictatorship under Franco. The party's main concern was with consolidating democracy in the country and it placed most other policies around attaining that aim.

In Greece, PASOK offered a version of social democracy that won elections on a populist-nationalist agenda but swung between Keynesian interventionism and neoliberal economics. The culture of the personalization of politics found its nadir in the reign of Papandreou and the highly centralizing influence he exerted over both party and state.

The PSP in Portugal has failed to make major inroads into the political system despite being the first government to take office after the end of the dictatorship. Early election triumphs were not capitalized upon in the 1980s and it took until 1995 for the party to re-enter government.

The social democratic approach

In all the countries the overriding split has been between labour and capital, Left and Right. Although other cleavages have played important secondary roles, such as religion in the case of the Southern European countries, none has surpassed the former. The parties selected also fall into the category of 'Socialist Party' created by Budge, Robertson and Hearl[11] in their examination of election programmes of 20 countries. Their analysis provides the justification for considering that the thesis is concerned with parties of the same 'family'.

Further evidence of the existence of a socialist/social democratic political family is provided by Ware's (1995) use of Klaus von Beyme's *familles spirituelles* and their continued relevance. Ware uses Laver and Hunt's data from the end of the 1980s when they asked experts to locate the positions of party leaders and voters on policy issues. Ware makes use of two of their scales, the role of the state in the economy and the rights of individuals *vis-à-vis* the state.

The first scale relates the leaders' positions on the public ownership of the means of production. 'Where the experts perceived a party as pro-

Socialist and Social Democratic parties

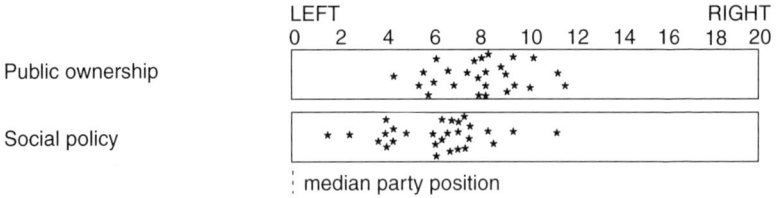

Figure 0.2   Position of socialist and social democratic party leaders

moting maximum public ownership they were instructed to return a score of 1; where they perceived a party to be opposing all public ownership of business and industry they were to return a score of 20.'[12] The second scale considered leaders' positions on social issues. An adherence to permissive policies including abortion and homosexuality scored 1, and total opposition to such policies brought 20. From such an analysis a convergence can be noted around the socialist/social democratic grouping on both scales. On public ownership they were located in the middle of the spectrum, whereas on social issues, while there was slightly more polarization, the parties still adopted a generally liberal position (see Figure 0.2).

The contention is that by merely adhering to neoliberalism they are conceding ground and consigning the values of social democracy to history. The changes to more neoliberal policies by social democratic parties since the 1970s is supported by the primary evidence of recent party documents and publications, including policy statements, election manifestos and programmatic statements, along with interviews. They tend to suggest that the market-oriented, low inflation, low taxation/state spending policies representative of the neoliberal approach are those being adopted by social democrats. Reference to the synthesis of secondary source material sustains this line of argument with the apparent subsumation of social concern beneath economic considerations. As a result of the acceptance of neoliberal policies, social democracy has a number of problems and dilemmas.

The first chapter examines varieties of social democracy, in particular the distinction between Northern and Southern European models. The characteristics of each model are set out in detail and a number of internal problems identified; such problems are directly related to the manner in which each version operated. The chapter also identifies a series of external problems which are common to all social democrats.

Chapter 2 reviews the main published theories about the social and economic failures of social democracy and the manner in which its traditional elements have been undermined. The theories developed to explain these changes can be divided into four categories: economic, political, sociological and institutional, each of which will be summarized and evaluated.

An evaluation of the four types of approach to social democratic failures will demonstrate that economic considerations are at the centre of these problems and that many others arise as a consequence of the economic failures.

The third chapter examines the several national parties comprising the Southern European model of social democracy. France makes up the bulk of the discussion with a brief overview of the development of the Socialist Party, before a more detailed account of its period in office during the 1980s and 1990s under Mitterrand's presidency. The party's subsequent decline and then recovery under Lionel Jospin provides an opportunity to discuss its policy position and actions in government after June 1997. In Greece, Portugal and Spain, it is possible to note a general movement away from policies that emphasized 'socialism' to a more market-oriented, pro-European and financially orthodox approach.

Chapter 4 examines the parties of the Northern European model of social democracy. Sweden provides the main example serving as an illustration of the once dominant, but now declining, position of social democracy. Germany, Denmark and Norway provide additional support in identifying retreats from the Northern model of social democracy and the greater acceptance of the market, pro-Europeanism and financial orthodoxy.

The investigation of each party will be informed by the conclusions from Chapter 2, the examination of the theories for the decline of social democracy. It suggests that it is the economic ideas and policies that largely determine whether social democrats are adhering to an agenda of their own making. Each party's economic policies, therefore, will be examined in terms of its three most important elements. Firstly, on taxation the traditional social democratic approach was one of progressive taxation, with higher rates for higher earners so as to pay for improved social services and increase the level of equality within society, whereas a neoliberal approach looks to reduce taxation to provide incentives to work and entrepreneurial initiative. Secondly, in the past, social democrats would have employed state intervention in order to alter the social and economic conditions of the country. The neoliberal critique of the state suggests that it 'crowds out' the private sector and interferes with the smooth running of the market. The welfare state, instead of being protected, is reduced under neoliberalism to prevent 'crowding out' and avoid disincentives to work. Thirdly, in the labour market social democrats traditionally defended the role of trade unions and collective action. This took the form of collective bargaining for wages, minimum standards in the workplace and the right to undertake industrial action. All these could now be viewed as illegitimate by those who see interference with the operation of the market as constraining economic growth, preferring instead a flexible labour market where wages reflect input more accurately and labour does not enjoy security of tenure.

The data sources used for each country take the form of recent election manifestos and party programmes. Such publications provide both an outline of the aims of the parties as well as a description of the policies they intend to follow. Where possible the policies have been traced over time in an attempt to detect changes in the language employed and the policy proposals.

The fifth chapter comprises a detailed account of New Labour and its development as the party that most accurately represents 'new' social democracy. Shifts in policy positions over time demonstrate that there has been an acceptance of the neoliberal political and economic settlement. This chapter is largely supported by a series of interviews with Labour politicians and specialist commentators or analysts in the area of Labour politics, and enables an examination of the approach of New Labour and of early indications of the time spent in government.

A series of unstructured interviews were conducted from 1995 to 1997 with various individuals (see appendix) whom, it was felt, could throw light on elements of the subject. These were mostly British Labour Party Members of Parliament (MPs), but others' opinion was also sought. Some academics and journalists with a special interest in the subject were interviewed, as were Members of the European Parliament (MEPs). British Labour Party conferences between 1995 and 1998 were also attended.

Chapter 6 describes the 'new' form of social democracy, which emerges from the examination of the case studies. 'New' social democracy retains the values of 'classic' social democracy but has taken note of modern economic, social and political developments so that it may remain attractive to the electorates. The components of 'classic' social democracy and 'new' social democracy are compared, to show that they vary but there are, however, some which they retain in common.

The chapter then provides a summary of the areas in which social democratic parties' actions are failing to coincide with their 'classic' values before going on to examine the record of achievements of those social democrats who held office during the 1980s and 1990s.

The evidence supporting claims that social democratic parties are not behaving in a manner consistent with their aims is borne out by an examination of opinion poll data, which suggests that the citizens of countries under social democratic government do not feel hopeful about the future, by economic data that show that they have not counteracted rising unemployment or inflation, and by spending figures which show a general downturn, or a failure to improve, in areas of social democratic concern.

The opinion poll data is taken from the Eurobarometer series published by the European Commission which tracks attitudes over time in the European Union countries. Swedish census data has also been examined and this, while not covering the same questions as the Eurobarometer surveys, does ask similar ones and this allows for conclusions to be drawn. Economic and statistical data are drawn from the Eurostat series, therefore, guaranteeing consistent measurements of the variable over time.

A further failure is provided by an examination of the United Kingdom's New Labour electoral coalition. As the most advanced party of 'new' social democracy it shows how unstable and heterogeneous its electoral coalition is and the problems the approach has caused with the core social democratic electorate.

The position of the parties of the Australasian countries, Australia and New Zealand, are also given consideration here because they pre-empt many of the changes made, in policy terms, by the Northern parties and because they fit the characteristics of the Northern model.

The Conclusion contains a summary of the thesis and the proposition that social democrats have conceded ground to the neoliberal agenda in order to win office. A model of the influences on social democratic parties is discussed which takes into account the internal dynamics of the parties themselves along with the wider environment such as economic conditions, interest groups and political competitors. The form of social democracy that exists at the present time is no longer a distinctive model and is thus open to hijacking by political competitors. The political evidence and the experiences in each country show that a new approach is required and this is discussed in relation to the new economic setting.

1
Diversity and Change in Models of Social Democracy

Introduction

When authors discuss the evolution of parties of the Left in Western Europe they employ an idealized model which may be termed 'classic' social democracy. This is useful in providing an overall framework within which to place these parties so that we are able to consider parties of the same 'type'. It is, however, misleading because it removes or ignores many of the differences that are evident between the two complementary systems of Northern and Southern European social democracy. While both are social democratic as they share the same basic values and beliefs, the histories and cultures of the countries result in differing organizations of their political systems and parties. So to merely consider 'classic' social democracy is inaccurate.

The chapter explains the nature of the social democratic dilemma before going on to suggest that a more accurate way of viewing social democracy is to consider Northern and Southern European models. These models more accurately reflect the characteristics of the countries and parties involved. Each model is subject to a series of internal constraints that relate to the social, economic and political institutions of the countries. However, both models share a series of economic and political problems which influence the development of social democracy.

The social democratic dilemma

The social democratic dilemma lies primarily in the abilities of parties which hold such values to work within the capitalist system. In the past this meant the abandonment of their revolutionary programmes and the adaptation to capitalist institutions. In some countries the parties split into two competing parties over this issue, leading social democrats into open competition with Communist parties for the same electorate, the blue-collar working class. For those with a Communist perspective the role of social democratic parties has been to undermine the possible achievements of the working class and leave them at the mercy of the exploitative capitalist system.

It can be argued that there is a degree of consistency regarding the social democratic dilemma. When considering Bernstein's challenge to Marx, Peter Gay (1962) recognized the ongoing debate between principles and power. For social democrats this has much to do with the adherence to liberal democratic political institutions which forms a core of their approach. By following this line, it is argued that social democrats have gradually diluted their principles in order to achieve power. This achievement of power is said to enable the parties to implement policies that advance their core beliefs, but it also provided social democrats with access to the power of the state. Without the achievement of a position of governmental power, social democrats would not be able to forward their cause. If the concept of class dealignment is accepted then parties of all types are having to compete for electors who are less inclined to identify with a particular party and are located in the centre of the political spectrum. If neoliberalism has been accepted by the electorate then it could be argued that there has been a shift in attitudes to the right, thereby making the social democratic approach less attractive and causing these parties to further dilute their principles. An additional element, consistent with the past, would be the debate concerning liberty and equality. The two are said to be in conflict meaning that if social democrats advance equality they will necessarily impinge upon the liberty of some. If the example of progressive taxation is employed then it can be seen that those who pay higher rates of taxation have their liberty restricted to advance the liberty of those further down the income scale. Social democracy has, therefore, been open to accusations of 'levelling down' but they viewed this approach as increasing the overall level of freedom. 'In order to find a way of providing the maximum freedom for all men, they had to think in terms of restricting freedom, at least in any sense of the word that resolved itself into the *laissez faire* conception.'[1] This would increase freedom in a system governed by industry.

A highly simplistic summary of the development of social democracy may look to highlight the desire of early social democrats to alter their environment while lacking the tools to do so. During this time they became increasingly concerned with electoral reform which would gain the working classes greater representation. But splits emerged between revisionists and those who sought adherence to Marxist beliefs. There was a gradual realization that socialism was required but *within* the capitalist system, meaning that elections, parliamentary debates, trade union action and cooperative activity were preferable to revolution.[2] By the 1940s/1950s the advent of Keynesian economics (together with the confidence that the Scandinavian social democrats provided to others) provided the policy tools necessary for them to proceed with the social, political and economic alterations they desired. The use of the market was explicitly recognized and accepted by social democrats. However, by the mid-1970s these tools were removed and social democrats lost much of the intellectual confidence they had gained in the immediate postwar era. Social democracy became more defensive and less radical.

However, there have been a series of disjunctures which mean that the dilemma for social democrats in the current period is somewhat altered. If the nature of the electorate is considered (as it is set out in greater detail in Chapter 2) then the previous numerical domination of what could be said to be the core electorate of social democrats, the working class, has come to an end. This makes the adherence to parliamentary means more likely to produce a further dilution of principles. The institutions upon which social democrats came to rely, i.e. welfare states or socialized/nationalized industries, have either come to an end or have been undermined through social, economic or political changes. The intellectual confidence of the postwar era, or the optimism of the early part of the century, have been removed leaving social democrats with limited horizons. Social democracy was seen to have failed by many electorates, hence the long periods out of office for some and the adoption of elements of the neoliberal agenda by the parties. The hope that had existed previously vanished. The triumphalism of Crosland (1956) appeared increasingly hollow.[3] In addition, if the globalization thesis is accepted then the version of capitalism, ownership, business relations and competition that social democrats now face has altered substantially. The dominance of the neoliberal agenda provided an effective victory of desires for liberty over equality, hence the widespread debate centred around a backlash against taxation. The neoliberal agenda also brought industrial considerations to bear against equality in terms of its adverse effects upon entrepreneurial spirit and the operation of the labour market. The environment facing social democrats, therefore, has shifted markedly but it retains some of the old dilemmas.

The abandonment of revolutionary policies meant that social democrats could work within the existing structures and institutions of capitalism. Yet, as has been recognized in recent years, capitalism is not one homogeneous structure but has a number of varieties which operate along the same market-based lines. Each, however, gives a different role to individuals and groups. The role that social democrats adopted was one of gradual reformism. On some occasions the institutions were augmented, i.e. through the provision of a welfare state and the public provision of goods and services. These were normally materially beneficial, and protective, to the working class, and helped maintain public confidence in the state structures. Those social democrats who did well electorally, tended to be those who fulfilled the role of provider to the market. This provision tended to take the shape of a trained and adaptable workforce. The 'left-wing' element of the programme was provided by the equalization of society, i.e. preventing extremes of income and wealth disparities. To do this within the existing state structures meant the use of the taxation system and public service provision. In this manner the working class and the middle class were afforded opportunities to have a share in society. Social democrats also maintained cohesion within the system by bringing labour and capital together in corporatist arrangements.

Disparities in power within society were only given minor consideration, seen as a by-product of the consideration given to wealth and income redistribution, and were not addressed directly. Existing power relations in society remained in place and social democrats attached themselves firmly to parliamentary means to achieve their aims. To disturb the existing power relations would have undermined their ability to bring all sections of society together to follow the reformist ideal. Social democracy was aided by economic growth which ensued after the Second World War, ensuring that finance was available to fund the welfare state. Consensus was possible because of the common aims and objectives of the working and middle classes.

But this historic settlement came to an end with the development of a new era of capitalism. The name employed for this period varies – post-Fordist, late modern – but this shift represents a serious challenge to the programme of social democracy. New forms of competition and the perceived impact of globalization have ended the former stable economic system, which was based upon full-time, male employment in industrial communities with national governments employing the economic levers at their disposal. This new economic environment presupposed a neoliberal view of the world with free markets at the forefront of development.

The new economic environment has affected social democracy in many ways. Firstly, it fragmented the blue-collar working-class core electoral base of social democracy, the work environment of small flexible units being less conducive to the development of a collective conscious and less likely to be welcoming to trade union intervention. The work-place has become more volatile with changes in social mobility, technological change, higher unemployment, the need for people to change occupations several times within their working lifetime, etc. The electorate has become more heterogeneous in nature.

Secondly, the new forms of competition are placing an emphasis on reduced social and labour costs to allow firms to compete competitively. This has led to the recasualization of the workforce and a constant pressure to reduce wage levels and working conditions. Firms consider social costs to be high and, therefore, impinging upon their competitiveness. They prefer these to be borne by the welfare state, but any such shift means that the taxpayer takes the burden. As the costs on taxpayers rise, the level of benefits they gain from the welfare state come into question. This leads on to the third impact, the role played by the welfare state. The new era of economic development suggests that the welfare state acts as a drag on people's aspirations. It holds them in a cycle of dependency and the higher the level of benefits the less likely they are to deem it necessary to find employment. Hence, the scope of the welfare state is called into question. On this, social democrats have not been aided by the common perception that welfare states are bureaucratic and unresponsive. But the more the welfare state is liable to cutbacks, the more the middle class is excluded from it as the eligibility for benefits is tightened. Their exclusion undermines the tax base of the welfare state as they become less willing to pay for falling benefits. This logic suggests that this group could move to private provision to replace the lost insurance that the welfare state once provided, placing further pressure for cutbacks as they become still less willing to pay for a welfare state in which they have little stake. The lower levels of economic growth achieved in this era of economic development also places greater pressure on the tax base to pay for the welfare state. Even the structure of the welfare state is considered, by some, to be unsuited to the flexible labour market that capitalism requires. Fourthly, the flexible labour markets required to allow wages levels to accurately reflect productivity and the scope for discretion required by firms who compete internationally mean that trade unions are viewed as illegitimate actors. Their traditional role of defending the interests, wages and conditions of workers can be considered incompatible with the new era of capitalism which is more conscious of costs. Fifthly, the role of taxation is questioned because of the adverse impact it has on attempts to attract inward investment and on work incentives for employees. Sixthly, redistribution, as it may involve taxation of the better-off sections of society, is, therefore, deemed to be inappropriate. To pursue the equalization of wealth and income in society impairs the workings of markets which rely upon inequalities to act as their dynamic.

The neoliberal agenda is largely incompatible with a social democratic agenda as it undermines the fundamentals of its approach. It challenges the role of redistribution, equality, taxation, the state, trade unions and minimum standards of employment. Most worrying for social democrats is the impact on the welfare state. Welfare state retrenchment effectively means cuts. So the balance between social and economic welfare which existed in the postwar era is moving in favour of the latter.

The impact of many of the above items can be challenged, but their importance is recognized by social democratic parties. The new economic era, more so than past eras of capitalism, does not allow a 'classic' social democratic agenda to be forwarded. The challenge for social democrats, therefore, is to formulate an approach which coincides with the new economic environment. The danger is that such reformism will effectively mean the abandonment of social democratic values in order to maintain the support of the electorate. This is a variant of the power versus principle argument. However, the social democratic dilemma is that the new economic era is leading to the breakdown of institutions necessary to implement a social democratic agenda. Without alternatives and with a value system that is being undermined the path which social democrats are choosing to follow is one of continual compromise. This dilemma can be illustrated by a consideration of the two major models of social democracy, their difficulties and the recent change to a 'new' model of social democracy, detailed in Chapter 6.

Characteristics of the Northern and Southern models of social democracy

Both the Northern and Southern European constructs are themselves ideal-type models and, as a result, are not fully able to track all the differences in every Western European country. Some countries will fit the models more accurately than others. The models are not pure types. The role of the models is to enhance the simplified 'classic' model so that the characteristics of the countries can be more accurately highlighted, even though it is still appropriate to employ 'classic' social democracy as a shorthand for the values and aims of the parties. This was the case in the postwar period, but from the mid-1970s problems began to emerge and the 'classic' model started to break down.

The Northern model

The Northern model of social democracy broadly covers the countries of Northern Europe, the Scandinavian countries, Germany, Austria, Britain and the Benelux countries. The Austrian case is a slightly special one because of its long periods of Grand Coalition rule and the nature of its highly structured and institutional societal and governmental relations.[4] The Northern model's characteristics are laid out below.

Firstly, it involved the existence of a powerful social democratic discourse. Some of the parties were aided by the absence or weakness of a communist presence, but in some countries the communist influence acted as a left-wing anchor. The Left gained legitimacy in the immediate postwar era for standing against Nazism in the Second World War. Whereas social democratic parties in Southern Europe had to compete for this enhanced legitimacy with Communists, this was much less so in the North where the dominant social democratic parties took most of the credit. In this era parties used the state in cooperation with, rather than in opposition to, capitalism, in order to plan the economy and ensure full employment, growth, stable prices and higher wages, and to redistribute. The belief that ownership was the only means of effective control led to the nationalization, or socialization, of key sectors of the economy. This, combined with a growing welfare state, ensured a substantial role for the state in terms of spending, but also provided social democrats with a basis of electoral support.

Secondly, the parties had a leadership, not personalist, approach. The membership of the parties believed that they were able to contribute to policy-making and that the party leadership could be held to account by the members. Rather than having a personalist approach that placed the leader, or leaders, of the party in effective sole charge, they had to make reference to the wider membership.

Thirdly, the consensual nature of the countries led to corporatist decision-making procedures. Labour, business and governments came together in order to fulfil social and economic objectives in a non-conflictual manner. This operated successfully because all the actors concerned wished to achieve similar outcomes. Strong, organized trade unions were recognized as legitimate actors and they worked with business to achieve economic growth which benefited both groups. Social democratic parties viewed one of their roles as being to facilitate this cooperation and to support the market while allowing for their social objectives and values. The parties often had close, if not organic, links with the trade unions. Agreements between the trade unions and these governments ensured unity, a solid base for economic reforms and a high level of penetration of society. The high level of union density made pacts with the social democratic parties in government easier to enforce, as they could ensure implementation, and such corporatist arrangements aided the success of the social democrats' economic policies. The strong civic culture with high levels of association enabled pressure groups, peak organizations and political parties to maintain their strength. This consensually based, corporatist system led social democrats to offer a programme of gradual reformism.

Fourthly, the welfare states had a large element of universal provision of goods, services and benefits. Esping-Andersen (1990) provides a more detailed outline of three varieties of welfare states: liberal, conservative and social democratic. Although the latter two categories can be said to exist in Northern Europe, there has been an underlying trend of solidarity and universalism common to both. This was especially true of the social democratic welfare states of Scandinavia with their extended social rights, where 'the social democrats pursued a welfare state that would promote an equality of the highest standards'.[5] The conservative model was dominated by the preservation of status differentials. The state would provide welfare in place of the market. The redistributive element, while low, helped to preserve traditional family structures. The liberal welfare state is more firmly based upon means-testing and benefits of a moderate level, which 'cater mainly to a clientele of low income, usually working class, state dependants'.[6] Under this model the state openly encourages the use of the market in welfare provision.

The Southern model

The Southern model of social democracy broadly covers Spain, France, Portugal, and Greece. The Italian system shares some of the characteristics of its Southern European neighbours but has much more distinct political institutions and political parties, so in many ways is an uneasy bedfellow. The trajectory of the parties of the Left in Italy and the subsequent creation of the Party of the Democratic Left (PDS-DS) make it a somewhat special case. Yet, in an idealized model, it can be placed in the broad Southern movement. Unlike the other Southern states France did not suffer at the hands of a dictatorship and was more 'advanced'. Many of the characteristics of the Southern model have most relevance to those countries that came out of a period of dictatorship in the 1970s.

Firstly, there was limited social democratic input in the creation of the states, having for the most part been created by fascist or military dictatorships. This was less applicable for countries such as France and Italy, but they had still to overcome a fascist legacy. However, parties of the left gained added legitimacy for having positioned themselves against the dictatorships' state, making them anti-centralist (hence decentralization) and reformist in areas where the state was involved. The practice of clientelism and of making openly partisan appointments, in order to maintain loyalty, was a characteristic of the dictatorships which continued under the new democracies. The political parties retained a dominant position because of the need to consolidate democracy after periods of instability but also as a result of clientelism. Social institutions had to be built, or at least attempts made to build them, in an era of low economic growth, with an economy which required restructuring and with an international political environment which stood against the use of collective institutions. The countries' social networks were largely underdeveloped. With weak or absent union–party links, social democratic ideas and beliefs found it difficult to penetrate society. The social structure consisted mainly of conservative social classes, including a large agrarian sector and a relatively small industrial working class, which undermined moves towards structural change. As a result of the inability of peak organizations to organize themselves effectively, consensus between groups was more difficult to achieve and often broke down.

Secondly, such states had a strong communist tradition which undermined the social democratic discourse and denied socialist parties a monopoly on radicalism. Social democrats were associated with anti-clericalism and a general hostility towards the Catholic church. Catholics, therefore, avoided voting for parties of the Left. Very often there existed competing right-wing parties that reflected their religious position and combined it with a 'social' element. The

Southern model thus involved electoral competition for the Left's 'Marxist' constituency.

Thirdly, the personalization of politics meant that influence lay in the hands of the party leader. This led to the parties being governed in a largely presidential manner with patterns of party management centred around a single leader who enjoyed flexibility, could impose a strategic vision and controlled policy. Strict methods of control within parties ensured that the party either reported directly to the leader or the leader enjoyed patronage within it. Personal attributes can be important in such control, but there may, in addition, be other sources of power such as electoral victory or a close team of personal advisers. The leaders of the parties enjoyed visibility because of the level of media attention. The emphasis on leaders has a historical precedence and is often aided by political institutions, i.e. a presidential system in France aided the subordination of the party. There was a low level of party membership and an absence of trade union links. In a study of Mitterrand, Cole (1994) considers that:

> The study of political leadership, in France and elsewhere, must be appreciated in terms of the interaction between leadership resources (personal and positional) on the one hand, and the constraint imposed and opportunities offered by particular socio-economic and political systems and sets of historical circumstances on the other.[7]

Fourthly, the welfare state remained, in Northern terms, under-resourced. It was based around a system of selective benefits and was more traditionalist, as demonstrated by their reliance upon strong, cohesive family units as the basis of welfare support. In terms of Esping-Andersen's (1990) work the welfare state fitted into his conservative category. The tradition of family dominated, with these groups adopting the role of major edifice in welfare provision.

Fifthly, the desire of the Southern European parties was to achieve 'modernization', to 'catch up' with the more socially and economically developed countries of the North. The parties differed in the ways in which they set out to achieve this goal, but in those countries recovering from a period of dictatorship this modernization was coupled with moves towards the consolidation of democracy. A strong military establishment temporarily attracted resources in the early phase of democratic consolidation, in the former dictatorships, in order to prevent a return to instability.

Internal problems of the Northern and Southern models

Each of the models outlined has a series of specific internal problems. These relate to their social, economic and political institutions and impinge upon the nature of the political debate under each system.

The Northern model

One of the main problems is that the high degree of consensual decision-making in the social, economic and political institutions of these countries reduces the degree of flexibility in the systems, and as new problems arose they were unable to deal swiftly with them. In economic terms the process of corporatism came under attack for its failure to cope with falling levels of productivity and rising inflation. The strong peak organizations involved in producing the consensual outcomes began to divide and came into conflict with one another. It has been argued that social democratic parties under such corporatist systems performed well because of their ability to bring labour and capital together, but that once this ability was lost the parties declined in strength and popularity. The factionalizing of trade unions and the perceived increase in the power of capital meant that these two groups could no longer agree on the way forward as they had been able to do during the golden era of capitalism (approximately the mid-1950s to mid-1970s).

Pressure groups have begun to act as a rival for political parties in terms of members. The falling levels of membership for political parties has heightened awareness of the collective action problem. This problem centres around the unwillingness of individuals to participate in campaigning for a political party, although they benefit from the rewards if the party reaches office. Parties, therefore, have always offered a selection of incentives to encourage this participation – material, solidarity and purposive.[8] Some parties have become successful at regaining members, i.e. the British Labour Party, because of the incentives offered to members. It could be argued that the fall in membership has encouraged political parties to increase the movement of power to the leaders and use more media contacts to counter the lack of grassroots activity and the associated adverse impact this may have on the level of the vote.

It has been argued that the presence of trade unions within the parties constrains them in developing new links.[9] These links may be with other social groups and could, therefore, cause conflict with the traditional partner. The trade unions must confront their own problems of legitimacy because of a falling level of membership and increased factionalism between unions. In this sense, trade unions can be seen as a burden upon social democratic parties.

The traditional instrument of Northern European social democratic action, the state, has been increasingly viewed as inappropriate in both social and economic spheres by political parties and neoliberal economists, as its outcomes are not always that which are intended (hence the backlash against state-centred welfare provision). It retains a role, but a much reduced one.

The Southern model

The dominant position of the party leaders meant that their interests and those of the wider party may diverge.[10] The leaders have often abused their position of power so that they acted in a dictatorial manner and this often led to a problem of succession. Personalization revealed a lack of suitable lieutenants, with leaders often working to maintain their positions and prevent the rise of rivals. The clearest example of such actions was Mitterrand's relation to the PS. His use of internal factions, and the personalities which led them, to cement his own leadership in the 1970s continued into the 1980s to prevent a rival from challenging him for the presidency. The zenith of this approach was the 1990 Rennes congress in which the party turned in on itself, as the rival leaders bid for power when it became clear that Mitterrand could not stand for a third term.[11]

Gillespie and Gallagher (1989) suggest that the dominant position of parties, at the expense of competing actors, undermined debate, leading to a 'high level of public cynicism, a low level of participation and low membership of organisations'.[12] Their dominance meant that they controlled the political agenda and the political institutions. The latter was achieved through the continuation of clientelism. Such practices do not appear to coincide with the desires for modernization and democratic consolidation.

There is a perception by some commentators that economic and social progress has been slow. Even after some extended periods in office many of the problems that faced the Southern European countries have yet to be rectified, i.e. the 'underdeveloped' welfare states or the comparatively high levels of poverty. Democratic consolidation may have been achieved, but modernization is far from complete.

The degree to which each party fits into the idealized models varies. However, the models do provide a more accurate reflection of the versions of social democracy that operated in Western Europe from the Second World War until the late 1970s/early 1980s when they began to give way to neoliberalism.

The breakdown of 'classic' social democracy

There was a certain degree of dynamism between the Northern and Southern models, so that each noted lessons from the practice of the other. Just as the Southern countries took note of the collapse of Keynesian economics in the North in the 1970s, the Northern model is taking note of the Southern model's failure to solve economic problems such as unemployment in the 1980s. This has led towards more general agreement between the two formerly competing models[13] and, therefore, to a 'new' model of social democracy that abandons many of the tenets of the past in an attempt to adapt social democracy to the modern economic environment.[14] The Northern and Southern models' solutions and themes are converging to produce 'new' social democracy. There remain nationally specific factors which will always control the options and language employed by each party, but the 'new' model does provide a description of the direction of social democracy in Western Europe at the present time. There are a number of common external problems and constraints, in addition to the internal problems, that have helped to lead along this path of convergence.[15]

End of the economic settlement

The rise of inflation and the associated failure of policies to solve economic problems has been a key element in the 'decline' of 'classic' social democracy. The supposedly successful Keynesian economic policies which social democrats had relied upon since the end of the Second World War could not counteract inflation, and neoliberal economic policies merely lowered it at the expense of other variables such as unemployment. None of the economic policies on offer appeared to provide social democrats with the guaranteed economic growth which they required.

Yet the degree to which the so-called 'golden age' of social demo-cracy, from the mid-1950s to the mid-1970s, was a consequence of Keynesian economics may be questioned. The economies were aided by the international economic environment of the postwar situation: for instance, the use of Marshall Aid by the Americans provided investment in a war-ravaged Europe. It provided capital stock which enhanced the spending capabilities for workers and, as part of the conditions for the Aid, prevented the countries from moving towards a planned economy. Once these problems of production capability had been rectified there was a pent-up consumer demand (because of rationing) to be satisfied so that firms could produce goods which would always be sold, even if they were not of a high quality. Firms earned high profits, and workers enjoyed a rising standard of living.[16] Although Keynesian economics may not have directly enhanced the economic situation, the stable environment and intellectual justification which it provided was of special value.[17] It provided social democrats with a theoretical underpinning for their social beliefs. Firms were able to invest and produce in the knowledge that the government would try to provide a stable economic environment. The rise of inflation and Keynesian economics' inability to deal with it brought to an end this stable environment and with it much of the understanding between firms and government.

With economies moving into recession the traditional core electorate of the social democrats, the blue-collar working class, began to decline in numbers as traditional industries crumbled. It is, however, to be noted that the electoral coalition was never as clearly defined as this, as there were middle-class voters who supported the social democrats, and working-class voters for right-wing parties. But the general point remains clear: the working class was viewed as the core electorate of social democracy.[18] The fall in the numbers of the blue-collar working class also undermined the trade unions as they declined in strength, leaving capital increasingly unopposed. The growth of a service sector, and the associated rise in the white-collar middle class, aided the fragmentation of the trade union base. A proliferation of unions, all with competing aims and interests, splintered the once centralized system ensuring that unions found it increasingly difficult to be an effective partner of government. The fragmented unions found it difficult to adhere to an incomes policy and maintain solidarity in wage negotiations. The resulting inflation further undermined the solidarity in wage settlements. In exchange for unions restraining the wages of their members, the government would offer improvements in the level of the social wage, i.e. higher welfare benefits, changes in the taxation system that would prove beneficial, or improved social services. Unfortunately, in an era of limited economic growth, governments found themselves unable to maintain this position and so the unions did not feel obliged to continue their wage restraint.

The position of women in the workplace also became of increasing importance as their opportunities for work, mainly in the expanded service sector and education, increased. As a result of all the above changes in the workforce the electoral position which social democrats confronted altered rapidly from its original homogeneous full-time, male-dominated, unionized employment situation.

End of the political settlement

Just as the traditional economic settlement collapsed, so did the political settlement. Many of the goods, services and redistributive policies that social democrats delivered relied upon economic growth (which began to falter) and taxation. As taxation rates rose to cover the increased demand for public services and to cover the decline in revenue as growth faltered, the political consensus around taxation began to crumble. Social solidarity and community initiatives, which after the Second World War helped create the hope for a better society bringing people together, faltered as living standards rose and poverty decreased. As individuals, people felt that taxation was too high, whereas as a community they had perceived the benefits.

Yet, the manner in which social democrats delivered equalizing measures primarily through the welfare state came under attack.[19] As part of the taxation backlash, it was viewed as too expensive and, more importantly, not delivering its promised goods. The public sector became a byword for inefficiency and bureaucracy. The role of the state in economic and social matters came under scrutiny; the welfare state was no longer delivering the improvements demanded in the social standards, at the correct price; and state intervention in the economy appeared to merely move economies further away from the position required to attain growth. The state's role in 'second-guessing' the market appeared to come to an end.[20]

Social democrats did not react quickly to the rise of 'post-materialist' issues such as environmentalism and feminism, so their broad appeal was undermined. These concerns gave rise to, mainly environmental, political parties which challenged for the electorate of social democrats but also altered the political landscape by challenging some of the movements' core assumptions: for instance, concepts of the welfare state had always been male dominated in their assumption of male full-time employment and the hierarchical family unit, and the growth in the provision of public services owed much to economic growth the very essence of which was contested by the ecology movement.

Conclusion

Although the definitions of 'classic' social democracy (outlined in the Introduction) provide a useful guide to the aims and values of the social democratic parties in Western Europe, consideration of the Northern and Southern European varieties provides a greater degree of insight into the characteristics of the parties. In the discussions of the two models of Southern and Northern European social democracy, the internal and external problems of each were highlighted.[21] The external problems are common to both but because of the differing characteristics of the models their internal problems differ. It is, therefore, the internal constraints that may help to explain any differences in the courses of development between the Northern and Southern models of social democracy.

A further examination of the social democratic dilemma, the parties' reactions to it, the changes in social democracy and the explanations of such change require an elaboration of the parties in the Northern and Southern models.

2
Theories to Explain the 'Decline' of Social Democracy

Introduction

The most appropriate approach when dealing with the many theories put forward for the 'decline' in social democracy is to divide them into four categories – economic, political, sociological and institutional. Each category will be divided into a series of subsections within which the relevant theories will be expounded. The theories will be compared critically so that a synthesis of the four types of approach can be developed. The economic category examines the movements in the economic system; the political offers reasons based upon the actions of actors within a system; the sociological examines some of the changes in class and work categories; and the institutional considers the organization of political systems and party structures. The theories selected form the most influential work concerned with the problems of social democracy. The aim is to draw together the theories so that a synthesis may be determined which sheds greater light on the topic under consideration.

The final synthesis suggests that economic determinants are playing a large role in the development of social democracy. These economic changes are impacting upon the other three categories, so it is a largely economic approach to which social democrats now adhere.

Economic theories

The shift from Fordism to post-Fordism

The nature of capitalism has altered, as we no longer live in a 'Fordist' economy characterized by full-time male employment relying mainly on industrial production. The Fordist economy was typified by a 'mass production and mass consumption society with a high emphasis on minimal unemployment, an active state and a commitment to social democracy and some form of social equity'.[1] This style of system sat with the objectives and the means which social democrats had at their disposal, especially with Fordism's role for government intervention in the market in the pursuit of employment and growth, and a welfare state including education and health in order to achieve greater equity.[2] Fordism entrenched collective solutions through mass consumption and mass production and allowed for agreements between capital and labour.

But as capitalism has 'matured' it has brought with it a series of innovations which have undermined the basis of social democracy to leave a post-Fordist economy that represents a change from full employment, high growth and increased equity to 'the niche production, high unemployment, low growth and hierarchical society' of post-Fordism.[3] In a post-Fordist setting flexibility and a dual labour economy (which place those on paid contracts outside of the remit of traditional wage relations through trade unions) depend upon skills to ensure production; competitive individualism replaces equity; and traditional class relations are thrown into disarray.[4]

Pontusson (1995) demonstrates that the decline of European social democracy can be viewed as a product of two structural-economic changes: (1) the shift to smaller units of industrial production; and (2) the growth of private non-industrial employment.[5] He also suggests that the size of the public sector has a positive impact on the magnitude of social democracy. However, post-Fordism enhances the structural-economic changes and, therefore, reduces the size of social democracy. Crewe (1991) is able to show how the impact of smaller units of production adversely affects social democracy.[6]

Moves towards deregulation and privatization, the encouragement of a business logic, the opening of the economy to foreign competitors, the dealignment of the state and of social democratic parties from organized labour and the view of the role of the state all aided the process of the movement to post-Fordism.[7] The Fordist mode of capitalism allowed social democrats to pursue policies in line with their aims of a more equal society achieved through cooperation based on universal benefits, full employment, state activity and the rights of citizenship in health and education. But post-Fordism is hostile to these aims.

The death of Keynesian economics

Keynesian economics, which provided social democrats with the means to pursue their objectives, effectively ceased to operate after the 1970s. Keynesian economics gave governments the perceived ability to achieve full employment through the deliberate use of fiscal and monetary policies in order to alter aggregate demand in an economy – i.e. through taxes, government expenditure and borrowing.[8] Once it was perceived that these methods could not contend with inflation the focus fell on the need to follow a new line of economic theory. The 'end' of Keynes undermined the confidence of social democrats and left them with few effective policies to achieve their aims.[9]

The Keynesian approach did appear to work well in the 1950s and 1960s but Skidelsky (1979) suggests that 'Keynesianism was perhaps always an unstable, or transitional stage in the control of economics'[10] while Ormerod (1994) puts its success largely down to good fortune.[11]

The role of the United States altered dramatically in the 1970s as it withdrew from its impartial international role to pursue its own economic objectives and this undermined the world economy. In the immediate postwar era America took upon itself the task of leading the 'free' world by preventing Communism from spreading. It did so by providing aid on a massive scale through the Marshall Plan and allowing the dollar to be used through the fixed exchange rate Bretton Woods agreement.[12] The end of the Bretton Woods agreement ended the dollar's dominance in the world's currency markets and undermined economic stability. Just as Britain led the earlier *laissez-faire* world,[13] the 'world Keynesianism' set up in the postwar era was held together by an open US economy. But whereas Britain had an empire to tax and a surplus-producing manufacturing base, the US had neither. Thus its hegemony lasted only around thirty years.

The rise of globalization[14]

Many of the economic changes which have occurred can be seen as a part of the process of globalization. Its impact is said to undermine social democracy because the ability of the nation state to control economic matters has weakened. The term globalization is often widely abused, being employed to suggest that the market is all-powerful and cannot be operated against. Advocates of globalization claim that multinational corporations (MNCs) are able to insulate themselves from the fiscal and monetary policies of government. With multinationals having companies in many countries they can easily switch production between them. These companies can easily play countries against one another in order to gain the best deals. So if a country imposes fiscal measures, a devaluation or other monetary measures, the multinational merely moves to where the environment is more suitable. The hands of government have been effectively tied. 'It is no longer possible to implement socialist policies in an isolated nation state in the modern world economy.'[15]

Some intellectually sound definitions of globalization are provided by Campanella (1993), Held and McGrew (1988) and Camilleri and Falk (1992). Campanella cites the OECD definition of the term globalization, it being dominated by three factors:

1   the entrance of new powerful actors such as the transnational corporations (TNCs) onto the political scene;
2   the rapid diffusion of soft technologies in communication and information;
3   the approval of deregulation policies in several OECD countries.[16]

Held and McGrew see globalization as having two interrelated dimensions 'scope (or "stretching") and intensity (or "deepening")'.[17]

> Social, political and economic activities are becoming 'stretched' across the globe such that events, decisions and activities in one part of the world can come to have immediate significance for individuals and communities in quite distant parts of the global system. On the other hand globalization also implies an intensification in the levels of interaction, interconnectedness or interdependence between the states and societies which constitute the modern world community.[18]

This leaves globalization as a multidimensional process, with its effects said to be evident in economics, politics, the military, cultures, etc. But it must be noted that the impact of globalization is not a uniform process and varies between, and even within, countries.[19] This is because a country's location, its trading partners or its infrastructure will all have an impact.

Camilleri and Falk fully accept the globalization thesis, as they highlight the following features:

> It has taken the stock market crash of 1987 to bring home to many the multifaceted character of economic globalization: the rapid flow of

information made possible by new electronic information systems; the availability of large funds which can be moved from one corner of the globe to another at a moment's notice; and the integration of national economics into 'one increasingly seamless global market'. Techno-logical change, particularly in the field of computers and electronics, has vastly reduced the physical and financial obstacles to global trans-actions and stimulated the creation of a bewildering array of financial instruments which enable investors and borrowers world-wide to trade around the clock and react almost instantaneously to each other's moves. The sharp rise in the velocity of money, the vast capital flows across national boundaries and the complex linkages of the world's leading financial centres are but the most evident symptoms of the rapidly changing economic landscape.[20]

Malcolm Waters (1995) defines globalization as 'a social process in which the constraints of geography on social and cultural arrange-ments recede and in which people become increasingly aware that they are receding'.[21] Peter Jay (1996) suggests that 'recent changes in the organisation of the world economy tend to the result that any entrepreneur anywhere can draw on savings accumulated anywhere and on technologies and managerial skills located anywhere to create a productive unit elsewhere, employing local labour, and selling its products anywhere to everyone'.[22] Paul Kennedy looks to globalization as the 'inter-connectedness of capital, production, ideas and cultures at an increasing pace'.[23]

For the nation-state policies of social democrats, in particular, the downgrading of the state is of great importance. In the world economy 'there is a disjuncture between the formal authority of the state and the spatial reach of contemporary systems of production, distribution, and exchange which often function to limit the competence and effectiveness of national economic policies.'[24] The advance of 'interdependence' between countries undermined the fiscal and interventionist politics of Keynesian economic policies. Financial markets throughout the world can work together, outlawing the use of Keynesian demand management policies because of the undesirability of debt incurred in their implemen-tation. The tax system is undermined by the international mobility of capital and people. Globalization has also impacted upon the ability of trade unions to negotiate for labour, as firms may simply choose to relocate. Governments may still retain formal economic powers but the power of the international financial markets and of private institutions are such that these powers are effectively discredited.[25] If true, this view calls into question the abilities of national governments to influence domestic economic and social policy.

Kennedy is part of the pessimistic school of thought which believes these changes will place billions of workers into the market at wage rates which will make most of the developed world uncompetitive.[26] This will, he argues, lead to a political and ideological backlash.[27] However, Hirst and Thompson consider the whole globalization thesis to be vastly overstated. They point to some evidence of regionalization, especially in Europe, and of inter-national economies but provide data to counteract globalization. This includes the fact that there has been no change in the terms of trade since 1973, signifying no alteration in the structure of trade between countries, whereas under globalization they would have been expected to increase,[28] that there has been a concentration of foreign direct investment (FDI) in the developed countries (US, Europe, Japan) and an absence of truly footloose transnational companies (TNCs). It has also been suggested that multi-national corporations (MNCs) tend to be nationally based. They also contend that much of the consideration of globalization also fails to explain the increasingly decentralized nature of MNCs and the levels of cooperation which exist between them.

Vandenbroucke (1998) provides an important link between the social democratic agenda and globalization claiming that the latter constrains the pursuit of a set of objectives termed 'egalitarian employment policies'. He provides a full exposition of the work of authors in the area[29] and concludes that governments can still follow domestic strategies in successful egalitarian employment policies.[30] Vandenbroucke's exposition of the globalization thesis gives weight to the continued ability of national governments to pursue domestic agendas.[31]

Gray (1998) sees a regime of global economic governance as essential to manage world markets and promote the cohesion and integrity of nation states. He recognizes the instability of a single free-market world economy and the impact it has on workers who bear the cost of technology and free trade. But, Gray claims, the state retains a role in monitoring the impact on the natural environment and in limiting the exploitation of natural resources. The state's other role is in 'preserving and fostering cohesion in society'.[32]

The emergence of varying forms of capitalism

For many years there was considered to be only one type of capitalism. The realization that there is more than one variety has led some advocates of globalization to suggest that one of these varieties, a low-cost, low-tax, individualistic, Anglo-American model is becoming dominant. It is said to be the version most compatible with growing international competition. The other models, Rhennish and Confucian, are claimed to be economically bankrupt because of low growth, high unemployment and unproductive firms. The unseen pressure is, therefore, to follow a more Anglo-American path. This model is the least appropriate for social democracy because of its short-term nature and exclusion of groups such as trade unions whereas the Rhennish and Confucian systems are largely based around a social democratic settlement – employment, inclusion and the restraint of the market.

The theory of 'stakeholding' provides a comparison of the versions of capitalism to enable a critique of the manner in which Britain and other countries, especially America, pursue short-term economic advantage and development. In addition, it offers a set of possible reforms to ensure an economy based around social democratic values. Each model of capitalism is accepting of the central capitalist tenets of the market, competition and profit, yet each operates in a different manner to achieve these outcomes.[33] Stakeholding leans towards Rhenish and Confucian capitalism as they encourage long-term, inclusive decision-making that benefits large swathes of society as opposed to narrow sections. Stakeholding builds on the strengths of each model to derive political and economic reform.

Will Hutton (1997) places an emphasis upon the culture of the country in influencing the style of its markets.[34] The three models differ in the manner in which they treat individuals and collectives. The main conclusion is that for an economy and society to operate effectively and efficiently individuals have to adopt a long-term approach and be actively involved in strong collectives. They may act either as individuals or as collectives, but this still makes them stakeholders in companies and in society. Each organization has a variety of stakeholding groups, but how much value is placed upon them varies in each model.[35] Any decision taken by a firm 'will be informed only if it draws systematically on all those whose information is relevant'.[36] This realization of the worth of employees and of other stakeholders to improve a company's performance provides a key lesson.

Anglo-American capitalism

It is a model which stresses individualism and places firms and their shareholders at the heart of the system, with the profit motive acting as its driving force. Primacy is given to shareholder value with other stakeholders not being considered, leading to a constant requirement to maintain dividends which undermines a company's ability to invest. Social welfare spending is kept to a minimum and this is reflected in low social security contributions, personal taxation and welfare entitlements. The labour market is deregulated to ensure easy movement between occupations and flexibility in terms of cost. Although job creation is high, inequalities are rife. But the model does contain strengths such as liberalism in personal conduct, flexibility of the firm, high levels of innovation and an ability to attract inward investment.

Rhenish capitalism

This version is normally associated with Germany and places the emphasis upon social solidarity and balance. It is statist and bureaucratic, giving greater powers to groups in addition to shareholders. There is a high level of consensus over the desirability of a 'social' element in economic policy. Labour is provided with enhanced powers and works in partnership with management through supervisory boards and works councils. Banks are locally based and build a close relationship with each company by lending long term to allow investment. The welfare system is encompassing, 'a protective social instrument to promote social inclusion, and allow capitalism its much-needed flexibility to build-up and run down industries without worrying about the social consequences'.[37] The political system diffuses power allowing for individual input. Workers and capital recognize each others' legitimacy and this sense of cooperation pervades companies. This version of capitalism is underpinned by a system of legislation.

Confucian capitalism

This third version of capitalism is often termed 'peoplism', because of its high level of labour input and employee sovereignty. It places great emphasis upon loyalty, effort, teamwork, 'trust, continuity, reputation and co-operation in economic relationships'.[38] Social balance takes precedence over the needs of the individual. This system is underpinned by tacit understanding and tradition. Companies know that they have an obligation to the wider society. The state plays a large role in organizing industry and in developing a coherent strategic industrial policy but without owning productive assets. An intricate series of cross holdings exists between banks, industries and companies which helps to prevent collapse and also lessens the fear of takeovers. Fast technical change is enhanced because of employee participation. Welfare provision is left in the hands of the private sector and families.

An examination of the strengths and weaknesses of the systems provides stakeholder theorists with an economic, social and political agenda which involves all citizens. Stakeholding is concerned with involving every citizen. It allows them a social and economic stake through companies and allows for enhanced participation. Individuals must have the power to make an input in social and economic decision-making processes. The two key phrases are empowerment and inclusion. These, it is claimed, will enable firms to operate more competitively, counteract insecurity and fragmentation, and improve social justice.

The realization of a link between societal strength and economic performance suggests that to enable economic growth and development a society must be inclusive. The most effective manner of achieving this is to encourage stakeholder groups to participate in the firm. Politically, they must also have rights and procedures to allow them to voice their position effectively.[39]

Criticisms of economic theories

The categories of economic reasons for the 'decline' of social democracy appear to offer plausible explanation. They illustrate the apparent lack of intellectual confidence demonstrated by social democrats from the mid-1970s onwards. Yet each theory is somewhat deficient and fails to adequately explain 'why' social democrats have adopted policy positions.

The shift to post-Fordism can be viewed as the new phase in the development of the capitalist system and as such social democrats must learn to work within it. Social democratic strength lies in working within the system, so post-Fordism represents a new challenge. It is, therefore, a case of social democratic adaptation just as it was to Fordism.

The perceived death of Keynesian economics presents a more serious problem. It may have been the case that the success of these policies was due to a special and unique period of economic development. But their decline removed the confidence from social democrats that they could alter the economic system to operate on their own terms. However, the death of Keynesianism has been much exaggerated, and the foundations on which it lies may not be dead.[40] It has been suggested that the former hegemonic role of the United States could be fulfilled by the economically integrated European Union.

Globalization appears to offer both opportunities and restrictions to social democrats. It is an ongoing process but the focus of the debate centres around the extent and speed at which it is taking place. But the evidence presented suggests that globalization has been exaggerated and that regionalization is a more important concept. Globalization fails to give great credence to the influences, other than costs, around which investment decisions are based. The institutions of each country and the availability of finance varies and these impact upon the operations of a firm. Globalization also fails to account for the continuation of varieties of capitalism.

Stakeholding provides the justification for the rearrangement of social, economic and political institutions to achieve social and economic advancement. However, neither the Rhennish nor Confucian systems are without problems, such as high levels of unemployment and a perceived lack of flexibility.[41] But it is not the case that one can pick elements at will from the more inclusive societies, even if one could decide which were the most important. Gradual change rather than wholesale adoption should aim to improve a country's system.

The pressure on countries to adopt a more Anglo-American style may involve political implications which clash with their heritage.[42] Stakeholding is also open to criticisms of increasing bureaucracy and of institutionalizing interest groups, especially trade unions. Problems arise over who constitutes a stakeholder and how their input should be made effective. It is also doubtful whether the term is one which has much appeal to the electorate, as is ably demonstrated by the abandonment of the term by the British Labour Party.[43]

Political theories

The collapse of the Soviet Union

Many of the problems which social democrats had were based on being too closely associated with the disgraced and collapsed regimes of the former Eastern bloc and Soviet Union. It is the case that the revolutions discredited socialism in the eyes of many. The Left is still undergoing a period of soul-searching for even it viewed the Soviet system as deeply flawed yet proof that socialism could succeed against capitalism. The collapse left a hole, not only in Europe, but in the ideology of the Left.

The end of history

To Francis Fukuyama (1992) the revolutions proved the complete opposite, that socialism's time was over and the end of history had

come with the triumph of liberal democracy. He claimed that no ideological challenge to liberalism any longer existed. To Fukuyama, all
human societies have a common evolutionary pattern which leads
toward liberal democracy. There have been cycles and discontinuities
(i.e. socialism) along the path to liberal democracy but everybody has
now arrived at that endpoint. Fukuyama states that economic liberalism allows for poorer countries to become rich, the openness of the
economic system allowing them to take advantage and create new
wealth. Inequality is acceptable to Fukuyama, who argues that because
of modern welfare states and social mobility inequality is nowadays
due to the natural distribution of talents.

Fukuyama accepts that the face of the Left has changed, having
moved away from class to other forms of inequalities, i.e. sex and race.
He recognized the absorption, by the Left, of the liberal democratic
agenda by saying if a future left-wing threat were to emerge it would
wear the clothing of liberalism while changing its meaning from
within rather than staging a frontal attack on basic democratic
institutions and principles.[44]

The culture of contentment

J. K. Galbraith (1992) believes that developed countries have their
own elite, the contented. They form a majority of the electorate in
democratic societies and employ that position to further their own
cause. An underclass exists who are essential to perform tasks which
the contented will not do for themselves, the underclass being very
often made up of immigrants and of people who do not vote. Their
concerns are, therefore, marginalized. Any party which advocates the
underclass's concerns, such as the traditional social democratic calls
for redistribution, is doomed to failure. So political parties when
appealing for votes look to the contented rather than the non-voting
underclass.[45] Spending on this underclass is kept to a minimum and a
great tolerance of huge inequality in incomes exists. The individual
pursuit and possession of wealth has replaced notions of the collective. A move away from achieving full employment to achieving low
inflation is another sign of 'the culture of contentment' as inflation
eats into wealth and savings. There is a desire to promote independence in individuals and continuity in families. The easiest way to do
this is to make savings attractive and thus inflation has to be
eliminated. Keynesian economics of tax and spend which, it is
claimed, increases inflation has become a victim of the culture of
contentment.[46]

Galbraith's culture of contentment effectively rules out the prospect of victory for a social democratic party which advocates enhancing the position of the poor. Hence it appears as though the historic mission of social democrats has to be abandoned if they are ever again to gain political office.[47]

The electorate

In the following section, which considers sociological changes as represented by the altered nature of the social democrat electorate, it becomes evident that electoral tactics of social democratic parties had to alter. All of these have had the effect of diluting their traditional policy positions and, therefore, demonstrates the 'decline' of social democracy.

The decline in social polarization has gone hand-in-hand with a decline in political polarization. Kirchheimer's (1990) 'catch-all' party model suggests that due to the affluence of the postwar period and the rise of a consumer-oriented society the political parties had to alter. The 'catch-all' party carries a minimal amount of ideological baggage, has a strong leadership, reduces the role of their membership, avoids specific links with classes or groups and attempts to secure access to a variety of interest groups. For social democrats, the 'catch-all' party model suggests an abandonment of class politics and of policies that do not appeal to the majority of the electorate.

Anthony Downs (1957) is based upon the understanding that the parties and the voters are rational actors who vote/act in accordance with what they see as their best interests. The voters have preferences about the types of policies they want the government to enact and these preferences can all be located on a single, left–right, spectrum. A vote will be gained depending upon the level of benefits that a party can provide to an elector. The parties seek to maximize their share of the popular vote and hence must appeal to a broad spectrum of the population and adopt policies to suit. The parties may make use of ideology to simplify the message to a mass electorate and keep information costs low. In a 'normal' distribution of voters with two parties, both will converge towards the centre to leave parties with few policy differences.

Budge and Farlie (1983) contend that the parties 'own' certain policy areas and that these are the areas upon which they concentrate their resources, meaning that not all policy areas are open to all. Once the electors have decided upon salient issues, support for the political party follows. The political parties, therefore, attempt to make their concerns, i.e. their areas of strength, most prominent in the minds of the electors. By examining a series of election manifestos Budge and Farlie compile a list of policy areas and the type of party (either from the left or from the right) that benefits from each. They suggest that the parties are selective in their choice of issues, leading the electors to decide on which issues are salient and which party 'owns' them:

1   Civil order – bourgeois
2   Constitutional – bourgeois
3   Foreign relationships – erratic
4   Defence – bourgeois
5   Candidate reactions – erratic
6   Government record and prospects – erratic
7   Moral-religious – bourgeois
8   Ethnic – bourgeois
9   Regional – bourgeois
10 Urban-rural – bourgeois
11 Socio-economic redistribution – socialist
12 Government control and planning – bourgeois
13 Government regulation in favour of individual – bourgeois
14 Initiative and freedom – bourgeois.[48]

Electors work along the lines of these categories in order to simplify their decisions, so the saliency of an issue decides the vote. But, according to Budge and Farlie, the only policy area that socialists can call their own is socio-economic redistribution.

It is not the case that a socialist party can adopt the position of the bourgeois party. Budge and Farlie claim that this would merely depress the party's vote rather than enhance it. To abandon a policy position would leave the electorate with the impression that the party was incapable of consistent thought. Socialist parties have to persuade the majority of the electorate that they will benefit and the answer is not simply to 'steal the clothes' of their bourgeois competitors.

The rise of individualism

Individualism is the ethic of neoliberalism and the antithesis of socialism, and as Barry (1988) says it 'is best seen as, both historically and analytically, the generalisation of the case for capitalism to non-economic matters'.[49] 'Individualism represents a desire for, and a belief in the moral superiority of, greater independence – for more control over work, home and social life – which is seen as necessarily rejecting the need to depend on others.'[50] As Barry suggests it is the application of the market to social life. It is often considered that the individual is alien to the Left, but this is a misreading. Policy measures, such as privatization, associated with individual advancement did not fit well with traditional socialist beliefs, but the working-class electorate found them appealing. Although evidence on whether these measures actually lessened votes for the Left is ambiguous,[51] there is no doubting that the culture of Western Europe has moved towards individualism. Related to the loss of faith in Keynes' economic methods, adherents of individualism portrayed taxation as a means of stifling personal initiative and destroying individuality.[52]

Brian Barry sees social democracy as a product of the immediate postwar era in Europe. The common experiences of the war produced social harmony and common expectations. 'The moral basis of the (British) post-war welfare state was laid in the experience of the Second World War and in particular the sense of common vulnerability and interdependence generated by the blitz.'[53] Social solidarity unfortunately diminishes over time leaving those on the left with little basis for support.[54]

The five dimensions of socialism

As presented in a previous chapter, David Marquand (1993) sees socialism as having five dimensions. But to Marquand in practice all that remains of socialism is its ethic, the value of fraternity, fellowship and community. The other aspects have either been invalidated or completed. The economic theory of socialism is not practised anywhere in the world, even by the Chinese who long ago moved to a more market approach. The neoliberal revolution with its associated privatizations has meant that the most a left-wing government is now allowed is the regulation of private companies. The 'social science' of socialism has fared equally badly, its evolutionary nature having been halted and social engineering being considered not only flawed but dangerous and undesirable. Socialism has lost much of its former working-class constituency, and that which remains is considered a liability. Trade unions, viewed as a blockage in the now desirable free market for labour, are seen to cause unemployment. The decline of the working class in absolute numbers has left socialist parties with a shrinking electorate, leaving them to speak the old language of the victims of society to a newly expanded white-collar middle-class electorate. Hence, socialism's power as a secular religion has also declined. But, to Marquand, the socialist ethic remains and appeals to the public.

Post-materialist values

'It has been argued that the increased economic development and prosperity of advanced Western industrialized societies during the past decades has transformed the basic value priorities of succeeding generations.'[55] Hence the rise of new politics of the post-materialist era, many of which compete with social democracy. Technological innovation, changes in occupational structure, economic growth, the expansion in education and the development of mass communications have led to a decline in the legitimacy of hierarchical authority, patriotism, religion, etc. which meant a declining confidence in institutions. At the same time it led to the political expression of new values, i.e. environmentalism and feminism,[56] and a movement away from materialist concerns such as jobs, income and production. The perceived inability of existing parties and institutions to adapt to new causes led those who hold such values to form their own political parties, i.e. the Green Party.

According to Muller-Rommel (1989), 'a radical realization of "new political issues" is beyond the reach of socialist parties.'[57] The core working-class electorate of social democratic parties is traditionally hostile to many of these ideas, but the smaller this core becomes the easier parties find it to adopt the new issues.

After social democracy

John Gray (1996) believes that an advancing social democratic consensus is emerging in Britain but that it is based upon assumptions that are no longer valid. Neoliberal policies and global economic and technological developments have undermined these assumptions. Gray argues that:

- the historical context in which social-democratic conceptions made sense has ceased to exist;
- a communitarian liberal perspective is a natural successor to neoliberalism and social democracy;
- the social-democratic commitment to egalitarian principles must be abandoned and replaced by concern for norms of fairness which are local, in that they dictate different distributions of goods in different contexts or domains, according to the shared social understandings we have of these goods.[58]

Gray sees that the economic policies which social democracy pursued have ceased to be effective because of the release of numbers of skilled workers through the collapse of communism and the disappearance of barriers to the global mobility of capital. The class base of social democracy has gone, it cannot return to its former policies and institutions and the role of national governments has steadily been reduced. Former calls for equality fail to recognize the conflicts among equalities and will only serve to sustain the class system and anti-elitism. Gray goes on to suggest that social democracy has suffered because globalization ends the ability to offer distributional goals, has affected the labour market's conception of community and removes policy levers.

Criticisms of political theories

The political explanations for the 'decline' of social democracy provide a greater insight as to why certain *policies* and *policy areas* were adopted or abandoned. They illustrate the options available to social democratic parties but fail to explain how the changes came about.

The collapse of the Soviet Union, while symbolically important, had little direct impact on social democrats. Fukuyama's *The End of History* is a text of liberal triumphalism and has failed to keep track with recent developments. Many writers have been critical of Fukuyama's 'end of history' argument. Eric Hobsbawm (1992) points out the existence of market-orientated authoritarian states who do well economically and wonders how they fit Fukuyama's model. Miliband (1992) notes unemployment, poverty, the lack of collective services, insecurity, illiteracy and alienation as some harsh internal contradictions in liberal democracies. Fred Halliday (1992) regrets the exclusion of an ecological or feminist perspective from Fukuyama's work, as they are two of the major issues facing the world as it moves toward the twenty-first century. Radhakrishan Nayar (1992) criticizes Fukuyama for failing to give a coherent historical analysis, to treat political ideas with precision or to consider the contemporary scene with realism.[59]

Galbraith's 'The Culture of Contentment' is highly plausible in explaining the perpetuation of inequalities in society and the reasons for the prioritization of certain issues in modern society. However, he does downgrade the possible role of political institutions: for instance, if the electoral system is a proportional one then the 'minority' may well be able to exert a disproportionate influence. Galbraith tends to treat the 'contented' and the 'underclass' as homogeneous blocks which have clearly defined agendas and contain little or no dissent.

On the approaches that parties may adopt, Kirchheimer's 'catch-all' model assumes that all voters are rational and are open to any political party. This explicitly accepts the notion that voters have become dealigned from parties but to some parties their ideology or class basis prevents large-scale movement. Wolinetz (1991) suggests a series of problems for the catch-all model including that voters want ideology, that as ideology falls in importance it is merely replaced by issues and images as the basis for competition, that it changes the nature of the relationship between the party and its members, and that as one party adapts to the model then others will follow.[60] The catch-all model finds it difficult to explain some recent events such as the rise of the ecology ideology.

The 'Economic Theory' as laid out by Downs has several serious flaws and many writers have criticized its key assumptions. Alan Ware (1996) outlines Patrick Dunleavy's criticisms which relate to a party's ability to influence the preferences of voters, that they are not exogenous, which in Downs' model is impossible. Those in government have the opportunity to use the state apparatus through partisan social engineering, altering the position of groups in the social and/or economic order of society to strengthen support for a party and the manipulation of situations to confer partisan advantage.[61]

In addition to the above, Downs' thesis can be criticized because he does not consider the role of party identification, realize that the interests of leaders and activists may not be the same or that politics do not just occur on a left–right spectrum.

David Robertson (1976) criticizes Downs mainly because the adoption of purely vote-maximizing strategies by parties can be questioned as other strategies are available.[62]

The rise of new issue areas is a continuous process, but Budge and Farlie's model of the 'ownership of issues' does not explain how a party will acquire the new issue as their own. There is, in addition, no role for trust in their process, and this is an aspect that political parties are constantly trying to strive for.[63]

The rise of individualism can be viewed as a consequence of the advance of neoliberalism, but the opinion poll data, such as the British Social Attitude Surveys, do not suggest that the ethic of individualism has become ingrained. Barry's perception of the war acting as a channel for collective feelings does not explain how long such emotions last or how to get them to return, if they can.

Marquand's five dimensions of socialism provide a compact guide to the changing nature of the left. However, Marquand fails to highlight, in his dismissal of the socialist economic theory, that the fundamental dichotomy between the state and the private sector still requires to be overseen. The private sector continues to produce outcomes that may not always be socially desirable and does not produce some goods at all. So there will continue to be a role for the public sector in either the provision of goods or in encouraging socially desirable private sector outcomes.

The rise of post-materialist issues has provided another issue area where parties can compete and it is open to parties both of the left and the right. But in an era where increased economic prosperity is meant to have made lives more comfortable, then the continued domination of economic concerns by the electorate requires explanation.

Gray in *After Social Democracy* begins his argument by stating that there is an emergent social democratic consensus yet fails to outline its basis or characteristics. He rejects the application of Rhine capitalism and, therefore, does not allow for the possibility of alterations in market cultures. These have, historically, occurred and to argue that Rhine capitalism is no longer appropriate because of its 'difficulties' is to underestimate its strength, especially in the post-reunification period. Changes may be forthcoming because of exogenous shocks. A serious omission from the work is a more detailed discussion of the role of collectives in the new form of social democracy, which the author advocates, to complement his discussion of equality.

Sociological theories

Alterations in the structure of the electorate

The Left has yet to come to terms with its shrinking electoral base. The working class formed the core electorate for social democratic parties. They were often not large enough to put a party into power on their own, but with some middle-class, or peasant, votes they could do so.

Economic and technological changes, and to some the rise of globalization, exposed traditional industries to new competitors and new forms of competition. As a result of these developments manufacturing industry has crumbled. In this sense globalization can be viewed as a cause of the collapse of the working class.[64]

Western Europe also witnessed the growth of service industries. There has thus been a rise in white-collar middle-class jobs accompanying the decline of the blue-collar working class – both of these developments are illustrated in Table 2.1. This new middle class

Table 2.1   Percentage of economically active population in manufacturing and social services

| | *Manufacturing* | | | | *Community, social and personal services* | | | |
	1960–1	*1970–1*	*1980–1*	*1992–3*	*1960–1*	*1970–1*	*1980–1*	*1992–3*
Denmark	28.5	25.9	17.2	19.9	22.2	24.2	32.0	35.0
France	27.0	25.8	22.3	18.9	20.1	20.1	25.4	27.8
Germany	39.5	37.6	32.7	28.2	18.8	19.0	n/a	26.5
Greece	13.4	17.2	18.7	18.8	12.1	10.8	15.0	18.9
Norway	25.5	26.7	20.2	14.3	18.4	20.2	30.4	37.2
Portugal	23.3	21.7	24.1	23.7	14.6	14.3	19.2	24.1
Spain	17.7	25.4	24.4	19.0	14.1	15.7	16.0	20.0
Sweden	34.2	28.3	24.0	16.8	19.9	26.1	34.0	37.1
UK	34.8	32.4	20.6	18.9	24.3	27.3	23.7	25.5

Source: D. Sassoon, *One Hundred Years of Socialism*, p. 652.

is less likely to vote for a party of the Left and has failed to join the bastions of the Left, the trade unions. The decline in support for trade union membership is shown in Table 2.2. The middle class are less ideological in their approach to politics and more likely to be aroused by certain topics such as green issues, often termed post-materialist issues.[65] So as well as the Left losing its traditional electorate it is attempting to come to terms with the 'new' middle class.[66]

The decline of the blue-collar working class therefore reduced the class identity and culture fostered by the 'close-knit' communities as these disappeared. Greater social mobility weakened the link between home and work, lessening the sense of community. According to some theories of voting behaviour these working-class communities would build up support for the left-wing parties by influencing those around them – a sociological approach. With the end of these communities voters became 'free'.

Class identities have decreased so that there has been a general dealignment of the electorate.[67] The number of those that identify strongly with a political party has fallen, and although some may still feel an allegiance it is not strong enough to prevent them voting for another party at an election. The electorate is more open to outside influences such as image and is, therefore, more volatile.

The rise in dealignment has meant electorates that are more open to influences such as the media, so the manner in which the media

Table 2.2   Trade union density rates in Western Europe, 1970–90

	1970	1980	1990
Denmark	60.0	76.0	71.4
France	22.3	17.5	9.8
Greece	35.8	36.7	34.1
Norway	51.4	56.9	56.0
Portugal	60.8	60.7	31.8
Spain	27.4	25.0	11.0
Sweden	67.7	79.7	82.5
UK	44.8	50.4	39.1
West Germany	33.0	35.6	32.9

Source: D. Sassoon, *One Hundred Years of Socialism*, p. 655.

presents a political party becomes more important. Leaders have to be 'media friendly' as witnessed by the increase in 'spin doctors' who attempt to manipulate the media. Voters do not automatically vote in the manner of their parents or in a way consistent with their upbringing. Issues now exert a greater influence.

The working environment has also undergone a transformation with the rise of female and part-time employment. Most of the increase in female employment has been in the part-time category but Table 2.3 shows that part-time female employment in Western Europe varies considerably. Table 2.4 gives a clearer indication of the increase in female employment, and Table 2.5 shows that it did not occur in the traditional industrial working class. Their participation, therefore, occurred in the non-manufacturing labour force where trade unions are weak, as is left-wing ideology. This change appeared to undermine the basis of the welfare state. It assumed a 'family with a full-time, stably employed male breadwinner with a wife primarily devoted to family social reproduction, and it was assumed that citizens' life-cycles were orderly, standardised and predictable, with little job mobility.'[68]

Whereas the traditional industrial working class acted as a reasonably homogeneous group, the middle class is a more heterogeneous grouping. It contains citizens from a variety of backgrounds and belief structures.

The above illustrates the highly diverse nature of class relations since the 1970s and the difficulty parties, especially of the Left, have in contending with this.

Table 2.3   Women and part-time work, 1992–3

	A: *Part-time employment as a proportion of total employment*	B: *Women's share in part-time employment*	C: *% of women employed in part-time work in the European Community, 1993*
Denmark	9.1	89.1	
France	12.7	83.7	23.8
Germany	14.1	91.0	30.7
Greece	4.8	61.3	8.0
Norway	26.9	80.1	
Portugal	7.2	67.4	10.0
Spain	5.9	76.8	11.9
Sweden	24.3	82.3	
UK	23.5	85.2	43.6

Source: D. Sassoon, *One Hundred Years of Socialism*, p. 659.

Problems with alteration in the structure of the electorate

It is impossible to dismiss the impact that changes in the class structure, the nature of the workforce and the impact of feminization have had on social democracy. But the question of the extent to which class is still an important factor in voting remains. A number of theories of voting behaviour exist, some of which see the electorate as rational, others which view party identification as the prime motive. Each of the theories of voting behaviour has its drawbacks. However, the definition of classes employed can effectively decide whether class remains a

Table 2.4   Women's employment, 1960–81

	Female population (% of total active population)		
	1960–1	*1970–1*	*1981–2*
Denmark	30.8	36.6	44.2
France	34.6	34.9	40.9
Greece	32.8	28.0	27.1
Norway	22.8	27.6	41.4
Portugal	17.7	25.2	35.3
Spain	18.2	19.6	24.8
Sweden	29.8	38.1	45.0
UK	32.4	36.5	38.9
West Germany	37.1	34.9	38.5

Source: D. Sassoon, *One Hundred Years of Socialism*, p. 433.

Table 2.5   **Women's employment in the working class, 1960–81**

	Female working class (% of industrial working class)		
	1960–1	*1970–1*	*1981–2*
Denmark	17.1	15.1	16.9
France	33.3	15.6	16.2
Greece	17.5	14.6	16.8
Norway	11.0	11.3	15.0
Portugal	17.6	23.1	22.7
Spain	n/a	13.3	11.8
Sweden	14.6	16.6	14.5
UK	18.2	18.4	16.1
West Germany	19.7	17.6	n/a

Source: D. Sassoon, *One Hundred Years of Socialism*, p. 433.

statistically valid influence in voting behaviour. One perspective suggests that class voting is dead, whereas another suggests that it is not and it is merely the number of classes that has altered.[69] Heath et al. (1985) reject absolute class voting, preferring instead relative class voting, drawing their evidence from a redefined class structure. They reject the concept of the decline in the level of partisanship among the electorate. Dealignment has a number of explanations but most centre around the increased level of education and the rise in television viewing, both causing increased political awareness. To advocates of dealignment the altered class structure has lessened class consciousness and fragmented class interests. Such changes appear to place more emphasis on the concept of issue voting.

Institutional theories

The state we're in

Will Hutton's book, *The State We're In*, illustrates how the impact of a country's institutions can have consequences in other areas. He builds on the belief that social, political and economic institutions interact with one another to produce a final outcome. If one fails then this adversely affects the others and for any fully functioning society the three have to be in some form of equilibrium. Hutton's thesis is based firmly on the British example. Its political system is malfunctioning, according to Hutton, with monarchical powers in the hands of the ruling party in the House of Commons that can ensure loyalty through its extensive powers of patronage.

Conservatism, Hutton contends, is the natural order in British society and is supported by the monarchy, church, law, City, army, aristocracy. Entry into the elite is only via education or family background. This Conservative tradition manifested itself in a gentlemanly ideal still pursued by the financial institutions. He complains that the Labour Party in government never tackled the social or political order, preferring instead to use the majority position in the House of Commons to pursue a limited agenda. The values of these institutions prevented Labour from ever fully implementing a left-wing programme.

Hutton goes on to describe that the free market ethos has been pushed into all aspects of life and that the trade union reforms undertaken by Thatcher have left workers with no real means of ensuring their protection. He claims that the market revolution has not succeeded in bringing benefits in that area and 'unemployed males are as likely to stay unemployed as they ever were'.[70]

These economic reforms have led to social consequences in what Hutton calls the 30–30–40 society. Thirty per cent of the population are disadvantaged, either out of work or economically inactive. Thirty per cent are marginalized and insecure with poorly protected jobs and few benefits. The rest, the other 40 per cent, are privileged and their market power has risen since 1979 because they are in secure jobs with a high wage. So a majority of the population, 60 per cent, find themselves badly off with an associated loss of civil liberties. The social consequences of the extended scope of markets is most clearly felt in the rise in income and wealth inequality and job security.

Hutton believes that Britain's social and political institutions have affected the manner in which its version of capitalism performs. From the early period of industrialization banks have refused to lend large sums with long-term returns for fear of collapse. Share issues allowed larger sums to be raised by firms but these required high dividends. This system of lending has continued to the present day. It forces firms to look for profits to finance investment themselves.

Hutton helps to explain Britain's failures and also those of social democracy. The British state is a fundamental cause of its economic and social problems and the state is fundamentally opposed to any type of increased intervention or anything that interferes with the running of the market. The City and the Treasury remain the cornerstone of this orthodoxy and, therefore, the centre of anti-social democratic feeling. By illustrating the weakness and flaws of the system Hutton shows that the only way forward for social democracy in Britain is to redesign the British state and bring its financial system up to date.

The transformation of European social democracy

Herbert Kitschelt in The *Transformation of European Social Democracy* (1994) adopts an approach which considers a wide range of issues relevant to a political party. Kitschelt believes that demands for economic redistribution have given way to new ideas, with parties more concerned about production and consumption rather than distribution. His main argument is that the future of social democracy lies in the hands of party leaders and activists. It is mainly internal constraints and competition which shape the adjustment, while class is not so important because new coalitions can always be built.

The decisions that people make concerning politics are shaped by their everyday lives. It is market experiences that have a fundamental effect; an individual will be less market orientated if they rely on a wage rather than profit or interest for income, work in the public sector and are less exposed to competitive pressures, both international and domestic. Those exposed to the global economy are more pro-market and, therefore, support those who advocate this approach. An individual's work environment, i.e. its ability to offer autonomy or enhance communicative skills, will dictate their view of other citizens and of enhanced levels of participation. 'Organisational experiences, then, are not primarily related to people's political dispositions on the distributive, socialist versus capitalist dimension, but to a libertarian versus authoritarian dimension that relates to cultural conceptions of identity and appropriate political collective decision making.'[71] Parties now battle upon left/right beliefs and authoritarian/libertarian beliefs (see Figure 2.1). As world competition increases workers become more hostile to government regulations, but those who 'lose' under the process call for subsidies and protection. Worker solidarity is, therefore, undermined. The degree to which the authoritarian/libertarian alternatives are championed varies with affluence, education, the sectoral composition of labour markets and the welfare state.[72]

Social democratic parties have adjusted themselves so as to move from a moderate socialist and neutral libertarian position to a more capitalist and libertarian one.[73] It is, therefore, apparent that social democratic parties do not choose between a pure class and a cross class strategy but look to mobilize different segments of the working class. The process of strategy choice depends upon the conditions and internal rules of the party but also the language and ideas that have informed the party's past. The more leadership autonomy increases the easier parties can drop the traditional left social and economic policies, Keynes and the welfare

Libertarian politics
(high education, women, symbol
and client processing)

Socialist politics
(public and/or domestic
sector, non-owners)

Capitalist politics
(private and/or internationally
competitive sector, owners)

Authoritarian politics
(low education, men, processing
artifacts and documents)

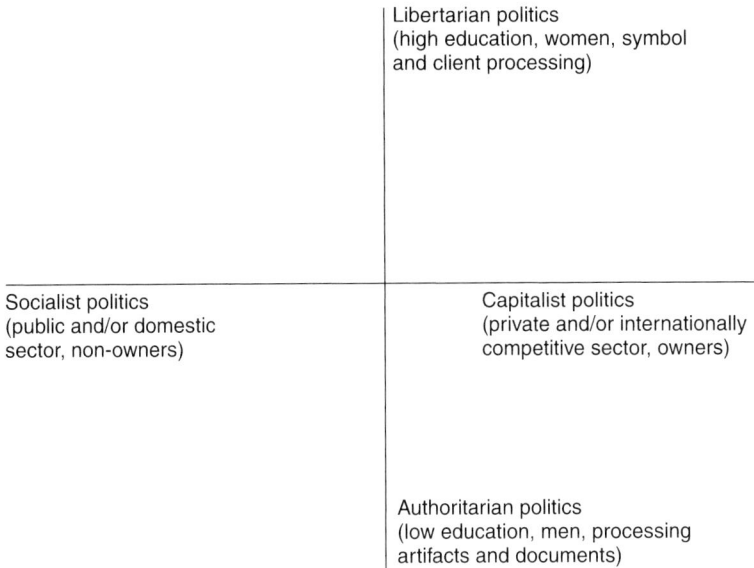

Figure 2.1   The party strategy space
Source: H. Kitschelt, *The Transformation of European Democracy* (Cambridge: *Cambridge University Press*, 1994).

state. The positioning of other parties determines the appropriate strategy for a social democratic party.[74]

Kitschelt believes that social democratic parties must compete on the distributive and communitarian dimensions but that their opportunities lie in advancing positions in the communitarian dimension on regulation, participation and the autonomy of the citizen. Social democratic parties must, above all, redesign their programmes to take account of the desire for individual choice and self-governance. For this to be the case leaderships require greater autonomy and reduced party links with trade unions. They must abandon the specific working-class programmes emphasizing libertarian objectives and market efficiency to build a new coalition.

The 'hollowing out' of social democratic institutions

The political institutions which a party faces in each country will have an impact upon their choice of strategy. A presidential system normally enables a run-off between a candidate of the left and right, placing social democrats as invariably the largest party on the Left. The nature of the electoral system and the number of political competitors will also prove an influence, i.e. a divided Left will constrain the policy options of the social democrats. A proportional electoral system places the leadership of a political party in an enhanced position because of the nature of the electoral competition. A proportional system normally means a structured and centralized party. Being involved in a coalition government is necessarily less effective than operating in government alone. The structures and organization of the state can prove a constraint or an aid to political parties. The Southern European tendency to engage in 'clientelism' ensures little opposition to governmental proposals and a state bureaucracy ready to argue the case of government.

The most dramatic events have been the 'hollowing' out of the social democratic institutions such as the welfare state and trade unions. With right-wing governments in power, or with social democrats pursuing an agenda that is not their own, these institutions have seen the basis of their support removed and been subject to financial cut-backs. Neoliberal economic policies, as outlined earlier, do not see a role for collective institutions. So when social democrats reach government they are helping to undermine sources of their own strength.

Problems with the institutional theories

The institutional theories provide a greater understanding of the environmental and internal restrictions which social democratic parties confront.

Hutton's critique of the British system tracks its development from early industrialization through to the present day. However, critics of his approach highlight the diversity of the British system as one of its key strengths and dismiss his claimed economic results. Much of the criticism of Hutton is couched in populist political terms, that market flexibility has brought more benefits than costs, that he is living in the past, is too pro-trade unions and wants to copy the rigid German system.

Kitschelt's work is of great value because of its comparative nature and its sheer scope. It covers many different areas and sheds much light on the strategic choices facing social democrats and the nature of their electoral environment. Kitschelt places greater emphasis upon the internal decisions and the processes by which they are arrived at than the external economic environment. As a result he places supreme power in the hands of the leadership and downgrades the role of the activists, believing that they cannot make the correct strategic choices and that they limit the flexibility of the leaders. This assumes a membership that plays a very limited role and this would not coincide with the libertarian concerns of the members. The personalization of the leadership may lead to a choice of strategy which is inconsistent with the good of the nation or the good of the party. The outcome should be the selection of a rational electoral strategy; however, it is doubtful whether a single rational strategy would be available. In the case of the voters, Kitschelt assumes a rational choice model of voting, as suggested by Downs, which can be criticized. The role of political messages and appeals is not considered in any great detail.[75]

Conclusion

An examination of theories to explain the decline of social democracy indicates that there can be no mono-causal explanation; rather, by bringing the economic, political, sociological and institutional explanations together it may be possible to fully explain the problems faced by social democracy. However, the driving force behind many of the changes is the alteration in the economic situation. These economic determinants are impacting upon the other categories and are, therefore, shaping the options available to social democrats.

Thus the undoubted changes that are occurring in the economic environment with altered patterns of policies and of physical production and trade lead to an altered political, sociological and institutional environment. Politically it means an altered selection of policy options available to social democrats and affects the desired outcomes of the electorate. The opportunities for social democratic 'success' in office change and the economic environment also impacts upon the values of the electorate. Most noticeable is the effect that economic change has upon the class structure. Recently this has meant the decline in numbers of the blue-collar working class, the rise of the white-collar middle class and the feminization of the workforce. This directly impinges upon the traditional electorate of social democrats and makes their opportunities for electoral success increasingly difficult. Institutionally, the market-driven economic changes have been seen to alter the nature of social democratic institutions such as the welfare state and trade unions. For Kitschelt (1994) the changes have complicated the nature of electoral competition and the nature of the electorate. But, as Hutton's thesis expounds, domestic institutions remain important and political parties have still to operate within them.

However, economic change is not an autonomous process and it has institutional and political imperatives. Political decisions have driven many of the changes in the economic institutions and here it is especially relevant to mention the impact of the neoliberal agenda as demonstrated by Thatcher and Reagan.

By paying attention to the manner in which the social democratic parties respond to the economic environment we should also be able to understand their reaction to political, sociological and institutional changes. Economic policies should, therefore, form the basis of the examination of social democratic parties because of their overlap with other concerns. Economics are driving forward the other changes as the market agenda dominates.

3
The Southern European Model of Social Democracy

Introduction

The characteristics of the Southern model of European social democracy are outlined in Chapter 1. This chapter examines the aims and
policies of social democratic parties in a selection of Southern
European countries. The majority of the discussion will revolve
around a description of the development of the French Socialist Party
(PS). It acts as a party which has made limited moves along the path
to neoliberalism and is relatively constrained by the internal characteristics and institutions of the French system. Therefore, the case of
the PS demonstrates the impact that internal dynamics have and how
constrained some parties find themselves. The PS is particularly
affected by the presence of a Communist Party to its left, a heritage
which is state-centred, and a party structure which for many years
defended the existence of factionalism. The Greek PASOK, Spanish
PSOE and Portuguese PSP are more advanced in their advocacy of
neoliberalism but have also to contend with internal constraints.
Many of these initially revolved around the desire to consolidate
democracy and achieve modernization. This has often led the parties
to be firm advocates of a pro-European Union stance. The early stages
of the development for the parties, in the face of recently defunct
dictatorships, was to pursue radical left-wing policies. These soon gave
way to more market-oriented modernization policies. The perceived
failure of the Northern European model, and the lack of corresponding institutions, led them to adhere closely to the prevailing
orthodoxy which hoped to remove the sclerosis caused by state intervention. Much of the traditional agenda for social democrats in the
postwar period had revolved around extensive state ownership and

public service provision. State ownership had been discredited by the dictatorships and public services were largely undeveloped. So the dictatorships, their actions and policies formed part of the internal constraints upon social democrats.

The discussion of the parties will revolve around the issues identified from the synthesis of the theoretical models in Chapter 2. So economic impacts, how the parties have reacted to them and if they stand against them are of prime importance. This involved a study of the parties' economic policies and of the associated welfare policies. Attempts will also be made to track the development of party thought over the period to demonstrate that the aims and values of the parties have shifted in the direction of neoliberalism, though not all at the same speed or from the same starting point. The conclusion to the chapter contains a synthesis of each of the parties, summarizing both the development towards neoliberalism and the reasons for it.

From the study of the countries it can be noted that the Southern European model of social democracy is accurate in its composition. It can also be seen how important internal constraints can be and how the forms they take can vary.

France

Pre Fifth Republic developments

The electoral victories for the French Socialist Party (PS) in the 1980s marked a return to power after over thirty years, and the first period of office during the Fifth Republic. Many of the problems for the PS in this period were caused by the existence of a rival party on the Left, the French Communist Party (PC). Under the previous regime, the Fourth Republic, the two had worked together, but during the early part of the new period they refused to do so. Not until the 1970s and the election of François Mitterrand as leader of the PS did this situation alter. His rapprochement with the Communists paved the way for a new era in the Socialist Party, in the manner in which it operated and in the nature of French politics and the party system.[1]

The 1936 Popular Front alliance of the Communists and Socialists (with the Radicals) lasted only two years, with Leon Blum as premier.[2] During the Popular Front the Socialists looked to implement substantial social reforms but Johnson (1981) terms it 'a dismal failure'.[3] A similar picture for the Socialists emerged during the Fourth Republic (1945–58).[4]

The Fifth Republic

The advent of the Fifth Republic signalled a period of political stability in France and the 'solving' of the Algerian problem. For the Socialist Party, faced by a powerful de Gaulle installed as President of the new Republic, it meant an extended period out of office and a search for an approach that would allow it to regain national office.

The new two-ballot electoral system did not suit the SFIO and relieved it of its pivotal position in the political system.

After the 1962 approval of the direct election of the President, two strategies began to emerge in the SFIO to regain popular votes. The first was based around Guy Mollet and his wish to preserve the autonomy of the party but with a form of alliance with the Communists, whereas the second, based around Gaston Defferre, considered the way forward as a Third Force which encompassed everything between the Gaullists and the Communists. Mollet's approach was eventually implemented, which meant making contact with the Communists as well as the smaller left-wing clubs which had emerged since the beginning of the new Republic as these groups took the political initiative.

The 1965 presidential election saw this approach come to fruition with Mitterrand as the candidate of the United Left, but with careful distancing from the Communists. By forcing de Gaulle to a second round, Mitterrand proved that this approach was feasible. The following presidential election, 1969, was very much a case of an opportunity missed. The left was not as united because of their uncoordinated responses to the May events of 1968, and many of the leaders were arguing among themselves. The derisory level of the Defferre vote in 1969, 5 per cent, illustrated the need for a more united socialist party. The SFIO had become identified with the failures of the past and its limited achievements, meaning that its image was permanently tarnished. A Congress in July 1969 at Issy-les Moulineaux founded the Parti Socialiste (PS) and Alain Savary became its leader. The approach of the party was to adopt a leftist agenda, and to have no alliances with centrist parties.

It was not until the Epinay Congress in June 1971 that more of the political clubs joined the PS, such as Mitterrand's CIR. Within several days Mitterrand had skilfully managed to become leader, as a result of his ability to make coalitions within the party between Defferre, CERES and his own supporters.

Mitterrand's coming to power in the PS provided it with a pragmatic leader who recognized the importance of working with the Communist

Party in order to gain votes and leave the PS as the major party on the left. With the left-wing CERES group steering the party on its study groups, the party programme eventually arrived at relied heavily upon concepts favoured by the Left. The more important element was not the programme itself, 'Changer la vie', but the bargaining position in which it placed the PS in relation to the PC. Mitterrand aimed to forge an alliance with the Communists to unite the Left, and then move the PC voters across to the PS. The nature of the Presidential system made this approach necessary, favouring a Socialist candidate who could draw a wide range of support in the second ballot.[5] The nature of the two-ballot electoral system also made cooperation sensible in parliamentary elections. Echoing the requirement for unity in order to gain power, the Common Programme brought the PS and the PC under a single banner.

It was to be the 1974 presidential elections that sealed the approach of Mitterrand as the only one that the PS could follow. With the Right divided, the Left put forward Mitterrand as their candidate. He followed a personal campaign and relied very little upon the parties, distancing himself from the Common Programme and the PS. Mitterrand won the first ballot, and came close to beating Giscard in the second round. The last of the major political clubs joined the PS shortly afterwards, the PSU led by Michel Rocard. Their joining the party relieved Mitterrand of his reliance upon CERES for support of the executive of the party, meaning that he could lessen the left-wing element of the party's programme.[6]

After the 1977 municipal elections, the Common Programme had to be updated since, in the opinion of Mitterrand given his new internal coalition, the old draft was too left-wing. The PC came forward with its own updated programme, and it was obvious that the interpretation placed upon the document by the two parties varied enormously. Negotiations failed and 'la rupture' occurred. The result of the 1978 parliamentary elections saw the PS become the largest party on the Left for the first time.

The Mitterrand governments

Mitterrand's candidature for the 1981 presidential election was approved by a special congress which adopted his policy statement, '110 Propositions', which was less left-wing than the PS's 'Projet Socialiste' programme. Mitterrand ran the campaign under the slogan 'Force Tranquille' and was also able to exploit the economic crisis, differing social aspirations and the overwhelming desire for change.[7]

His presidential victory was followed by a parliamentary majority for the PS providing the Socialists with complete control over the central institutions. Mitterrand introduced several PC members into lowly ministerial positions in order to illustrate their subservience to the PS and to ensure that the PC would be associated with all aspects of government policy.

The new government followed a reflationary economic strategy, out of favour internationally at that time and deemed highly radical. Much of French industry and all of the banking system were nationalized, power was decentralized, labour relations reformed, redistribution took place and advances also took place in civil rights. Public expenditure rose at the expense of an expanding budget deficit, while increased consumption occurred because of the higher levels of social security and a higher minimum wage. Investment was encouraged through the use of interest rate subsidies. Employment levels were further aided by the lowering of the retirement age to sixty, a reduction in the working week and tax incentives allowing firms to take on extra staff. Nationalization helped in the plans to decentralize firms and was employed as a tool of industrial policy but, in reality, it helped to boost the government's budget deficit because of the 100 per cent acquisition of capital and undermine its economic policy. But as with nationalizations elsewhere, many of the firms taken over were loss-makers and their structures, responsibilities and finances were all poorly defined and their objectives remained unclear.

The budget deficit grew at a faster rate than expected and the balance of payments deteriorated, a devaluation of the franc of 8.5 per cent against the deutschmark being unable to reverse the situation. The government was forced into a 'U' turn, initially resisted by Mitterrand, and entered a period of 'rigueur'. Further devaluations and a tough package of cuts characterized the phase of *rigueur* and austerity. In this the nationalized industries came to the forefront as the government attempted to streamline these industries. They refused to bail out companies and set them the new objective of becoming competitive on the world stage. Such industrial restructuring was termed modernization and to many commentators such strenuous efforts would have been impossible in the private sector. The reconstruction of firms to improve profitability, productivity and competitiveness went ahead even at the expense of job losses. The government policy shifted from job creation to the control of inflation. State control loosened under a mild form of privatization. From this juncture the PS managed capitalism by presiding over an orthodox economic and social policy.[8] In all areas of society liberalization, commercialization and privatization occurred. This newly implemented orthodox economic policy came from a man who earlier stated that 'anyone who does not accept ... a rupture with capitalist society, cannot be a member of the Socialist party.'[9]

During Mitterrand's second presidential term (1988–93) a minority government led by Michel Rocard followed by Edith Cresson and then Pierre Bérègovoy maintained a favourable economic record with low inflation, steady growth, rising productivity, a strong exchange rate, a moderate budget deficit and a balance of payments surplus by 1992.[10] But on reducing unemployment the PS faltered and after 1992 the French economy slipped into recession with low growth and a rising budget deficit. Economic policy revolved around sound money and price stability, in an attempt to make France competitive with Germany. But the strong franc (*franc fort*) meant high interest rates were required to hold its level, limiting the scope for reducing unemployment.

> What the party promised, up-to-date management with a human face and a European future, differed very little from what a modern centre-right could offer; only its prospectus came shop soiled with rising unemployment, urban insecurity and visible corruption. It is not surprising that the conservative alternative seemed preferable.[11]

That is what the electorate voted for in the 1994 European and, more importantly, the 1993 legislative elections in which the parliamentary PS was reduced to a rump.

In other areas such as foreign policy the PS followed in the Gaullist tradition of a strong France but with Atlantic solidarity and a new Europeanism. De Gaulle's policy of military independence continued in the development of nuclear weapons. Mitterrand took an active role in European development especially during his second term. Two policies which took on prominence in the first administration were decentralization with the *autogestion* programme, and the attempts to secularize the education system. The Savary Bill which was to implement this merely revived the anti-clerical tensions within France. Mass mobilization and demonstrations against the proposals forced Mitterrand to withdraw the proposals.

The constitution, it was thought, was threatened in 1986 when the PS lost the legislative elections to an RPR–UDF coalition meaning that, for the first time, a President of one party would have to work with a government of another.[12] Mitterrand named Jacques Chirac as Prime

Minister and so began the first period of 'cohabitation'. Mitterrand confined himself to being an arbiter in domestic affairs, only becoming involved in areas of public concern, preferring instead to concentrate upon foreign, defence and European matters. He portrayed himself as 'above' politics, promoting the nation beyond all else. This was the ploy he also used in the 1988 presidential election but the following legislative elections did not provide the PS with a majority.[13] The concept of broadening the Socialists' appeal found its voice in the appointment of Rocard as Prime Minister and the inclusion of centrists in his cabinet. Understated reform on a guaranteed minimum income, New Caledonia, education, a wealth tax, reform of the legal system and public sector modernization were often overlooked as Rocard struggled to keep the Socialists in power. From the point that Rocard was replaced by Cresson, Mitterrand's popularity fell. Appointing the first woman prime minister could have been a popular measure but her abrasive style alienated non-socialists, and her unpopularity reflected upon Mitterrand and his political judgement. The regional election of 1992 saw socialist support plummet (18.3 per cent) and Cresson replaced by Bérègovoy. His premiership, only eleven months, was over-shadowed by political corruption and Mitterrand's decision to hold a referendum over the Maastricht Treaty.[14]

The direction of the PS has been, to a large extent, dominated by its internal factions.[15] The internal workings of the party led to intra-party groupings piloted by rival politicians. These politicians battled over personality as disputes, policy, ideologies, strategies and organization were minimal. Each faction supported its leader in his or her battle to become the presidential candidate and/or control the party. With the leadership being elected by proportional representation on the basis of signed resolutions an estimate of faction strength could be made. These resolutions were published, debated, amended and then voted upon. If a resolution gained more than 5 per cent of the activists then its backers gained representation on the Directing Committee which elected the National Secretariat.[16] Mitterrand, from the outset, recognized how to use the factions to his own advantage. In the early stages of the Party's existence Mitterrand allied his own *courant* (the Mitterrandists) with CERES, a left grouping led by Jean-Pierre Chevènement. By the 1975 Pau Congress CERES had grown in strength so felt more able to bargain with Mitterrand but with Rocard's PSU joining, they provided Mitterrand with a new ally, one more hostile to the Common Programme enabling Mitterrand to marginalize CERES. This arrangement lasted until Rocard's criticism of Mitterrand in the run-up to the presidential nomination of

1981. Mitterrand reincorporated CERES to help put down Rocard's propositions at the 1979 Metz Congress. With Mitterrand as president all internal dissent was easily quashed until after 1988 when it became apparent that Mitterrand would not stand again for the presidency. The Rennes Congress of 1990 typified the internal state of the PS as it put on a show of disunity and public retribution which alienated the electorate.[17] The Mitterrand faction had split into two, between those who supported Fabius and those who supported Lionel Jospin. If a clear successor emerged then this would have hindered Mitterrand, so he contributed to the divisions even though this adversely affected the popularity of the party. For the first time no policy statement was agreed. The Special Congress of 1991 was arranged to ratify a new project entitled 'Un nouvel horizon', 'a celebration of long-scorned social democratic reformism'.[18] It was a project to unite behind and importantly it was the first document which had not revolved around Mitterrand. Fabius became party secretary a few weeks later as his faction came into alliance with Rocard's enabling the latter to become the 'natural' presidential candidate. This worked well until the disastrous 1993 general election whereupon Rocard formed a coalition of other leaders to remove Fabius from his position.[19] He promised a new type of PS open to non-socialists, centrists, ecologists and disaffected communists (a strategy which Lionel Jospin pursued in 1997). Rocard's takeover as First Secretary caused Chevènement, leader of CERES, to leave the party, and those on the left became led by Henri Emmanuelli. Further poor election results in the 1994 European elections ended Rocard's chances of becoming the presidential candidate, leaving Emmanuelli to become First Secretary. His more left-wing policy pro- posals were endorsed by the Party at the 1994 Lievin Congress. This programme went against the political beliefs of Jacques Delors, the man thought most likely to be the Socialists' presidential candidate. When he declined to stand for the presidency, the Party was left with no other of equal stature. Emmanuelli and Jospin stood for the nomination with the latter successful in a vote of party members at a special congress providing him with a legitimacy lacked by others.

It is notable from all the above that the PS's programme was devised firstly to make it the dominant party on the left and secondly to allow Mitterrand to become President. The Party was very much dominated by the leadership, as a result of the presidentialization of politics – 'the effective concentration of real power and patronage in the presidency incited each of the party's factions to fall into line behind President Mitterrand's choices, except in a few well-publicised instances.'[20] Mitterrand's position weakened during the second period of cohabitation (1993–5), due to his dissipated power, the Right's large electoral mandate, a small PS presence in the National Assembly, few disagreements with the Prime Minister and ill health which reduced his fighting capabilities. This led to a new leadership coming to the fore to do battle over the presidential nomination.

Trade unions have never held much sway over the PS. They are internally weak, have few members and are badly divided. They are often antagonistic towards one another because of their different political leanings and different economic strategies. This has meant that occasions when they operate together are rare. Their decentralized decision-making processes and the lack of employer cooperation means that corporatism remains unlikely. The measures passed by the PS in the early Mitterrand period met with some trade union approval, such as decentralization and the Auroux Laws, but the economic *rigeur* ensured unemployment and, therefore, weakened the trade unions still further. Relations between the PS and the trade union confederations remain slight.[21]

The Jospin era

The 1995 presidential election provided the Socialist Party with the necessary opportunity to prove that it had recovered from the Mitterrand years and Jospin's position in this was aided by the very low expectations of his chances of winning the presidency.[22]

The danger for the Socialist Party was that the two candidates from the Right would enter the second round and leave no real choice for the electorate, but Jospin's 'C'est clair' (It is clear) slogan and an effective campaign gave him the opportunity to move into the second round. The battles between Chirac and Edouard Balladur enhanced Jospin's appearance as an *homme d'Etat* (statesman), but it was his objective of 'rassemblement' (union) of all socialists[23] and of uniting all progressive forces behind his candidature in a 'New Left' that ensured his, still unexpected, victory in the first round.

Lionel Jospin's presidential election platform, 'Propositions pour la France', was broad in its appeal. It contained many left-wing elements but opened itself to other ideas. In many instances it can be viewed as similar to the 1997 parliamentary agenda in terms of working hours reduction and the rebuilding of French democracy. But it also took up the themes of managerialism. There was an emphasis on the role of the individual and the control of their own lives as opposed to social considerations. These were made less of in 1997. In 1997, the left-wing elements were more 'extreme' and are given greater emphasis.[24] The results of the second round confirmed the great strides that Jospin had made in making the result a close one, but Chirac's most potent weapon was the fear of another seven years of 'socialism'.

The task facing Jospin in the period, after the presidential election in which he had built his reputation was to construct a new French 'third way' for the Socialist Party. According to Pierre Rosanvallon, this 'third way' can be distinguished by four characteristics:

1   a change of generation to be clearly made – with people such as Martine Aubry, Daniel Vaillant (a Socialist deputy in Paris), Bertrand Delanoe (president of the Socialist group on the Council of Paris), Pierre Moscouici (who managed the finances of the presidential campaign and the face-to-face debate), Dominique Strauss-Kahn, Catherine Tasca, Elisabeth Guigou, Catherine Trautmann (Mayor of Strasbourg), Jean-Marc Ayrault (Mayor of Nantes) and Bernard Poignant (Mayor of Quimper) coming to the fore;
2   the split with Mitterrandism to be established;
3   a culture of government to be created along with the image of a project reformer – so that the new project does not just become a rejection of *rigeur*, but of a genuine idea of progress, i.e. practical as well as principled;
4   by his political style, Jospin is innovative – he has an undeniable authenticity and is a 'brilliant' orator. There is little doubt that this style helped to rally the Left around his candidature.[25]

Jospin used his surprise result in the presidential election as a source of legitimacy in the party and acted to move it forward both programmatically and structurally in order to rebuild belief in the use of government, the PS and in politics. Rather than using the factions in the party as Mitterrand had done to obtain his position of power, Jospin created an alliance of 'renovators' as opposed to a faction of his own.[26] His own supporters were placed in key positions of power and the other factions were represented in the leadership but were not permitted to choose their own candidates. The promotion of a new generation of politicians, and of more females in the party through the use of quotas, ensured the diminution of the power of former power-brokers. This was also aided by the 1997 parliamentary election where few of the new deputies aligned themselves to a tendency.[27] The policy review occurred through a series of consultation exercises revolving around three policy committees – European policy, democratic policy and economic policy. Each contained a large membership so as to minimize the arguments, but the most important element to emerge was a more sceptical view towards Europe, with its acceptance but only with conditions.

The reconstruction undertaken by Jospin and the Socialist Party in the years after the presidential election, were very nearly thrown into chaos by President Chirac's early dissolution of the National Assembly in 1997. Despite the large right-wing majority and with the parliamentary term still having another year to run, Chirac decided to renew his party's mandate in the run-up to difficult decisions as France prepared to enter the Single European Currency. By doing so he hoped to catch the Socialist Party unawares and with an incomplete policy programme.

The Socialist Party did produce a manifesto, 'Let's Change the Future', which undermined the first element of Chirac's plan. The Socialist programme had to balance two objectives: to distinguish itself from the right-wing government, and to maintain the support on its left, made more complicated by the importance of the PC. The two left-wing parties at the election issued a suitably vague joint statement. It deliberately glossed over the main issue on which the two did not agree, Europe. The Socialists, for the first time, also agreed an electoral pact with Dominique Voynet's Greens, the largest of the ecology groups. This operated in the same manner as the (mutually desisting) agreement with the Communists.

Chirac's major failing in calling the election was to underestimate how unpopular his government, and in particular Prime Minister Juppé, were. The results of the first round placed the Socialist Party ahead of all the others, up 8 per cent on 1993, despite Chirac's unprecedented use of his office to openly campaign for the RPR-UDF. The second round of voting left France with a third period of 'cohabitation', but the first between a Socialist government and a Gaullist President. Chirac's gamble failed spectacularly as the PS became the largest party in the new National Assembly, gaining 190 seats on 1993, but without enjoying a majority. The Socialist-led government, therefore, relied upon the Communists, the Greens, the radical Socialists and the (ex-Socialist) Mouvement des Citoyens. The Left did well mainly because of the vote-splitting impact of the National Front with their entrance into 132 second-round battles, combined with the unpopularity of the Juppé government.

The 1997 policy programme

The policies on which the Socialist Party fought the 1997 general election were portrayed by the British media as left wing and out of touch with modern thinking. This was not wholly true but, as may be expected, some of the policies were more to the taste of a country still wedded to the power of the state and having the constraining influence of a Communist party. So in building a policy programme the PS had to have a wide-ranging appeal that extended to centrist voters, National Front supporters on the Right and Communist voters to the Left. The two-ballot electoral system and a presidential system makes this approach a prerequisite for winning power. A programme at a presidential election has to be more centrist so as to ensure a wide appeal, whereas for a parliamentary election the programme should be more leftist to ensure that the Communist vote is not alienated.

1997 – 'Change the Future: Our Promises for France'

There were four parts to the election document: change the economy and society; change the everyday life of the French; change Europe; and change our democracy.

Many of the themes were derived from Jospin's attempt to become President in 1995, especially the desire to create employment, solve social divisions and improve the democracy of the country. The three headline policies that were emphasized at the 1997 election were the party's more left-wing elements (as listed below). However, beneath these the Socialist Party built on the policies that they implemented when in government during the 1980s around an acceptance of the market and unhindered international trade. The three headline policies were:

1   a reduction in the working week from 39 to 35 hours per week without any loss of pay;
2   the creation of 700 000 jobs for the young within two years, half financed by the state;
3   four conditions before the Single European Currency should be implemented, following a more sceptical line towards Europe because of the perceived adverse impact on employment.

The creation of employment was that part of the programme that appealed to the whole of the country. State spending was part of the perceived solution but working with the private sector was seen as important. The creation of employment in this sector would be enhanced by the reduction of social deductions on work, i.e. lower social costs and tax rates. Government would cease to increase tax on firms and would subsidize employment in the private sector. Although a wealth tax was advocated, income tax was to fall. There was a belief that the concentration of taxes on middle and low incomes should come to an end.[28] There was deemed 'too much unemployment, too many inequalities, too much tax, too much exclusion... '.[29] The control of inflation and the balance of payments was part of the sound financial set-up that the party wished to pursue, and it claimed that it would not stop enterprises from operating.[30] The idea was to prevent moves to a fully deregulated market system and, therefore, the party rejected the harsh capitalism of the Right. Enhanced intelligence was the way forward in the new economic climate, which meant a greater emphasis upon education. Small businesses and new services needed workers who were innovative, creative and flexible. This required, from the viewpoint of the firm, a fiscal environment that was favourable to investment, risk-taking and saving. Small businesses were placed at the heart of this new logic.

What was more to the Left in the Socialist programme was the role of the state. In some instances it was to aid the equipping of business. But, the PS still believed in the state as a provider of social services and benefits. The emphasis was on a 'better state', not 'more' or 'less' state activity.[31] The quality of public services had to improve. In health there had to be a reduction in the level of waste, but equality of access had to be retained. Although public spending was not given specific mention in the programme, the desire to reduce the public deficit was. The party remained liberal in social policy and promised to cancel the anti-immigration Pasqua-Debré laws.

For many, the four new conditions for achieving entrance to the Single Currency optimized the party's left-wing rhetoric in the election. These conditions were:

1   that Italy and Spain were to be included in the first wave of joiners;
2   that a 'pact of stability and growth' be adopted;
3   that an 'economic government' be set up to counter the European Central Bank;
4   that the Euro should not be overvalued against the dollar.

On privatization the party was to be guided by pragmatism rather than ideology so it was not to be ruled out. Rocard even stated that the party was 'not against the principle of privatization'.[32] What was ruled out were renationalizations.[33]

The Socialist project was intended to play to the realism of the situation in which France found itself. This realism meant that the party promised a public finance audit which would cover all aspects of government spending and a conference on salaries to examine how to implement the party's commitment to lower the working week without affecting wages.

The theme of increased democracy featured highly in the PS's pro-gramme, offering the electors a 'pact of change' to 'renew democracy' and create a more citizen-based state. This was thought to stand well against the inability of the RPR state to counteract the problems of the French system. The impartiality of the state, especially in relation to the operation of the justice system, was deemed important, but justice had to remain accessible. The new democratic state would encourage the capacity for dialogue and enhance plurality.

What is most noticeable about the 1997 programme was its balance between a more left-wing component, required by the presence of the Communist Party, and the need to be seen to offer a modern element. Therefore, the commitment to sound finances, low taxation and state reform was contained in the policies, yet details of how such changes were to be implemented and what form they would take was lacking. There were then the left-wing commitments, with little detail, on the 35-hour working week and the jobs creation programme.

The early period of the 'gauche plurielle' government

The General Policy Statement made by Lionel Jospin to the National Assembly shortly after the victory acted as an indication of the direction that government policy would take.

A proposal for a 'development and stability pact' to reduce unemployment, poverty, insecurity and inequality placed employment as a governmental priority. This would take place through a more social Europe to guarantee 'progress, peace and independence'.[34] If growth permitted, the new government would look to reduce taxes and social security contributions, and there was a keenness to at least stabilize them.

In a later statement to ambassadors (5 September 1997), Jospin gave increased emphasis to the state budget, to get it 'back on to an even keel and bridge the social security gap'.[35] Instead of implementing all the government's left-wing commitments a new promise of a national conference on employment, wages and cutting working hours was announced. Industry would be rationalized and the strong commitment to Europe was given greater credence.

The commitment to involving Europe in the creation of employment was to dictate the French bargaining position at the 1997 European Conference in Amsterdam, but the agreement which Jospin left with was hardly an achievement. In the face of pressure from other countries, the PS's views of employment were merely accepted as an aim, not as part of a definite plan of action. But it was the government's first budget that noted an alteration in its stance. It contained, firstly, a temporary increase in corporation tax from 36.6 per cent to 40 per cent until the end of 1997, with small business exempted. This was viewed as a 'Euro-tax', needed to prepare the country for the financial demands of joining the Single Currency, but it also placed the burden on large businesses which generate profits, without reference to either their investment or jobs. Secondly, income tax concessions promised by the previous Juppé administration for high earners were not reneged upon. Martine Aubry, the Employment Minister, had also accepted the Juppé measures to return to a balanced budget by 1999 at the earliest. Thirdly, state spending was not drastically cut, but instead the approach was one of gradual change, i.e. such as the abolition of the blanket payments of family grants[36] which have become means-tested. Changes to the minimum wage remained limited. 'The 1998 budget demonstrated the government's attempt to balance macroeconomic constraints with clear domestic political choices.'[37]

Although the attacks on big business provided both a scapegoat for France's ills and a basis for support for the Left, it does raise the question of whether these large firms feel able to raise wages, cut working hours and employ more young people, as the government desires. What was less pleasing to the Left were the announcements of the sale of state assets through partial privatizations. The chairman of Air France, Christian Blanc, resigned because the government planned to keep a majority control in the airline. But the trade unions considered strike action at the prospect of even a minority sale of assets to the private sector in France Telecom. The Airbus consortium was also placed on a market footing with its conversion into a 'proper' company. It can be suggested that the consensus-seeking and pragmatism that surrounds union–employer–government negotiations over privatization do change the parameters of the policies. The fact that Jospin is consulting is enough of a change from the style of Juppé to satisfy many of those involved. The government appears largely unwilling to alter its predetermined path during discussions. The costs of creating the 350 000 public-sector jobs would mainly take place in 'proximity jobs', and bring 'locally-based good neighbour services including home care, security, sports training and other activities organised by local authorities, schools and voluntary organisation.'[38] For the other 350 000 jobs in the private sector, it remained unclear as to what those firms would require from the government in terms of flexibility in wages and working conditions.

Denis MacShane (1997) sees three guiding principles behind the Jospin manifesto:

1 a post-ideological politics of governance from the centre, where results count above all;
2 a pragmatic engagement with Europe;
3 the French seeking to modernise their economy and make it globally competitive.[39]

Since being in government the Socialist coalition government has been subject to a series of strikes by workers unhappy with the failure to increase the welfare budget and unemployment benefit in particular. Despite a series of protests throughout the country Jospin made few concessions to maintain peace, claiming that to prepare France for the Single Currency prevented him from increasing public spending. Jospin also partially privatized a number of industries, most notably Air France, reversed his position on the Single Currency while being unable to force other European nations to take his employment proposals seriously, and ran into massive problems over the working week proposals. The impact that the reduction of the working week would have on employment rates was disputed by those who claim that it will lower employment. Although the measure was viewed as the centrepiece of the government's programme and proof of its left-wing credentials, many within the party were sceptical.[40] The bill that was eventually passed by the National Assembly on 10 February 1998 hoped to create between 300 000 and one million jobs by the year 2000, which was an optimistic figure. It did not force businesses to do anything before the year 2000, leaving the details of any agreement to the workers and the companies. Certain categories of workers were to be given extra days off instead of shorter working weeks and the issues of overtime payments would only be addressed in a follow-up bill. Therefore, the bill could be characterized by its vagueness and its business-friendly approach. However, business leaders were so against any changes that Jospin succeeded in alienating the CNPF (main employers confederation). This led to the coming to power of a new CNPF leader, Ernest Antoine de Seillière, who promised to destabilize Jospin's government. This was despite gaining major concessions from the government for business interests at the Conference and it appeared to destroy Jospin's limited attempts to consensus-build.

From the programme, and subsequent developments, it is apparent that the simplistic notion that Jospin was pursuing an old-style social democratic agenda has been shown to be incorrect. Jospin has attempted to move the country, and its state-based mindset, towards what he deems to be 'modernity' and 'the future'. There was an acceptance of much of the programme of the Right, while giving the more left-wing elements additional emphasis. There was a belief in the abilities of the market, and of firms to compete efficiently and unhindered. This was demonstrated by the acceptance of Renault's factory closure plans, even though Jospin initially ruled them out. From placing before the electorate an agenda which was sceptical towards the European Union, Jospin went on to claim a 'full and total commitment' to Europe. The public sector deficit was being reduced, privatizations continued, private pension funds were coming together, public sector wages were being held down, taxation would not increase for the rich and welfare benefits were not to receive any major boost. 'It is all in keeping with the orthodox, monetarist policies pursued by French governments, right and left, over the past fifteen years.'[41] There was pragmatism on the measures first implemented by the Juppé government on health service reform, reducing the size of the armed forces, etc. The new government promised to repeal the Debré-Pasqua laws which were seen by the left as racist measures. But once in government there was only a partial restoration of the *droit du sol* by 'giving automatic citizenship to those born in France from the age of 18, rather than from birth as legislation in place before 1993 had stipulated'.[42] They also failed to reverse the 'double penalty' of the deportation of immigrants if they are convicted of a crime. Even Jospin's view of the United States has changed:

> Contrary to what we (in France) have claimed, and indeed believed, the jobs being created in the United States are not only, or even mainly, low-paid, dead-end jobs, but skilled ones in the service and high-tech industries.[43]

This represents a large shift in the thinking of the PS and Jospin even gave consideration to learning from America's dynamism, the vitality of its research and innovation, its competitive spirit and capacity for renewal.

The PS has been aided in its return to office by the actions of Chirac. His opportunistic policies of the presidential election, splits within the Right over Europe, its proliferation of leaders, his calling of a snap parliamentary election, his actions within the campaign and his attitudes (and those of his former 'coalition' partner the UDF in the aftermath of 1998's regional elections) towards the National Front have all aided the cause of the PS. Jospin was attempting to build a new alliance between the market and the state which retained a social role for the latter. He claimed that there were large constraints but room for manoeuvre still existed. Resources go to the key sectors in the economy, such as education, but with companies being restructured so as to meet the challenges of the internationalized markets. Jospin's main problem lay in making a reformist platform appear attractive in a country where ideologies and 'big ideas' have previously dominated.[44]

Spain

If the ability to form governments is the only criterion of what constitutes a 'successful' social democratic party, then Spain's PSOE would be classed as one of the most successful. Unlike the other social democratic parties in Southern Europe, the PSOE has a long history, being founded in 1879. The party leadership moved into exile during Francoism, but came to the fore once again during the 1970s with Felipe González at its head. The coming of González and his control of the leadership from 1974 signalled changes in policy and in the public's perception of the party.

The 1976 Congress in Madrid (December 1976) illustrated how despite an outlook of realism and a recognition that the consolidation of democracy was the most important battle facing Spain, the party was still prone to rhetorical flourishes of radicalism. It defined the PSOE as a class party and rejected any 'accommodation with capitalism' calling for the socialization of the means of production, distribution and exchange and for 'mass mobilization', with grassroots activity to accompany parliamentary means. The legalization of the PCE and the introduction of universal suffrage represented the 'politics of consensus' in Spain when all the concerned actors came together; the same occurred with the writing of the new constitution. This consensus came through also with the Moncloa Pact. The Pact helped to persuade businesses that workers were moderate and that they could continue to make a profit under the new industrial relations system.[45] But as the PCE did not act in a radical manner at this time, it left the PSOE appearing as the main alternative to Prime Minister Suarez, while 'the various experiences of regained legal status, growing access to commercial media, increasing institutional participation, party growth, internal and external encouragement to act "responsibly", and the logic of electoralism, all encouraged the PSOE to be less doctrinaire and more pragmatic.'[46]

The outcome of two congresses in 1979 set the tone for how the PSOE operated from then on. González and Alfonso Guerra claimed that the party's Marxist image was costing votes but instead of revealing their intentions to the party, they first went to the press. Combined with a general lack of consultation over other decisions, the two came into conflict with the party. The refusal of the 28th Congress in May 1979 to accept the deletion of references to Marxism in the party programme led González to resign as General Secretary. The resignation threw his opponents into disarray, and without an alternative leader they floundered. However, González's use of the newly empowered regional levels of the party meant that at an extraordinary party congress in September 1979 he gained re-election.

This victory for a moderate left-wing agenda has been described as the PSOE's 'Bad Godesberg'. Power was placed firmly in the hands of González so that 'further shifts to the right could be expected from the new leadership which now accentuated the PSOE's electoralism'.[47]

The gradual movement away from class politics and the PSOE's desire to cement liberal democracy led to their eventual electoral success in 1982. It was the attempted coup of 1981 that fractured support for the UCD, leaving the PSOE to project themselves as a party of government. The PSOE did not promise radical change, but to make things operate effectively in a managerialist approach. So by the 1982 election it gained support throughout the country from all groups. The more moderate party programme of the 1982 election appealed to the right because nationalization had been dropped (except for the National Grid) and diluted ideology. To maintain support from the left an employment pledge of 800 000 new jobs within four years and a referendum on Spanish membership of NATO were promised. However, González's personality and appeal were relied upon heavily.

The party's election in October 1982 saw the social and economic liberalization of Spain. The new government moved to introduce legal aid, trial by jury, police reform, an extension of social security provision, educational reform, a proper career structure in the civil service, recognition of conscientious objection, the establishment of a network of family planning clinics, abortion on medical grounds and tax reform.[48] The extent of the welfare state prior to 1982 was limited and the quality was low. The government wanted to tackle the Basque problem (mainly through devolution of power to the regions), modernize the economy and, more generally, bring Spain closer to their Northern European counterparts in terms of rights and living standards. But to do this their first priority had to be to consolidate democracy. This meant the appeasement of potentially hostile forces – the armed forces, police and bureaucracy.

The promise of a referendum over NATO membership when the PSOE was in government was considered a sign of 'leftness', but a 'U' turn over their commitment to campaign for withdrawal was justified primarily with reference to continued stability and lasting economic recovery. The party's foreign policy lost much of its neutralist and 'third-worldist' leaning.

The new government was able, economically, to build upon a realization that the Spanish economy had to be rationalized and restructured. The UGT, the main trade union group, accepted moves down this path. Reduced pay levels were justified as a means of 'showing solidarity with the unemployed'. A Social and Economic Agreement (AES) by the employers' associations and the UGT, covering 1985–6, gave an impression of national unity. While inflation halved, growth rose and the balance of payments moved into surplus, but inequality rose and unemployment increased dramatically. The market-orientated monetarist economic approach of the PSOE came about because of several factors. Firstly, there was a lack of feasible public sector-led recovery packages available, especially given the experience in France. Secondly, Spain was attempting to internationalize its economy because of a lack of domestic investment, so there existed the need for foreign funds and technology. Thirdly, Spain was preparing for EC entry as a way of ending its isolation and providing stability for the new democracy.

Economic austerity lasted from 1982 to 1985 and included a currency devaluation, money supply reductions, tax increases and a reduction of the budget deficit. Industrial conversion sought to 'reduce spare capacity, cut labour costs, shift from labour-intensive to capital-intensive industries and dilute state involvement in the economy – relying instead on the initiative and investment of private capital'.[49] This provided an early indication of the move away from state involvement to allow a freer role for the private sector through privatizations, tariff reductions and reductions in labour market rigidities. The aim was to make firms competitive in the European market.

These measures, combined with a general world-wide economic upturn, entry into the EC and a fall in oil prices gave Spain an economic position which many envied, as both growth and job creation rose. The

1986 election victory showed that, despite persistently high levels of unemployment, the public believed in the manner in which the PSOE was acting. The party tried to balance 'economic efficiency and redistribution, a greater role for the market in the economy and an expansion of the state in social policies'.[50] Whereas other countries were cutting back on social expenditure, Spain's increased (1982–9) but from a low starting position.

As the 1980s drew to a close the workers in the UGT refused to sign any more agreements with the PSOE government, and there was a general strike at the end of 1988. The Izquierda Unida on the left, led by the Communists, began to win support, and the PSOE's own vote continued to decline. It was believed that an attempt at programmatic renewal would be helpful in maintaining support and control over the political agenda, so began the 'Programma 2000' process. Among some sections of the party it was hoped that the renewal would allow for a reappraisal of neoliberal and 'Atlanticist' policies. But the document produced at the end of the exercise contained more general principles than commitments. There was no alteration in the values of the party and only one paragraph was given over to the role of the market. But it did recognize the cross-class appeal of the PSOE by abandoning its claim to be a worker's party.

González's main aim was to prepare Spain for entry into the European Exchange Rate Mechanism (ERM) and in turn to the Single European Currency as part of the agenda for modernization. By 1992 there had been major fiscal revisions to tackle the public sector deficit and to encourage flexibility and deregulation, especially in the public sector and in the labour markets. The public sector was witness to prolonged funding reductions and efficiency drives. The government was in continued conflict with the trade unions over the labour market reforms and the clash led to a nation-wide general strike.

Entry into the ERM at too high a parity caused a tight credit squeeze at the same time as rising inflation, a worsening budget deficit and a widening trade gap.[51] Despite these factors and rising unemployment, the PSOE unexpectedly won the 1993 election; but with the PP showing strongly. The 'new' cabinet after 1993 contained seven 'independents' (technocrats), but economic problems remained with unemployment high, outside investment increasingly difficult to attract, and the continued drive for flexible work practices. 'All the government now appear to offer is a programme of substantial cuts in living standards and security, in the hope that this will make the country more attractive to investors.'[52] But the period from 1993 until the electoral defeat in 1996 proved to be one of drift.

The PSOE began in government as a party of 'change, not of convulsions' but started its move to the right before it entered government. Richard Gillespie has highlighted several reasons for the move rightwards including the consensus during the transition period, the precariousness of the new regime and the economic crisis and a rising unemployment causing labour militancy to decline thereby lessening social conflict. The party also relied on bank loans for its finances and this had two effects: firstly, with the loans being paid back through state subsidies, this meant that the party had to retain a high vote because this dictated the level of subsidy the party received; and secondly, it ruled out bank nationalization because of the 'close relationship' between the two.

But external circumstances were also decisive and the need for Western trade, technology and investment left their mark. The PSOE achieved some social and economic success and alongside these came parliamentary and democratic reform, a consolidated capitalism and a new party model.[53] However, a growing bureaucracy, high levels of unemployment (climbing to over 20 per cent) and uneven development did not aid societal development. The party has been left as a middle-class careerists' party with few young members, the leaders being 'more concerned with "powers, careers, spoils and rewards" than with "strategy, policy, or ideology"',[54] according to Gillespie.

The party could rely on four main factors for its support:

> first, its *moderate ideology* and its reformist programme which responded to a very large extent to the views of Spanish society as a whole; second, its *internal unity* and cohesion over many years; third, the *leadership* of Felipe González, reinforced by the importance of TV in Spanish politics and by the pattern of prime ministerial government; fourth, the *catch-all* orientation of the party.[55]

Yet the 1996 election showed that this was no longer sufficient. The rise in unemployment illustrated, to many, the lack of sensitivity of the party, and combined with its careerist appearance lessened its attraction to the electorate. The party could no longer rely on the media as it became more questioning, the cooperation of the unions could no longer be guaranteed and fourteen years in government proved to be a mixed blessing.[56] The PSOE's greatest strength remained the popularity of Felipe González.

PSOE policies

The policies placed before the electorate in 1996 looked to demo-cratic socialism to propose a political project based on the traditional values of solidarity and responsibility, and policy concerns of employment, housing and other public benefits that would be avail-able to all without exception. Unemployment was viewed as the main concern of the party but in creating jobs the financial strength of the country would also be enhanced. The party proposed change, but without destroying the achievements of their period in office: 'our goal is simple, to maintain what has been achieved.' The great strength of the PSOE during the 1980s was the perception that it enabled the consolidation of democracy and this theme was employed by the party in calls to strengthen the democratic system and lay at the heart of its explicit desire to attract the votes of the young. Such calls revolved around the strengthening of the system by cleaning up politics and expelling party members who had been seen to do wrong in this field.

The role of the market, even given the concern with social issues, did not come in for great criticism. Privatization was defended on the grounds that it guaranteed equal opportunities for all citizens. Yet there was a realization that health and education would require addi-tional support not provided in the marketplace. Such appropriations would be made only according to the state of the economy, inferring that economic growth would be the most important element of any moves to enhance social provision. This, therefore, downgraded the role that taxation could play. Nevertheless, an improved national health system, the building of an additional half a million homes between 1996 and 1999 and the tackling of existing problems of water supply and its availability to locations where its supply was needed were all given special attention. Along with equal rights for women, these social considerations were to be placed alongside the economic orientations of the party that looked to control the unbalanced economy through the reduction of inflation and of the public deficit. In addition taxation was to be set only in accordance with the condi-tions of an open economy, which meant as low a tax rate as possible.

The economy

The salaries of the workers were to be adjusted to the correct level for their jobs, therefore, maintaining the PSOE's commitment to a flexible labour market. Also in keeping with the policies of the earlier govern-ments the *comunidades autonomas* were to be allowed to consolidate their positions. This was viewed as a necessary part of the development of new activities in the economy, such as in new technology. These new firms were to be encouraged through the easing of procedures to start them and thus improve their share of the job market. Enhanced telecommunications were seen as a part of this approach to improve the economy.

For those without employment the opportunities they received to find work would be enhanced as unemployment offices were improved. More importantly, the PSOE would support the reduction of overtime working, the stimulation of the use of flexi-time and the employment of contract workers for new jobs, all in order to create new employment opportunities.

Health

The level of attention to be paid to patients was the key to the PSOE's policies. Patient-centred care would be at the expense of bureaucracy that had built up around the health system. Reduced waiting lists and new services would form the core of enhanced patient care. Other methods of improving the situation would include a new service where nurses visited homes, the incorporation of courses for nurses, doctors, etc., greater use of medical investigation and a better standard of medical centres and first aid attention.

Old people in poor health and the mentally ill came in for special consideration and the reform of hospitals was considered as urgent. The availability of low-cost medication for those who required it was one of the more important elements of a series of reforms which aimed to enhance the bond between doctors and patients.

Education

Education was mentioned as the other area that the market could not be assumed to protect. The guaranteed right of education for all was the bold statement that the party made. This would be performed through the building of new schools for secondary education and in the combination of work and study for the over-19 age category. The need to equip people with skills for the modern international market-place was considered by recognizing that everyone should learn a second language.

The PSOE's time in office provided many achievements in health, education, pensions, unemployment benefits, and social provision. Levels of spending on infrastructure rose, civil rights were extended, women's rights provided and abortion legalized. This, however, has to be placed against a background of falling living standards, rising insecurity in the labour force, the payment of subsidies to employers to hire non-union workers and the decline in political participation. While spending may have increased in some areas, progress remained slow. The public health system remained in debt, unemployment benefit eligibility was constrained and there was a rise in the use of temporary workers. In terms of economic policy neoliberalism and the use of the markets were embraced. The government did, however, try to maintain some control over privatizations and to intervene in areas of importance, such as the banking and energy sectors.

González unexpectedly resigned as party leader in summer 1997 and was replaced by Joaquin Almuía. It was suggested that Almuía would merely step aside to let González return at an appropriate time in the future, as he remains the most popular politician in Spain. The introduction of primaries to consolidate the Almuía leadership increased democracy within the party but had the opposite effect to that intended when Almuía was himself replaced by the more populist Josep Borrell. He acts as a break with the González era which was characterized by sleaze and corruption at the end of his period in office.

Portugal

The Portuguese Socialist Party (PSP) was formed in April 1973 by a small group in exile, a year before the authoritarian rule of Salazar and Caetano came to an end. Salazar attempted to preserve a traditional way of life through conservative means; industrialization was avoided in order to prevent the evolution of a working class, leaving the economy dominated by large family firms. But with no reform forthcoming a revolution took place instigated by 'middle ranking officers in the Armed Forces Movement (MFA)'. The very nature of an anti-Salazar state made it left-wing in orientation. The radical nature of the MFA government became evident as banks, insurance companies, industry, transport and basic services were all nationalized. Colonel Eanes, leader of the government, realized that a liberal democratic solution was the only way forward which would prevent civil war. This victory for the moderate branch of the MFA opened the way for democratic socialism to take control of government. The 1975 elections provided the pluralistic parties, the PSP, PPD and CDS, with a mandate to draft a new constitution.[57] The PSP obtained 37.9 per cent of the vote, making it the largest party but, importantly, with a spread of support throughout the country. Soares, the PSP leader, promised 'undogmatic Marxism' to create a classless society within a pluralist political framework.[58] The Constitution, largely shaped by the Socialists, represented a compromise between the radical left, the democratic centre-left, civilians and the military political forces.[59] The Constitution contained many Socialist concepts including a list of individual and worker rights including that of full employment and the socialization of the means of production.

The PSP government acted in a consensual manner in order to stabilize the political system, not moving wholeheartedly towards the Constitution's stated goal of a 'transition to socialism'. But the minority PSP government lasted only until 1977, when it entered into a coalition with the CDS. The government floundered over the issue of help from the International Monetary Fund in the face of severe economic conditions which had been inadequately tackled by Soares. Soares was dismissed by the President in the summer of 1978, and was succeeded by three technocratic, non-partisan governments. This event paved the way for the PSP's move to the right. By the party's third congress in March 1979 most references to Marxism had been removed. The adaptation of 'Ten Years to Change Portugal' signalled a break as economic policy placed the emphasis on 'the role of the private sector (but with an infrastructure based on the public sector) and judicious economic planning'.[60] The PSP rejected its 'Marxist, collectivist and etatist' leanings. The party was to follow the mixed economy, and allow redistribution through social reform, not socialization. Constitutional revision in 1982 removed much of the left-wing ideology, with socialism modified to 'pluralism and participation'.

After the revision procedure a PSP/PSD coalition came to power which, again, had to rely upon the IMF for loans to save the country's economy. This 'bloco central' government was forced to adopt a strict economic austerity policy, to counteract rising inflation and a balance of payments deficit which involved brutal public expenditure cuts resulting in large rises in unemployment. This coalition lasted two years, leaving Soares to preside over 'the most drastic austerity programme to be implemented by any Western socialist leaders'.[61] The PSD dominated government during the 1980s and 1990s only coming to an end in October 1995, when the PSP was able to get 43.9 per cent of the vote and form a minority government; but this left the Communist party in a position of some strength with 8.6 per cent of the vote. The PSP's victory was a culmination of moves made by a new party leadership to the right after flirtations with a bipolarization strategy in the late 1980s.

Decision-making authority lay with the party executive and emphasized the secretary-general's power. This kind of control made programmatic renewal much easier, and allowed Soares to pursue his belief that the PSP should act as a pivotal party in the political system with social reform as the primary goal of Portuguese modernization. 'De-colonisation, basic social reform, consolidation of pluralist democracy (in tune with the guidelines of the Socialist International) and a firm refusal of a permanent role for the MFA as military overseers of the polity were its first achievements.'[62]

The Guterres era

After Santos' poor showing in the 1985 elections, he was replaced as secretary-general by Vitor Constancio, a technocrat, who rallied the forces who previously stood against Soares. Constancio favoured a bipolar approach to politics and despite a relaunch at the Seventh Party Congress in February 1988 he was unable to replace the PDS in government. The current leader, Antonio Guterres, finally won an election in 1995 on a platform of consolidation and of building on the centre ground as opposed to making common good with the Communists. He built his appeal on three stages – change, assurance (no higher taxes) and 'new against the old'.[63] This approach achieved the highest ever PSP vote, 44 per cent. As a charismatic, right-wing modernizer, Guterres appeared more attractive than the PSD's Fernado Noguiera. After a decade of disunity and changing leaders, the party came together behind Guterres.

To most Southern Europeans modernization has included closer ties with the European Union. For Portugal, even though the country is a member of the EC, closer ties have also meant preparation for entry into a Single European Currency and being actively involved in decision-making processes.

On economic policy the PSP considers privatization a very necessary part of the agenda, but also that liberalization should have a human face. This is where the party's social democracy is said to enter the equation. The PSD also pursued privatization during their time in office, and the PSP have continued with these moves. 'The Portuguese electorate opted for a new governing team, not an alternative set of policies.'[64] But whereas the PSD looked to business interests only, the PSP has attempted to consider the other social partner, labour. Guterres believes in 'creating a climate where the social partners, business and labour, can reach accords that favour the economic climate while advancing equity'.[65] This is not say that the government will legislate for such accords.

Guterres aims to reach the convergence criteria for a Single Currency – reduced inflation and cuts in the budget deficit and level of public debt – and these act as part of the justification for privatizations as they provide the revenue for the economic platform. But justification is also provided by the argument that privatization protects the citizen and the consumer. 'Socially our strategy is based on an agreement with the moderate trade unions and the entrepreneurs'[66] to ensure that the government remains committed to what the society desires. The PSP also looks to cut red-tape and bureaucracy in the state sector and improve the justice system, and, most importantly, education acts as a key priority in the modernization of society and the economy.

Guterres has a 'dialogue approach' in which all parties are consulted and a consensus is attempted. This has worked on some occasions, whereas on others it has merely meant the permanent delay of decision-making. Portugal is seen to have gained much from the competitive edge that Europe provides, as well as having gained lucrative financial settlements from the EC because of its formerly weak economy and its position on the periphery of Europe. In addition, Europe's image of providing democracy for Portugal aids the PSP's drive towards the greater devolving of power within Portugal.

Along with New Zealand and Britain, Portugal has privatized the most in terms of its GNP (Gross National Product). Only 20 per cent of industry remains in public hands, and the drive continues in all aspects of Portuguese life with private roads, railways, the electricity market, the banking sector, etc.

The role for the state in the eyes of the present government lies in public/private partnerships in order for Portuguese firms to gain a niche in the European market and search for opportunities abroad. Even though the government views its main task as being the liberalization of the economy and the maintenance of low taxation in order to draw in business,[67] it retains social responsibilities that social democrats have to perform. As a result of this, there has been the introduction of an experimental minimum wage and a slight increase in the pay of nurses and teachers. However, the welfare state has not seen a deal of reform except for some moves towards efficiency. The tight rein on government spending is a constant theme of the Guterres government and any extra resources have to come from efficiency savings and the clamping down on the 'tax-dodging' professional classes. Yet, unemployment is rising (although it remains relatively low). There exists a consensus in Portugal over the desirability of deregulation, the decline of state power, incentives for capital, the internationalization of the economy and a flexible labour market. Yet the economic structures of the country have remained largely intact.

Greece

Greece's period of dictatorship was much shorter than that of other southern European countries. The era of 'the Colonels' lasted from 1967 to 1974 and, therefore, the political system had a more recent heritage to build upon. The regime's own incompetence largely ensured its downfall, eventually leading to the former premier Constantine Karamanlis being summoned back from exile to re-establish democracy. But Andreas Papendreou's 'Pan-Hellenic Socialist Movement' (PASOK) portrayed itself as a radical new party having no ties with the past, exploiting the political space between left and right, viewing the battle as one between a small privileged minority of foreign interests, multinationals, the US and monopolies and the rest of the non-privileged population. The party's 'Declaration of the 3rd September' gave it a radical image. Four slogans summarized its political agenda: 'National Independence', 'Popular Sovereignty', 'Social Liberation' and 'Democratic Procedure'. The party looked to a socialist transformation of Greece through socialization, worker participation, decentralization, social reforms, welfare policies and 'the achievement of national liberation and the implementation of a non-aligned foreign policy by withdrawing Greece from NATO and negotiating the country's position in the E. C.'[68] PASOK wanted 'an end to exploitation of man by man' and looked to transform the structures of wealth, power and property. Social democracy was merely 'capitalism with a human face' and 'the subservient agent of US foreign policy'.[69] This nationalism built upon a widespread anti-Americanism in Greece, whom PASOK blamed for Greece's dependency on others.

By 1977's elections Papandreou had altered PASOK's image from one of protest to one of a serious party capable of acting as a government. The party's first conference took place in the summer of 1977 by which point much of the opposition to Papandreou had gone, and so the party was able to move away from ideas of the Left and adopt a new constitution. The centralization of power around Papandreou accelerated, fired primarily by a desire to obtain office. Its electoral programme toned down references to classlessness, and a 'socialist transformation' became 'social change'. This lessening of socialist commitments and a widening of the party's appeal illustrated its chosen path to power: closer relations with the EC, a dislike of monopolies but not capital *per se* and appeals to the middle classes, while retaining an independent foreign policy and stance of national independence. Modernization and *allagi* (change) became the watchwords for a pragmatic PASOK. By 1981 it did well among all social groups winning the election, but it inherited an appalling economic situation of rising inflation, falling real wages, low investment, rising unemployment and a burgeoning trade deficit, along with an inefficient and inflexible civil service and problems in the education and justice systems. Papandreou introduced Keynesian economic policies as the answer to these problems and by 1983 had introduced a 'Five-Year Plan for Economic and Social Development' which protected labour markets and increased the size of the public sector. Wages, salaries and pensions all rose, being indexed in the government's first year. This raising of incomes aimed to create demand and, therefore, enhance investments. Price controls would protect those on low incomes, and a clamp-down on tax evasion would improve the country's financial position. Rationaliza- tion of sectors was acceptable and others were 'socialized' in order to counteract monopolies but socialization extended only as far as the phar- maceutical and military sectors. The stimulation of demand, however, did not affect the economy in the desired manner. Its lack of competitiveness led to a rise in imports. The government resorted to borrowing, which made the country's debt worse and was deemed an 'irresponsible' manner to provide extra goods and services. It eventually changed tack drastically and undertook a series of austerity measures beginning with a devalua- tion and an incomes policy. Austerity increased in intensity after the party's re-election in 1985. After initial resistance to foreign capital came attempts to encourage it in the form of investment, while removing restrictions in order to allow for labour and capital markets to operate without hindrance. These economic problems ended *allagi* and the party adopted a neoliberal approach after 1985.

Social and administrative reform took precedence in order to deflect from the unpopular economic policies. The government established a National Health Service, and tackled the state administration. How- ever, in these two areas PASOK showed an unpopular trait of Greek politics, for 'patronage, centralisation, unethical partisan practices, arrogance, an unaccountable and incompetent management and an overall authoritarian statism were the basic traits of the PASOK administration';[70] the 'PASOK state' took over.

The PASOK government's line on foreign policy provides a clear illustration of how its rhetoric varied considerably from its actions. On coming to power it promised 'to end dependence on the USA, withdraw from NATO, adopt a non-aligned policy, renegotiate EC membership terms and dismantle US military bases'.[71] However, on entering office moves towards all of the above were minimal. In 1983 the government reached an agreement with the Americans which allowed for the continued presence of their military bases. PASOK has ensured Greece's continued loyalty to the EC and has taken advantage of grants on offer to it especially in the agricultural sector. It has not substantially altered the structures and arrangements which it blamed for Greek dependency, i.e. the USA and NATO.

If outside groups sought to expound views contrary to the government's then both the state and the party apparatus would interfere to undermine their actions, as was the case with the trade unions. After initial pro-labour reforms the government went on to ban the right to strike in the public sector[72] and referred strikes to binding arbitration. PASOK intervened to alter the composition of the GSEE Council (the main trade union confederation) to place its supporters on the board. Yet, for all the above, its failure to win 1989's election was due more to the occurrence of scandals which resulted from the way PASOK operated in government.

PASOK modernization

During the period in opposition from 1989 to 1993 the party began to consider its organizational modernization as activists realized that its centralized, personalist structure had helped contribute to its defeat. Papandreou was effectively accountable to no one, and the Executive Bureau which decided party policy was appointed by him. But there were moves towards some form of party modernization – a lifting of some secrecy from internal procedures with limited criticism being tolerated.[73]

Michalis Spourdalakis (1992) also detected a new trend towards modernization of the party structure with constitutional amendments being passed such as 'the announcement that PASOK will set itself on course to become a party with concrete institutional and ideological principles' and minimum levels of women's participation in the Central Committee. The most important change was the creation of a Secretary-General elected by the Central Committee to challenge the president's position, and by removing responsibilities and offering an alternative source of power, to help in moves away from a personalized power structure.[74]

The party's re-election in 1993, however, relied very much upon Papandreou and nationalist charges about the danger posed to Greece by

Macedonia. PASOK's economic programme at this time, the 'Regeneration Programme', remained fairly Keynesian yet began to move towards the modernization of social and economic institutions, including moves to decentralize. It did stop the privatizations of the public utilities carried out under the previous New Democracy government and supported public investment in schools and health. Papandreou's extended stay in hospital when he refused to relinquish control of the government illustrated his unaccountability.

The party has often, however, shown itself unable to follow a consistent political line, especially over the modernization of the economy because of its populism and attempts to build support on all sides. This populism attempted to aid the development of PASOK as a classless, catch-all party. It appealed to the electorate on the basis of individuals being part of a collective and thereby suppressing class divisions. The party began in government as pro-labour, but this moved towards a pro-capital line. This belief in populism left the party with a core of support whose 'material interests are based on the reproduction of the unproductive facets of the Greek economy (e.g. subsidies, tax deferrals, protectionism)' and who articulate themselves politically as being a 'progressive force' and 'anti-right'. The 'anti-right' rhetoric is exemplified by PASOK's populist ideology.[75] The lack of economic development helps to explain why Papandreou relied so heavily upon populism and clientelism. 'In essence, Papandreou pursued what can be described as "heterodox orthodoxy" – the pursuit of political power on the basis of a mixture of traditional clientele-patronage organisation and radical populist-nationalist rhetoric.'[76]

PASOK did achieve many progressive social reforms in family law, the introduction of civil marriage and divorce by consent, decriminalization of adultery, the abolition of dowries, improvements in the position of women, education reforms which encouraged increased numbers and junior staff, and movements towards universal medical and pension coverage.[77] Yet, since early radical announcements promised much these could be viewed as limited achievements. It made few changes to the state's repressive behaviour and reduced divisions to a 'simple social and political cleavage'[78] to suit the party.

The death of Papandreou and his replacement as party leader by Costas Simitis signalled a change in approach for PASOK. Instead of adopting the Papandreou method of employing absolute control and expelling those who did not agree with him, Simitis has allowed for a measure of dissent by not dismissing opponents from their ministerial positions. This measure has reduced the impact of any criticism.

Simitis has attempted to integrate Greece with the rest of Western Europe and as a result has placed all the emphasis upon joining the Single European Currency. To do this meant agreeing to a 12.1 per cent devaluation of the drachma in March 1998, pursuing privatizations and reducing the budget deficit. This could bring the government into conflict with the trade unions. Simitis has been open about PASOK's new view of the power of the state:

> The state can no longer satisfy various social demands. Its weakness leads to frustration and to fears that vested interests will be undermined. Social groups intensify their struggle in order to defend their position. Political parties, to retain their clientele, are under pressure to resort to populism. But populism creates new hopes, new demands and the crisis deepens. This vicious circle must be smashed. The answer to the crisis cannot come only through party antagonism between populists and modernisers within the parties themselves.[79]

As well as accepting that the state can longer fulfil its previous functions there has also been an acceptance of the role of globalization. The Congressional Theses of the fourth party Congress which took place in June 1996 accepted that globalization removed the state's power to act as an organizer of social provision, so that on the welfare state 'its institutions should be incorporated in the whole process of development and restructuring of productive activities'.[80]

Conclusion

Each of the parties examined above have been subject to a series of internal constraints (including the role of trade unions, the political processes and competing political actors) and these, along with the histories of each, have dictated the policies and options on offer to them. However, the examinations of the parties in the Southern model show that these constraints appear to be of limited importance and that the parties have been able to adapt to neoliberalism. The exception to this is the PS, so that its development, while not swift, is nevertheless progressing. The other parties are 'freer' to pursue the aims of the leadership because of the lack of constraints. But they have all, to some extent or another, embraced the neoliberal, market-driven agenda. The extent to which the neoliberal agenda has been adopted has been less in France than in the other examples of Spain, Greece and Portugal.

The French PS from the early 1980s came – if unwittingly – to regard the neoliberal agenda as their own. Mitterrand wished to forward a political vision of modernization to help keep the PS, and himself, in power. His wish to leave a legacy meant that he promoted a vision of European integration which required the assistance of right-wing politicians, both at home and abroad, which meant dialogue, compromise and agreement with them. The cohort leading the PS in the early 1980s, including such figures as Fabius and Delors, were also more open to market-led ideas. In the modern context, Jospin has engaged in an ongoing struggle to distance himself from the Mitterrand legacy. Part of this approach brought business interests to the heart of government, and, therefore, required neoliberalism to be seriously considered. However, for the PS, some internal constraints weigh heavily. In particular the continuing role of the PC and of the state in French society limits the room for manoeuvre for the party. Yet other aspects aid movement, such as the concentration of power in the hands of the leadership, the power of the centralized state and the weakness of groups outside the party, especially the trade unions.

The PS, despite its protestations, has attempted to maintain a balance between a modern market environment and the need to maintain cohesion in its (post-1997) 'pluralist-left' coalition government. The PS also desires to maintain France's claim to be a 'special case' or reflect 'exceptionalism'. The role of state intervention (*dirigisme*) and a strong welfare state are cemented in French politics because they are shared by Left and Right alike. French exceptionalism has increasingly become a misnomer as the centralism, state intervention in economic management, high inflation and economic growth of the model came to an end.[81]

For the other Southern European parties – Spain, Greece and Portugal – much of the adoption of neoliberalism was due to the wish to 'modernize' their countries and consolidate democracy. To be viewed as developed meant 'catching up' with their more socially and economically 'advanced' Northern European neighbours. They came into power at a time when the Keynesian model was becoming discredited and came to adopt neoliberalism as the accepted version of events. The cohort of politicians and the importance and power of certain political leaders proved important in acting as the vanguard for change in policy orientation. The social democrats in Spain, Greece and Portugal benefited from the lack of internal constraints, with little standing in the path of the wholesale embrace of neoliberalism: political competitors disappeared (such as the UCD in Spain); the trade unions had few links with the parties and exerted comparatively little influence over the wider society; and the parties enjoyed a considerable degree of leadership control. It can be claimed that the greatest success for any of the parties in the post-dictatorship period was to consolidate democracy.

The parties of the Southern model are largely willing to let the economic structure impact upon the political, institutional and socio-logical characteristics of their countries. The French would have to be said to be, to an extent, standing against its more extreme impact, but their intransigence has been questioned.

'The Spanish and Greek experience (where governments of the centre-right ruled in the initial democratic phase) confirms the inability of the first democratic governments to satisfy popular expec-tations and keep up the momentum of change released by the demise of authoritarianism'; the Greek and Spanish parties 'got a chance to produce an organisation capable of assuming power and hammering out a strategy to cement its authority'.[82] The Portuguese party was not in such a privileged position and was unable to cope with the release of expectations from the dictatorship period.

The successes of each of the Southern parties remains fairly impressive, especially for those in the period of democratic consolida-tion. However, many institutions remain underdeveloped: for instance, the levels of per capita welfare spending in Spain, Greece and Portugal remain the lowest in Europe. In economic terms in particular there has been a distinct move in all of the countries in the neoliberal direction. Jospin attempted to maintain that there exists scope for manoeuvre but others willingly accept the constraints imposed on them by the European agenda. This acceptance of the external constraints impacts upon the policy options available to them.

4
The Northern European Model of Social Democracy

Introduction

The characteristics of the Northern model of European social democracy are outlined in Chapter 1. This chapter examines the aims and policies of social democratic parties in a selection of Northern European countries. The largest section of the chapter consists of a discussion of the Swedish SAP. The Swedish model has often been cited as one for other social democrats to emulate because of its electoral pedigree. It was, however, based upon a close relationship between the centralized trade union organizations and the party itself. The SAP placed most of its emphasis on equipping business interests and over a period of time managed, through policy innovation, to maintain its electoral coalition. It is important in the case of the Scandinavian countries to examine prewar developments because that is the period in which the foundations were laid for their successes. The Swedish party has undergone a series of policy reversals during the 1980s and now attempts to bring together calls for greater equity along with more market-oriented demands. The Danish SD has not been as successful in winning elections or forming governments but the electoral space in which they compete is much more factionalized and has been impacted upon more heavily by the role of issues such as membership of the European Union. The Norwegian DNA has also been faced by particular issue problems but the party has a more consistent electoral record. In recent years the party has been able to follow a line of improved social conditions because of the flexibility provided to it by revenue from the oil industry. While this simplifies the economic situation in which the DNA finds itself it has also aided the party to maintain cohesion with business and labour groups. The further example of the German SPD shows a party which has played an influential role in social democratic developments yet has a poor electoral record. During the 1980s and 1990s the party has been a spectator at national level and relied upon its strength at state level.

The discussion of all the parties will again revolve around the synthesis of the theoretical models in Chapter 2, as was the case in relation to the Southern parties in Chapter 3. The economic impacts, how each of the parties has reacted to them and if they stand against them are of importance. The development of each party will be followed by an examination of their economic and welfare policies. Attempts will be made to track the development of thought within each party to show to what extent the values of the parties have shifted in the direction of neoliberalism.

From the examination it can be noted that the Northern model is an accurate construct. The role of internal constraints, although acting in the same manner as in the Southern model, led to different outcomes for these countries. Not all of the parties are moving at the same pace towards neoliberalism, but the direction of movement is common. The SAP represents a party which lies somewhere between the two extremes of 'classic' social democracy and neoliberalism, while the DNA is more firmly rooted in the 'classic' model because it has yet to deal with the new economic environment or the lack of welfare state funding.

Sweden

The Swedish Social Democratic Party (SAP) was formed in 1889 as the political organization of the trade unions, and it was this close relationship which aided the growth and survival of the SAP in government. After a brief spell in government (1917–20) which achieved an eight-hour working day, the political system divided into bourgeois against socialist power blocks. The party came to pursue practical reforms which centred around the entire population, not just the working class. The foundations were laid for the *folkhem* (People's Home) policy, which regarded democracy as the party's ultimate goal,[1] and adhered to the belief that 'the emergent Social Democratic state should be like a home, a family, in which solidarity is natural and mutual help instinctive'. The SAP won the election of 1932 by putting forward a programme for economic recovery which included employment relief and state unemployment insurance, an early form of Keynesianism but without the nationalizations which might have alienated business interests. The SAP and capital cooperated, with government taking the role of redistribution while accepting that private ownership created wealth.

By 1933 the Agrarian party had joined the SAP government because of promises of support for farmers.[2] The social democrats also brought to government the legitimacy of the Confederation of Trade Unions (LO). The tradition of Swedish class politics ('little spontaneity of militancy in word or action but competent organisation, through preparation, caution, willingness to negotiate, stubbornness, and perseverance'[3]) built upon the close working relationship of the LO and SAP. The 1938 Saltsjöbaden Agreement strengthened the centralization of industrial relations, with the LO and the SAF (Employers' Federation) establishing a code of conduct which constrained individual unions, leaving the LO in control of ensuring wage solidarity and reducing disparities in wages and conditions.

In the postwar period social side universal child allowances were introduced in 1947, obligatory health insurance in 1955 and, most importantly from a point of view of continued electoral success, a National Supplementary Pensions Scheme (ATP) in 1959. The idea of a 'universal earnings graduated second tier pension' appealed to both white-collar and blue-collar groups. Much of the success of the SAP was due to its ability to maintain its electoral coalition through the evolutionary nature of its social and economic policies.[4]

However, by the mid-1970s, the SAP had lost its central platform, the ability to maintain full employment, while the welfare state struggled to maintain equality and was increasing in cost forcing up taxation. 'In short, the system failed at once to satisfy (especially trade unionist) calls for more equality and middle-class demands for less taxation and greater income differentiation.'[5] The SAP lost power in 1976, the first time since 1932.[6] However, the bourgeois parties followed a very similar line to that of the Social Democrats, even undertaking nationalizations.

The Meidner Plan for wage-earner funds was suggested to the SAP at this time by the LO as a means to obtain shares in companies, the first moves towards socializing the means of production. After regaining office in 1982 the version of the wage-earner funds finally implemented was very diluted from that originally intended by the LO because of the funds' unpopularity among employers and the media.

The SAP fought the election of 1982 on a platform of social commitments combined with secure management of the economy, with the priority being to generate economic growth. It did this by shifting the emphasis to the private sector, profits and market forces. Olaf Palme (Prime Minister at the time) devalued the currency by 16 per cent but also restored welfare entitlements, increased taxes on wealth and inheritance, undertook a public investment programme and implemented the wage-earner funds (however mildly). The government still relied upon the LO to deliver wage restraint. Increasingly supply-side measures were introduced. 'Subsidies to industries were cut; public sector companies issued shares and were sold off, rationalized and decentralized; financial markets were deregulated; taxation was reformed;[7] and an application was made for European Union membership.'[8]

However, the central role in Sweden's corporatist institutions held by the LO began to decline. The SAP recognized the increased inability of the LO to guarantee wage restraint, realizing that this might hinder the battle against inflation and lessen the benefits accruing from devaluation. The LO lost power for several reasons. Firstly, there was the rise in importance of the SAF and their rejection of corporatism as signified by their removal of representatives from state bodies. Secondly, there was the rise of white-collar unions, challenging the legitimacy of the LO as the voice of workers, such as SACO (which covered professional, managerial and administrative workers). Thirdly, there were divisions within the LO along public/private sector lines as emphasized by the 1983 breakaway from central bargaining by the metalworkers (demonstrating a lower level of solidarity). Fourthly, there were public disagreements between the LO and the SAP over the role of indirect taxes. Fifthly, there was pressure for wage negotiations to be decentralized. Sixthly, de-industrialization contributed to a fall in membership within the LO.[9]

The shift in emphasis by the SAP had several sources but mainly revolved around the failure of left strategies to cope with the problems of the 1970s, combined with the coming to prominence of a new group of party intellectuals educated in economics and open to neoliberal ideas. They looked to keep unemployment low through investment incentives and an active labour market policy, while accepting some inflation and avoiding large welfare state cuts.

Yet by 1989 inflation has risen to a level where action was required. Its cause was deemed to be wage growth and not the recently implemented financial deregulation. A subsequent SAP coalition with the Liberals implemented public expenditure cuts. The reforms promised in the 1988 election were all deferred.[10] The government made their priority, for the first time, the control of inflation as opposed to full employment.

The crisis of 1990 helped lead to electoral defeat in 1991. 'The crisis of 1990 had also lost the Social Democrats their electorally valuable reputation for competence.'[11] The new bourgeois coalition government implemented policies of public expenditure cuts, tax cuts, benefit reduction, deregulation and privatization. The trade unions came under 'attack' through the withdrawal of state funding for some activities, the abolition of investment funds and the raising of fines for illegal strikes. These moves were the clearest indication that the social democratic hegemony was over; the bourgeois parties no longer felt they had to adhere to its previously indisputable cornerstones. The SAP agreed to the governments' budgets of 'increased charges, reduced benefits, taxation increases and expenditure cuts, in a spirit of national co-operation to defend the Krona'.[12] It did, however, remove its cooperation after hostility from the wider labour movement.

The SAP returned to power in 1994 but with no real alternative to the austerity policies of the right. It fought the election on a pro-gramme of getting the unemployed back into work and stabilizing the economy, while defending the welfare state. Public works schemes would provide a one-off boost to domestic demand but a realization occurred that the private sector had to create jobs, so appropriate meas-ures were included.[13] Tax increases and public expenditure cuts were required to counteract the high level of public debt.

The political weakness of conservatism and a divided right has greatly aided the SAP in its electoral successes.[14] The SAP also gained through its ability to build bridges between demands by capitalists for growth and the general desires of the wider labour movement. The party has been adept at keeping the bourgeois parties divided and demoralized, for instance through the use of referenda in both the ATP and nuclear energy issues.[15]

The decline of Sweden's industrial base has hindered the govern-ment's ability to provide welfare and has led to austerity measures, bringing conflict between classes. Sweden's industry has become increasingly export orientated since the 1970s, leaving the economy less responsive to demand stimulation. Companies such as Volvo, Aga and Electrolux have taken to investing heavily abroad and 'advising' governments on how best to maintain employment domestically.

The Swedish social democratic model has been undermined to a degree which throws its historic means and objectives into serious doubt. The party's ability to remain in office rested on its ability to represent the nation but the situation now places capital against labour, white-collar against blue-collar workers and unions against one another in a more factionalized society. As a result conservatism has increased in importance.[16] The economic situation has weakened the ability of the SAP to successfully finance a comprehensive and univer-salistic welfare state. 'If the welfare state no longer promotes equality of the highest standards and all universal cover, why should everyone feel obliged to pay?'[17] The SAP relied upon the LO, whether it be to deliver wage restraint, supply a large party membership, aid the cre-ation of policies or maintain the party's reformist instincts. Structural changes have undermined this relationship and the end of collective affiliation lessened formal collaboration.[18] It has been suggested that the 'Swedish model' has come to an end.[19]

The 1998 election saw the SAP fall to an even lower ebb. Although the party maintained its position in government it now requires the help of the Left Party and Green Party. This is because it received its lowest share of the vote since the First World War. The SAP, therefore, finds itself constrained by a Green Party that wants redistribution. Despite SAP Prime Minister Goran Persson's promises of the spending of any budget surplus on health, education, pensions, employment, children and families, the party lost support from among the public-sector workers and women. The party, in its election manifesto, claimed credit for bringing Sweden out of its worst economic crisis but it appears that the electorate gave greater consideration to the sacrifices made in its achievement.

SAP policies

During the 1990s the SAP have gradually reduced the role of the state, and the relationship the party has had with the business sector and the labour movement has shifted in favour of the former. The aim of the party, in 1996, was to 'build a society where people will enjoy security and a sense of safety in their daily lives, and where they will have a strong trust in the future. It is a society where each and every person, regardless of social background and financial resources, will have equal opportunities to develop and grow as a human being.'[20] The emphasis on individual security has increased in importance, and represents a movement away from collective security and safety.

In economic policy sound public finances were the first priority; to achieve this security payments have been reduced and to an extent taxation has been raised (although this has to be placed in the context of large cuts to it in the late 1980s and early 1990s). The desire to achieve sound finances was given a social democratic justification by saying that budget deficits were a very bad form of redistribution and large interest payments mean that the state has less money to spend on welfare.[21]

The party maintains that there have been no reversals in ideology and that cuts in welfare payments are not part of a grand ideological plan. It is noticeable that the SAP has continually adhered to the belief in the wealthier parts of society making the greater sacrifices, that universality should remain a cornerstone of the Swedish system and that society shares a responsibility for democracy, work, social equality and equality between the sexes. The central values of Swedish social democracy remain freedom, equality and solidarity. But equality would come about more through the distribution of knowledge and competence in society, hence a much greater prominence assigned to the role of education in the modern agenda with promises of 'a second educational revolution for Sweden'.[22]

Universal welfare was to be retained but otherwise the aims of the party were very much reduced from those of the past. Instead of full employment, the party looked to reduce unemployment or increase employment; instead of equality, society could now look forward to a more equal distribution of income and wealth; and benefits would be of a reasonable level, and tax based on the ability to pay, with the word progressive not stated.

The party also appeared to accept the tenet of the New Right that the state could not grow any further, so that there was little room for any general tax rises, so that even after sound finances were restored, the public sector's share of GNP (Gross National Product) would not rise substantially, so much so that the party wished to introduce a ceiling on expenditure in the public sector. Small businesses and the private sector were viewed as the engines to economic recovery and growth would pay for any rise in benefits or the level of services. While the SAP's battle against inflation is not new, the priority given to it, above unemployment, is relatively recent. This constitutes a shift in emphasis from that of the past. This makes for an interesting comparison with the 1990 programme that considers the problems of capitalism. It explicitly criticized the 'exploitation of human beings, raw materials and energy. Environmental destruction followed in its wake. Workers were forced to put up with unhealthy working conditions.'[23] The party, at this stage also promised to restrict the powers of private owners. The aims of the party considered class inequalities a problem, and desired greater equality, solidarity and fair shares. Commercial interests were said to exploit people, 'thereby obstructing their achievement of independence and social participation'.[24]

Flexibility has always been an element of Sweden's active labour policy. Rights and obligations formed the basis of the policy so that there was an expectation that employment would be accepted if it was offered, in exchange for high levels of universally provided benefits while out of work. There has been, however, an enhanced emphasis on flexibility with shorter periods of entitlement available with eligibility limited. Even working hours are viewed as part of the process of flexibility, being adapted to the needs of the individual employee and 'the conditions prevailing in work places'. Whereas the majority of the party's policies are, at the present time, geared towards the individual, on wages the concept of the collective remains. There has been a realization that the internationalized economy places a restriction upon economic policy, and for that reason wage increases should be approximately comparable with those of other European OECD countries.

The SAP has placed a great emphasis upon the global level as a means to influence the economy, so while they see less role for the domestic state this has been replaced by a higher authority and more international agreements.[25]

The philosophy of the party has altered radically, even since the beginning of the 1990s. The self-reliance of workers, the wish to transform society progressively and the desire to counteract the effects of capitalism have all been discarded. Political, economic and social democracy, achieved through legislation if necessary, are very much reduced in scope. The previous commitments to progressive taxation and full employment have both been maintained but only as general guides to policy. The role of the public sector is downgraded. Yet the actions of the SAP in government, and their altering of the dominant beliefs in society combined with the shift in emphasis towards equipping citizens to perform in the marketplace, are themselves part of the process of undermining the state sector. The actions of the party, the rise in importance of the individual and the falling role for collective solutions have arguably not aided the solidarity for which the SAP has always stood.[26] With the above, it must be asked whether the consensual nature of Swedish society is in danger of collapse. The winning of the 1994 election was considered to have occurred precisely because the party made no promises of reforms or improvements.[27]

Denmark

The Social Democratic Party (SD) in Denmark was established in 1878 with the aid of trade unionists. The 'September Accord' set up a judicial system to regulate between employers and employees following a series of conflicts. 'The Accord laid the basis for centralised bureaucratic organisations of labour and of capital, while at the same time facilitating smooth co-operation between them, and between the state and class associations.'[28] The slow early pace of industrialization and thus the continuity with pre-industrial society made Denmark more pro-capitalist and pro-market than other countries.[29]

The 1901 move to parliamentarism aided the SD by creating splits between existing parties and creating a new possible coalition partner in the Radical-Liberal Party (RV) in 1905. With both parties looking for social reform and income redistribution, this facilitated a coalition between workers and farmers. The SD regained office in 1929 in coalition with the Radicals. This partnership would last, largely unhindered, until the mid-1960s. An economic crisis package of agricultural subsidies and trade union wage restraint allowed both the Liberals (with a constituency of large farmers) and the Radicals to support the measures building the image of the SD as a 'people's party'. After the war increased Communist party support radicalized the SD causing it to place Marxist ideology at its heart and speak of the 'confiscation of large companies, banks and insurance companies'.[30]

As a result of re-entering government in a minority position after the war, the SD was unable to pursue its radical policies because of the dominance of other parties. The liberalization of foreign trade aided an integration into the Western system causing a reappraisal of planning and a movement towards greater belief in economic growth with the state redistributing any associated rewards. There was little support for selective intervention in industry, for active labour market policies or for state enterprise to supplement private production because of the overriding importance of small-scale industry and the agricultural sector.[31] But the SD achieved some notable reforms in the extension of workers' holiday period to three weeks, in reducing the working week from 48 to 45 hours and in the introduction of a universal flat-rate pension.[32] In order to maintain economic success, the government changed normal employer–employee collective agreements by becoming actively involved and dictating terms such as low pay increases and a price and profits freeze.

A period in opposition from the late 1960s until 1971 was spent reorganizing the party, providing for greater participation and more grassroots activity. On the programmatic side, 'economic democracy, worker participation in industry, greater public control of savings and investments, active manpower policies, more social housing and, above all, more equality'[33] were promised. The refusal of LO to cooperate in wage restraint with the bourgeois government led to their loss of office in 1971 and its replacement by a reconstituted SD/SF coalition which achieved several social reforms.[34]

This period was, however, overshadowed by a referendum on joining the EEC. The socialist left parties and nationalistic right fought against entry, while the SD and main bourgeois parties fought for entry. The result in favour led to changes in the upper echelons of the party in an attempt to regain unity. The resulting 1973 elections proved catastrophic for the SD as new parties gained votes and rising taxes and prices affected the SD's working-class constituency, sealing a 12 per cent fall in the SD vote.[35]

The Social Democrats returned to power as a weak minority in 1975. Attempts to solve the economic problems meant a series of incomes policy agreements with non-socialist parties. These led to intervention in the collective agreements of 1975, 1977 and 1979. The only perceptible difference the agreements made were to party–union relations, with the latter angry at the 'something for nothing' approach adopted by government. Cooperation between Social Democrats and Liberals in government heightened the distrust. From this point until the early 1980s the Social Democrats attempted unsuccessfully to gain parliamentary agreements. Defeat in 1982 led to Denmark's first Conservative prime minister of the twentieth century.

From 1982 until 1993 the bourgeois parties operated along neoliberal lines implementing wage freezes, cuts in unemployment benefit, deflation, deregulation and privatization. The SD saw its task as maintaining and defending the role of the welfare state. A general strike in 1985 aimed to prevent welfare state cuts, but it was provoked by government intervention in free collective bargaining and it brought people onto the streets outside of parliament. The strikes' defeat helped tame the public sector. While inflation remained low, the trade deficit was eliminated, the currency stable and growth achieved, unemployment rose to what many perceived as 'unacceptable' rates. Yet it was a scandal which brought the Schluter government down. An SD coalition formed with Poul Nyrup Rasmussen as Prime Minister. This occurred after the referendum on acceptance of the Maastricht Treaty which many social democrat voters rejected. The SD came to power promising to overturn the 'no' vote and did so with a referendum on a 'national compromise' which allowed for Danish opt-outs in some areas.

The deradicalization of the Socialist People's Party has led to closer cooperation with the SD in the Folketinget. But the SD has made a conscious effort to work with smaller parties in the centre. A new party programme in the late 1980s accepted the role of the market but humanized it with social and political rights for the individual. Socialism was no longer mentioned.

The Danish Social Democrats' biggest problem has been its inability to find a stable coalition partner and realign itself effectively since the demise of the farmer alliance. This has meant that the party has struggled to offer a clear identity.

Another factor that has undermined the party is its record of conflict with its own constituency, the working class. Although enjoying close relations with the LO, the party has not always pursued policies which were palatable to the unions and this has led to conflict. The SD has never been able to command a parliamentary majority, having had to seek coalition partners. Unlike in other countries Denmark never enjoyed a united working class, having had to operate in a petty bourgeois society and with an electoral system which does not prevent new competitors from entering the frame. The SD's problem lies in failing to have a distinct identity in a crowded political arena. Electoral victory in March 1998 owed much to the economic state of the country but this did not overshadow the perceived problems of the country's welfare state. Yet the composition of the government remained unchanged as did the holders of its major portfolios and its fiscal policies.

SD policies

Recent examples of party policy place at their heart the ability of individuals to use their potential, but to accept responsibility for themselves, the community and the future. The task of the Social Democratic Party is seen to be to provide freedom, opportunities and equal access so that individuals are able to find self-fulfilment. The state retained the role of creating a secure and safe society and a strong and dynamic welfare state in which people would be encouraged to get back onto their feet.

The principle of full employment remained a key part of the party's agenda, but to do this required an international agenda because 'the individual countries are not able to tackle the great challenges of the times by themselves and in isolation'.[36] The party looked to a national and international agenda to ensure improved welfare and a better environment, 'to put up frameworks, and to adjust the market economy to ensure a socially just and sustainable development'.[37] Part of this agenda was the favouring of 'green growth', whereas in the past the party considered ecology to be more important than the economy.[38] To gain full employment required good opportunities for the development of business, and for government to act to improve education and training. Cooperation between businesses and pay-earners would also create opportunities that could be exploited but this had to be placed alongside a greater 'focus upon research, the development of new products, and investments as well as better and more future-oriented planning of staff and training requirements'.[39] This economic growth would enable government to pay back the debt that it had accumulated over the past years. Employment creation would have come from the public sector, taking a lead in relation to the long-term unemployed, but the private sector had also to take a role in this.

In principle the party was against privatization but stated that only health, social affairs and public transport should remain part of the public sector. Investment in the education and training of the workforce was the first step towards a more effective economy, running on the basis of low interest rates to ensure a dynamic business sector with well-functioning markets. To ensure that markets were well-functioning the policy would be one of replacing subsidies and of creating transparency and real competition in order to create the lowest possible prices for consumers. The value of small- and medium-sized industries was recognized in the process of job creation and would be encouraged through the rise of entrepreneurs.

Healthy public finances were viewed as the starting point for any improvements in the public sector and in the environment of the country. There would be lower taxes on earned incomes, but increased taxes on resource consumption and pollution, thereby adhering to the strong environmental theme of their thinking. The basic rate of taxation would be the first to be lowered as this was said to affect the poorest in society; the party promised 'effective' taxation for those on top incomes and large fortunes, thereby maintaining a vague adherence to progressivity while not advocating increasing the taxes on the rich. Many other aspects of the parties' policies were also geared towards improvement in the operation of the labour market such as its family policy, and child-care arrangements would allow parents to 'function in the labour market'.[40]

In the public sector the contracting out of services to the private sector was mooted as a possibility, but the party believed that some sectors would remain within the public sphere. The role of citizens' involvement in the public sector was to be increased with the adoption of service targets to make sure that the service fulfilled its responsibilities. These moves appeared to be part of attempts to force the public sector to act in a more market-oriented manner.

In 1992 the party claimed that 'democratic socialism represents the opposite of any dictatorship and of the inequalities of capitalism',[41] directly criticizing the economic system that by 1996 it was attempting to pacify. 'We do not support the view that economic gaps between people promote growth and a dynamic society.'[42] Once again, this was stronger language than is currently commonplace, and it does not bear any relation to the later position. Political, economic and social democracy were also part of that agenda, but were not advocated in the later document. The party in 1992 wished to see co-ownership, co-determination and participation in the workplace as well as in the local communities.[43] But there remained the concept of setting the framework within which business operated – i.e. on working conditions, social welfare and such like – and in promoting initiative and talent in the business sector. By 1996 these were in the hands of the business sector themselves. But the stable and financial basis of the welfare state and a shift in the burden of taxation were both recognized at this stage.

On Europe, the Social Democratic Party believed that the extension of the single market should be accompanied by improvements in the position of employees. By 1996 there was no consideration of equality, redistribution, increased spending, class or the trade unions as independent actors in the system. Promises made in 1992 were either abandoned or diluted. Privatization and contracting out were both part of the agenda to move private sector ethics into areas where they have traditionally never been witnessed. The main agenda appeared to be one of equipping the markets to act in the manner that they desire, leaving the role of the state as one of managing a controlled and limited welfare system.

Norway

The Norwegian Labour Party (DNA) was formed in 1887 with the aid of the trade unions. But late industrialization led the country to have a diverse export sector but a high level of foreign ownership, meaning that there was no urban working class until the turn of the century. The DNA unlike other Nordic social democrats adopted a more populist and pragmatic appeal to gain the support of the peasantry, forestry workers, fishermen and the working class. But from 1919 to 1923 the DNA was a member of the Comintern and radicalized itself. Nevertheless in January 1928 the party entered government for a mere 18 days as a massive flight of capital ensured near financial collapse. Defeat in 1930 again on a revolutionary agenda strengthened the reformist wing of the party which developed a crisis policy of 'employment creation, welfare reform and subsidies to the farmers'[44] in the face of growing economic problems and a rural debt crisis. With support from the Agrarians, the DNA formed a majority government in 1935. This had been preceded by a pact between the trade union confederation (LO) and the employers' association (NAF) which created industrial peace.

The DNA acted as a resistance party in exile during the Second World War and used this time to build a new long-term political project based around growth, balanced trade, full employment, stable prices and egalitarianism. To achieve these objectives, 'labour–capital relations would be based on a long-term ratio of wages to profits'[45] combined with an active regional policy and planning. The party won a majority as the first postwar government.

Organized labour and Keynesian economic planning were the key elements in creating a more equal society, and traditional notions of the 'socialization' of the means of production were removed. All the bourgeois parties agreed to this, bringing to an end the polarized political conflict which characterized the prewar era. Unfortunately, this social democratic hegemony in the Norwegian case led to stagnation[46] and was part of a gradual process of deradicalization.

Two areas of policy seriously undermined the immediate postwar dominance of the DNA: defence and EEC entry. Despite a deal of internal opposition the DNA agreed to Norwegian membership of NATO. In 1960 a breakaway by those against the membership saw the formation of the Norwegian Socialist People's Party (SF) and they helped to bring down the DNA government in 1963. The question of membership of the EEC was to prove an even larger problem. The official DNA line was pro-entry; however, in a bid to maintain loyalty, the leadership allowed individual party members to campaign in line with their own views. All semblance of unity was lost, especially after anti-entry members of the party broke away to affiliate with the newly formed

Socialist Election Alliance (SV). The vote went against membership and (the following) 1973 elections devastated the DNA, but with SV support it remained in office. Hegemony had effectively ended as had the historic alliance.

The traditional order began to return in 1977 when the DNA regained much of its lost electorate. A shorter working week, early retirement and growth in the public sector were used to aid employment. Austerity measures comprising wage and price freezes along with a devaluation of the currency were the tools used as the government attempted to counteract a consumption boom. Higher taxation alienated middle-income earners and as a result large numbers of the middle class moved across to the Conservative Party in the 1980s.

To counteract this drift in support the DNA appointed its first woman leader, Grø Harlem Brundtland and made moves towards a more pragmatic programme, shifting away from socialism as a goal and the socialization of financial institutions in order to aim for freedom, democracy and equality. A one-party conservative government took office in 1981 to pursue a neoliberal agenda. They benefited from oil revenues enabling them to cut taxes, and they deregulated and privatized the economy. The ensuing boom and overheated economy left the government to 'apply the brakes'.

After 1985 the party undertook an internal debate entitled the 'Freedom Debate' 'to "recapture" the concept of freedom for the labour movement'[47] and ensure they had a response to the five years of the bourgeois parties' talk of the individual, the market and the private sector. The realization that the party had lost political hegemony drove many into the arms of reform. Very little internal opposition came forth. The 'Freedom Debate' continued a collectivist logic, but the individual rose in importance. To keep the party's support high the debate aimed to open up the party to new groups.

A Brundtland government, which entered office in 1986, pursued a tight fiscal policy, tax reform to make credit more expensive for high-income earners and a tight monetary policy with an increased rate of interest in order to strengthen the already devalued krone. By 1988 a moderate two-year wage settlement was agreed by the LO, and the government enjoyed general support for what was seen as a necessary modernization process. Brundtland attempted to build upon her campaign themes of a less ideological approach to policy with greater flexibility and 'to cater for consumer as well as the producer interests'.[48] That campaign placed the emphasis firmly upon individual choice served by market solutions. The minority status of the government meant that deals with the centre parties were required and this ensured the continuation of moderate policies.

High unemployment and the deflation of assets meant that by 1989 a new centre-right government was formed.[49] Re-election in 1993 left the DNA with a minority. However, the party suffered in the 1994 referendum on whether to join the EU as the SV benefited from the anti-entry referendum result.

The DNA government led by Thorbjørn Jagland (as a replacement for Brundtland) has not put through the public expenditure cutbacks that other social democrats promised. This appears to be for two reasons: firstly, massive oil revenue; and secondly, the fact that the country is not subject to the Maastricht criteria. In the 1997 election Jagland promised to resign as Prime Minister if the party did not obtain at least the same vote as they had in 1993. This led to his replacement by a pragmatic Christian People's Party Prime Minister.[50]

The DNA was very late in beginning its internal debate; whereas the Swedish SAP foresaw the end of its farmer–worker coalition and looked for new partners, the DNA preferred to wait until being forced into action. The DNA were slow to react, but they cannot blame disaffected activists because until the 1970s it was a highly centralized party. The party culture altered substantially with the 'old left', which would complain about the party being bourgeois, being sidelined. The party was more open to the media, and there were more party bureaucrats and fewer members. There was an extensive use of surveys, while electoral volatility and volatility among its members rose meaning that reform could eventually take place.[51] Inside the Storting, the DNA relied upon the SV in the 1970s but had an understanding with the parties of the Right in the 1980s.[52]

DNA policies

The 1996 'Co-determination: Statement of Principles and Action Programme' did note a change of tack for the party, but largely it still adhered to many of the desires and policies of its heritage. The values of the party remained 'freedom, equality and solidarity' through cooperation so that business and government could work together in a market economy with a *certain amount* of political control.[53] Full employment remained a commitment. The DNA also deemed international co-determination an element of economic growth.

The role of the individual was highlighted, being aided by developments in the labour market and the provision of employment with a good working environment, encouraged by teamwork between labour and capital. The working hours of employees would be suitable for their lifestyle, allowing the role of the individual to develop. Capital was for the common good and not just for profit, but this attitude had to be encouraged so a strong trade union movement and the government ownership of certain businesses and industries were deemed essential. Yet this was more boldly stated in 1992 as 'the state must take an ownership stake'.[54] In terms of economic policy, full employment could only be achieved by a stable cost level and a binding approach in incomes policy. The party was not averse to an expanding public sector as long as job creation occurred in health, welfare, education, the environment and culture sectors. Public sector budgets would be employed to counteract recessions and relieve wage pressures. Taxation policy also constituted an important element in the creation of employment, contended the DNA. Tax levels, however, had to remain unchanged over a period of time so as to avoid speculation, uncertainty and, as a related consequence, an unwillingness to invest. The DNA, therefore, realized that taxation could not alter as it should not attract capital and assets away from investment in jobs. There should be 'no increases in the total tax level relative to the trend in competing countries'.[55] The earlier 'Togetherness' programme insisted upon a 'relatively high taxation level';[56] this was no longer appropriate given the competitive element in the newer policies.

A further element to the creation of employment was the responsible management of the country's economic resources. The party stated that it was opposed to market liberalism and that what was required was a strong public sector that used and controlled the market. Responsible economic management meant tight control over both income and expenditures in the public accounts. The 1992 programme stated that 'in the new industrial era we have entered into, there is still a need for a social democratic will to use the state'.[57] This was diluted by 1996. A similar move occurred on the environment: while still featuring heavily in the 1996 programme, the earlier document suggested that growth was not a goal in itself and that the environmental impact had to be taken into account, meaning that the content of growth should be altered.

By 1996, the DNA wished to maintain a strong public sector and welfare state, one that encouraged 'participation, belonging, responsibilities and commitment'.[58] To gain solidarity for the welfare state it was imperative that living conditions were equalized. There would be a fair distribution of resources as this would create a secure society and prevent social and ethnic antagonism, helping to control crime. Public services had to become more user-friendly in order to avoid distance and bureaucracy, and this also entailed the increased efficiency of the public sector. Individuals had to take control over their lives, but with a welfare state that was too bureaucratic this was not possible; there needed to be greater individual input into the public sector. In the 1992 programme there was a stronger emphasis upon the democratization of corporate organizations so that each individual could use his or her own abilities and skills in the company's day-to-day operations. By 1996 this was no longer offered. The improved utilization of resources was necessary as new needs and opportunities became available. Efficiency was the key to a reorganized public sector with a greater focus on results with performance-related financing. Global solidarity was viewed as a necessary element in most of the major decisions that faced nations and the party considered the cooperative bodies not to be strong enough.

The Norwegian Labour Party still retains a social democratic agenda but it is still the case that the agenda is less radical than had been the case at the beginning of the 1990s. Yet it could still retain some of its elements because of the oil-rich nature of the economy. The policies towards the control of private enterprise have been lessened, preferring instead to give it a freer hand, and taxation has become part of a more cautious attempt to create employment through competition and economic growth, but nevertheless the DNA has retained a large role for the state. Flexibility and efficiency are aimed for and will be, the party claims, provided by a labour market which retains access to education and training. However, the key measures are an incomes policy and solidarity in wages policy.

The neoliberal overtones are much more explicit by 1996, on taxation, competitiveness, sound finances and individual input into public services. Increased levels of spending are not offered, but they can claim some ability to move public money counter-cyclically; yet this may largely be because they do not have to borrow to perform this task. The party in the later programme appeared split between a classic social democratic and a neoliberal approach, and contented itself by placing before the electorate the main elements of both.

Germany

The German Social Democratic Party (SPD) is often cited as an example of how left-wing parties should evolve ideologically and operate in government. But its postwar period in government lasted only from

1966 to 1982, since when it has struggled to compete as a serious party for national government. The party regained office in 1998.

Founded in 1861, the SPD operated on a platform of Marxist rhetoric, but with a series of reforms and aims to be achieved within the capitalist system. In the immediate postwar years Konrad Adenauer, leader of the rival Christian Democratic Union (CDU), successfully established a cross-class appeal for his party which led them to electoral success.[59] As a result of this pressure the SPD made an effort to move itself from being a 'workers' party' to a 'peoples' party' (*Volkspartei*), a process which culminated in the successful congress at Bad Godesberg in 1959. The party 'explicitly disowned its Marxist heritage, emphasizing instead an eclectic array of sources for democratic socialism in the Christian ethic, classical philosophy and humanist tradition'.[60]

Bad Godesberg saw the SPD coming to terms with weakening class politics. Ideology declined in importance, so socialism's replacement by 'freedom, justice and solidarity' appeared appropriate. Bad Godesberg accepted private ownership but within a just social order, 'improving and reforming, rather than abolishing, the system of free competition'.[61] The banning of the Communist Party in 1956 removed a competitor on the party's left leaving a larger electorate open to it and allowing for a wider appeal to the centre without fear of losing votes on the left. The party entered government in 1969 in coalition with the FDP after having been a member of a Grand Coalition from 1966 to 1969.

The 1970s proved to be an era of mixed achievements for the party. Brandt's 'Ostpolitik' made moves towards Eastern Europe and ensured international approval. But internally the party tried to integrate the growing numbers of dissenters. This influx of members of the APO generation meant that ideological conflict came to the fore during the 1970s. The new activists were also concerned with increasing the level of democracy within the party and this conflicted with the party's hierarchical nature.[62] The New Left challenge occurred in the party through the Young Socialists (*Jusos*) and also at the parliamentary level. Brandt's tactics were to allow discussion and integrate the groups, allowing them to become functionaries and involve themselves in programme-making. The process of integration helped to lessen dissent by exposing groups to pressures to conform and to act in unison.[63]

Brandt's successor, Schmidt, was less accepting of dissent and made opposition views increasingly difficult to voice. The 1976 election left the coalition with a majority of only 10 which made parliamentary management more difficult and strengthened the role of the FDP. Recession deprived the Left of support and their claims for zero growth appeared inappropriate. Schmidt was able to maintain the party's position in government as conservatism rose through a close relationship with the trade unions and a more authoritarian approach to leadership.

Schmidt viewed the DGB's importance at this time mainly in terms of being able 'to control inflationary wage settlements and assert his government's autonomy from the party'.[64] But, despite retaining office in 1980, increasingly austere economic policies coupled with rising unemployment brought rank and file union members into conflict with the government while the union leadership strived to maintain wage discipline. Schmidt preferred budgetary stability and gave very little emphasis to improving the lot of workers. Despite public expenditure cuts, social spending cuts, reduced taxation on businesses and a tight money supply, inflation, the budget deficit and unemployment all rose. The FDP removed itself from the government coalition because the measures taken were not deemed harsh enough. The SPD also alienated post-materialist support because of the stationing of intermediate-range nuclear weapons in West Germany. As a result, the early 1980s witnessed the rise of the Green Party. The party's problem since 1982 was seen to be its inability to pursue a coherent strategy, undermining its credibility. An initial period from 1980 to 1984 with Brandt as party chairman saw him make calls for the reintegration of post-materialists. Instead, the party reaffirmed its industrial nature and referred to Greens as 'irresponsible utopians'.[65]

From 1984 to 1989 the party attempted programmatic renewal, an ambitious effort to 'reappraise and reformulate the basic values of Bad Godesberg'.[66] A first draft of the process was released in 1986 but it was characterized by a reluctance to break with the ideals of the past. Its release was overshadowed by the 1987 election. A redraft was heavily criticized for its philosophical tone and pessimism, appearing too 'corporatist' and Keynesian. It was also said to fail to address the 'affluent majority' and individual opportunity.[67] Phase two of the process was more purposeful and concerned itself with the previous drafts' inability to overcome the dichotomy between social solidarity and individual opportunity. With elections due in 1990, the review was concluded, with a draft approved in January 1989.

Revisionist ideas were given scant regard. On economics, Bad Godesberg's fundamentals were reiterated: competition but planning where necessary. The role of the state was downgraded but onto this was 'grafted the new politics issues of environment, the humanisation of the workplace, gender equality, and commitments to a "critical" dialogue between elected representatives and citizens'.[68] There was a clear endorsement of the power and legitimacy of the free market.

The election results of 1990 proved to be disappointing, despite the new programme. The election was dominated by the reunification of Germany which had also overshadowed the release of the new 'Basic Programme'. The Left was ambivalent about reunification and this attitude did not sit well with public opinion. Chancellor candidate Oskar Lafontaine ran a more 'new left' campaign combined with appeals to workers.

Bjorn Engholm took over as party leader bringing ideas for organizational reform, hoping to integrate social groups through cooperation using the SPD as a forum for debate. Engholm, forced to resign after a scandal, was replaced by Rudolf Scharping who favoured a low-key, moderate outlook while making overtures to the centre and business. Few expected electoral victory in 1994, but the party managed only a meagre 36.4 per cent. Scharping was replaced at the 1995 Mannheim congress by Lafontaine who favoured cooperation with the Greens and the PDS. Although the SPD performed badly in federal elections in the 1980s, it has retained a solid base through its consistent results at the *Länder* (state) level allowing the party continued experience and expertise in government and also to work with other parties, especially the Greens.

The party began to accept international competition and market dominance with Schmidt as Chancellor but returned to Keynesian demand management policies when in opposition. In 1983 and 1987 the party tried to mix economic growth and ecological concerns but with unconvincing results. The German social market economy has only just begun to question itself. Its solidarity and the political consensus surrounding it meant that extreme neoliberal economic and social ideas have not, until recently, had to be contended with. This has led to problems of the SPD being able to offer a distinctive policy package.

The party had to re-examine itself because of the rise of postmaterialism but has been unable to formulate an electoral strategy or define relations with other parties. But these problems have been created very much through its own inability to adopt and build new coalitions. The adoption of Gerhard Schröder as 'Chancellor-candidate' for the 1998 election provided the party with a more dynamic, media and business-friendly leader, one viewed as capable of challenging Kohl. Schröder's appeals, based around the 'new centre', hoped to bring in floating voters to enhance the role of consensus. Given the nature of the German electoral system the ploy is a necessary one, but it complements the need to keep his rival Lafontaine on board and maintains the cohesion of a party that has been historically divided because of its federal nature.

SPD policies

The 1998 election manifesto 'Work, Innovation and Justice' attempted to revise the basis of Germany's economic and social strengths. The social market economy, since its postwar inception, has brought together economic growth, full employment and low inflation. Employment creation remained the 'highest priority', especially since reunification, as the former East Germany has struggled to cope with the change to marketization. However, the means by which this employment was to be created has altered. The SPD never employed Keynesian techniques to the same extent as other Northern model parties but the shift to neoliberalism is nevertheless noticeable. Consensus in the system remained important with capital, labour and government all retaining a role but the social market economy is recognized to require reform. This reform would be based around 'market powers and the people's willingness to perform ... on social partnership and social stability'.[69] This would mean the removal of excessive regulation and bureaucracy which burdens both the public and private sectors.

Germany has always enjoyed great strength among its medium-sized firms but they were deemed to require additional advancement, in terms of innovation and flexibility. For Germany to regain its position as a foremost economic power, in addition, required a competitive economy to secure jobs, prospects and social security. Greater entrepreneurial spirit and energy, therefore, would have to be achieved to ensure the full use of the opportunities presented by globalization and European unity. For the opportunity to be utilized flexible solutions had to be sought in wage policy and labour policy. When the party considered labour market regulation it merely looked to outlaw 'unfair' practices. For the country to be able to take advantage of the new economic situation, new technology and product advances, lifelong learning and improved education were deemed essential.

Many of the criticisms of the German social market economy have centred around its perceived high levels of costs. The SPD recognized this and promised the 'reduction of statutory secondary wage costs',[70] and to aid tax reduction on both the firm and the individual (with the top rate of income tax falling). Reductions would take place in bureaucracy and in social welfare constitutions.

The SPD viewed itself as the 'new German centrist party' which adhered to a strict budget discipline and aimed to reduce the national debt. To ensure this, an audit of public finances and funding restrictions would take place and the manifesto also contained the stark warning that 'not everything that is desirable can also be funded'.[71] Yet the social welfare state remained important in the German social market system. Self-responsibility and personal initiative were the aims of this welfare state to provide a humane economy balancing the market economy. Private provision was recognized as a legitimate element in pensions.

The German state was to become a partner of citizens rather than their 'guardian'. Heightened awareness of the desirability of democracy was shown by the adherence to increased importance of the *Länder*, the use of referendums and a 'constitutional amendment to strengthen direct public participation'.[72] The supranational level was recognized as a legitimate actor. The SPD would seek German achievement of greater European cooperation in a social EU setting, a Europe of employment, social justice and social stability.

The post-materialist agenda was an important element of the SPD's programme. The environment came in for special attention, i.e. as the party promised to phase out nuclear energy, with women, the family, immigration and young people also deemed worthy of special consideration.

By 1998, the SPD criticized Kohl for aiding the decline of consensus and claiming that it was 'time for a change'. However, some of the policy themes were in evidence in the previous 1994 election manifesto. Social costs, the role of entrepreneurs and debureaucratization all featured. But by 1998 the calls were stated more boldly and were couched in the explicit recognition of the need for revision to the social market model. Fiscal rectitude was an ongoing theme but was given an explicit aim in the reduction of the national debt, while taxation instead of falling for lower income earners would fall for those on higher rates. The new left agenda was given less scope in the later manifesto.

The SPD stands for tax cutting and careful spending, and as a pro-competition, pro-business, efficient, debureaucratized and environmentally friendly party which aims to revise the social market model. The message has become one of 'modernity', 'social responsibility' and 'an alliance for jobs and education'.[73] At an SPD campaign congress Schröder spelt out his themes as 'renewal, justice and modernisation' promising at its heart the battle against unemployment. Globalization has been accepted as an opportunity. 'The SPD is the party of the new centre, putting jobs, innovation and justice together. Those are the policies for a new majority, ending division and putting society back together.'[74]

The electoral victory of 1998 provided the SPD with its best result since 1980. However, early indications have shown a split between Schröder and finance minister Lafontaine. While Schröder has appointed a businessman to the position of economic minister and continues to talk of lower non-wage costs, a partnership with business, supply-side reforms and an economic policy 'for the modern politics of the social market economy',[75] Lafontaine is pushing a Euro-integration agenda based around Keynesian economics. The battle between the two has yet to be fully fought out but does illustrate how the federal nature of the German system is also played out at the national level.

Conclusion

The internal constraints (as referred to in the Introduction), such as the role of the trade unions, the political processes and competing political actors, to which the parties of the Northern model have been exposed have generally been stronger than those of the Southern model. These have, therefore, acted to slow the rates at which the parties have adapted to neoliberalism. The former importance of many of these constraints is now subject to deliberate dilution so that the parties are more able to develop as the party leaderships deem appropriate. Where this is less true we see a greater adherence to 'classic' social democracy, i.e. the Norwegian case. Yet even here it is possible to detect some movement towards neoliberalism. In the SAP there have been deliberate moves against the constraints, i.e. by placing much of the media emphasis upon a single leader in an attempt to provide it with greater scope for independent action. During the 1980s the parties were perceived by some to be constrained by their image of being in favour of the welfare state and public sector expansion, trade union power and equality.

The Scandinavian parties have seen their model undermined and this enabled the neoliberal agenda to be forwarded. They witnessed declining labour market participation, foreign investment outflows, tightened eligibility and levels of benefits, falling taxation rates as well as marginal rates and the collapse of centralized bargaining structures. 'No longer is it a prominent goal to maximise labour market participation.'[76] But Norway remains different: it has retained centralized bargaining procedures, has invested its oil revenue in a State Petroleum Fund to cover future pensions, and the opposition parties have not advocated neoliberalism to the same extent as those in Denmark and Sweden. Where all the parties retain a similar characteristic is in their expansion of active labour market policies, proving that employment remains important in their programmes.

During the course of the 1980s the SAP's right-wing competitors came together to provide an effective opposition in the country, as well as an alternative to SAP government. The collapse of the central bargaining procedures in Sweden came about for two reasons: not only did the trade unions lose their cohesion but business people also came out against the manner in which the economy operated and threatened to move their enterprises abroad.

For the Danish SD and Norwegian DNA, two constraints have been dominant from the 1970s: the question over whether to join the EC, and the rise of factionalism within the party system. General economic problems, such as rising unemployment, along with high taxation, environmental concerns and others, caused the rise of new parties both to the left and right of the party systems. For the SPD, the 1980s provided many problems, such as being confronted with Kohl as leader of the CDU while it had 'weak' leaders, being subject to four electoral defeats and its constant changing of policies.

The Northern parties often relied heavily upon corporatist institutions, but these have been declining, with Norway once again acting as a possible exception. The great strength of the parties of the Northern model was their ability to facilitate the desires of both capital and labour. Unfortunately, these desires no longer coincide in the same manner, making consensus more difficult to achieve. The desire for profits in the international market environment placed pressure on wage levels, social conditions and working practices. Capital wished for flexibility on the part of the labour force and powers for themselves to follow market developments 'as necessary'. These are not necessarily the desires of the working population.

The parties of the Northern model have been more willing to try to work with the economic actors in an attempt to alter its political, institutional and sociological characteristics. This caused all the parties to build welfare states, operate in a stable political environment and enjoy economic growth.

5
The British Case: the Development of New Labour

Introduction

New Labour has been accepting of the neoliberal agenda. It has embraced the market and an Anglo-American approach to economic development at the expense of its traditional means. Tony Blair, who is the incarnation of New Labour, led the party to a massive parliamentary majority in 1997 after 18 years out of power.

This chapter will analyse the movements that have been made by New Labour in terms of their policies, organization and internal reforms in order to ascertain how the New Labour acceptance of neoliberalism evolved and why it did so. The path of modernization has had much to do with the placing of power in the hands of the party leadership and insulating it from previously important internal constraints. Arguably, these constraints have merely been replaced by new ones such as business concerns. These issues will be explored in the same analytical terms as in Chapters 3 and 4. An account of the modernization process of the party and some reflections as to the government's performance will help illustrate the direction of movement for New Labour.

From the analysis it becomes clear that the development of New Labour is an ongoing process which does not have a particular starting point. Some contend that this particular phase of development began under Neil Kinnock, but it took on a new dynamic under Blair and this has led to a change in the party's culture. The construct of New Labour is, therefore, more than just an electoral strategy and represents a true change in Labour's politics. This change, however, is not accepted by all of the parliamentary party or the wider membership and this schism may lead to conflict in the future.

Development of the Labour Party

The New Labour project can be characterized as an acceptance of the role of the individual and the market, a reforming of the party's internal mechanisms, and a revision of its perception of the role of trade unions and the public sector.[1] These can be aggregated into the term 'modernization'; to some this is the abandoning of old ideals, to others it is the coming to terms with the modern era. To understand how and what New Labour is and how it arose, we have first to examine Old Labour, the latter often viewed as a model of 'classic' social democracy.[2]

The ideological development of the Labour Party has had very little to do with socialism and more to with a pragmatic approach to British politics which places the parliamentary system and the House of Commons at the heart of its thought.[3] The Labour Party has been a political party not much interested in ideas, preferring instead to follow the interests of the trade unions, which are fundamentally linked to the party.

The time before New Labour up to Neil Kinnock can be divided into four periods:[4]

Rhetorical socialism (from the party's birth to the 1930s)

In these earlier years Shaw claims that the party did not have a vision of a good society and its policies were not geared around an analysis of social and economic trends.[5] The early thinkers in the party tended to congregate around Fabian desires for gradual and constitutional change, through the use of collective ownership, control and regulation of economic and social life.

The leadership employed socialist oratory and looked to alleviate squalor and poverty, but had little to say on economic policy. The pronounced belief was that a socialist society would emerge, but within the confines of the British constitution, at all times adhering to a financial orthodoxy of a balanced budget, free trade and a strong pound.

Socialism (1930s to late 1940s)

The move to this second stage came about because of Ramsay MacDonald's creation of a National Government and because of economic crisis, which forced the party into opposition in 1931 and devastated it electorally at the following election. Thereafter, the party came to a socialist analysis which challenged Britain's failings and for the first time gave the party a coherent set of policies. The belief was that to get full employment, social justice and an improved standard of living, the system needed radical alteration. This more collectivist approach consisted of four main elements: public ownership, planning, Keynesian demand management and a collective system of welfare provision. The party began to look to intervene in the way that the market operated and change the ownership of some elements of the economy. By introducing planning into industry and finance, the Left were able to reconcile themselves to a system that otherwise believed in capitalism and disavowed redistribution.

Keynesian social democracy (1950s to the mid-1970s)

To the Revisionists (as they were known) Keynesianism meant that public ownership was no longer necessary. Through the use of fiscal and monetary policies, governments could fix the level of demand to ensure growth, full employment and rising living standards. The main thinker of this generation was Anthony Crosland who believed that management was more important than ownership, that those who did own industry were now constrained by greater democratization, the role of the public sector and trade unions, and that the welfare state meant that citizens were free from the vagaries of the market because their basic needs had been fulfilled.

Most famously, Hugh Gaitskell attempted but failed to institutionalize these changes in thinking into the party's constitution by seeking to alter Clause IV. What Crosland had done was to provide an intellectual justification for the pursuit of equality and social justice within a privately owned market economy.

Revisionism was never to enjoy quite the same degree of open support from the leadership after the death of Gaitskell and his replacement by Harold Wilson. By the 1974–9 government (Wilson resigned as leader in 1976), the party appeared to have lost its sense of direction, struggled for intellectual justification and much of the electorate lost faith. There was an inability to overcome entrenched interests at the Treasury, a placing of overseas interests at the head of government concerns which put burdens upon public spending levels, and a defence of an overvalued pound at the expense of British industrial capacity, demand and public confidence.[6]

Decline of Keynesian social democracy (mid-1970s until the election of Kinnock as party leader)

By 1974, many of the certainties upon which Labour thinking was based had begun to disintegrate, leaving James Callaghan (who replaced Wilson as party leader and Prime Minister in 1976) to say to the 1976 party conference (28 September):

> We used to think that you could spend your way out of recession and increase employment by cutting taxes and boosting spending. I will tell you in all candour that that option no longer exists, and that insofar as it ever did, it only worked on each occasion since the war by injecting a bigger dose of inflation into the economy followed by a higher level of unemployment as the next step.

During the period the party spent in opposition (1970–4) alternatives to Keynesian social democracy developed and the Left organised itself mainly around the figure of Tony Benn. With the Left in charge of vital parts of the party's organization and decision-making processes, the party stood in 1974 on a much more left-leaning agenda of state intervention, nationalization planning agreements and promising to redistribute power and wealth to the working people of Britain. Part of this left-leaning agenda was the Social Contract between the trade unions and the Labour Party which demonstrated a new era of corporatism in Britain. Once again a Labour government oversaw a devaluation and had to apply to the International Monetary Fund (IMF) for a loan. This imposed on the government public expenditure cuts which alienated the party's supporters and lost support among trade union leaders, leading eventually to the Winter of Discontent and the downfall of the government in 1979. The early 1980s, up until 1983, saw Bennite socialism which had been an undercurrent of thought throughout the 1970s dominate party thinking, leading to the 1983 general election manifesto dubbed 'the longest suicide note in history'.

The movement to the left began in the 1970s because of the belief that the leadership had 'betrayed' the membership by not pursuing their preferred policies. The Left hit upon three reforms of the party organization and rules which would ensure that the leadership did not dominate the party again:

1   the mandatory reselection of MPs;
2   an electoral college for the election of the leader and deputy leader;
3   NEC authorship of manifestos.

It was when the trade union leaders came behind many of the planned reforms at the party conferences that the prospects for the Left improved.[7] It was this movement away of the leaders of the unions from the line pursued by the leaders of the party that the Left gained victory on reselection and the electoral college.[8]

These moves caused a breakaway Social Democratic Party (SDP) to be formed providing an extra competitor for the party in the 1983 election. Between the years 1979 and 1983, the party engaged in a series of internal fights, including an especially hard-fought battle between Benn and Denis Healey for the Deputy Leadership in 1981, and the impact of the rise of an entryist group of the Left, Militant. On policy, the party entered the 1983 election with a manifesto, 'New Hope for Britain', which stood more as a rebuttal to the Wilson–Callaghan governments than the Thatcher one. The party advocated an Alternative Economic Strategy (AES) which would have committed Britain to the status of a siege economy, with imports controlled through trade management, national plans, planning agreements, state holdings through a National Enterprise Board, greater use of nationalization and controls on multinational companies.[9] The commitment to reducing unemployment to a million in one parliament appeared unattainable, the unilateralist defence policy was out of step with public opinion, and withdrawal from the EC appeared, to many, unrealistic. It was only the 'first-past-the-post' electoral system that ensured that the party with only 27.6 per cent of the vote gained a disproportionately high number of seats in the House of Commons (32 per cent). Labour's 209 seats dwarfed the 23 obtained by the SDP–Liberal Alliance (with their 26 per cent of the vote) and enabled them to maintain their position as the main opposition party.

New Labour

The Kinnock period

The development of New Labour has been a continuous process from the point when Neil Kinnock became leader in 1983, but it took on a new dynamic when Tony Blair took over.[10] Kinnock realized that to regain public support a more moderate and pragmatic line was necessary and so slowly he began to remove the unpopular left-wing policies. Kinnock was a man of the Left who had gradually come to realize that the way forward did not lie with Benn and the 'hard' left, but with a more pragmatic line that worked with the grain of public opinion rather than against it.[11]

Kinnock's moves to reform the party both in terms of policy and organisation took several steps backwards because of the Miners' Strike of 1984–5 and the revival of the battles over the Militant Tendency at the 1985 party conference. He employed the battle against Militant to re-establish the power of the leadership over the party, as this would then give him enhanced power to move forward on the policy alterations that he deemed desirable. Kinnock realized that coalitions were required and the building of bridges with the 'soft' Left of the party demonstrated this to be the case.

From this point onwards, Kinnock began to shape the party into the image that he deemed appropriate for the winning of elections. Opposition to his plans gradually lessened and the leadership reasserted control over candidate selection, with the NEC obtaining the power to replace unsuitable candidates. Apart from the changes in policy orientation, the most important moves that Kinnock made were to place power and authority back in the hands of the parliamentary leadership of the party.

The Labour Party became a more marketable and professional product during the later 1980s with the appointment of Peter Mandelson as the head of the 'Campaigns and Communications Directorate'. The red flag was replaced by a red rose, and opinion polls were employed to select policy change and identify areas in which the party could improve itself. Policy-making arrangements moved into the hands of the parliamentary leadership in Joint Policy Committees between the NEC and the Shadow Cabinet. However, few moves on policy were achieved before the 1987 election.

A further defeat in 1987 gave Kinnock more power in his battle against the party and an enhanced ability to move policy stances. The subsequent 'Policy Review' was not driven by ideological considerations but by the need to make Labour electable with the whole process coordinated from Kinnock's office.

The groups responsible attempted to move the party away from the perceived position of being hostile to everything that Thatcher had introduced. This was an attempt to try to remove the image of the party being hostile to prosperity. The party, therefore, was reacting to perceptions rather than addressing the causes of its unpopularity. Despite a few minor problems, the review process proceeded according to Kinnock's plans.[12]

On the economy, the party took note of the Conservative-inspired tax and public spending agenda and learnt from it. Commitments to full employment and nationalization were abandoned, and the market mechanism enthusiastically endorsed. The fight against inflation became the prime economic battle and fiscal prudence took over from state spending. Wealth taxes and nationalization were replaced by a fairer income tax system (with new bands) and public–private partnerships. The former Euro-sceptic party became the most enthusiastic of the main parties after the Review.

Kinnock's personal image became a problem for the party in the 1992 election. The 'Kinnock factor' left an impression of a politician who suffered from a lack of intellect and gravitas. Yet despite modernization in terms of policy and presentation, both the problem of leadership and the tax-and-spend image haunted Labour, and the electorate failed to trust them. John Smith's Shadow Budget at the start of the 1992 election campaign played many of the traditional Labour themes such as increases in spending on Labour priority areas and slight tax increases for the better off. This was cited, by the modernizers, as one of the reasons for Labour's failure to make a breakthrough in 1992.

The Smith period

Kinnock's replacement, John Smith, did not sit comfortably in the mould of modernizer. He came from the more traditional right-wing of the Labour party which believed in the link with the trade unions, looked to full employment and Keynesian-style economic policies. To those who sought to move the party 'forward', Smith represented much of the 'comfortable' thinking into which the party had fallen during the 1960s and 1970s. They believed that this type of approach was no longer adequate. What was required was to question the tenets of social democratic thinking and bring party thinking into the modern era. Smith was more wary of alienating traditional supporters and trade unionists, especially the latter to whom he owed his large victory in the leadership election. His style was more consensual, he acted in a more tolerant manner to his adversaries than Kinnock had done and looked to a range of opinion when making decisions. He rewarded loyalty and long service rather than those who simply agreed with him.[13]

Ironically, however, Smith's moves to introduce 'One Member, One Vote' (OMOV) in candidate selection and leadership elections brought him into conflict with the trade unions and nearly ended his leadership. The trade union leaders were largely opposed to moves towards OMOV as it threatened their power. At the 1993 party conference the chance of a victory for the leadership appeared slim. It was the placing of all women shortlists for candidate selection on the same motion as well as an intervention from John Prescott, a 'friend' of the unions, that swung the votes behind the leadership to ensure a narrow victory. The reforms passed with a majority of 0.2 per cent.

Smith's premature death in 1994 ensured that his legacy would never be questioned and that his name would be employed as justification for future policy moves, giving them legitimacy. The opinion polls suggest that Smith did improve the party's image on issues such as taxation, trust and prudence with the finances of the state, and his personal popularity and that of the party maintained high levels during his time as leader. With regard to policy, however, the party's programme remained relatively thin, Smith having had time only to set out some ideas and set up commissions and committees but not to lay out any amount of detail.

The Blair era

Smith's death opened the way for one of the leading modernizers to take over the leadership of the party. Under the new OMOV leadership election rules Tony Blair went on to win easily.[14] This enhanced legitimacy gave him greater scope and power to move the party forward as he saw fit. If Smith was the last of the 'old right' leaders of the Labour party then Blair was the first from a younger, postwar generation who entered parliament during the Thatcher years. Blair's movement of the party away from its traditional thinking has been dramatic, with even the policies of the 1992 election and those held by Smith up until 1994 being discarded. The organisation of the party has been altered, the relationship with the trade unions downgraded and even greater emphasis placed on leadership, discipline and obedience.[15]

Although some of the changes were already under way before Blair became leader, the manner of their implementation has been more provocative and less consensual than in the past. One of the most noticeable elements of Blair's Labour Party is the degree of personalization involved; the battles have become personal crusades and many of the initiatives on policy come from himself or those close to him.

Clause IV

Blair's first great move was to change Clause IV of the party's constitution, enabling him to give early substance to his rhetoric of reform, revise the party's values and bury one of Labour's political myths.[16] To Blair, this aspect of the constitution was open to misinterpretation and represented the Old Labour tradition. He claimed that Clause IV emphasized nationalization, a policy which New Labour would never contemplate and believed that its revision would remove a source of tension between the leadership and the activists. Blair, however, miscalculated the degree to which the old Clause IV acted as a potent symbol for those on the Left, signifying the power of the state and the degree to which the Labour Party was still a socialist party. They viewed Clause IV as the 'soul' of the party and the manner in which the change had been sprung upon the party at the Conference, after little or no consultation, angered many. Radice and Pollard (1993) had earlier claimed that the alteration of Clause IV would be 'a potent symbol of Labour's modernisation'.[17] It would prove to be the decisive break between Old and New Labour and would prove Blair to be a strong leader.

When Blair realized that his battle over Clause IV was to be more difficult than first anticipated, he brought forward the idea of membership consultation. This coincided with his wider project for the party, which was about 'designing a left-of-centre agenda that gained the trust of the British people'.[18] Part of the 'project' was concerned with moving power away from the activists and giving it to the wider membership. It was assumed by the leadership that a national consultation and then vote by the constituencies over Clause IV would provide Blair with the win he desired. Given that the wider membership appeared more in favour of Blair than some trade unions, their votes gave Blair a chance to appear democratic, yet also to ensure victory. By giving the membership a vote, this also helped to distance New from Old Labour, where the activists were said to control much of the party. The main danger of defeat appeared to come from unions that did not ballot their members, contrary to the recommendations of the Blair team. The Transport and General Workers' Union (TGWU) and Unison both came out against the new clause. This gave Blair the opportunity to portray the battle as one between Old and New Labour, one in which Blair would not make deals with union barons.[19] Blair did appeal directly to the Scottish party conference during his national tour of Britain, but, given the size of his vote on becoming leader, his national popularity and his popularity among the media, it was never really in doubt that his version would win through. Interestingly, while much of the debate on the clause was being conducted there was no word as to its replacement – this only came later. By closely controlling the alternatives, Blair was once more working to ensure victory. There were only two alternatives on offer: the existing statement, which was associated with the past and was strongly rejected by the newly installed

leadership; and the alternative, written mostly by Blair and symboliz-
ing all that his project stood for. A special conference, held on 29 April
1995, passed the new version of Clause IV (see Appendix 3). The
victory was gained with two-thirds of the total vote, with the constituencies voting 90 per cent for the change.

The decline of internal dissent

Once Blair had decisively won his battle over Clause IV, it became
obvious that most of the opposition to his style of leadership and the
content of that leadership was finished.

This was most vividly demonstrated at the following 1995 party conference in Brighton where there were two leadership 'battles' with the
Left – one over the deselection of Liz Davies as a parliamentary candidate for Leeds North East and the other with Arthur Scargill's resurrec-
tion of Clause IV after threatened legal action. Davies, holder of an
editorial position on Labour Left Briefing, claimed that her rejection
had been based on purely political grounds, and this was largely accurate. What Blair demonstrated was that just as left-wingers in the 1980s
employed the party's constitutional arrangements to rid the party of
right-wing MPs, Blair used those instigated by Kinnock to rid the party
of those he saw as potential rebels from the Left.

The second battle for the Left, over Clause IV, illustrated the Left's
demise even more graphically. Scargill's impassioned plea for the rein-
statement of Clause IV drew little support from the delegates. Only a
decade previously Scargill had been the darling of conferences, being
widely supported on whatever topic he chose to speak. This conference
highlighted how the mood had altered within the party. On a card
vote the amendment was lost by 88.7 per cent to 11.3 per cent.[20]

Combined, the above debates were the final stand of the Left before
the 1997 general election. After this point, a tight discipline surrounded the party, with those on the Left not wishing to shoulder the
blame for another loss if they chose to speak out against the party line.
The tight leadership line can be shown by the alterations in the
conduct of the party conference and the changes in the structure of
the party organization.

During the party conferences of 1995, 1996, 1997 and 1998, the
leadership did not lose a single vote. The docility of the Conferences of
1995 and 1996 illustrated the desire of the party to win the 1997
election.

The introduction of OMOV meant that an appearance of democracy
has been given to the whole procedure, yet the union delegations still

vote as a block rather than as individuals. Although the unions' percentage of the total vote at conference has diminished to 50 per cent, to the modernizers this is still too high and at the 1997 conference a document, 'Labour into Power', came up for discussion which considered altering the nature and structure of conference still further as well as that of the National Executive Committee. The emphasis has become one of the control of elements within the party by the leadership, the dilution of the union link, and of using the conference as the American parties use their conventions, as a media rally and support-gaining mechanism at which dissent is not tolerated.[21]

The bypassing of the trade unions was noticeable during the 'Road to the Manifesto' campaign where Blair put his policy proposals directly to a vote of the membership. The choice was one of accepting the document as a whole or rejecting it – there was no option of rejecting individual policies – and with Blair claiming that these were the policies on which he would fight the general election, he was bound to be successful.

The fear of a low turnout among members who expected the document to be passed forced the party to engage in extensive telephone canvassing in order to raise the level of voting. If only a limited number of the membership voted then this would have undermined the public relations exercise surrounding it. The eventual result was 95 per cent in favour, with 61 per cent of members taking part.[22] By appealing to the individual members, once again, the trade union leaders found their hands tied when the document came to be passed by conference.

Modernization

Blair's most daring ploy was to portray all the events before his arrival as Old Labour by labelling his movement New Labour.[23]

> Old Labour, it is argued, was deeply suspicious of market forces, which it sought to trammel by means of centralised economic planning and heavily interventionist policies... Convinced of the superiority of public ownership it sought steadily to expand its frontiers at the expense of the private sector. It favoured the entrenchment of the power of the trade unions in government on the grounds that they represented the working class... Finally, it tended to be loose with the nation's finances, too often giving way to the temptations of the

'quick-fix' solution of 'tax, spend and borrow' rather than seeking more sober and considered approaches.[24]

The move from Old Labour to New Labour occurred through the process of 'modernization'. But some on the Left have been fearful of what this process entails.[25]

Colin Hay[26] outlines the modernization thesis in a summary of four related hypotheses:

1   that by questioning the assumptions of the Keynesian orthodoxy of the postwar period, Thatcherism has transformed the terms of the contemporary political debate in Britain;
2   that in doing so Thatcherism has in fact facilitated the necessary accommodation of the Labour Party to the new constellation of global economic relations, and specifically to the emergence of the increasingly globalized flow of capital in an unbounded capitalist market place of open economies;
3   that as a consequence, Labour's Policy Review should be seen, somewhat ironically, as the product of the party's years in the electoral wilderness during the 1980s and the requirement to face up to the future that this imposed; and
4   that the Review should not therefore be seen as a concession to Thatcherism, but rather as a long overdue modernization that had previously been prevented by the cloying influence of the trade unions and the inertial pull of the extreme left.[27]

Eric Shaw defines 'modernization' as 'the "marketisation" of Labour's economic outlook and a corresponding abridgement in the role of the state, and a weakening of the links with the unions'[28] and 'a detachment from Labour's established values and objects and an accommodation with established institutions and modes of thought'.[29] Yet, 'modernization' can also be said to define a series of attitudes:

1   a more centralized style of leadership and the downgrading of the influence of activists to the benefit of the wider membership (with the party's structural reforms and moves to mass plebiscites);
2   a professional attitude to campaigning (under the auspices of Peter Mandelson);
3   the use of the media to achieve desired ends (there being an extensive use of media spin doctors);

4   a more open and pluralistic society (having policies concerned with decentralization);
5   a willingness to work with others (i.e. as demonstrated by the presence of Liberal Democrats on the Cabinet committee examining electoral reform).

The characteristics of Old Labour have variously been criticized as being as follows:

1   Economic policies based around 'tax and spend'. The party spent too much public money and taxed for the sake of taxation. The use of Keynesian economic policies and, mainly, the use of fiscal policy did not allow the economy to modernize as necessary and did not provide economic growth at the level required. 'Stop–go' policies did not achieve a stable economic environment and this discouraged investment. The use of high taxation prevented entrepreneurs from developing and discouraged hard work. The instrument of the state was thought of by the party to offer many opportunities to run the economy and society more effectively.
2   The welfare state encouraged dependency and did not equip people to cope with the modern economic environment.
3   The party saw itself as class-based and one that looked after the interests of the working class. That class showed solidarity through trade unions, and these unions had a direct link to the party leaving the party as unrepresentative of other sections of society.
4   Intellectual stagnation meant that thinking was not updated.
5   Parliamentary socialism saw the party look to use the full powers of the existing state.[30]

The culture of the Labour Party

Blair has attempted to change the culture of the Labour Party and has been quite explicit about this desire.[31] Earlier writers such as Drucker (1979) refer to an ethos of the party which covers its spirit, traditions and habits.[32] To Drucker the ethos of the Labour Party has four elements: the party is loyal to those that serve the party; the party expects sacrifices from its leaders and employees; the party saves its money; and the party has a belief in formal explicit rules.[33] This leads to a defensive character within the party which is expressed in the touching belief in its manifestos, its insistence on treating its own elected representatives as delegates, and its loyalty to leaders.[34]

Adam Lent (1996), as one of the few other authors to consider the party's ethos, attempts to take the analysis a stage further by deconstructing ethos and producing a series of different ethoses. He believes that Kinnock communicated a 'willingness to carry out the necessary modernisation for the sake of electoral success while simultaneously affirming the grand traditions and goals of the Labour movement'.[35] This is something that Blair does not pretend to adhere to and he explicitly wishes to move away from these traditions. Lent also detects a 'defend the people ethos' which attempts to 'defend the rights and welfare of the most vulnerable and the most exploited'.[36] New Labour does not adhere to this ethos either; instead it wishes to enable the most vulnerable and exploited in society so that they can defend themselves. The role of the Labour Party is no longer viewed as a defensive one. This may be less true of some sections of the party than others, but the belief is that leaders are in the position to lead, and must, therefore, run some way ahead of the membership on issues. It is not the case that all the elements of the ethos that Drucker describes have been abandoned, but there is no doubt that the broader culture of the party has. Blair would argue that the culture of the Labour Party did not alter for many years, so that just as one can note a definite change in policy style between Old and New Labour, there has also been a change in culture.

It is possible to suggest that the Old Labour culture was:

- accepting of existing social, economic and political institutions;
- workerist, being centred around the working class, large industries and communities;
- based around the triumvirate of state, collectivity and progressive taxation;
- democratic, in that members whilst wary of the leadership felt that they could hold them to account (even if this was not always the case in practice);
- organically linked to the trade unions who carried a large weight in the party but normally followed the line adopted by the leadership;
- fixated with a sense of moral destiny and a desire to develop the ideals of socialism;
- aiming to build a new Jerusalem.

On the other hand, the New Labour culture is:

- leadership led;
- media dominated;

- centralized;
- ruled by the triumvirate of market, individual and low taxation;
- aimed at maximizing the vote;
- one which tailors policies to suit the electorate.

There have been several elements to this transformation to a new culture. Firstly, there is the alteration of Clause IV as described above. Secondly, there has been the opening of the party to working with other groups and individuals. This has been the case with close work with the Liberal Democrats on certain policy issues. A group of sympathetic MPs has formed a group called 'LINC' (Labour Initiative on Cooperation) who advocate much closer cooperation between the two parties. This movement is part of what Blair says are attempts to forge a new politics, a centre and centre-left movement. But there is some disagreement within the party that this is an appropriate measure. One of the key demands of the Liberal Democrats is for the introduction of an electoral system based upon proportional representation. Hence, the inclusion of key Liberal Democrats on the Cabinet committee examining the possibilities of such change.[37]

More disturbing to some of those within the party is the consultation with groups that have traditionally been viewed as the 'enemy' such as Conservative politicians and business leaders. Significant members of the business community now openly support the Labour Party and many have been concerned in the designing of party policy. After the general election victory of 1997 Blair attempted to appoint a leading businessman as head of his Downing Street policy unit and many are members of leading government committees.[38] Blair even went to Hayman Island, Australia to address the NewsCorp Leadership Conference and build bridges with Rupert Murdoch. As far as Conservative politicians are concerned, Blair consulted Margaret Thatcher after becoming Prime Minister on foreign affairs and negotiation tactics and has Chris Patten aiding the Northern Ireland process. Blair had often spoken favourably of what Thatcher achieved during her time in office and promised not to reverse policy in many areas.

Thirdly, there has been a move away from the power of activists to that of the empowerment of the wider membership. The sidelining of activists in policy-making and candidate selection is part of an attempt to make the party appear less 'extreme'. The role of activists is largely confined to campaigning in elections but even this is open to direction through the employment of a more professional media elite. Although there was a key seats strategy in the 1997 election, the emphasis was placed on a national media profile and on Blair himself.[39] Yet the activists cannot be completely ignored. Some commentators claim that activists are needed to help the party win constituencies.[40] As Alan Ware (1992) points out there is a constant stress on shared symbols and values to inspire the membership to work for the party[41] and Tim Bale (1995) believes that Blair still relies upon the symbols of community and social justice to maintain the loyalty of activists.[42] Yet the rhetoric of the modernizers constantly moves away from these symbols, especially given the pronouncements concerning the power of the individual and moves away from higher rates of taxation. These, along with the other changes in the party's culture discussed here, appear to indicate that the party members are becoming more accepting of change. There are certain sops that they still require, as was illustrated by the government's promise to spend extra funds on health and education. Yet examples of *changes* in policy being forced upon the leadership are becoming less common. Whiteley and Seyd's (1998) examination of New Labour members notes that they are more conservative in orientation and less active than Old Labour members, so that they are mainly used as a source of funds, to campaign in elections and to weaken the opposition to further reforms. They are also less strongly attached to the party than Old Labour members. But there has been a 'softening' of attitudes from all members on the key touchstones of nationalization, redistribution and class politics.[43]

Fourthly, the changing structure of the party means that, internally, the Labour Party has witnessed a gradual movement towards the strengthening of the position of the leadership through its policy-making process,[44] its campaigning techniques, the revised Standing Orders of the Parliamentary Labour Party (PLP), the direct election of the leadership and the manner in which OMOV has been implemented. The use of OMOV to set concrete power in the hands of the leadership through mass plebiscites does not appear to have been the original intention of the reform but it is how it has developed. Some of the above reforms were initiated in the pre-Blair era but were enforced under his leadership. Previous leaders approached the implementation of structural reform with caution, if at all. But Blair pursued his ideas for reform with single-mindedness even if this brought him into conflict with groups, i.e. MPs or trade unionists.[45]

The release of the 'Labour into Power' document, passed by the NEC in January 1997, and the revised version 'Partnership in Power', in July 1997, illustrates the future direction of the party structure. After a series of discussions at constituency level, 'Partnership in Power' was released, and the document was passed at conference will little opposition.[46] The plans included:

- cutting the five days of policy-making at the annual conference to two, with the three days devoted to talking-shop discussions;
- reducing the conference's power by stopping it from passing judgement on the performance of a Labour government. It would no longer discuss all the big policy issues each year; instead, it would look at two or three issues in depth and produce long-term options for the government;
- inviting outside experts such as businessmen and academics, including people who do not support Labour, to address delegates to show the party is in touch with the real world;
- getting cabinet ministers to brief delegates in informal private sessions from which the media would be excluded;
- transferring detailed work to policy forums which already meet during the year. They will be given extra powers, even though that are regarded as merely a talking shop by Blair's critics.[47]

Conference would become a smaller segment of the policy-making process of the party with more scope being given to Policy Forums and a new Joint Policy Committee[48] in the two-year rolling programme, in which the submissions made by internal and external groups are of equal importance. Trade unions, therefore, no longer enjoy any greater degree of say. The leadership controls the Joint Policy Committee which effectively runs the National Policy Forum process. The conference will instead 'set out and publicise Labour's achievements and plans'.[49] The 'Partnership in Power' proposals effectively enhance the leadership's control over policy and limits the scope for dissent. By placing policy-making in the hands of the National Policy Forums effective power is removed from the conference. In addition to the above alterations in the composition of the party conference, the National Executive Committee has lost many of its policy-making abilities and will become more of a system of management of the party. The revision of the NEC, and the prevention of MPs from standing in the constituency section, was an attempt to head-off a source of left-wing strength. The Left relied upon this section, in which members vote, to gain some representation on the NEC. Those that stand in this section will be local politicians, without the power resources to challenge the parliamentary leadership.

The Labour Coordinating Committee, a group sympathetic to the cause of the modernizers in the Labour Party, launched a report on party democracy. Its interim report talked of Labour needing to transform itself 'from being an unwieldy federation of committees and interest groups into a dynamic network of progressive individuals'.[50] It believed that party members should decide on policy through OMOV and thus strip out the role of delegates in this area. The party conference should become a showcase for selected policy themes. The concentration of power in the hands of the leadership should be enhanced through the creation of a list of suitable candidates for public office from which the local members could then decide. It would appear from the interim report that members were mostly in place to support the leaders. While these were not the policies of the leadership it helps to provide an illustration as to the direction favoured by the modernizers within the party.

From the opposite side of the spectrum a pamphlet by two Labour MPs, Derek Fatchett and Peter Hain, advocated an enhanced role for the membership through cooperation with the leadership rather than subservience to it. They highlighted the Labour Coordinating Committee's Report and singled it out for much criticism, especially over its hostility to the trade union link. 'Their [the LCC's] approach constitutes a neat, sectarian way of keeping internal control over the Party' and that under the LCC members would provide 'a sounding board for the development of new strategies and ideas by progressive politicians'.[51] Fatchett and Hain claimed that the members should participate in the direction of the Labour movement; this would mean accountability and communication between the members and the leaders. 'The organisation exists to perform a number of tasks: to facilitate internal Party business; to provide opportunities for members to discuss and to develop ideas; and to encourage the skills and the activities whereby the Party's political message can be taken to the broader electorate.'[52] These publications neatly summarize the positions adopted on either side of the debate on the direction that party organization should take.

The concentration of power

The element that is most noticeable about the changes is the increasing degree of concentration of power in the parliamentary leadership. Many of the reforms pursued by Blair have been justified in the name of greater democracy within the party, but this is not how they have operated in practice. Within New Labour there lies a paradox: between the promotion of the parliamentary party above all other levels, and the desire to see increased participation in the country. The Labour Party is being more tightly controlled from the centre, yet it claims to stand for plurality and a more open and cooperative style of politics in the country.

The extension of voting to provide the membership with a vote on key issues is an accepted element of New Labour. OMOV has ensured that whereas in the past party members had little direct input into the selection of parliamentary candidates, the election of the party leader and policy-making, they have a regular ability to be consulted. The question remains whether such votes constitute the wider use of democracy because of its inherent desirability, or whether it merely occurs because it limits the influence of the more left-wing activists. General Management Committees (GMCs) who used to wield control over the selection of parliamentary candidates were generally dominated by the left-wing activists and trade unionists. Placing power in the hands of the more moderate members has ensured generally more moderate perspective candidates. The use of a referendum for the 'Road to the Manifesto' document can be criticized on several levels:

- For its timing – as it took place approximately six months before a general election and thereby left the members with little choice but to vote in favour for fear of destroying the party's electoral prospects;
- For its failure to offer any options – the document could not be accepted or rejected in its entirety;
- For using the voters as a means to bypass Conference – the former 'parliament of the party' was reduced to merely ruubber-stamping the decision.

Conference merely acted as a rubber-stamp for the passed document. The move to the direct consultation of the membership implicitly criticized delegatory democracy, which was the basis of the British Labour movement.[53]

The influence of the trade unions has been reduced, with the agreement of the union leaders, since the Kinnock leadership. This has occurred at all levels – at conference, with OMOV, in parliamentary selection procedures and with their sponsorship funds being switched from MPs and candidates to the constituency parties. This sidelining of the unions is ably demonstrated by the lack of union rights contained in the 1997 manifesto.[54]

There is a tendency by the parliamentary leadership to make policy without reference to the wider party. The best examples of this practice are the policy reversal over the imposition of VAT on school fees (after a newspaper interview with Shadow Employment Secretary David Blunkett) and the changing nature of the policy on the party's wish to join a Single Currency. The problem of entry into a Single Currency became inflamed during October 1997 when a series of apparently contradictory stories circulated in the newspapers. An interview with the Chancellor, Gordon Brown, in *The Times* was interpreted as a reversal of party policy and was taken to rule out entry for the lifetime of the parliament. But this had been preceded by a story in *The Financial Times*, several weeks earlier, that had appeared to suggest that the party was moving closer to monetary union.[55] This episode acts to illustrate not only how easily the leadership can alter policy without wider reference, but also the amount of power that party 'spin doctors' have with the media.

The standing orders of the PLP places the leadership in a position of power. Files are also kept on the MPs so as to keep track of any potential troublemakers. Ministers and senior civil servants also have to report any lunches that they have with journalists to the Number 10 Press Office, so that an element of control is maintained. At the first meeting of the new PLP after the 1997 election, Blair said to the new MPs 'Listen, it's not your job to tell us what to do.'[56] This states his position clearly, and this domineering style pervades through to the Cabinet level, where in 1997 he had two inner Cabinets. The first included Brown, Prescott and Cook as well as Blair himself. The second was a strategy group comprising of Blair, Brown, Peter Mandelson, Alastair Campbell and Jonathan Powell, who devised the overall approach of government. Blair retains a close group of policy advisers, including business friends but not trade unionists. The NEC passed a motion (May 1998) to agree to draw up a list of endorsed prospective parliamentary candidates from which constituencies can choose. This will reduce, still further, the chance of dissent from the leadership's line.[57]

The New Labour method

Many theories have been put forward to explain the New Labour strategy.[58] It appears mainly as one to maximize votes. However, we can place this within several theories, although they do not fully explain the changes undertaken by the Labour Party. Several further explanations have, therefore, to be examined. A Downsian strategy suggests that the Labour Party has attempted to reconnect the party with the median voter.

Budge and Farlie's[59] concept of the 'ownership' of different policy areas suggests that the Labour Party could rely upon welfare issues and the public sector as natural areas of policy strength and public support, while those on the right, the Conservative Party, could rely upon law and order, defence and the economy. What Blair did with the Labour party was to move its horizons and appeal to those issue areas that the right traditionally maintained.

There is a battle between those who believe that Blair is engaged in preference-accommodation and those that see preference-formation.[60] Somewhat unexpectedly, normally supportive MPs, from those interviewed, agreed with the perspective that New Labour was accommodating itself to an agenda that is not their own.

Blair claims to be winning the battle of ideas; however, there is little innovative thinking being adopted by the leadership. Blair's language and policies fit within the Thatcherite settlement to an extent that was not the same for Kinnock and Smith. What Kinnock, Smith and Blair have done is to move the party back into a consensual system, just as the parties operated in during the postwar era. The major difference between that settlement and the Thatcherite settlement is that the former was a social democratic settlement; the latter is not.

The characteristics of the postwar social democratic settlement can typically be viewed as:

1   Keynesian economic policies and the pursuit of full employment as the primary goal;
2   acceptance of strong defence and the maintenance of overseas interests;
3   collective institutions;
4   the use of taxation as a means of redistribution and public spending to maintain a public sector;
5   a belief in the use of the public sector to equalize life chances and an understanding that the market required intervention in order to operate effectively, through the use of nationalization and consultation with outside groups such as trade unions;
6   the primary British institutions did not require alteration.

On the other hand, the characteristics of the Thatcherite settlement were:

1   neoliberal macro-economic policies and the pursuit of low inflation as the primary goal;
2   acceptance of 'strong' defence and the nuclear deterrent;
3   individual liberty;
4   rhetoric of low taxation and low public spending;
5   a lessening of the role of the public sector and a belief in the power of the market which meant the lessening of adverse influences on markets such as trade unions;
6   the primary British institutions required modernization.

Kinnock and Smith did not adhere to the Thatcherite settlement to the same extent as Blair.[61] They maintained more of the traditional policies of the Labour Party, not as they had existed in the early 1980s but as they existed in the 1960s, when the party occupied government. Blair moved beyond this scope to a position which was more accepting of the key tenets of Thatcherism.[62] Many of the policy areas that have been deemed unpopular or unsuitable have been abandoned, and other policies that cannot be dropped because of the significance they hold with party members or that are required for the party to maintain a distinct identity have been diluted – such as the national minimum wage. A claim that New Labour has adopted a purely preference-accommodating strategy does not explain the maintenance of policies, in whatever format, that do not sit comfortably with the Thatcherite settlement. This can be explained only through the internal dynamics of the party and the necessity of New Labour to maintain a distinct profile.

The clearest charge of preference-accommodation can be made against economic policy as laid out in the 1997 election manifesto and the absence of redistribution. In this the party continues to outline a new approach to spending and taxation in which it spends the public finances wisely, saves to invest, taxes fairly and takes no risks with inflation. Most importantly the party, in its election manifesto, pledged to stick to planned public spending allocations for the first two years of office.

If we compare the party's policy positions between 1992 and 1997, we see a dilution of commitments, less state intervention, less regulation, less spending and no tax increases, which gives body to the opinion that in 1992 the party was still pursuing a traditional left-wing agenda, and that the real changes came about with Blair. A full comparison of the policies is made in Appendix 4. Under these policies, it is the power of Blair's rhetoric which gives the party direction. Given that this is where many place the emphasis in modern politics, it is likely to be the most effective method. The policy alterations removed the powerful ammunition that the Conservatives once had with which to damage the Labour Party. Other policy areas have also seen the removal of potentially damaging elements: the renationalization of water (and possibly other former public utilities) has given way to tougher regulation; from being against schools testing pupils, the party has now accepted it, with refinements; and the promise to replace student loans with a full grant system has given way to repayment of costs on an income-related basis.[63] Labour in 1992 still offered a social democratic agenda, but New Labour has either removed the items or reduced their effectiveness.

Reasons for the shift from Old to New Labour

New Labour has been labelled as various different types of movement, but for many it is an election-winning machine without any sign of principle. Blair claims to be restating the principles of the Labour Party in a modern setting, that the only way for individuals to realize their full potential is through the growth of a strong community. The main problem with New Labour is its limited horizons. This was partly for electoral reasons, given four election defeats and the desire to avoid hostages to fortune in a general election campaign, but this spilled over into the way the party has conducted itself. Thatcher had the middle classes at the forefront of her revolution for Britain, but Blair does not have a similar vanguard. The only vaguely comparable sympathetic group that is evident with New Labour is the mythical 'Middle England' which is more of an electoral grouping than a distinct class with a set of easily identifiable aims, values or policy perspectives.

The Labour Party today stands for the market, public–private partnership, the individual within a community setting, fairness, efficiency and competition. Very few of the values of Old Labour remain and even the language has altered; full employment has been abandoned, social justice is now the task of the individual and equality has become fairness, a much vaguer concept.

The question to pose is why these changes occurred. Why was there a movement from Old to New Labour?

Firstly, there was the loss of four elections. The impact of 1992, although delayed by Smith's leadership, had a profound effect on the party and its members. The programme that was put forward was mildly redistributional but the voters rejected it even at a time when the Conservative Party was viewed as vulnerable. Even though the party was not perceived as being as 'extreme' as it once was, the changes were still not 'enough' for the electorate. So there was a sense of desperation to win office and as a result a pliable membership. These four election defeats enabled Blair to take the lead and for members to follow him. There was a realization that without party unity, images of division from the early 1980s would never be eradicated. The diminishing of the role of the trade unions aided this process as they lost their ability to act as an alternative to the leadership or support those who followed this line.

Secondly, New Labour was deemed the only way to win office. Given the political atmosphere elsewhere with the collapse of the Soviet Union, defeats for other social democrats and victories for the right, globalization and the rise in income inequality, it appeared that New Labour was the correct approach. The more left-wing alternatives had been largely discredited or ignored by the wider public. The ideas of the Right were dominant, with the Left being unable to forward a coherent alternative, so New Labour portrayed itself as a halfway house between left and right. Many of the Conservative policy moves were viewed as permanent and irreversible by the Labour leaders. New Labour also ensured the defeat of the Left internally with its stand against the old Clause IV, its disciplinary procedures as set out in the new Standing Orders of the Parliamentary Labour Party and through the vilification of such individuals as Liz Davies.

Thirdly, there was the dominance of the media. The British newspaper media has for many years stood against the Labour Party and in favour of the Conservative Party. The impact of this effect is widely disputed, yet this is the atmosphere and agenda within which the Labour Party has had to operate. The claim can be made that because of this created atmosphere, the Labour Party had no choice but to adhere to this right-wing agenda. But a key element of the New Labour approach was the open cultivation of the tabloid press.

Fourthly, there was the poor standing of the Conservative government. During the post-1992 era the Conservative Party collapsed, in terms of its electorate, its policies and its continual loss of membership. With a large section of the electorate left open to be attracted to a different political force, the Labour Party stepped into the gap and provided a new home for disillusioned Conservative voters. The most vivid illustration of the manner in which the Conservative Party lost its way was the humiliation of sterling's withdrawal from the Exchange Rate Mechanism. That event is widely believed to have led to the loss of the image of the Conservatives being strong on the economy.[64] The Conservatives' other problem was the destruction of their credibility as a unified party. By employing traditional right-wing themes, as described above, the Labour Party was able to attract disgruntled Conservative supporters and members. The breakdown of one-nation Conservatism provided a political space for the Labour Party at a time when its own paradigm was breaking down.

There has been an acceptance of much of what Thatcherism did to Britain, a perspective with which the 'modernizers' interviewed agreed. Elements of the neo-liberal agenda may prove to be of use to the Left. Individual empowerment is a key element of the New Labour project, and Blair claims a heritage for this through Tawney and other socialist writers. If it were not for the moves that Thatcher made, making the individual the centre of her political philosophy, the Labour Party could well still be defending the rights of a centralized state. With Thatcher making the nationalization of industry inadmissible, the Labour Party has been able to move away from an area that was deemed inefficient and bureaucratic and consider the use of regulation rather than ownership. Changes in some of the vested interests in Britain by Thatcher, such as the civil service, has legitimatized the role of government in reconfiguring the British institutions, leaving Labour able to go further. Thatcher showed that many of the institutions taken for granted for many generations were no longer legitimate.

Fifthly, New Labour represents a new generation of leaders untainted by past failures, first elected to parliament during the 1980s and heavily influenced by the Thatcherite decade and agenda. The leadership of Old Labour was part of the party's problem – unappealing leaders who were associated with weak leadership, inconsistent policy positions and untrustworthiness.

New Labour's ethics

New Labour looks to economic development at the expense of all other concerns. Old Labour placed an emphasis on the social side of human development, the building of a civil society through collective institutions. All of the social services and education are geared towards providing the individual with the skills necessary in the marketplace. There is no emphasis given to their social development, especially in educational terms. The assurance of social liberties through higher taxation and spending by government has given way to economic liberties and the gaining of employability. The methods of redistribution have become indirect instead of the more direct methods of the immediate postwar era. New Labour's sole concern with economic matters places a contradiction at its heart of market versus community (or individual versus collective). The values of the two are fundamentally at odds with one another: the marketplace requires self-interest whereas a community requires altruism.[65]

Blair seeks to balance the two, yet it is doubtful whether enlightened self-interest is applicable in the marketplace. It can be questioned whether companies will operate in an enlightened self-interested manner in the marketplace, unless they are instructed to do so, i.e. through legislation. There are reforms for democratic redistribution, but no such reforms in economic circles. The variety of individualism that New Labour wishes for is 'accompanied by self-identity, personal responsibility and a consciousness of the impact of one's actions on others'.[66] New Labour offers a 'collective individualism' that 'enables and empowers people' thereby offering 'a new synthesis – of market and state, public and private, individual and collective, rights and responsibilities'.[67]

The fourth of the four principles of the Social Justice Commission provides an indication of how far the party has come in its acceptance of markets: 'inequalities are necessarily unjust but unjustifiable inequalities should be reduced and where possible eliminated.'[68] The welfare state has become an individual's escape route from poverty, and support for those that use the welfare state has become provisional.

The link between community and the public sector is overlooked. The public service element is downplayed by New Labour; it also does not make clear how communities are to be rebuilt and through what institutions this will occur. According to Michael Ignatieff

> the model is no longer egalitarian, it is civic. It says what will hold us together is decent public services that people can afford. That means when you get on the bus, or go to the NHS, or use the public sphere, it is decent, efficient, perhaps even market-driven. But it can co-exist with great social inequalities.[69]

The moralism of the party has shifted from having a set of values – looking after one's neighbour, co-operation, mutual respect, etc. – to preaching about the manner in which people should live their lives.[70]

This comes through especially clearly in the social policy of the party, from being the party of liberal social policy (the legalization of homosexuality, abolition of the death penalty and so on) to one which appears to punish those that find themselves in an unfortunate situation (single mothers and the unemployed).

If we place New Labour within the trinity around which socialism has traditionally operated then we can note the following distinctions between Old Labour and New Labour:

Old Labour:

- Equality was designed to equalize life chances directly through taxation and services, and to support those who could not support themselves.
- Liberty was freedom from the excesses of the market.
- Fraternity was provided, to all, by close-knit communities, normally based around a large industrial manufacturer or an industry.

On the other hand, according to Kampfner, with New Labour:

- Equality is now confined to giving individuals equal chances to make use of the opportunities provided for them.
- Liberty is the freedom to exploit those opportunities in the market.
- Fraternity, or the community, is the sense of inclusion for those that have made the most of their opportunities.[71]

New Labour in government

With the size of majority that Labour obtained in 1997 and the manner in which the British political institutions operate, it has the ability to be a radical, reforming government but it is doubtful whether this will be the case during a first term. The promises that Blair made in the run-up to the election can be criticized for not being 'radical' or 'inspiring' enough, especially given the amount of time the party was out of office.[72]

There appeared to be a fascination by the New Labour government with public relations and the power and control of the media; interviewees from the Left were particularly wary of this. It is understandable, given Blair's pronouncements concerning the arrogance in power displayed by the Conservatives, that he did not wish to abuse his large parliamentary majority. However, he appeared reticent to employ it in any large pieces of legislation. The promise of legislation came in politically correct areas such as the banning of blood sports, lowering the age of consent for homosexuals and banning tobacco advertising.[73] In addition to these, the main announcements from the government appeared to be very trivial items such as allowing children into Downing Street, or how the Cabinet would not address each other by their official title but by their Christian names. Gordon Brown wished to walk to the House of Commons to conduct his first budget, and had a new Budget box made by apprentices in the Rosyth shipyard in his constituency. The Department of National Heritage has been renamed the Department for Culture, Media and Sport; Blair walked to the Queen's Speech; the ban on trade unions at GCHQ was lifted; the Home Secretary announced a fresh enquiry on the Hillsborough disaster; the government announced that an annual report, 'Britain plc', would be released to show how well the government had been performing. This symbolism attempted to set the tone for the new government, but there is little of substance. However, the symbolism which works with the public is not of the same variety that the party requires. Come difficult times for the government the question has to be posed 'what is there to hold it together?' In the past Clause IV, public ownership, etc. performed this role, but these have been removed and the party no longer has symbols that will hold the allegiance of its members.

However, on more substantial matters the government began to give some idea as to the direction it intends to take. At conferences on Europe, the environment and the G7 summit, Blair and Brown talked of the priority being given to the creation of jobs, the importance of the environment (with Blair announcing self-imposed targets for the reduction of CO_2 gases) and a new constructive role for the European Union, with employment viewed as a priority for this organization.

Gordon Brown's budgets have given small businesses and investment a high priority to please the City, and extra resources for health and education have aimed to give hope to traditional supporters as well as to head-off any possible backbench revolt.

Conclusion

Blair has altered the culture of the Labour Party. Although the processes at work are not new, the dynamic under Blair marks a major break with the party's historical traditions.[74] We can look to the culture of the party as the manner in which it conducts its business, the relationship between leadership and members, how debate is viewed, where power lies, formal rules and symbols, and customs and manner of campaigning.[75] Kinnock's left-wing background prevented him from challenging Clause IV or the fundamentals of the operation of the party; Blair has no such qualms. The party's old procedures, symbols and alliances have fallen by the wayside as the parliamentary leadership attempts to separate itself from the party's other institutions. Whereas Kinnock used and cajoled the party, Blair challenges it. Blair's reforms have been carried through with a confidence and a verve not shown by previous Labour leaders. Outside groups are actively encouraged to participate in policy-making. This acts as a direct challenge to former allies. The 'dominance and self-confidence'[76] of the modernizers has been helpful in forwarding this dynamic.

Blair has been single-minded in his reforms of the Labour Party, yet seems reticent to set out a reformist agenda for the country. For the country, there have been steps towards a new constitutional settlement with devolution for Scotland and Wales and a mayor for London. However, there are constant suspicions, expressed by some, that New Labour is not wholly committed to further change. For those that look for a radical edge to the New Labour project, the constitutional agenda is where they try to seek solace. It is an inexpensive way to provide a radical agenda and it can be argued that democratic redistribution has replaced economic redistribution as New Labour's *raison d'être*.

The element that is most noticeable about Blair's New Labour Party is the degree to which power is concentrated in the leadership. The use of referenda, the bypassing of conference, the reduced role of the trade unions, the tendency to make policy without reference to the party and the subordination of the PLP all leave Blair with more scope for action. The level of personalization has increased, with each battle viewed as a personal campaign by Blair (i.e. the Millennium Dome) and many policy initiatives come from himself or those close to him. Blair's concern with the media and effective public relations, which were used to great effect with the party, have also entered his government. The media is used to build expectations in advance of official government announcements.

The size of Labour's victory in the election came as a surprise to many, especially for those critics on the Left who claimed that New Labour would be lucky to win at all because it did not enthuse the electorate. With Blair's approach proving so popular in the opinion polls, the Left finds itself having to wait for the government to make mistakes so it can come in from the cold. From the interviews conducted it became obvious that there is a lack of any fully developed alternative agenda or leader. Those in the PLP who do defy the leadership's line can be silenced by the invoking of the Standing Orders of the PLP which can lead to their expulsion from that body in extreme circumstances.[77] The Left find themselves alienated in the party largely because of the pro-market direction that Blair has taken the party. Members, activists and those discontents on the Left will have to wait to see how New Labour in government acts to see whether they will be disappointed or not, but given that Blair has already stated how his government will act it will be difficult for anybody to feign surprise or disappointment.[78]

6
The Failures of 'New' Social Democracy

Introduction

From the examples of the social democratic parties examined in this study it can be noted that social democrats in Western Europe are failing to act in a manner compatible with their social democratic values. The previously applicable models of Northern and Southern European social democracy are becoming less distinct and there is convergence around a 'new' model of social democracy which is more neoliberal in orientation. This shift represents a reaction to the internal and external problems faced by the Northern and Southern models, and reflects the influential position of economics and the failure by the parties to respond to economic change and development, as suggested in Chapter 2. 'New' social democracy is an idealized model which represents the direction of movement for social democracy in Western Europe. In several ways it is a hypothetical endpoint in the development of social democracy and its adaptation to neoliberalism.

Given the values of social democracy it is possible to construct a series of measures of success for both 'classic' and 'new' social democracy. These can be divided into two broad categories: intellectual and electoral, and social and economic. Many remain common as the 'new' model of social democracy emerges, but in the latter category differences have emerged as a result of the altered aims of 'new' social democracy.

Some parties adhere more closely to the 'classic' tenets than others, but many are on their way to failing to implement them at all. It is the Norwegian party that remains closest to the 'classic' model of social democracy, largely because it can afford to on account of the huge revenue Norway gains from oil sales. The Swedish party attempts to make reforms within a set of social democratic priorities so that cuts are not as severe in areas of high priority. There remain attempts to retain the universal element of the welfare state, but this has not ended the process of cutbacks. Most countries are congregated somewhere between the two models – France, Spain, Portugal, Greece, Denmark and Germany – but all are moving in the direction of the 'new' model, especially those formerly of the Southern model of social democracy.

If we compare 'classic' to 'new' social democracy it is possible to note a series of retreats. There have been three main areas of failure for 'new' social democracy:

1   a failure to implement or give consideration to the 'classic' aims of social democracy in their programmes, such as equality and collective action;
2   a failure to fulfil the expectations of the electorate and promote confidence in the future, as is demonstrated by the presentation of economic data and opinion poll data;
3   a failure to build a stable electoral coalition. The electoral approach of 'new' social democracy, as most ably demonstrated by New Labour, is a fragile one with little cohesion. This failure may hinder the consistent achievement of governmental office and add to the already existing electoral volatility.

The Australasian examples of the Australian Labor Party and the New Zealand Labour Party had, in the past, many characteristics in common with the Northern model of social democracy. They are introduced at the end of the chapter to provide further illustrations of the record in office of social democratic parties which followed a neoliberal agenda. The party that exhibits the highest number of 'new' social democratic characteristics is the British Labour Party. Tony Blair, as leader, has done much that was required, such as enhancing the power of the leadership, for a party to survive in the modern era. But he has only a tenuous grasp on the two elements that a party must adhere to in order to remain social democratic: furthering equality and collective action. Since entering government, both appear to be in danger of coming to an end as the party grasps a policy agenda that is not of its own making.

'New' social democracy

From the examples of the parties employed above it can be seen that by the 1990s the institutions formerly necessary to provide social democratic parties with success had broken down: the class structure had altered in nature, nationally based economic policies appeared less fruitful, the welfare state was under financial strain and traditional political institutions were questioned. 'Classic' social democracy had come to an end.

The distinctive characteristics of the Northern and Southern models are weakening, and in terms of policy there is a greater degree of convergence. A new model of social democracy has emerged with altered means and aims. It is less ambitious than 'classic' social democracy, but retains the two common elements which enable it to continue the name of social democracy, namely collective action and equality. The values of social democrats mean that they have to offer collective action as a means of solving social and economic problems. Collective action normally means forms of state intervention, either directly or in the creation of welfare institutions. Social democratic concerns with greater equality have altered in scope. 'Classic' social democracy employed taxation as its means of redistribution, whereas 'new' social democracy relies more heavily upon economic growth; but given the fragility of this in recent years it may be that equality becomes less achievable. There has been a shift in emphasis from material equality to equality of opportunity, as is demonstrated by the constant repetition of the value of education. Failure to achieve equality is placed at the door of the individual. 'New' social democracy continues to adhere to collective action and equality but both have been reduced in significance, so the link with social democracy is tenuous. Communal action has given way to individual initiative and responsibility, and with equality becoming 'fairness', it is less extensive in its scope. Equality in many ways, appears incompatible with the market-driven economic policies of 'new' social democracy which demands inequalities to ensure incentives and initiatives in work. This analysis also places a question mark beside the role of the welfare state in a market-driven system. 'New' social democracy, therefore, has a set of characteristics which are less exclusive than in the past. These six characteristics are as follows.

Firstly, social democrats encourage the use and aid the development of markets. They prevent the public sector from impinging on the scope of markets and merely intervene in the private sector at the margins to prevent extremes of hardship for the population. A level of partnership and cooperation between the public sector and the private sector has been encouraged. For markets to operate successfully it has been deemed necessary to build international institutions such as the EC and GATT which institutionalize the market prerogative.

Secondly, the public sector has been witness to cuts in 'unnecessary' expenditure while social democrats claim to comply with their values. There has been a shift in the delivery of public services to be more consumer-based, affordable and responsibility-based. These new forms of public-sector service delivery look to the private sector for 'best-practice' techniques and the market may even gain a role in public provision.

Thirdly, 'save and invest' based economic policies have replaced 'tax and spend' policies. This new approach aims to achieve high and stable employment levels with an emphasis on ending long-term unemployment, on non-inflationary economic growth, on wages that reflect reward levels, skills and position in the labour market, on low inflation and on enhanced skills and training that equip people for their changing lifestyles.

Fourthly, the parties aim to follow national policies that reflect the interests of the whole of the population. This it is hoped will replace the notion of some social democrats being too closely associated with sectional interests such as the trade unions.

Fifthly, an improved level of fairness in society in terms of wealth, power and income is the hoped-for outcome of social democratic policies. The aim is no longer of merely reducing poverty but of limiting the time people spend in poverty.

Sixthly, it was realized that post-materialist concerns could be incorporated into social democratic appeals without great conflict through approving an improved openness to democracy and environmental sustainability.

The role of the state is a very much reduced one but it still facilitates the market. 'New' social democracy now wishes for work at any price, even if this means low wages with the state providing 'top-ups'; its macro-economic policies assume some level of unemployment. Gamble (1988) realized this role for the state when he considered the development of Thatcherism, summing up the process as the free economy and the strong state. This is the attitude towards the state adopted by 'new' social democracy. Those social democrats who enjoyed success in the past did so, it has been said, because they facilitated the market. This role is not, therefore, new, but the priority given to it above social considerations is. The whole notion of collective goods is being removed from economic policy.

The moves towards 'fairness' will not occur through direct redistribution but by providing individuals with the opportunities, through education, training and skills enhancement, to improve themselves. It is a reliance upon equality of opportunity and gives a lower emphasis to the role of the welfare state. Cuts to the welfare state, however, adversely affect the middle class and continual exclusion may leave it exposed to further cutbacks. The move has been from the welfare state as a rights-based institution which assumes the good in people, to a responsibilities-based one which says that if individuals do not use the opportunities provided to them, their rights will be removed.

The welfare state's problem is two-fold: a funding problem and a systemic problem through its inability to cope with new patterns of behaviour. The state's ability to levy taxes, it is argued, is no longer an effective weapon because of its adverse impact on inward investment which requires low overheads, and if imposed on personal taxation it would merely serve to drive people away from the country. The parties' perception of the reluctance on the part of the electorate to pay higher taxes effectively rules out traditional social democratic means of redistributing wealth and providing collective services. It also rules out a branch of economic policy leaving social democrats to rely on monetary policy.

The welfare state's funding problem has its roots in the demographic changes that mean a large ageing population being supported by a younger generation itself shrinking in size but the implicit consensus remains that the welfare state can no longer be afforded.[1]

However, the manner of operation of the welfare state is under review by 'new' social democrats, the paternalistic welfare state being replaced by one in which individuals as consumers are placed at the centre. The welfare state as envisaged in the Beveridge model was dominated by the image of the male breadwinner involved in lifetime employment. This, while appropriate in the golden era of capitalism, fails to take account of changing work patterns, the increased participation of women in the workforce and the rise in part-time employment. Social citizenship rights, as envisaged by T. H. Marshall,[2] were a mainstay of 'classic' social democracy but are reduced in importance under 'new' social democracy. Marshall claimed that social citizenship constituted the core idea of the welfare state. The move in values to accept neoliberal prerogatives has shifted the social democratic emphasis away from social citizenship.

There are many measures of social democratic success and these vary over time depending upon the social and economic contexts within which the parties operate. Those measures which take priority will also vary from country to country depending upon the political context and culture. But it is noticeable that the 'successes' of 'classic' social democracy were inviolable and more absolute than is the case under 'new' social democracy. 'New' social democracy holds elements in common with 'classic' social democracy but it is a scaled-back project. In summary the aims of the two can be compared as follows:

Aims of classic social democracy:

- equality
- collective rights
- expansion of the state to counteract the ills of capitalism
- redistribution
- state as a provider
- ethic of cooperation.

Aims of new social democracy:

- fairness
- individual rights
- aid the market
- individual initiative to achieve enhancement
- state as enabler
- community.

Measures of success

If consideration is given to these aims then it is possible to consider criteria for measuring the success of social democratic parties under both the 'classic' and 'new' models. Any measure of success has to relate to the aims of a party. Therefore, the altered aims between 'classic' and 'new' social democracy has meant a change in the measures of success. The measures are divisible into two broad categories: intellectual and electoral (which both refer to the space within the political systems), and social and economic (which refer to outcomes). There is a degree of consistency between the two models, as we should expect if we are considering parties of the same 'type'. However, there is some degree of divergence between the two on social and economic measures.

Common measures of intellectual and electoral success

There is a series of common intellectual and electoral measures of success for 'classic' and 'new' social democracy.

- The importance of the party within the political space will be enhanced if it holds a pivotal position, i.e. if it is regularly able to form a government either on its own or in coalition. If the party is the largest party on the Left then this will provide it with enhanced opportunities for electoral success, e.g. as Mitterrand discovered in France. If the party is regarded as important by outside groups, i.e. opinion formers or other political parties, then it will enjoy media coverage. To hold institutional positions in the media or wider state structures will aid a sustained political presence.

- Intellectual cohesiveness will aid the setting of the political agenda, the terms of the debate and the political language employed. If the party is prone to factionalism, this may undermine its electoral appeal.
- The retention of vote share, or of a position in government, are the ultimate objectives for any political party. Once out of office a successful party must be construed as one that can still present itself as an alternative government.

Common measures of social and economic success

There is a series of common measures of social and economic success for 'classic' and 'new' social democracy.

- All social democrats look to provide good quality and widely available public services in terms of housing, education, health care and retirement in good circumstances.
- Social democrats wish to prevent social exclusion and offer an improved quality of life and standard of living which tackles insecurity, fear of crime and pollution. A social democratic party looks to alter the social and economic environment of a country to suit the expectations of the electorate. Expectations and outcomes must illustrate some congruence so as to ensure continued electoral support.
- A social democratic foreign policy is one based upon a progressive role centred around the maintenance of human rights, international peace and security and the relief of poverty abroad.
- A party which purports to subscribe to equality has to exhibit liberal tendencies on social issues so as to equalize the life-chances of all citizens of whatever social or economic background.

Some of the above measures are more easily quantifiable than others, but all relate to the aims of social democracy. The most important success lies in the political agenda: if a social democratic party sets the terms of this agenda then this is the ultimate sign of intellectual success, whereas if they adhere to someone else's framework then they have failed.

'Classic' social democratic measures of social and economic success

Some divergence exists between 'classic' and 'new' social democracy on measures of social and economic success. Those for the 'classic' model are:

- to build up a strong public sector through the use of nationalization/socialization which delivers rights-based welfare entitlements. However, the perspective adopted in the delivery of services was that of their producers rather than their consumers. The extended use of state apparatus was employed to achieve the desired ends of the parties;
- 'tax and spend' Keynesian economic policies to ensure growth, full employment, high wages and stable prices (these being viewed as the keys to economic success);
- to bring trade unions into corporatist arrangements to ensure economic success and strengthen the position of the working class in society;
- to directly intervene to improve equality in society in terms of wealth, power and income.

'New' social democratic measures of social and economic success

The measures for the 'new' model of social democracy are:

- to make extended use of markets and to aid their development while preventing extremes of suffering for the population. There is a level of partnership and cooperation with the private sector which aims to encourage small and medium-sized businesses;
- to cut unnecessary expenditure within the public sector while complying with the values of the social democratic parties. Delivery will, therefore, be shifted to a consumer-based, affordable, responsibility-based welfare state and public sector;
- to use 'save and invest' based economic policies to achieve high and stable employment levels with an emphasis on non-inflationary economic growth and ending long-term unemployment. Wages should reflect reward levels, skills and position in the labour market, and will be accompanied by skills and training programmes that equip people for the changing lifestyles;
- to adopt a national policy that is not open to vested interests, which includes all elements in society, not just those traditionally close to social democratic parties;

- to foster an improved level of fairness in society with extremes of wealth, power and income disparities lessened which moves towards not just reducing poverty but also the time people spend in poverty;
- to increase the level of democracy and further citizen participation and environmental sustainability.

There are many measures of success and these will vary over time, as will those that take priority. But it is noticeable that the 'successes' of 'classic' social democracy were simpler and more absolute, i.e. to reduce poverty. 'New' social democracy holds much that is similar to 'classic' social democracy, as suggested in the lists of measures of success, but it is generally a diluted model.

The failures

A comparison of 'classic' and 'new' social democracy reveals a series of failures in some areas on the part of the 'new' version.

Failure one – the aims of social democracy

The adherence to equality and collective action has become increasingly limited and as a result social democracy is losing its distinctiveness. Competing parties may fit into this version of social democracy making the position of social democrats in the electoral marketplace less competitive. The justifications for this 'modernization' can vary between countries: in Portugal it is because of the requirement for European integration, whereas in the United Kingdom it is more explicitly an acceptance of the demands of competition and the markets. But neoliberalism is homogenizing the mainstream social democratic left in Europe, so that it no longer looks to:

1   actively restrain the free market;
2   rebuild belief in the state;
3   persuade the electorate that taxation can be beneficial;
4   convince that more and greater use of democracy, in the workplace and in the party's internal relations, is necessary and desirable;
5   use direct intervention to improve equality.

Restraint of the free market

Traditionally the Left has stood against markets, but with the acceptance of globalization and the 'benefits' which come with it, this is a role from which they are moving away. To ensure that citizens are placed before markets in accordance with social democratic values, a form of governance is required. Globalization, therefore, offers the prospect of closer international cooperation which social democratic governments are in a position to guide because the concept of collective action is a fundamental tenet of the Left. Social democrats need to be seen to be challenging globalization, not to be retreating in the face of markets but working with them through global institutions.

If there are further moves towards an Anglo-American style of economy this rules out greater cooperation because of the demands on national economies to compete effectively with one another, i.e. to bid down wages and conditions.

The policy goals, the instruments that the governments employ and the settings in which these instruments operate are the same regardless of whether a neoliberal or social democratic government is in office.[3] By accepting the primacy of the market the state ceases to be social democratic, for the consequences are that it allows poverty and inequalities to rise, allows public services to be dismantled and lessens people's standards of living (not just in the economic sense).[4]

Rebuild belief in the state

One of the key areas in which social democrats have been unable to forward their thinking is in the reconciliation of their style of state (i.e. interventionist) and the neoliberal state which demands less intervention and small government. There is also the associated debate over how the role of the market should coincide with the unbreakable commitment of social democrats to a welfare state. Neoliberalism does not claim that the state cannot be used but that its scope should be lessened while still facilitating the market. Social democrats are interpreting this to mean coercing citizens into employment, i.e. through workfare schemes (although this term is not always used). The state, therefore, becomes a method of coercion as opposed to one of ensuring freedom. Social justice has, therefore, shifted from concerns about equality to more liberal values of fairness and individual opportunity.[5]

The role of taxation

All the parties have accepted the need for a stable financial environment and low taxation, and to let markets operate more freely. Once that argument over taxation is accepted, it is only a short step to arguing for lower costs in terms of labour because that has similar effects. The withdrawal of belief in the benefit of higher taxation is a

164 The Social Democratic Dilemma

retreat that leaves the social democrats unable to defend wage levels, social costs and the role of the welfare state. With services centred around the individual, the concept of 'standard collective provision' falls in significance. Driver and Martell (1996) believe that 'fragmentation of common and equal experience and divisiveness in forms of provision may undermine communities'.[6] If the welfare state loses its legitimacy then so does the whole project of the Left.

Democracy

The democratic agenda has taken many forms for social democrats. Its has had aspects concerning state institutions, political arrangements, the workplace (and trade unionism), internal party structures and employment. At all times social democrats wished to encourage activism, participation and empowerment. But there have been retreats in the thinking of social democrats in this area.

An agenda for the workplace is one that the mainstream Left is not examining and incorporating into policy in any great detail. An illustration of how many on the Left have capitulated to the power of the markets and have, therefore, dropped ideas such as reduction in the length of the working week is provided by the ridicule endured by the French PS at the hands of the British media and by the Labour Party, after its election in June 1997 when it made such a suggestion.

'New' social democracy centres itself on the power of its leaders, but this is often at the expense of input from members. The members are often consulted in a very *ad hoc* manner on an agenda that has often already been decided upon and against a backdrop of pressure to centralize power in an attempt to control the media. The people of greatest importance in political parties, generally, are not the members but the media consultants, or to employ a term that is increasingly being used, spin doctors.

Equality

Social democrats in power at the present time are failing to prioritize equality. There exists a desire to witness long-term egalitarian outcomes but this aim does not enjoy any degree of exclusivity. Employment is the major consideration but little emphasis is given to wage levels, standards of work or to the psychological costs of coercing citizens into employment.

Employment has become an end in itself, as opposed to the 'classic' position whereby it was viewed as a means to alter and alleviate levels of poverty. All social objectives now appear to be gathered around the requirements of the market and employment, so that education is

Table 6.1 Unemployment rates: France, Spain, Greece and Sweden, 1981–96

	France	Spain	Greece	Sweden
		Unemployment rate (%)		
	France	*Spain*	*Greece*	*Sweden*
1981	7.3			
1982	8.1	16.8		3.2
1983	8.3	18.6		3.5
1984	9.7	20.6		3.1
1985	10.2	21.9	7.8	2.8
1986	10.4	21.5	7.4	2.2
1987	10.5	20.7	7.4	1.9
1988	10.0	19.5	7.7	1.6
1989	9.4	17.3	7.5	1.4
1990	8.9	16.3	7.0	1.5
1991	9.4	16.3	7.7	2.7
1992	10.3	18.4	7.8	4.8
1993	11.7	22.7	8.6	8.2
1994		24.2	8.9	8.0
1995		22.9	9.1	7.7
1996		22.2		8.0

Source: Eurostat, *Yearbook 1996*.

merely a means of equipping individuals for the rigour of the market-place. To concentrate solely upon the redistribution of political power to increase participation requires a corresponding economic redistribution; without it individuals may not have the ability to take up the greater political opportunities. For political redistribution to be effective inequalities in wealth, income, education, social standing etc. have to be tackled.[7]

Unemployment is rising (see Table 6.1), although the rhetoric is concerned with its reduction, and as it is a major source of inequality this, according to their values, is unacceptable to social democrats. In addition there exists a rise of in-work poverty, that is employees who still require state support even though they are in employment because of the very low wage they receive from their employer. As things stand social democrats are taking part, and in some cases actively encouraging, the bidding-down of wages and conditions in the belief that this is the way to national prosperity. There is also a rising trend of work-poor households, that is of households where neither partner is working. Apart from their human consequences, these trends further inequality.

Failure two – the record in government

In terms of policies, the achievement of social democratic aims is limited, yet it may be useful to ask whether the position in terms of outcomes is different. The following section examines the actual achievements of several of the social democratic parties which enjoyed an extended period in government in the 1980s and 1990s – in France, Spain, Greece and Sweden (some other countries are mentioned merely to provide some basis for comparison). The time periods adopted help to overcome any time lag problems whereby policies implemented by the previous administration were still effective several years into any new government. Such an examination helps to ascertain whether or not these parties achieved outcomes compatible with their social democratic aims. From the evidence presented it is obvious that there is divergence between what social democrats seek and what they actually achieve in office. The 'success' of these parties in government must, therefore, be questioned.

All the parties oversaw huge increases in unemployment. Over the period 1985–95 inflation rose considerably (see Table 6.2) except in France, growth rates were not high (see Table 6.3) and the economies shrank in several years; overall the picture is one of volatility. There has also been no real change in the working hours of people in Europe and exclusion from the labour market is rising (see Table 6.12 below).

Social democrats have also been unable to improve the operation of the labour market, as is shown by the general rise in the number of people no longer in the labour force. In Sweden, the periods of time

Table 6.2   Inflation rates

	France	Inflation (1985 = 100) Spain	Greece	Sweden
1985	100.00	100.0	100.0	100.0
1986	102.7	108.8	123.1	104.2
1987	105.9	114.5	143.2	108.6
1988	108.7	120.0	162.6	114.9
1989	112.7	128.2	184.9	122.3
1990	116.5	136.8	222.6	135.1
1991	120.2	145.0	266.0	147.8
1992	123.0	153.5	308.1	151.1
1993	125.6	160.6	352.6	158.2
1994	127.8	168.1	391.1	161.6
1995	129.9	176.0	427.4	165.7

Source: Eurostat, *Yearbook 1996*.

Table 6.3   Growth rates

	France	Spain	Greece	Sweden
	Yearly growth (gross domestic product at market prices) *as % of previous year*			
1985	1.8	2.6	1.8	4.1
1986	2.4	3.2	0.4	2.3
1987	2.2	5.6	1.9	3.1
1988	4.2	5.2	18.5	2.3
1989	3.9	4.7	4.0	2.4
1990	2.4	3.7	−0.8	1.4
1991	0.08	2.3	3.4	−1.1
1992	1.1	0.7	0.4	−1.4
1993	−1.5	−1.1	−0.5	−2.6
1994	2.7	2.0	1.1	2.2
1995	3.1	3.1	1.6	2.8

Source: Eurostat, *Yearbook 1996*.

spent in unemployment has risen during the 1990s, the number in part-time work has increased and associated with these movements is the rise of spending on social welfare, but only to cover the problems of labour market movements.

The level of growth in social spending has been low, especially considering the 'underdeveloped' nature of the welfare systems of those countries formerly under dictatorships. Social protection budgets have seen only limited growth (except in Greece) but with the costs of unemployment rising steadily, this implies that benefits may be being reduced or that eligibility is tighter (see Table 6.4[8]). Sweden's increases in social spending reflect the rise in unemployment which has meant rising taxes and cutbacks on benefits while spending on health has also been reduced (see Table 6.5). In Greece spending on health (see Table 6.6) has risen but as a proportion of social protection it has fallen quite considerably (from 26.0 per cent to 18.7 per cent in the period 1980 to 1992) (see Table 6.7). This has also been the case with family/maternity benefits but less so with pensions. If this move was towards increased pensions then that would be social democratic (aiding the reduction of inequality); however, if it is a reflection of the general trend in the rest of Europe then it has more to do with an ageing population. The rise of unemployment in Greece, Spain and France has meant increased social spending in this area, which is not social democratic because it means that other priorities suffer and taxpayers finance economic failure. If a government acts in a social democratic manner then when it takes over

Table 6.4   **Social protection current expenditure as a percentage of gross domestic product at market prices**

	France	Spain	Greece
1980	25.4	18.1	12.2
1981	26.7	19.6	13.6
1982	27.9	19.4	16.3
1983	28.3	19.5	17.2
1984	28.7	19.4	18.2
1985	28.8	19.9	19.2
1986	28.5	19.5	19.4
1987	28.1	19.6	20.2
1988	28.0	19.8	19.5
1989	27.6	20.1	20.7
1990	27.8	20.7	
1991	28.7	21.4	

Source: Eurostat, *Social Protection Expenditure and Receipts 1980–1991.*

from a right-wing government its spending priorities should alter, but in Spain and France we see little change in the composition of social spending. The growth in the level of education spending has been disappointing especially in Greece, but in Spain and France at least the moves were in a direction congruent with social democratic aims (see Table 6.8). But we must question whether, in an era of rapid economic change, the levels are adequate to allow their economies to compete.

The record on poverty of the social democrats in power has been most disappointing (see Table 6.9). Over the course of the 1980s there were only limited moves in the direction of greater equalization in society. In Greece, the problem has become worse, and this is certainly not social

Table 6.5   **Sweden's social spending (as a percentage of GDP)**

1980	32.0
1985	33.3
1986	33.7
1987	35.2
1988	36.0
1989	35.2
1990	35.8
1991	37.6
1992	40.0

Source: Commission of the European Community, *Basic Statistics of the European Community.*

Table 6.6   Health expenditure

	France	Spain	Greece	Sweden
		Total health expenditure as a proportion of GDP		
1985	8.5	5.7	4.9	8.9
1986	8.5	5.6	5.4	8.6
1987	8.5	5.7	5.2	8.6
1988	8.6	6.3	5.0	8.6
1989	8.7	6.5	5.1	8.6
1990	8.9	6.9	5.3	8.6
1991	9.1	7.1	5.3	8.4
1992	9.4	7.2	5.5	7.6
1993	9.8	7.2	5.7	7.5
1994		7.3		7.0

Source: Eurostat, *Yearbook 1996*.

democratic. Income distribution has become more dispersed during the 1980s and 1990s with Britain under Thatcher leading the way (see Table 6.10[9]). Earnings dispersions act as a partial explanation for this growing inequality, where even in Sweden, which attempts to remain true to social democratic values, this is the case (see Table 6.11[10]). Levels of exclusion from the labour force have risen (see Table 6.12[11]) and this has made any attempted moves towards equality more difficult to achieve because the numbers requiring help have increased.

Table 6.7   Social protection benefits by group of functions

	France	Spain	Greece
		Percentage of total expenditure	
Health (1980)	35.6	36.9	26.0
(1992)	34.6	36.6	18.7
Old Age/Survivors (1980)	43.9	40.8	61.9
(1992)	44.1	41.3	69.0
Family/Maternity (1980)	12.7	4.4	4.5
(1992)	9.5	1.8	1.7
Unemployment (1980)	5.1	16.2	2.5
(1992)	7.7	18.5	5.3
Other (1980)	2.7	1.8	5.1
(1992)	4.1	1.9	5.3

Source: Commission of the European Communities, *A Social Portrait of Europe*.

Table 6.8   Spending on education (at current prices as percentage of GDP)

	France	*Spain*
1985	5.6	3.8
1986	5.5	3.8
1987	5.4	4.0
1988	5.3	4.0
1989	5.2	4.1
1990	5.4	4.2
1991	5.5	4.4
1992	5.8	

Source: Eurostat, *Yearbook 1996*.

All these figures have to be placed into the context of the time, but the circumstances of the late 1990s are where many of the constraints on spending are set by the governments, both domestically and internationally, and where firms make very large profits but governments tolerate unemployment and social problems. Social democrats do not appear to work against these constraints.

If we consider the time periods when social democratic parties were out of office in the above countries there are few significant differences. In the case of Spain such observations are not possible because the opposition right-wing party only came into government in 1996 and figures are not, therefore, available.[12] There is a problem of time lag involved when considering the often short periods when the social democrats were out of office in these countries as reforms may take time to come to fruition. General observations, however, suggest that the trends between Right and Left, on the whole, varied little. Unemployment (Table 6.1) generally became worse under right-wing rule but when the social democrats re-entered office they failed to solve the problem. With inflation (Table 6.2) and growth (Table 6.3) the records were just as bad.

Table 6.9   Poverty (percentage of adults with income under 75% of EU average) (% of households)

	France	*Spain*	*Greece*
1980	18.0	20.3	20.6
1985	14.8	17.8	17.4
1988	14.0	16.7	20.6

Source: Commission of the European Communities, *A Social Portrait of Europe*.

Table 6.10   **National studies of income distribution: Gini coefficients from 1970**

	France	Germany	Norway	Sweden	UK
1970	39.8				25.5
1971					26.2
1972					26.5
1973		25.4			25.5
1974				24.7	
1975	38.4			21.3	23.8
1976				20.9	23.7
1977				20.4	23.4
1978		25.4		20.0	23.5
1979	36.4			19.7	24.8
1980				19.4	25.3
1981				19.1	25.9
1982			23.4	19.4	25.8
1983		25.5		19.4	26.4
1984	37.2			20.4	26.6
1985		26.0		20.5	27.9
1986			22.6	21.4	28.8
1987		25.2		20.5	30.2
1988				20.4	32.0
1989			24.4	21.0	32.4
1990		26.0		23.5	33.7
1991				24.7	33.7
1992					

Source: A. B. Atkinson, *Incomes and the Welfare State: Essays on Britain and Europe*, pp. 60–1.

But in Sweden, growth under the right-wing government was even lower. Social protection (Tables 6.4 and 6.5) may even have been a little more generous than under the social democrats. Spending priorities varied little between the governments, such as in education (Table 6.8) and health (Table 6.6), and the respective trends in each country remained constant. Exclusion from the labour market (Table 6.12) demonstrated the same trends, except for Sweden where the opposite occurred and exclusion rose under the right-wing government. The same divergence in income distribution (Table 6.10) took place under governments of both right- and left-wing parties.

If the trends between right- and left-wing governments varied then it could be suggested that in a country-specific context social democrats were adhering to their aims. Yet when few, if any, differences are evident it becomes difficult to state that social democrats are behaving in a manner which contrasts with their right-wing competitors.

Table 6.11 Trends in earning dispersion, 1970–94 (comparison of D9 to D5 group)

	1979	1980	1981	1982	1983	1984	1985	1986	1987	1988	1989	1990	1991	1992	1993	1994
France	1.94	1.93	1.93	1.94	1.94	1.93	1.95	1.96	1.97	1.97	1.99	1.99	1.99	1.97	1.99	1.99
Portugal							2.14				2.24		2.24	2.48	2.47	
Sweden		1.57	1.55	1.53	1.50	1.52	1.59	1.57	1.57	1.56	1.57	1.52	1.55	1.57	1.59	

Source: OECD, Employment Outlook, July, 1996.

Table 6.12   Exclusion from the labour force

	France	People not in the labour force, aged 15 to 64 1985 = 100 Greece	Sweden
1985	100.0	100.0	100.0
1986	98.7	101.9	98.0
1987	100.7	103.5	96.8
1988	102.4	103.0	94.6
1989	102.9	103.6	92.2
1990	104.2	107.4	91.0
1991	107.3	112.5	97.4
1992	106.4	110.6	109.2
1993	106.1	111.1	124.0
1994	105.9	109.6	133.8
1995	105.9	108.0	131.0

Source: Eurostat, *Yearbook 1996*.

Some of the most important information about the performance of any government is the attitude of the electorate to certain key questions about personal security and attitudes to the future. This constitutes the second failure outlined in the introduction to the chapter, that social democratic parties are not providing a sense of optimism and rising expectations among the electorate. In the examples of the Euro-barometer and Swedish data presented here (see Tables 6.13–6.17) it is clear that, in general, the time spent by the social democrats in office failed to convince people that the future would be better and that a difference could be made. They have, therefore, failed to build themselves a base of support. Social democracy requires raised expectations and their periods in office in Spain, Greece, France and Sweden have served only to dash them. The archetypal Left/Right divide is one between radicalism and conservatism so the history of 'left-wing' parties means a hope that improvements and changes will be made. Expectations, therefore, are higher for the Left than for the Right. When asked to consider how the general economic situation had developed over the past year, the general impression was of a situation that had got worse over the period of social democratic rule. There was no perceptible alteration in patterns of attitudes towards improvements in the finances of households and this also applied to the future prospects over the coming next year. The general expectation was of a situation that would continue to get worse.

Table 6.13   Perception of general economic situation:

(a) **From October 1990: 'Compared to 12 months ago, do you think that the general economic situation in this country is... ?'**
(b) **From October 1982 to November 1989: 'How do you think the general economic situation in this country has changed over the past 12 months?'**

France (*a*)

% of sample	1982	1983	1984	1985	1986	1987	1988	1989	1990	1991	1992	1993
a lot better	1	1	1	1	1	1	1	2	1	0	0	0
a little better	13	16	11	19	19	15	31	19	13	5	7	8
same	29	26	24	33	45	34	39	38	30	31	29	27
a little worse	35	33	36	31	23	35	21	26	40	37	37	37
a lot worse	20	21	26	14	8	12	6	9	13	24	25	26
don't know												

France (b)

% of sample	1994	1995
a lot better	1	1
a little better	8	18
same	27	41
a little worse	26	13
a lot worse	26	13
don't know	2	2

Spain (a)

% of sample	1985	1986	1987	1988	1989	1990	1991	1992	1993	1994	1995
a lot better	3	3	3	4	5	4	6	1	1	1	2
a little better	24	28	31	35	28	25	27	7	5	5	18
same	26	28	36	33	33	28	34	15	15	16	31
a little worse	28	29	22	20	21	31	20	43	41	42	30
a lot worse	12	7	5	5	10	6	7	31	36	36	18
don't know										2	2

Greece (a)

% of sample	1982	1983	1984	1985	1986	1987	1988	1989	1990	1991	1992	1993
a lot better	10	7	6	2	5	4	5	2	3	2	1	2
a little better	38	31	29	6	21	21	21	7	15	12	8	16
same	23	21	25	20	22	22	27	21	20	15	18	42
a little worse	18	26	21	36	30	27	25	25	36	36	40	23
a lot worse	5	10	11	30	18	22	15	35	22	30	30	10
don't know												

Table 6.13 *continued*

Greece (b)

% of sample	1994	1995
a lot better	2	1
a little better	16	12
same	43	25
a little worse	23	39
a lot worse	10	21
don't know	7	2

Analysis of the tables confirms that social democratic governments are not achieving outcomes that are compatible with their aims and values. Rising unemployment, growing income inequality, no clear indication of where social spending priorities lie, rising social protection spending mainly due to higher unemployment and rising exclusion from the labour market are not compatible with social democratic desires for a 'better society'. The effectiveness of welfare states in achieving this outcome was undermined by their faltering base of finance due to the failure of economic growth. Social democratic governments have also failed to convince the public that social and economic improvements will be forthcoming meaning that, according to the public, a 'better society' will not occur. Social democratic parties are often still rhetorically social democrat, but increasingly less so in terms of their governmental performance.

Failure three – the electoral coalition

The third failure of 'new' social democracy concerns its unstable electoral coalition. Such instability may hinder the consistent achievement of governmental office and could add to the already existing levels of electoral volatility. The nature of the New Labour electoral coalition at the 1997 British general election is characteristic of the approach of 'new' social democracy. Far from being a class-based approach, it was a highly heterogeneous grouping and typical of the national appeal Blair attempted to project. In addition, it signified a reversal of fortunes for the Labour Party, rebuilding traditional sources of support but also gaining ground in groups which had hitherto been hostile. The Blair approach looked to move beyond the 'rainbow' coalition of the poor and disaffected groups in society to achieve middle-class inclusion.

Table 6.14   Perception of financial situation:

(a) From October 1990: 'Compared to 12 months ago, do you think the financial situation of your household, now is…'
(b) October 1989 and before: 'How does the financial situation of your household now compared with what it was 12 months ago?'

France (a)

% of sample	1982	1983	1984	1985	1986	1987	1988	1989	1990	1991	1992	1993
a lot better	1	2	2	1	2	2	3	5	4	2	4	2
a little better	9	8	5	9	9	8	13	14	16	12	11	10
same	38	33	29	35	39	43	44	43	43	43	46	40
a little worse	35	34	38	35	35	30	28	25	26	26	25	33
a lot worse	14	21	24	18	13	15	10	11	9	14	12	13
don't know												

France (b)

% of sample	1994	1995
a lot better	2	2
a little better	10	12
same	40	48
a little worse	33	26
a lot worse	13	11
don't know	2	1

Spain (a)

% of sample	1985	1986	1987	1988	1989	1990	1991	1992	1993	1994	1995
a lot better	3	1	2	2	2	3	2	2	2	2	1
a little better	14	13	18	21	19	25	23	13	10	10	13
same	51	52	56	52	47	54	54	51	52	52	56
a little worse	22	24	16	18	23	15	14	27	28	29	22
a lot worse	8	5	5	5	9	3	2	6	7	7	7
don't know										1	1

Greece (a)

% of sample	1982	1983	1984	1985	1986	1987	1988	1989	1990	1991	1992	1993
a lot better	10	7	7	2	7	4	7	2	4	2	2	2
a little better	32	25	26	11	23	32	36	11	16	12	8	16
same	36	35	40	39	32	32	36	48	27	25	29	56
a little worse	15	23	18	28	23	22	20	18	34	36	38	19
a lot worse	6	10	8	18	14	20	11	16	18	24	22	5
don't know												

Table 6.14   *continued*

Greece (b)

% of sample	1994	1995
a lot better	2	2
a little better	16	15
same	56	29
a little worse	19	29
a lot worse	5	15
don't know	2	1

But the fragility of this approach can be demonstrated by an examination of the New Labour support and its limited sources of cohesion. The election provided New Labour with its largest ever parliamentary majority but not its largest share of the vote. The electoral system, on this occasion, aided the party, as did the propensity of the electorate to vote tactically to defeat Conservative MPs. This places part of the explanation for Labour's historic victory in the hands of the Conservative Party, their loss of support and the loss of their image for economic competence after sterling's withdrawal from the ERM.[13] 'Labour recovered most in areas where the party had been weakest throughout the Thatcher years, storming back in Greater London: the South East and the Midlands.'[14] Table 6.18 illustrates the decline of the North–South divide in British politics and the national appeal of New Labour's victory.

The swing from the Conservative Party was 10.5 per cent, the highest since 1945. Two million voters moved directly from the Conservatives to Labour, and one-fifth of Liberal Democrat voters moved to Labour.[15] The sources of Labour's 1997 vote are shown in Table 6.19.

Constituencies with a high concentration of professional and managerial workers moved sharply to Labour. The skilled non-manual (C1) group which had acted as the bedrock of Thatcherite success also voted New Labour. The Blair approach was successful in maintaining the support of Labour's core electorate but also added to that the middle classes. The decline of class voting can be traced over time, and the shift in Labour's support likewise. Table 6.20 illustrates the decline of class voting and the rise of Labour's all-encompassing appeal. With the level of party identification falling as well, this appears to give credence

Table 6.15   Perception of the future:

(a) **From October 1989: 'As far as you are concerned, do you think that the next year (...) will be better or worse than (...)?'**
(b) **From 1980 to 1989: 'So far as you are concerned, do you think that next year (...) will get better or worse than the year that is ending?'**

France *(a)*

% of sample	1980	1981	1982	1983	1984	1985	1986	1987	1988	1989^I	1989^{II}	1990
better	15	32	18	17	15	26	26	24	30	33	43	29
worse	29	32	42	46	41	21	19	25	17	12	14	30
same	35	28	36	31	36	45	47	43	48	48	30	34
no reply	11	8	4	6	8	8	8	8	5	7	13	7

France (b)

% of sample	1991	1992	1993	1994	1995
better	24	29	25	25	33
worse	25	28	38	38	19
same	40	36	31	31	39
no reply	11	7	6	6	9

Spain (a)

% of sample	1980	1981	1982	1983	1984	1985	1986	1987	1988	1989^I	1989^{II}	1990
better	26	53	37	29	33	38	35	37	47	38	35
worse	39	13	25	34	25	15	14	16	11	14	23
same	22	24	26	28	28	28	36	35	30	33	29
no reply	13	10	12	9	14	19	15	12	12	15	13

Spain (b)

% of sample	1991	1992	1993	1994	1995
better	49	21	33	33	41
worse	17	46	31	31	23
same	23	25	27	27	29
no reply	11	8	9	9	7

Greece (a)

% of sample	1980	1981	1982	1983	1984	1985	1986	1987	1988	1989^I	1989^{II}	1990
better	39	72	59	50	53	26	36	32	39	49	47	36
worse	39	6	18	27	21	45	37	33	24	22	16	43
same	13	9	10	15	14	19	17	23	23	11	18	13
no reply	9	13	13	8	12	10	10	12	14	18	19	8

Table 6.15 *continued*

Greece (b)

% of sample	1991	1992	1993	1994	1995
better	29	26	47	48	22
worse	46	50	19	19	60
same	14	17	20	20	15
no reply	11	7	14	4	4

Source: Eurobarometer, *Public Opinion in the European Union* (various years).

to the concept of 'voters as consumers' leaving parties to forward policy and managerial packages.

Norris (1997) shows, with reference to the Alford index, that its stepped shifts in values indicates that 'the explanation lies in the changing pattern of party competition, notably New Labour's shift towards the ideological middle ground with a classless appeal, rather than a steady secular slide due to long-term social trends.'[16] Owner occupiers, the young and first-time voters all looked to Labour; only among the over 65s did they not make gains. Table 6.21 presents the full details of the electoral coalition.

But the maintenance of this heterogeneous coalition may prove to be difficult. According to David Marquand (1997) the coalition is a fragile one. 'Wide ranging coalitions are almost bound to be fragile: their fragility is a condition of their capacity to range widely. But this coalition is more fragile than most.'[17] He views the coalition as being held together by an antipathy towards post-Thatcherite Conservatism and this would appear to be born out by the calls for the 'time for a change' (see Table 6.22). Apart from this issue, the wishes of the coalition diverge, and at the extremes may come into conflict with one another, i.e. the demands for fiscal rectitude may hinder the party's ability to deliver on the NHS. Table 6.23 shows a large concern for the problems faced by the Conservative Party and John Major as Prime Minister when deciding whether to vote for the Labour Party, although the changes made by Blair to Labour and the characteristics of Blair himself were also important in the electoral victory, as were some of the specific expectations of his party in government. The most urgent problems which the electorate saw were divergent (see Table 6.24), with a large section seeing health as by far the most important, followed by unemployment and education, and then Europe and law and order before some minor concerns are noted.

Table 6.16   Perception of economic situation (Sweden):

Over the past year has your personal economic situation got better or worse?

				% of respondents			
	1986	1987	1988	1989	1990	1991	1992
better	24	24	27	24	21	22	15
worse	17	18	18	19	31	25	34

Apart from the inability of the Conservative Party to portray itself as a credible political force, Labour gained support because of perceived changes in its own structures and policies (see Table 6.25).

Labour were the party which would be 'good for all classes' (see Table 6.26) and they also raised expectations but only slightly (see Table 6.27). The Labour Party achieved the 'successful minimisation of expectations'.[18] Tony Blair as leader also provided New Labour with an electoral asset (see Table 6.28).

Labour has to be aware that there was a substantial decline in turnout among all sections of the electorate. The data presented by Denver and Hands (1997) also suggests that there was a tendency for past and potential Labour supporters to stay away from the polls in larger numbers. Therefore, the endorsement of New Labour was not a full one. Those voters from inner city areas and the poor showed a large amount of disaffection. Rising volatility among the electorate may also undermine the coalition (see Table 6.29).

The victory was achieved on the lowest electoral turnout since the Second World War and it fell most sharply in Labour areas.[19] Blair's centralization of power left few buffers between himself and the blame when things do go wrong,[20] and short-term support is always more likely to defect in times of difficulty. Blair could comfort himself in

Table 6.17   Perception of the past year (Sweden):

Over the past year has the economy of Sweden got better or worse?

				% of respondents			
	1986	1987	1988	1989	1990	1991	1992
better	32	32	30	12	2	3	3
worse	20	16	16	38	81	80	94

Source: S. Holmberg and L. Weibull, *Perspektiv På Krisen*, Samhälle Opinion Massmedia.

Table 6.18 Party shares of votes and changes in vote shares in standard regions (%)

Region	Con.	Lab.	Lib. Dem.	Nat.	Oth.	Change 1992–97		
						Con.	Lab.	Lib. Dem.
Scotland	17.5	45.6	13.0	22.1	1.9	–8.2	+6.6	–0.1
Wales	19.6	54.7	12.4	9.9	3.4	–9.0	+11.4	0
North	22.2	6.9		13.3	3.7	–11.2	+10.3	–2.2
North West	27.1	54.2		14.3	4.5	–10.7	+9.3	–1.5
Yorks & Humbs	28.0	52.0		16.0	4.1	–9.9	+7.6	–0.8
West Midlands	33.7	47.8		13.6	3.7	–11.7	+10.4	–1.6
East Midlands	34.9	47.8		13.6	3.7	–11.7	+10.4	–1.6
East Anglia	38.7	38.3		17.9	5.1	–12.3	+10.3	–1.6
South East	41.4	31.9		21.4	5.4	–13.1	+11.1	–2.0
Gtr London	31.2	49.5		14.6	4.7	–14.1	+12.5	–0.6
South West	36.7	26.4		31.3	5.6	–10.9	+7.2	–0.1

Source: D. Denver, 'The Results: How Britain Voted', in Geddes and Tonge (eds), *Labour's Landslide*, p. 11.

President Clinton's ability to maintain the same form of coalition in his re-election and in the persistent failures of the Conservative Party. Clinton owed much of *his* victory to the problems of the Republican Party.

Whereas the SAP, for many years, did maintain a national coalition it was done under very different economic, political and social circumstances. It too benefited from the absence of a united opposition and the party delivered on many of its aims. There was, however, a larger degree of unity on these aims and this does not appear probable with the 'new' social democratic approach. The new coalition may be transitory because of its rejection of a party or a set of policies, as opposed to an embrace of the social democratic alternative.

Table 6.19 Sources of Labour's 1997 vote

	%
Old Labour voters	65
Ex-Conservatives	12
Too young, abstained	15
Ex-Liberal Democrat	6
Other, don't know	2

Source: R. Rose 'The New Labour Government: On the Crest of a Wave', *Parliamentary Affairs*, p. 752.

Table 6.20   Occupational class and vote, 1964–97

	1964 Nonmanual (%)	1964 Manual (%)	1997 Nonmanual (%)	1997 Manual (%)
Conservative	62 (a)	28 (c)	38	29
Labour	22 (b)	64 (d)	40	58
Liberal Democrat	18	8	18	12

	Absolute class voting index (A)	Relative class voting index (B)
1964	76	6.4
1966	78	6.4
1970	64	4.5
1974 (Feb)	64	5.7
1974 (Oct)	59	4.8
1979	52	3.7
1983	45	3.9
1987	44	3.5
1992	47	3.3
1997	29	1.9

A: $(a - b) + (d - c)$
B: $(a/b) / (c/d)$

Source: D. Sanders, 'The New Electoral Battleground', *in New Labour Triumphs: Britain at the Polls*, p. 220.

The Australasian experience

The Australasian parties of the Australian Labor Party (ALP) and New Zealand Labour Party (NZLP) both maintain characteristics of the Northern model and act as examples of parties which won elections and followed a more openly market-dominated agenda.[21] The NZLP followed neoliberal theory to the greatest extent and as a result it has lost much of its previous influence. However, the ALP has been able to rebuild itself after the difficult later years of the Keating government and appears well placed for future governmental office. Australia and New Zealand pursued the market agenda to an extent that other social democrats did not. They looked to deregulate their economies, introduce the market into new areas, cut back the powers and scope of state intervention, and incentivized the welfare state and taxation systems. They hoped to encourage the market while retaining the social democratic egalitarian element.

Table 6.21   Vote by group (%)

	Con. 1997	Change since 1992	Lab. 1997	Change since 1992	Lib. Dem. 1997	Change since 1992
All	*31*	*−11*	*44*	*+9*	*17*	*−1*
Men	31	−11	45	+8	17	0
Women	32	−12	45	+11	17	−2
18–29	22	−19	56	+18	18	+1
30–44	26	−15	49	+15	17	−5
45–64	33	−14	43	+9	18	+1
65+	44	−3	34	−1	17	+1
AB voters (managerial/ professional)	42	−14	31	+11	21	0
C1 (white collar)	26	−15	47	+15	19	−4
C2 (skilled workers)	25	−13	54	+13	14	−2
DE (semi-skilled, unskilled, state pensioners)	21	−16	61	+15	13	−2
Own home outright	41	−14	35	+10	16	−2
Mortgage-payers	31	−16	44	+15	18	−2
Council tenants	13	−8	66	+1	15	+4

Source: P. Kellner, 'Why the Tories Were Trounced', *Parliamentary Affairs*, p. 617.

Table 6.22   The Conservative record:

Q: 'Which of the following comes closest to your view?'

	All.	Con.	Lab.	Lib. Dem.	Ex-Con.	New Lab.
'It's time for a change: the Conservatives have done a bad job'	*44*	3	71	48	40	60
'This is no time for a change; Labour wouldn't do any better'	*32*	92	3	9	8	3
'No matter how well or how badly the Conservatives have done, its simply time for a change'	*23*	5	26	42	51	37

Table 6.23 Reasons for voting Labour:

Q: 'I am going to read out some of the reasons people have given for voting Labour on Thursday. Could you tell me, for each, whether it was very important for you personally, fairly important, not very important or not at all important?' (Labour supporters only)

	Very	Fairly	Not very	Not at all	Don't know
Labour, under Mr Blair, became more moderate and sensible	66	23	6	3	2
The Conservatives were sleazy and corrupt	62	17	13	5	8
It was time for a change	65	14	13	6	3
Labour will improve public services like the NHS and education	90	7	1	1	2
The Conservatives broke too many promises	75	14	5	2	2
Labour will lower unemployment	74	19	3	2	2
Tony Blair will provide strong leadership	78	16	3	2	2
Mr Major's government was accident prone and could never seem to get anything right	53	24	13	6	3
John Major was a weak leader	43	24	18	11	4

Source: Gallup, *Political and Economic Index*, May 1997, p. 22.

The market reforms carried out in the two countries went further in New Zealand than they did in Australia and the results were far from convincing.[22] Hawke in Australia adopted a more consensual approach whereas the New Zealand method was characterized by the phrase 'crash through or crash', i.e. the reforms would either solve New Zealand's problems or they would fail completely. However, the two countries did pursue a series of common reforms: economic protection was abandoned, the machinery of government was modernized, there was a shift away from centralized wage bargaining structures, female political participation increased, foreign policy shifted to place a greater emphasis on the Asia-Pacific region, and environmental concerns and the rights of indigenous minorities were given an enhanced role.[23]

Although both parties followed a similar overall pattern, variations appeared in the results that each party obtained. Both set a precedence upon which the right-wing parties that followed them into power could build. The interests that the ALP had to contend with, such as the trade unions (with their close institutional ties with the ALP), a federal structure and so on, did not exist in New Zealand, so the NZLP had a compar-

Table 6.24   The major problems facing Britain:

Q: 'And what would you say is the next most urgent problem?' (Includes most urgent problem)

	Today	Mar.	Feb.	Jan.	Nov./ Dec.	Early Nov.	Late Sep.
Health	41	40	42	42	37	27	34
Unemployment	35	39	33	38	42	41	48
Education	30	28	29	30	29	35	20
Europe	15	17	22	17	12	10	10
Law and order	14	13	13	15	13	26	18
Housing	3	7	5	7	7	7	9
Cost of living	5	4	3	5	12	9	8
Other economic issues	5	4	4	5	6	4	8
Pensions	5	3	4	5	6	4	5
'Mad Cow'	0	1	1	1	1	1	2
Immigrants	1	1	1	1	1	1	1
Environment	1	1	1	1	0	1	1
Defence	0	0	1	0	0	0	1
Council tax	1	1	1	1	1	1	1
International affairs	0	0	0	1	0	0	1
Other	21	22	22	19	14	17	16

Source: Gallup, *Political and Economic Index*, April 1997, p. 4.

atively easy task in pressing ahead with whatever they felt the country required. This degree of concentrated power in the hands of the government of New Zealand left them in a very powerful position. The man who pushed many of the reforms through, Roger Douglas, had business experience, whereas in Australia Bob Hawke with a background in the trade unions was brought up in the tradition of negotiating.

Table 6.25   Party ratings on the main issues (%):

Q: 'Which party do you trust most to take the right decisions about...'

	Conservative		Labour		Lib Dem	
	1997	Change since 1992	1997	Change since 1992	1997	Change since 1992
The economy	42	−11	44	+11	13	0
Income tax	36	−19	44	+13	0	+6
Schools/education	26	−14	48	+9	26	+5
Dealing with sleaze	23	n/a	49	n/a	29	n/a

Source: P. Kellner, 'Why the Tories Were Trounced', *Parliamentary Affairs*, p. 621.

Table 6.26   Party images (%)

Q: 'Regardless of how you voted today, do you think that the Conservative Party is good for one class or good for all classes? Regardless of how you voted today, do you think that the Labour Party is good for one class or all classes?'

	All Con.	Lab.	Ex-Conservative voters Con.	Lab.	New Labour voters Con.	Lab.
Good for one class	68	31	71	38	84	13
Good for all classes	32	69	29	62	16	87

Source: P. Kellner, 'Why the Tories Were Trounced', *Parliamentary Affairs*, p. 627.

Table 6.27   Expectations (%):

Q: 'If Labour wins the election, do you think that, overall, Labour policies will make things in Britain...'

	All	Labour policies... Ex-Con.	Lab.
A lot better	24	17	40
A little better	33	42	54
Would make no difference	11	18	3
A little worse	16	18	1
A lot worse	17	6	1

Source: P. Kellner, 'Why the Tories Were Trounced', *Parliamentary Affairs*, p. 622.

Table 6.28   Best Prime Minister (%):

Q: 'Regardless of how you voted today, who do you think would make the best Prime Minister?'

	1992 %	1997 %	Change
Neil Kinnock/Tony Blair	30	47	+17
John Major	45	33	–12
Paddy Ashdown	26	20	–6

Source: P. Kellner, 'Why the Tories Were Trounced', *Parliamentary Affairs*, p. 626.

Table 6.29   Pederson index of electoral volatility, average for 13 European party systems, 1948–94, and for Britain, 1948–97 (in percentages)

	1948–59	1960–69	1970–79	1980–89	1990–94	1997
European average	7.8	7.3	8.2	8.5	13.8	
UK	4.4	5.2	8.3	3.4	5.1	13.0

Source: D. Sanders, 'The New Electoral Battleground', *New Labour Triumphs: Britain at the Polls 1997*, p. 222.

The degree to which the absence of a role for the state hindered the performance, both economically and socially, of New Zealand can be disputed. Yet, by comparing the two countries, it is obvious that the one that maintained a role for the state, however reduced, achieved more economically. The Australian economy performed better that did the New Zealand economy. The New Zealand neoliberal experiment was carried forward to an extent that no other country attempted, and yet it failed to deliver what it promised. The interests of business and of the free market were allowed free rein at the expense of social considerations. The role of the state was dismantled and private provision came to dominate what remained of the welfare state.

The NZLP has undermined its own electoral base and can be said to highlight the underlying problems of social democrats using the market to the exclusion of all else. The ALP managed to combine its values with the use of the market by involving all the relevant actors in an Accord process with the trade unions.[24] The ALP also attempted to bring together business leaders, government ministers and trade unionists on a number of occasions. However, it was aided by the changing nature of the Australian economy with the decline in its traditional markets and the growing influence of the Asia-Pacific region. Keating suggested that the party had developed a new 'modern Australian social democracy'[25] but it more closely resembled 'pragmatic neoliberalism'.[26] Yet, the social achievements of the Labor governments have come into question.[27]

Both parties believed that international economic competitiveness would bring with it great social and economic benefits and that these would outweigh any short-term costs. The parties aimed to provide social cohesion within a competitive economy. However, the associated social costs remained in the minds of the electorate, especially in the case of New Zealand, and both parties have been left with the task of rebuilding support among their core electorate. Both parties effectively dismantled their country's postwar settlement, so much so that by the 1998 general election the ALP was having to make additional efforts to regain its blue-collar voters through some limited spending commitments on education, health and employment.

Conclusion

While confronted with a dilemma over the altered nature of the social environment, the new economic environment and the problems of strategy, the parties are conceding ground in areas that social democrats have traditionally held so that they are no longer adhering to their basic values. Social democratic parties no longer appear to know where they are going or what they are aiming for. 'New' and 'classic' social democracy enjoy slightly differing aims and, therefore, employ different measures of success. Through these the performances of social democratic parties in office could be measured and evaluated. This chapter has attempted to make a small step towards this.

The parties in government during the 1980s and 1990s failed to achieve their social democratic aims. Instead of improving the social and economic situation in each country the direction was generally the opposite. Yet there has not been a reaction against these failures of 'new' social democracy. Indeed, this model, as exemplified by New Labour, is taking the reforms a stage further. But one could look to the market reformism of the ALP and NZLP as former front runners in this field and note that the apparent social costs of this reformism has blighted their recent electoral records, especially in the case of the NZLP.

The electoral coalition forwarded by 'new' social democracy appears to be an unstable one because of the lack of a unifying cause. A heterogeneous coalition is more liable to breakdown than the former single-class approach, but the latter is no longer applicable. The new coalition lacks a concept of unity because social democrats have not forwarded a value or policy to act as the linchpin of such cohesion. Calls for 'a change' are necessarily self-fulfilling once a different party enters office and are, therefore, only temporary. In addition, if social democrats merely follow the policies of previous, usually right-wing neoliberal governments, then this lack of change will cost them support.

7
Conclusion

Introduction

'New' social democracy is failing to prove itself as a distinct political model and in order for it to play a role in protecting democratic systems and retain its electoral base this has to be rectified. Social democrats are conceding ground in areas that should be of concern to them and the examination of the parties proves this to be the case. At the present time, social democrats are merely replicating the neoliberal agenda and this is leading to a series of dilemmas. However, not all social democratic parties are equally guilty of following the neoliberal agenda. The Scandinavian parties do still attempt to adhere to their values and this is shown by the SAP's cutting of welfare benefits while at least maintaining their universality. The Norwegian DNA is aided by the country's oil revenue which helps maintain spending and the French PS is making some headway in its attempts to pursue a social democratic agenda by shortening the working week. The German SPD, at its party congress in 1997, did begin to put forward a social democratic agenda, at least in embryonic form.

Each party is open to a series of internal and external constraints, some of which are more powerful than others. The Southern model of social democracy has been more able to break with the 'classic' social democratic traditions because of the weakness of many of these constraints coinciding with a party structure conducive to strong leadership and a set of wider circumstances that enabled them to fully exploit this situation. However, France stands as the example where this is less the case. The Northern parties have been more dominated by the constraints and this has slowed their adoption of neoliberalism. But in some cases they have freed themselves from the constraints.

This helps to explain why some countries have moved towards 'new' social democracy more rapidly than others. The external common constraints have meant that there has been some movement in all of the parties.

While social democrats are increasingly directing themselves towards neoliberalism, it may not be the case that this path is inevitable. There are several signs of encouragement for those who wish for a more definite implementation of social democratic values. Most importantly for social democrats are the signs of weakness and collapse in the neoliberal ideology. Many of its core assumptions are unravelling. Several examples will suffice. Low costs are not the only incentive to investment; other factors are also important such as access to markets, a country's skills base and its level of infrastructure. A 1997 article in *Business Week* warned that 'production everywhere is running ahead of consumption ... today, for the first time in years, there is world-wide over-capacity ... and the excess supply will get worse.'[1] This demonstrates that markets are not automatically self-correcting as neoliberals claim they are. The concept of a free market in labour leading to flexible wage levels that reflect the market circumstances is challenged by Hutton (1995) among others. He shows that wages are not flexible in the manner considered by neoliberals. Hutton, Fukuyama (1995) and Driver and Martell (1998) all recognize the need for social capital in order to achieve economic growth. Those countries which have higher levels of social capital tend to have higher levels of economic growth. Wilkinson (1998) claims that inequality undermines moral codes, common public and social spaces, empathy and trust. He, therefore, believes that it is economically and socially efficient to have low levels of inequality. This forms the basis of an argument for higher levels of public expenditure to redress imbalances. Low equality societies have poorer health, more violence, less self-esteem and more discrimination. Recent events in the former Soviet Union, where markets have been introduced swiftly with little regard to existing social and political institutions, show neoliberalism's limitations. Instability, crime and violence have now grown up around their markets. The collapse of the East Asian financial markets in 1998 illustrated their instability and prompted former advocates of a free market approach to recognize the need for an overall reform of the system and the need for regulation.[2]

Some limited measure towards a possible move away from neoliberalism was presented by European finance ministers at the end of 1998, where open discussion was made of a form of Euro-Keynesianism.

A 'New European Way' statement suggested that money be spent on infrastructure projects and that coordinated action be considered on job creation. However, the existing neoliberal Maastricht rules and the hostility of the chief of the European Central Bank do not bode well for such plans. The statement did not outline the sources of funding for any Euro projects and did not challenge the basis of globalization which all the left-of-centre parties recognize. It appears that Keynesianism on a European basis is a replacement for Keynesianism at a national level. Domestically social democratic governments look to fiscal rectitude and lower taxation leaving sources of additional funding for Keynesian projects unclear. It must be noted that such Euro-Keynesian thinking remains in an embryonic form. There is, therefore, a definite intellectual challenge to neoliberalism and grounds for believing that it can develop as neoliberal thinking unravels.

Ironically, much of the thinking applicable to 'new' social democracy comes from the American Democratic Party. Although not a member of the social democratic family, it has enjoyed a close relationship with it and has been seen to follow a similar development path in recent years. The realization of the need for a distinct social democratic agenda and of the apparent political space for it means that a new cohesive progressive coalition can be constructed. Such a model, the need for it and examples of some of the early consideration it is being given by the Democrats and the SPD, will be described in this conclusion to the work along with the 'Third Way' which is attempting to act as a new model of social democratic thinking. Communitarianism, which suggests that society's problems can be blamed on the death of the active citizens and that morals can only be restored through the reconstruction of communities, will also be discussed as it has been forwarded as the foundation of a new social democratic approach.

The social democratic dilemmas

In this era of the neoliberal political settlement social democrats have been faced by a number of dilemmas.

The traditional electorate of the social democrats, the working class, was a numerical majority but has reduced in size. Appeals now made by social democrats operate around their belief in capital and market interests, thereby undermining what remains of their working-class base. Yet, such pronouncements prevent appeals to the middle class who face exclusion from the welfare state and bear the brunt of the adverse effects of globalization. So by adhering to a neoliberal agenda, social democrats are removing any semblance of an electoral coalition.

The absence of a basis of economic policy remains a problem for social democrats. Since the demise of Keynesian economics and their adoption of neoliberalism, the Left has been unable to pursue economic policies which are consistent with their values. A more fruitful approach would be to examine the details of the varieties of capitalism available.[3] This would enable them to look to the incorporation and well-being of the citizen into the heart of the economic and political process. This opens up an economic approach of participation, differing ownership structures and financial system alterations. The style of economics decided upon will also aid social democrats in their attitude towards the role of the state, and towards the degree of regulation and ownership in a market economy. One of the state's traditional roles was to aid the achievement of solidarity. But as the state, trade unions and collective institutions are reduced in size this solidarity is undermined. As a result there has been a greater reliance by social democrats upon parents, families, etc. and these are traditionally viewed as Conservative institutions.

Greater scope for action at the level of the European Union may be feasible if neoliberal economics were to be abandoned meaning that conflict between countries could be avoided. However, for this to occur European structures and policies would have to be revised in line with social democratic values.

A decision has to be made whether to advocate 'safe' social democratic issues, such as the welfare state, or to move to the opposition's territory. While adhering to an agenda that is not their own, the scope for pursuing 'safe' issues diminishes as cutbacks and the introduction of markets into the public sector undermine the credibility of such appeals. The type of party system in which the social democrats operate will decide whether or not this approach is at all possible.

The appropriate party structure for social democrats remains undecided. If democratic and constitutional reform is part of the agenda then it has to occur within the country and the party and at the supranational level, i.e. Europe. The challenge now is the creation of a relevant organization and membership for the next century.

The absence of a 'big idea' is a concern to some, but to others it is merely representative of the decline of political ideologies. If it is the case that there are now few differences between the parties of the Left and the Right, then this would imply that big ideas are no longer part of the agenda. If correct, then electoral competition is reduced to a debate as to which party is best able to manage the economy and a position in government. The credibility of a party and its policies may form part of the appeal but as such it does not provide a distinction between social democratic parties and parties of the Right. For social democrats part of outlining an alternative to the debate over credibility lies in being more self-confident and escaping from their defensive mindset.

Justifications for a new model

A brief reference to the example of the NZLP, as outlined in Chapter 6, is sufficient to illustrate the dangers of implementing a series of reforms that are hostile to one's own traditions. The party has been reduced to a mere shadow of its former strength because it has alienated large swathes of its traditional electorate and is finding it hard to rebuild its reputation and support. This has to be the 'worst' case scenario but it serves as a vivid illustration of the dangers of moving away from social democratic values for these parties.

The NZLP took office in 1984 during a period that brought into question the perceived role of the social democratic state. The party succeeded in destroying the economic base of its traditional electorate and heightened economic and social tensions. The extreme neo-liberalism of 'Rogernomics' included some of the most 'advanced' thinking in this area. Privatization, cuts in public expenditure (especially on the welfare state), financial deregulation, the enhancement of the role of business, etc., all took place in a brief six-year spell in office. But the benefits which such a policy direction was meant to attain were not forthcoming: GDP per capita fell, industry did not grow in strength, employment growth was zero and wage differentials grew. New Zealand became a less equal society in which few economic improvements occurred. The party alienated its traditional working-class electorate and lost trade union support. The improvements which the party promised never arrived, and splits within their own ranks merely served to highlight the divisive effect of such policies. The legacy of these governments' policies has been electoral defeat and decline. Some of those social democrats who adopted a more neoliberal position in the 1980s have fallen back on their more traditional electorate and appeals, but this is because those experiments lost them support and left them open to haemorrhages at the polls.

A second reason why a distinctive approach is required is shown by the danger to democracy represented by the apparent fragmentation in party systems because of a failure by mainstream political parties to deliver on their promises, their inability to make 'a difference' and to be different from one another. This, combined with a decline in trust in politicians and political 'sleaze' has undermined political parties. Not all of these criticisms are accurate but they have resulted in a fall in membership of parties with a corresponding rise in support for single-issue groups and pressure groups. In elections voter turnout is falling, and for people who do continue to vote, extremist parties appear more attractive. Social democrats are not solely to blame for these dangers but they do carry some responsibility. Table 7.1 shows that (except for Spain and Denmark) the general trend is one of falling voter participation. The rise of splinter and extreme parties can also be employed as evidence of problems within Western political systems, such as the PES and Republican parties in Germany, the FN in France and the various left-wing factional parties in the Scandinavian countries.

There does, however, remain scope for social democratic state action as demonstrated by the expanding role for regulation of the privatized industries and in the continued public support the public sector receives. In many instances there has not been a surge in support for the values of neoliberalism. The impact of Thatcherism on the British public is often overestimated. When asked to choose between a 'Thatcherite' society and a 'Socialist' society, the latter came out on top in all but two of the questions posed (see Table 7.2). On those where the 'Thatcher' society was preferred, it was only by a narrow majority. The poll, conducted in 1989, showed that even after a decade of Thatcherism 'the public remained wedded to the collectivist welfare ethic of social democracy – or so they said'.[4] Her self-help doctrine was not widely accepted and there was a growth in the rejection of her positions during the 1980s. Support for tax cuts over greater public service provision moved away from equal numbers towards a firm acceptance of service extension – to seven times as many by October 1991.[5] Attitudes towards trade unions provide a similar example: an increasing majority viewed them as a 'good thing' after 1985, while accepting Thatcher's elimination of union abuses.[6] Likewise, privatization began in 1979 as popular but lost support as the decade progressed. We can also consider the support that striking lorry drivers obtained in France in 1996 and 1997, and recent mass demonstrations in favour of increased unemployment benefits, as evidence that neoliberal attitudes have not taken a complete hold.

Table 7.1 Voting turnout in parliamentary elections (percentage of the electorate)

	1973	1978	1981	1986	1988	1993	1997
France	79.6	81.6	69.9	75.1	64.7	65.6	65.0

	1977	1979	1982	1986	1989	1993	1996
Spain	78.5	68.0	79.8	70.4	69.7	77.2	77.1

	1975	1976	1979	1980	1983	1985	1987	1991	1995
Portugal	91.8	83.3	87.5	85.4	78.6	70.9	72.6	68.2	67.1

	1981	1984	1989[I]	1989[II]	1990	1993
Greece	88.5	87.0	81.6	83.1	81.8	81.5

	1970	1973	1976	1979	1982	1985	1988	1991	1994
Sweden	88.3	90.8	91.8	90.7	91.4	89.9	88.3	86.7	86.8

	1973	1975	1977	1979	1981	1984	1987	1988	1990	1994
Denmark	88.2	88.7	88.2	85.0	82.7	87.8	86.1	74.9	82.2	84.3

	1973	1977	1981	1985	1989	1993
Norway	80.2	82.9	83.2	84.0	83.2	75.8

	1972	1976	1980	1983	1987	1990	1994
Germany	91.1	90.7	88.6	89.1	84.3	77.8	79.1

	1970	1974[I]	1974[II]	1979	1983	1987	1992	1997
Britain	72.0	78.7	72.8	76.0	72.7	75.3	77.7	71.4

Source: *European Journal of Political Research; Electoral Studies;* Francis Jacobs, *Western European Political Parties* (Haslow: Longman, 1989).

The death of Keynesian economics is also greatly exaggerated, as many budgets have been expansionary in a traditional Keynesian manner and much of the state spending on defence in America during the 1980s had an effective Keynesian multiplier effect. The Lawson budgets of the late 1980s in Britain, with the cutting of taxation at an inappropriate time, led the British economy to boom in what was the incorrect use of Keynesian economics.

Table 7.2   'Thatcherite' versus 'Socialist' ideals

Q: 'People have different views about the ideal country. In each of the following alternatives, which comes closest to the ideal for you and your family?'

	All (%)	Conservatives (%)	Non-Conservatives (%)
A country in which private interests and a free market economy are more important	30%	46%	21%
or			
A country in which public interests and a more managed economy are more important	62	48	69
A country which emphasizes the social and collective provision of welfare	54	34	65
or			
A country where individuals are encouraged to look after themselves	37	61	25
A country which emphasizes keeping people at work even if this is not very profitable	59	44	67
or			
A country which emphasizes increasing profitability even if this means people losing their jobs	29	44	21
A country which allows people to make and keep as much money as they can	48	65	40
or			
A country which emphasizes similar incomes and rewards for everyone	43	29	50
A society in which the creation of wealth is more highly rewarded	16	25	7
or			
A country in which caring for others is more highly rewarded	79	71	87

Source: I. Crewe, 'The Thatcher Legacy', in A. King, *Britain at the Polls*, p. 20.

Model of influences

The internal and external influences under which social democratic parties operate can be illustrated diagramatically, as in Figure 7.1. The degree to which these influences are effective varies between each country but all the political parties operate within the overall framework of the political culture and the wider political environment. It is possible for a party to affect its political environment given the opportunity, i.e. with the failure of a previous set of dominant ideas.

The social democratic parties themselves are influenced internally by their heritage, the influence and desires of the membership/activists and, most importantly, the degree of leadership autonomy. This autonomy is increasingly necessary in the face of instantaneous decisions and personality-based, media-run campaigns. Yet the members, under the libertarian and democratic order that social democrats claim to pursue, demand and expect an input.

Internal institutional influences include the nature of the political institutions in which the parties compete and its competitors; their actions will often open or close political opportunities. The state bureaucracy has often been viewed as uncooperative and even hostile to much of what social democracy has stood for and each party has a different relationship with it. Of increasing importance are interest groups, especially as many share similar values to social democrats and now stand as the main avenue for political participation for most citizens. Ecological concerns are now of such magnitude that they deserve their own separate heading.

The wider social environment includes the health and education systems but also popular culture which has proved significant as the media rises in importance.

External economic conditions are of particular importance to social democrats as many of their plans for the improvement of society, as well as the position of individuals, depends upon economic growth. This is influenced by a country's trading partners as well as the international business cycle.

Socio-economic cleavages are now largely determined by ownership and education, and these interact with economic conditions. The main economic policy of social democrats in the late twentieth century is education, equipping and skilling citizens to cope with economic conditions. Both the public and private economic sectors can be internationally competitive or domestically based, and interrelate with one another, no longer being viewed as polar opposites. Both also influence

198

POLITICAL CULTURE
Political Environment – Dominant Ideas

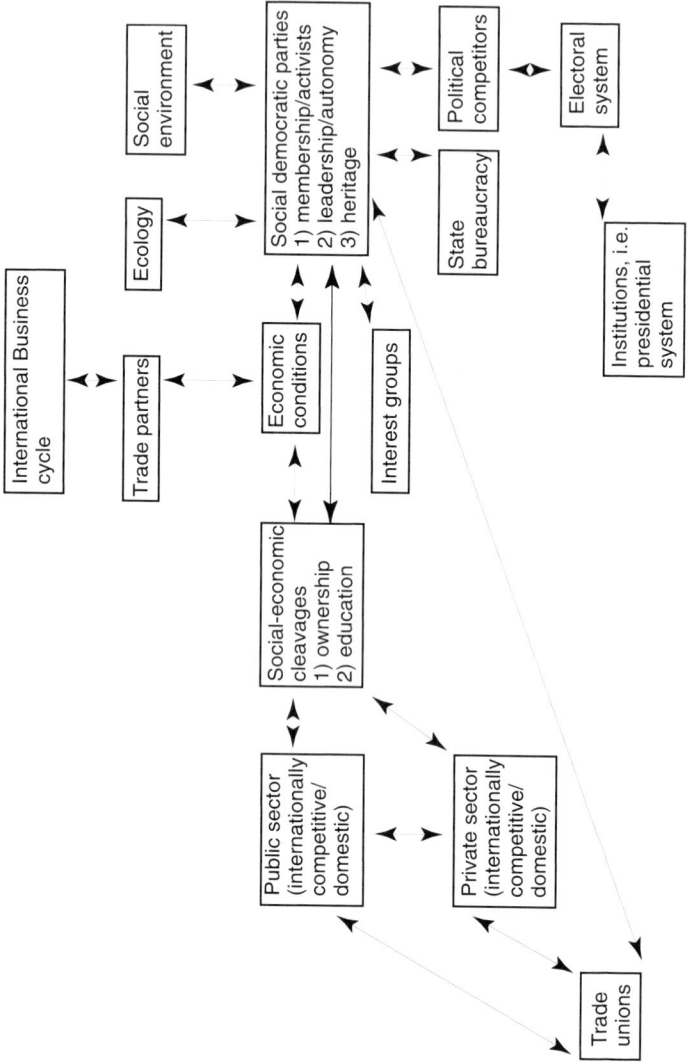

Figure 7.1 Model of influences on social democratic parties

and are influenced by socio-economic cleavages. Trade unions, which interact with both economic sectors, very often have a direct influence on social democratic parties. Yet for most, the degree to which this is the case has lessened, as they look to themselves as national parties. Trade unions are themselves declining in size and strength because of unemployment and a more diverse social structure.

The relationships between all the elements illustrated in Figure 7.1 are dynamic, interactive and two-way. None of the relationships are static.

A new progressive coalition

To get into a position where they can implement social democratic policies, the parties have to build a new progressive coalition. They can no longer rely upon a working-class electorate or even a vaguely defined class coalition. There are two complementary models that we can employ in explaining a new coalition: firstly, E. J. Dionne's 'Anxious Middle', and secondly, Will Hutton's 30 : 30 : 40 society.[7]

Dionne argues that in many ways the rise of the Right has been good for the progressive tradition because it has forced them to open up a defence of their first principles and to modernize their programme.[8] The existence of a moral crisis and economic opportunity coupled with economic dislocation has provided an opportunity for progressives to introduce the use of government to aid citizens. The American progressive tradition involves 'the careful but active use of government to temper markets and enhance individual opportunities';[9] the European tradition places more emphasis on the collective. Its task is to re-legitimize the use of government.

For social democrats, progressive values are their values – of individual progression within collective circumstances, as represented by the postwar era of greater personal security and a welfare state which everyone could use. For Dionne the 1990s are represented by the emergence of a large group at the core of the electorate which no longer adheres to traditional ideological and partisan loyalties.

Pressed by economic change and worries that the country is experiencing a moral and social breakdown. Angry at government, uneasy over the workings of the economic system. They crave self-reliance – and honour this virtue in others – but fear that both the government and the economy are blocking their own paths to sufficiency.[10]

The Anxious Middle's lack of partisanship makes them quick to punish those who fail to deliver what they want. It is radical in its disaffection with the status quo, holds deep worries about the failure, desires far-reaching changes and is highly critical of the current political and economic arrangements.[11] Dionne refers to them as the middle because it lacks the rigid definitions of left/right or liberal/conservative and because they are not utopian in their beliefs, merely pragmatic. It is an effective term because it helps to represent the great mass of those disaffected, and implies their beliefs are majoritarian positions. The Anxious Middle are motivated by the economic changes of unemployment, falling incomes and lost benefits.

Four causes of their anxiety can be put forward. First there is the *economic crisis*, where globalization and slower economic growth have created insecurity and are holding people back from progressing in economic as well as social terms. For many the overriding expectation was that they would achieve income and status through education, but this is no longer true. The *political crisis* involves a distrust of politicians and of big government, when the real problem is one of bad government. Yet, they still wish the government to take a role. An interesting shift in emphasis has occurred with government now seen to help individuals to help themselves rather than aiding them directly. There is also the *moral crisis*, as many see the moral decline of the country, family life and the work ethic. All three appear to be under threat. The *foreign policy crisis*, as of the country's place in the world, is questioned and nobody is sure what its post Cold War role should be.

Dionne refers to the Anxious Middle in a fairly abstract manner, although he does accurately highlight the concerns of a great mass of public opinion such as the causes of the crisis which face the Anxious Middle and the wish this group has for effective government to counteract personal, social and economic insecurity.

What brings greater detail to this area is the second model, Hutton's 30 : 30 : 40 society. Now that the economic environment has shifted, social democrats are in a position to gain support. Hutton's 30 : 30 : 40 society is characterized by 30 per cent that are marginalized, idle or working for poverty wages; 30 per cent that are insecurely self-employed, involuntarily part-time or casual workers; and 40 per cent that enjoy tenured full-time employment or secure self-employment.[12]

The changed economic circumstances of the 1990s means that the bottom 30 per cent and middle 30 per cent now enjoy a tacit bond of insecurity forming the Anxious Middle. This new alliance is volatile and lacks a common identity because of its highly heterogeneous nature. Above a basic common agenda of economic insecurity and political dislocation they hold little in common. The task for social democracy is, therefore, to cement the coalition. But while social democrats tamely adhere to the orthodoxy of the market and allow globalization to work unhindered, they are missing an opportunity to stand for this insecure group. Robert Reich sees this group as the 'vital centre', those that seek 'individual empowerment and security against the more brutal forces of economy and society'.[13]

Not only have work patterns altered with the rise of part-time, temporary and contractual employment, but the types of work and the sectors they occur in have also changed. The theories of Herbert Kitschelt (1994) (as outlined in Chapter 2) highlight the complex situation facing modern political parties when he augments the standard socialist/capitalist model to include libertarian and authoritarian concerns. If we interpret Kitschelt's theories in the light of current social democratic policies it can be noted that if social democrats continue to place the emphasis on training and education, this will move the electorate upwards along the libertarian axis. The same will occur if workplace experiences continue to be based in small, flexible units. However, these are largely based in the private and/or internationally competitive sector and, therefore, move people along the other axis, towards capitalist politics. The former move along the libertarian axis works in the favour of social democrats, but the latter along the capitalist axis against them. Moving along the capitalist axis makes it imperative for parties to marginalize their 'socialist' elements (see Figure 2.1 on p. 59 for a graphical representation).

But social democratic parties cannot follow policies that facilitate a continuous move along the capitalist axis if they wish to remain social democratic and adhere to their core beliefs. The task for social democracy is, therefore, to shift the agenda in their direction, by making appeals to the electorate on the libertarian scale. Social democrats have a heritage which becomes useful, of making markets work more efficiently (normally through intervention). The heritage can also be employed in order to justify claims of a social democratic ability to effectively counteract the effects of globalization.

The neoliberal interpretation of liberty as 'freedom from' is deemed less appropriate than the social democratic 'freedom to' as the scope of markets increases. So this provides a second manner in which social democrats can make appeals on libertarian issues, by enabling more 'freedom to' through democratic reform and political redistribution.

This would include an agenda of empowerment for women and ethnic minorities, and freeing people from constraints imposed by state institutions.

An economic agenda

Once the electorate's trust has been regained, social democrats can then move the agenda onto more sympathetic ground (along Kitschelt's socialist axis). This has to be done through the expansion of what, in neoliberal terms, would be called an 'inefficient' domestic sector with more regulation, a reconstituted public sector and the removal of the more extreme market elements.[14] This is required in order to restore public confidence and inclusion in the public sector and the welfare state. An 'inefficient' domestic sector will gain the support of the insecure Anxious Middle which will gather around the idea of a sector that creates jobs, maintains employment and works for the benefit of society. The domestic sector is country-specific, non-traded and not open to international pressures, i.e. services cannot be purchased abroad but have to be provided and consumed domestically. Running a domestic sector along these lines is useful as a counterweight to the internationally competitive sector. It is also useful as a fallback position if economic growth is not forthcoming. For any changes to be successful, governments require finance; this means an agenda which attempts to relegitimize the use of taxation.

The more privileged members of society would have the responsibility, in times of economic problems, to pay more. Those paying the higher rates of taxation benefit from lower crime, a higher quality of public services, more secure employment and better social conditions associated with a healthy economy. This short-term stabilization will enhance company profits, may provide for better pay and in this way will raise demand ensuring a virtuous economic cycle. The tax revenue would be spent in the public sector with the state acting as 'employer of last resort'. Once the public and domestic sectors were operating effectively and employing more people they would no longer need the extra revenue, and would cost the government less because they would absorb many excess unemployed workers. An expanded domestic sector can be justified both in economic and political terms: in economic terms because it will lessen unemployment, lower government spending on benefits and increase demand in the system to aid the development of a successful economy; in political terms because it will reinvigorate government action enhancing the electoral opportunities for social democracy and place them 'in charge' of the new agenda. In some instances large companies have to act as domestic monopolies, so that they can compete abroad competitively. Within the domestic sector, the public and private sectors must work together and avoid the previous animosities which existed between them. However, if the relationship is to be a social democratic one the public sector has to decide the scope of private-sector involvement rather than the market deciding the extent of its scope. The Left is now concerned with new means of intervention, regulation that, in the internationally competitive sector, does not hinder the market to the extent that its mechanisms cannot function effectively. This would merely serve to undermine the sector's ability to compete.

The argument that governments can no longer operate effectively in the field of economics is mistaken.[15] Social democrats should move away from a 'tax and spend' image because of the perception of penalizing initiative and of incompetent government which alienates the Anxious Middle. It is a more effective approach to tackle those at the upper end through closing loopholes, restricting tax relief, etc. Governments retain powers over working conditions, employment practices, spending, taxation and supply side matters such as skills enhancement, training and education. These have largely replaced explicit demand-enhancing policies. The 'international markets' are most concerned with profit, and as long as a system can prove that profits will be made, that system will be allowed to operate with little hindrance. There is still much scope for governmental action in such areas as 'the structure of public spending, the shape of the tax and benefit system, the corporate tax regime, the level of the minimum wage or the toughness of competition law'.[16] If, however, a system runs in an uneconomic manner with unsustainable budget deficits the international markets will punish it. For instance, the French experiment of the early 1980s is held as an example of how demand management can no longer be employed by governments, and how it is no longer possible to tackle unemployment. But it is really an example of how an economy cannot be run with unsustainable budget deficits.

The task of government is to create an economic environment in which business can operate, with each country playing to its own economic strengths. Governments have to aid the development of the internationally competitive sector through the advance of technology in support of large companies. But investment is not the only cure; it has less effect and impact as economies mature. Investment boosts should only be made counter-cyclically, when a gradual build-up will not hit capacity constraints.

A more cooperative economy is necessary in gaining economic success, as part of a wider stakeholder approach. There are, it is claimed, three approaches to labour markets:

> The first group wants to make the labour market more flexible by giving incentives to employers to offer wages closer to productivity levels ... The second camp opposes this and wants stronger social protection. The third wants to redirect the money government spends in benefits and use it instead for work incentives. Rather than paying taxes for training, individuals would pay this money into an individual learning account, which they can draw on for training needs. Those not in work would have their account topped up, while the contributions of the wealthy could be taxed. These policies incorporate both equality and efficiency.[17]

The points outlined above fall into this third category. The current trend for 'clearing-up' after the market is not providing the required stable social environment for firms. Corporatism, as advocated by Australia and the Netherlands, is also failing because it fails to deliver on the social side of the bargain. In the Netherlands, although economic growth has been favourable, the trade-offs between state, trade unions and businesses have not solved long-term unemployment. Only part-time employment has expanded, and unemployment benefit and eligibility have been cut. What should be aimed for is a stakeholder approach which aims to bring together elements of the Anglo-American, Rhennish and Confucian systems of capitalism. It would aim to 'guarantee income support, but at a level that will not inhibit the willingness of people to work at prevailing market wages', while increasing 'the monitoring of recipients in terms of unreported work and job search efforts, and improving aspects of programme integration and administration'.[18]

Collective action

Social democrats have to engage in new forms of collective action.[19] The definition of collective action has to be broadened into local, state and supranational levels. The welfare state must become less bureaucratic and more responsive to the needs and desires of consumers. Social democrats are in a position to advance this because of their historic links with the public sector and its trade unions. The neoliberal moves on this agenda have been to reduce welfare, in the belief that low tax economies are more effective,[20] to encourage middle-class opt-out and lessen support for social democrats. The deliberate removal of great swathes of the population from the welfare state merely increases the insecurity of the Anxious Middle. Collective provision is more efficient than market provision in welfare service delivery. Public funding is still the only way forward, as a majority of the population either cannot afford or would not obtain private insurance for such matters as health care. The expenditure involved in private provision for the middle class would be prohibitive. Recipients in the welfare system must deserve to receive benefits, so enjoy rights alongside responsibilities. These responsibilities are concerned with non-abuse of the system. These responsibilities also extend to firms who must represent the wider community and their own employees.

With inclusiveness as the aim, the fruits of growth have also to be more equally distributed. With profit concentrated in the hands of a few, inequality increases while insecurity and rejection rise and manifest themselves in alienation from the political system. A progressive system of taxation is desirable in practical terms to maintain the integrity of politics. Redistribution is essential for the continuation of existing political systems. Citizens must also have access to decision-making at all levels to prevent a similar reaction. For Colin Crouch and David Marquand the new collectivism must be 'pluralistic, diverse and internationalist'.[21] Instead of merely issuing commands from the centre, new collective action must make subsidiarity a major aim allowing for the innovation and initiative of individuals so as to encourage inclusion.[22]

Most actions must be performed at the local level. 'Classic' social democracy was historically concerned with the power of the centralized state, but by employing the principle of subsidiarity, social democrats can aid citizens through involvement. This will build the sense of community lacking from modern politics, reinvigorating it and rekindling citizens' perceptions of involvement and inclusiveness through community action groups or local housing associations. For reinvigorated community politics, these groups have to be reconstituted. Involvement has to pervade all levels of decision-making, in both political and economic circles. Many on the Left have attempted this agenda before, most notably Sweden and West Germany, but were thwarted by intransigent employer attitudes. These attitudes will change through the realization that modern companies need a degree of trust and worker involvement in order to compete globally.[23]

The local sectors can also be employed as economic engines, more responsive to the needs and types of economic problems faced by local communities than central government. At the local level economic niches are more likely to be discovered, so production should also occur there. So a 'freer' local approach builds individual initiative, allows entrepreneurial skill to develop and encourages innovation; in this way it builds upon both Rhennish and Anglo-American capitalism.

The revival of civic society, or community, is a central element in the building of a social democratic society. But this new community needs education as its foundation – teaching the new generation what is expected from them, what they can expect to gain from an active society, and how to actively engage in it. State action has to encourage voluntary associations and other intermediate institutions which determine the success of such a venture. Common values have to underpin the system, such as the recognition of equal rights, equality and the value of collective action. The task, therefore, is to ensure that values bind the community, and that each person has the necessary resources, opportunities and abilities to participate. Opportunity has to be extended beyond education to make it available throughout a lifetime, to protect the citizen from the instabilities in the market system, and make access to social services equally available to all. These should be enshrined in a series of citizenship rights, which make financial and social rights available to all sections of society.[24]

There will always be a role for the state in social democracy. The nation state has much to do in preparing its citizens for a social democratic version of globalization. It has to re-equip and retrain the workforce for the new industries and opportunities which arise. New industries will develop as old ones contract. The task for a social democratic government is to smooth that process, only intervening directly if the transition adversely affects a large section of the population. The welfare state has to view periods of unemployment as opportunities for skill enhancement. The financial sector also has to be revised to provide venture capital. In the British instance, the availability of mortgages to casual and temporary workers is poor. As this sector of the labour market increases in size, the British economy will lose its traditional motor of the economy, the bought housing sector. Re-casualization, therefore, demands a greater availability of rented accommodation. These are all areas in which the nation state remains the prime actor.

While social democrats have concentrated on the national context, they have also downplayed the role of the international setting. If economics and global finances become ever more internationalized, then so must the means to modify them. Social democrats prospered in the 'golden era' precisely because they were able to work with capital and allowed for economic growth within a context that improved the situation for the citizens of the country. If companies continue to operate as if the employees are a mere commodity then the social capital of the country breaks down, the demand for goods lessens and firms suffer.[25] The employees are the major asset of the firm and as such need to be treated with respect. The deregulated labour market has proved useful to women as they have entered the labour force *en masse* and it is not the case that social democrats should return to the time when full-time, male employment dominated. Yet instead of merely conceding the argument, they should engage in it. These new work situations offer unexpected opportunities for social democrats to reclaim ground they have lost since the 1970s. Emancipation is a social democratic cause, so in the new work environment they should continue to try to extend it. For instance, the nature of work constantly changes, so that at the end of the last century a 40-hour working week would have been considered part time. Social democrats should encourage a lower working week because of the improvements it brings in the quality of life, which means not being solely concerned with the term 'full-time employment'.

The primary international-level institution for social democrats is the European Union. Many on the Left clung to it as the last bastion of socialism, especially during the late 1980s and 1990s, when many social democrats found themselves out of power in national governments. Social democrats can, through common institutions and legislation, use the European level to pursue their aims, and their internationalist heritage provides them with justification in this. The European approach must ensure that countries do not compete directly against one another to lower wages and conditions: this is not a social democratic aim. At the present time neoliberal objectives mean that the European Union acts as a means of dismantling social democracy's achievements, especially in welfare state provision.[26] Such international cooperation that presently exists places monetary budgets at the heart of a European Single Currency, while social targets are limited to minor elements in the European Social Chapter. *Single market* Europe is stronger than *social market* Europe. From the citizens' point of view the European Union is an illegitimate level at which to conduct business because of their lack of identity with it and the absence of citizenship.[27] The nation state cannot be replaced as the focus of people's attentions, at least in the short term, and it remains the starting point for any moves towards international agreements and other levels of governance.

The examination of globalization by Hirst and Thompson (1996) puts forward a series of possible reforms that are open to social democrats so that they can be seen to be tackling the causes and consequences of the expanding markets. They believe that there is much scope for regulatory and management systems, arguing that the present highly internationalized system is not unprecedented and that genuinely transnational corporations (TNCs) are rare. Capital mobility does not appear to be producing a massive shift of investment and employment from the advanced to the developing countries so the world economy is far from being genuinely 'global'; flows of trade, investment and finance remain concentrated in Europe, North America and Japan. There remain major players in the world economy who have the ability to coordinate policy.[28]

Nation states will have to justify international cooperation to ensure that it retains its legitimacy. For businesses, international governance will provide the economic and social stability that they require in order to function efficiently, allowing for long-term investments because of the ability to plan more accurately for the future. Standing against globalization will also protect the integrity of nation states that are coming under increased pressure from internal ethnic, cultural and regional groupings who are bearing the brunt of swift economic change. A part of globalization that can be embraced by social democrats is the justification it provides for greater equality and more realistic pay structures. The value of employees rises in small, flexible firms which globalization creates because of the demands on local markets. To enhance employees' input, activity and creativity, effective remuneration is required.

Examples of new thinking

The above can be supported with reference to the policies and thinking of two parties: the American Democratic Party and the German SPD. Both are beginning to move the social democratic agenda forward. The Democrats' thinking is proving to be an influence on many of the European parties, especially on New Labour who have developed links with the party. The German SPD has begun to consider policy areas previously thought beyond the reach of social democrats, in policies such as those that consider working arrangements, but these found limited appeal with Chancellor candidate Schröder. They are broadening their horizons. A further ideology which was revived in the 1980s was communitarianism. It appeared to provide an intellectual justification for social democrats to revise their ideology in the light of economic and social events, while the 'Third Way' represents a coming together of social democratic parties along a new common line of initiative.

The American Democratic Party has forwarded an agenda which contains many new elements. They have made the running in developing an agenda which closes 'the door on the old left–right debate of the past' and appeals to a 'coalition of the centre'. This coalition is said to be a 'third way' beyond traditional liberalism and conservatism. The main outlets for this thinking are the Democratic Leadership Council (DLC) and the Progressive Policy Institute (PPI). For Clinton, this new approach is bipartisan and has enabled him to engage the Republican Party.

The 'New Progressive Declaration' issued by the PPI summarizes much of the Clinton approach: 'it offers a new governing philosophy – of equal opportunity for all and special privilege for none; of mutual responsibility; of civic empowerment.'[29] To the PPI the Information Age is weakening traditional societal relations and putting working families in turmoil. A market-led approach is the most appropriate method for creating wealth but five challenges make government action in creating equal opportunity, defending civil rights and renewing civic culture applicable: economic anxiety, social disintegration, political dysfunction, cultural fragmentation and global confusion.[30] The role of government is to enable citizens to respond rather than to impose solutions: it is the servant of society.

The ideals that the new Progressives look to are equality of opportunity, mutual responsibility and self-government. These require a rebuilding of social capital which, in turn, means the decentralization of power and greater individual choice. There is a substantial emphasis on the achievement of economic growth and the process by which it may take place. The agenda involves:

1   a shift from redistributing existing wealth to fostering conditions that enable people to create new wealth, i.e. through the use of public and private investment;
2   creation of policies and institutions to allow responsibility for managing individual careers and security;
3   enhanced learning;

4   business taking on new responsibilities and investing in developing human capital with corporate accountability and governance;
5   developing unions and new associations to enhance economic power and promote community self-help.[31]

The DLC built the policy bridge between the PPI and President Clinton which continues currently. There are many examples of innovative policies from this organization. Clinton's battle to achieve a balanced budget formed part of his attempt to shift the Democrats' image from that of 'tax and spend', which became a familiar charge by the Republicans. Such fiscal discipline is combined with providing Americans with the tools to succeed in the new economy. These tools largely revolve around training and education. The Democrats have advanced ideas around the stakeholding agenda such as ACORP, the Alliance Corporation between capital and labour. As well as distancing the party from 'tax and spend' the policies place the private sector at the heart of the Democratic approach at the expense of 'big government'. The desire is to place before the electorate a non-bureaucratic, activist government able to deal with the 'big challenges' that face America. This opened the Democrats to new sections of the electorate: middle classes, suburbanites, the young, 'knowledge workers who want leaders to govern in the national interest' and 'those who want a Democratic Party for the twenty-first century'.

Many of the initiatives put forward rely upon initiatives from lower levels of government. This is illustrated by the coming together of new jobs and new workers in 'regional skills alliances' – 'in which employers, public agencies, schools and sometimes even labour unions, are pooling resources to train workers for region-wide emerging job opportunities'.

According to Mark Penn (who acts as pollster to both President Clinton and the DLC), far from being alienated by this new agenda, traditional Democratic party voters are being drawn to the Clinton–Gore message. This message revolves around the values of fairness, opportunity, responsibility, community and freedom. Their goals are: speeding up economic growth, honouring work and family, improving education, preserving health and retirement security, engaging the world in promoting their values and breaking the cycle of inner-city poverty.

The German SPD have also forwarded policies which illustrate a realization that there are areas in which social democrats can follow an original and innovative line. On the environment, a long-term concern of the SPD, there was a realization that 'sustainable development' requires not only technological innovations but also for consumers to change their behaviour. Ecological tax reform could be used to reduce the use of energy and resources that harm the environment. The SPD also saw employment opportunities coming from ecological change. A link between the economy and society was fully expressed and so there was an emphasis upon employment creation and the use of the international level to ensure fair competition.

In the policy document, solidarity in international cooperation is necessary to improve trade, currency, research and technology policy. Such action at the European level would involve the harmonization of tax policy. Tax havens in Europe are seen to create divisions and so have to be eliminated. EU-wide labour regulations are deemed necessary in the upcoming information age so that standards of work legislation and protection at work are protected. A large element of the EU agenda, a Single Currency, is seen by the SPD as a challenge to globalized financial markets. International codes of conduct will ensure free and fair competition in order to reconcile economic clashes and combat environmental problems. The above recognized the importance of the European-level in ensuring that economic prosperity continues. In the document globalization is deemed to need action, not to halt it, but to ensure that its impact is appropriate in a national setting.

The SPD furthered the social democratic agenda through the consideration of working practices and citizen participation. The party recognized a change in working life taking place, with flexible working hours needed to allow for lifelong learning and with education and work losing their well-defined order of succession. Flexible, shorter and differentiated working hours, combined with a revaluation of the role of overtime would ensure a more 'flexible transition between work and education, career breaks and retirement'.[32] This new agenda realized the need to examine the relationship between family, work and social activities of both men and women. Any reduction in working hours would be flexibly designed to recognize the sovereignty of workers in relation to their own time. In the proposals employees and trade unions are viewed as legitimate actors in economic and social decisions. Such co-determination would be extended and given further 'quality' 'on the job, in the company, and in the management of large companies'.[33]

Communitarianism is mainly associated with the work of American sociologist, Amitai Etzioni. His primary work, *The Spirit of Community*, found favour with President Clinton and other political leaders, especially in Britain. Its thinking centres around the belief that the crises that societies face result from the decline of the active citizen. Communitarianism aims to rebuild social and personal responsibilities in order to reinforce the moral and social foundations of the community's institutions, emphasizing common values and collective responsibility while rejecting market-led ideologies and a sole emphasis on individual rights. The community and the individual enjoy a co-equal moral standing.[34] 'Communitarians call to restore civic values, for people to live up to their responsibilities and not merely focus on their entitlements, and to shore up the moral foundations of society.'[35] Communities are built around shared values and social webs, and comprise people with a core of common ethical values. It stands against extreme individualism by balancing the rights and responsibilities that an individual can enjoy.

This rebuilding of a moral community is said by the communitarians to begin with the family because it lays the foundations of moral education. Schools are the next block as this is where skills and knowledge are acquired. Social webs then bind individuals and these webs have to have their roles protected from intrusion from government and the national society must, in addition, ensure an encompassing and over-riding community. This consideration of the role of morals, community and rights and responsibilities is attractive to the Left. However, there are elements of communitarianism which are incompatible with the values of social democracy.

Communitarianism adheres to a deregulated market-driven system and does not give great consideration to the dynamics of the market or the impact that it can have on societal relations. What is important to the communitarians is to limit the role of the state.

Those tasks which the state used to carry out should be transferred to the private sector, non-governmental agencies or the communities themselves. If communities take over this raises the spectre of varying levels of provision within a country. The welfare state is not considered a worthy institution as it imposes a set of homogeneous norms and values. Its tasks should be left to the community to carry out if it deems necessary. But a community's first responsibility is to itself. The whole redistributive agenda is downplayed. The emphasis Etzioni places upon parenting and the family leads to an analysis which criticizes the role of mothers in working. He argues that this has helped to destroy the stable family environment required for the child's moral upbringing and represents 'the parenting deficit'.

There are, in addition, elements of a communitarian agenda which lack detail. The question of what constitutes a community is never fully addressed[36] and there is the question of which community one should adhere to. There is little consideration of the heterogeneous nature of most communities which may themselves contain conflicts and values. The structure and shape of national political institutions remain vague and the whole concept of a shared self-conception may not always hold intrinsic value, for instance with the Ku Klux Klan.[37] There is a danger of majoritarian rule and with it the suspicion that individual liberties may be subsumed. Whether communitarianism is compatible with social democratic values has to be queried.

For a political party such as the British Labour Party, communitarianism has been adopted to justify the use of terms such as 'rights' and 'responsibilities', to reduce the role of the state and to place a greater emphasis on the individual in a collective setting.[38] Communitarianism justified the use of sanctions against those who did not adhere to the responsibilities of accepting work and chose instead to depend on welfare.[39]

> Communitarianism social philosophy complements neo-liberal economics by providing a cultural rather than material account of social problems... . Communitarianism proves a counterpart to neo-liberal economic thinking.[40]

Much recent thought has been given over to notions of a 'Third Way'. The phrase is not new, having been employed by both Communists and Fascists to represent a new manner of thinking. This is also true for the social democrats who now employ the phrase. Although development of the 'Third Way' is still in an embryonic form, social democratic leaders throughout Western Europe appear eager to sign up to it. At a meeting in New York (September 1998), Clinton and Blair led the way in championing the concept but alongside them stood a number of other European social democratic leaders.

However, because of the early stage of its development, the 'Third Way', does not yet appear to have formed a coherent set of core values or policies. Indeed, it could be argued that it is merely an apology for market-based, neoliberal economic policies because of its failure to offer any alternatives in this area of policy. Yet its writers contend that it is a project of social democratic renewal and is a third way 'in the sense that it is an attempt to transcend both old-style social democracy and neoliberalism'.[41] Its intellectual foundations are, therefore, supplied by social democracy and this provides it with a heritage and a series of feasible policy positions and supporters. Yet it must be noted that the definitions supplied by the writers for old-style social democracy and neoliberalism are distinctly vague. They maintain that the 'Third Way' is part of the movement to the 'radical centre' or the 'active middle'.

Giddens (1998) and Blair (1998) have, to date, put forward the fullest accounts of what the 'Third Way' stands for. Its policies are a reaction to globalization, the rise of individualism, the deterioration of the environment, the 'decline of politics' and a belief in the fading distinctions between left and right.[42] Blair believes that its goals are of the centre-left but that it is flexible, innovative and forward looking. It is, however, easier to see the values of neoliberalism in the writings rather than those of social democracy. The balance is, very much, in the favour of neoliberalism.

The 'Third Way', much like 'stakeholding' before it, attempts to bring together many diverse elements of the modern political agenda, such as economics, political institutions and democracy, relations between the public and private sector, the role of the individual in civil society, etc.[43] There are, according to Blair, four broad policy objectives:

1   a dynamic knowledge-based economy founded on individual empowerment and opportunity, where governments enable, not command, and the power of the market is harnessed to serve the public interest;
2   a strong civil society enshrining rights and responsibilities, where the government is a partner to strong communities;
3   a modern government based on partnership and decentralization, where democracy is deepened to suit the modern age;
4   a foreign policy based on international cooperation.[44]

Blair believes that the values of the 'Third Way' are equal worth, opportunity for all, responsibility and community. These can be achieved through economic stability, democracy and modernization. Giddens' consideration of the 'Third Way' is rather more substantial and he believes it to be a method by which citizens can be helped to pilot their way through major revolutions such as globalization, changes in personal life and the changing relationship to nature. He sees the project's values as equality, protection of the vulnerable, freedom as autonomy, no rights without responsibilities, no authority without democracy, cosmopolitan pluralism (promoting social inclusion and fostering transnational systems of governance) and philosophic conservatism (pragmatism towards change). These can only be achieved, he believes, through one-nation politics, a reconstructed state, the renewal of civic society, a democratic family and a new mixed economy. The latter looks

> for a synergy between public and private sectors, utilising the dynamism of the markets but with the public interest in mind ... . It involves a balance between regulation and deregulation, on a transnational as well as national and local levels, and a balance between the economic and non-economic in the life of the society.[45]

Such changes in the economic sphere will also involve a redefinition of the nation state as a stabilizing force. Equality is, to Giddens, inclusion – meaning citizenship, civil and political rights with obligations, and involvement in the public sphere to produce an inclusive society. The reform of government and the state would, therefore, mean a 'deepening and widening of democracy'.[46] Improvements in education and entrepreneurial skills would also be of benefit to the cause of the 'Third Way'.

However, although the thinking is in its early stages it fails to break the mould of neoliberal dominated thinking, although it does, at least, demonstrate signs of life on the Left. Without a clear concept of political economy to replace, or at the very least supplement, the neoliberal thinking, the 'Third Way' is relegated to social support for the misdeeds of the market. Where consideration is provided to responsibilities that the public sector have, there is scant regard for similar responsibilities in the private sector. Partnerships between public and private are a core of the 'Third Way', yet the boundaries between these sectors are not dealt with. It realizes that the state cannot 'second-guess' the market but does not look to shape the manner in which businesses operate, i.e. corporate structures or forms of governance are not mentioned. According to Hall (1998), in Giddens there is a sketching out of significantly sociological shifts which are assumed to have major political consequences. There is an overall failure to recognize possible conflicts between groups, individuals or actors within political, economic or social systems. The writings do not tackle effectively the possible clash of values between neoliberalism and social democracy. The fact that the values can be combined is considered a 'given'.

The new agenda

The conclusions of this work highlight that social democratic parties are moving towards neoliberalism for a number of reasons that are largely centred around economic change (as was suggested in the conclusion to Chapter 2). Economic change has had several effects including:

- an altered nature and structure of employment. This adjusted the basis of class, meaning that social democratic change has had an electoral imperative as the definitions and size of the working classes and middle classes shift;
- changes in work have impacted upon the welfare state. Instead of welfare states operating from a foundation of full employment based on male full-time occupations, these have been complicated by female participation in the workforce and the decline of full-time employment and male participation. The balance between the role of the collective and of the individual, therefore, came into question;
- social democrats have failed to replace Keynesian economic policies which they relied upon to achieve their desired economic and social outcomes, and which also helped to sustain their intellectual confidence;
- the Anglo-American model of capitalism appeared attractive because of its ability to create employment and 'solve' the problems of state-based social democracy;
- the incidence of taxation and the impact that it had on work incentives and the ability of firms to operate efficiently came into question. Lower taxation called into question the scope and method of operation of welfare states. But welfare states were also seen to alienate some taxpayers because of the perception of bureaucracy, inefficiency and a failure to deliver services effectively.

The perceived increase in the freedom of action of social democratic parties along with the new thinking outlined above suggests that the problems are not insurmountable and that a social democratic agenda could be restored. What follows is not prescriptive but is indicative of the direction which social democratic parties could arguably pursue. The resulting form of social democracy could be more distinctive than that which is currently being pursued. Its aims are:

1   equality, with social democrats reclaiming control over the use of
    the word. Redistribution is required to allow for greater individual
    initiative. Unless power, wealth and income are redistributed then
    most individuals will never be in a position to pursue their own
    initiative;
2   individual rights in a collective setting as social democrats move
    away from the belief in the collective as the only means of action
    to that which balances this with the rights of the individual.
    This appeals to a large section of the population at a time when
    insecurity is rising;
3   stakeholding that realizes that the market mechanism is the most
    efficient method of allocation but that if capitalism is to operate
    effectively governments have to intervene and citizens have to be
    allowed a role in social and economic institutions;
4   the state as a provider and an enabler as it is appropriate to enable
    opportunities to be pursued, but also to provide for groups who
    are unable to take up these opportunities. The paternalism of the
    state as a provider should be supplemented by the state as an
    enabler;
5   cooperation in a community setting involves the devolution of
    power in democratic and economic matters – local cooperation is
    the way forward.[47]

These aims will direct the policies of a new social democratic
government. It is, therefore, appropriate to suggest new measures of
success.

   Markets should be overseen at different levels by different bodies.
Social democrats have to look towards local, national and international
markets where appropriate. A strong domestic sector is necessary to
complement a strong internationally competitive sector. But markets
should be removed from, or not allowed to enter, sectors where their
presence may be contrary to the public interest.

   The public sector should not be allowed to act merely as a safety net
and should retain a universalist approach. To do this social democrats
have to regain control over the concept of taxation and public expenditure. Welfare should be consumer-based, not producer-based. An
individual's control over their own welfare benefit funds would help
counteract fraud and abuse while also persuading the individual of the
requirement for greater personal taxation.

   Economic policies can achieve more than is often stated and taxation increases are not ruled out by international markets. Not all

instruments should be directed towards low inflation as employment is the social democratic priority. As long as the markets believe that profits will be made and that a country is not living beyond its means, then economic policies excluded during the 1980s return to the fore. Social democrats have to lessen unemployment and achieve economic growth to pay for their desired increases in public services, provide for fair wages and increase the skills base. This new economic approach can be both 'tax and spend' and 'save and invest' depending on the circumstances.

Vested interests should no longer play a role in social democracy. Instead, as part of a pluralistic approach, all groups should have equal access to government.

Libertarian concerns have to rise in importance for social democrats, providing them with scope to regain the political initiative.

There must also be a humanitarian foreign policy.

The problems caused by unemployment, insecurity and the Single Currency have given social democrats a platform from which to work, and this has been adequately demonstrated through their recent electoral victories. If social democracy appreciates its historic opportunity, there may be the chance to ensure a sizeable period of political consensus in line with *their* values, as opposed to the current neoliberal consensus.

Appendix 1
Profiles of Interviewees

The interviews took an unstructured format but were based around a number of core questions to ensure consistency in approach and allow for comparisons to be made. Flexibility in the questioning allowed the specializations of each interviewee to be explored. The core questions were:

- Why is it that Labour has only ever won two elections well?
- Is there a future for social democracy?
- Is there a danger that social democracy is emphasizing the individual at the expense of the collective?
- What constitutes a successful social democratic government?
- What are the core values of social democracy?
- Is there too close an association between the Left and the public sector?
- Are social democrats adhering too closely to neoliberalism?
- Should the Labour Party embrace proportional representation and closer collaboration with other parties?
- What will be Blair's main problems on entering government?

Hilary Armstrong (21/1/97)

Labour MP for North West Durham since 1987. Born in 1945 and educated at Monkwearmouth Grammar School, West Ham College of Technology and Birmingham University. Employed as a social worker and then lecturing at Sunderland Polytechnic in community and youth work before becoming an MP. Appointed as a frontbench spokesperson on education (1989–92) before becoming John Smith's PPS (Parliamentary Private Secretary). She returned to the frontbench as part of the Treasury team after Smith's death, became a regular member of the NEC and was appointed Minister of State for Local Government after the Labour victory of 1997. Member of MSF, having been sponsored by them, a holder of Christian Socialist values and a Tribunite.

Dr Roger Berry (13/11/96)

Labour MP for Kingswood since 1992. Born in 1948 and educated at Huddersfield New College and the universities of Bristol and Sussex. Worked as an economics lecturer for 19 years before entering Parliament. Former Avon county councillor and deputy leader and leader of the Labour group. Chair of the Full Employment Forum, a believer in Keynesian economics and rights for the disabled; a Tribunite left-winger.

Ken Coates (29/1/97)

Former Labour MEP for Nottinghamshire North and Chesterfield since 1994, being MEP for Nottingham (1989–94). Born in 1930 and educated at Nottingham University as a mature student having first been a coalminer and then going on to be a tutor in adult education at the University of Nottingham (1960–80). As an MEP he is a member on the committee on foreign affairs, security and defence policy, and of the subcommittee on human rights. Expelled from the Labour Party in the 1960s for his vocal views on comprehensive education and has recently left the Labour grouping in the European Parliament to join the Confederal Group of the European United Left/Nordic Green Left in protest at the policies of the Labour Party and their proposals for a new voting system in European elections. A member of the Institute of Workers Control and an author of many books from a left-wing perspective, especially on the role of full employment.

Jeremy Corbyn (21/1/97)

Labour MP for Islington North since 1983. Born in 1949 and educated at Adams Grammar School, Newport (Shropshire) and North London Polytechnic. Worked as a trade union organizer for NUPE before entering Parliament as a replacement for an SDP-defecting candidate. Member of the Social Security Select Committee since 1991 and keen campaigner against poverty; member of Cuba Solidarity and supporter of a united Ireland. One of the most irreducible left-wingers in the Labour Party.

Dan Corry (13/11/96)

Former Senior Economist at the Institute for Public Policy Research (IPPR) and founder of their journal of economic policy, *New Economy*. Recruited from an economics position examining public expenditure in the Treasury by the Labour Party to head their Economic Secretariat (1989–92), close to both John Smith and Margaret Beckett before joining the IPPR. Currently working as special adviser to Stephen Byers at the Department of Trade and Industry. An ardent Europhile.

Alistair Darling (13/11/96)

Labour MP for Edinburgh Central since 1987. Born in 1953 and educated at Loretto School (an Edinburgh public school) and University of Aberdeen. Was a solicitor and an advocate at the Scottish Bar, as well as being a Lothian regional councillor, before entering Parliament. Became Shadow Chief Secretary to the Treasury in 1996 after serving as a frontbench spokesman on both home affairs (1989–92) and Treasury affairs (1992–6). Initially Chief Secretary to the Treasury in the Labour Cabinet 1997–8, in 1998 he became Secretary of State for Social Security. Viewed as a serious-thinking Tribunite.

Donald Dewar (12/11/96)

Labour MP for Glasgow, Anniesland since 1978 (the seat being renamed, formerly Glasgow, Garscadden) having first been elected to the House as MP for Aberdeen South (1966–70). Born in 1937 and educated at the Glasgow Academy and Glasgow University. Worked as a solicitor before entering Parliament, an occupation that he returned to after first working as a social work reporter following his defeat in 1970. Worked as PPS to Anthony Crosland (1967–9), and was viewed as a right-wing factionalist. A spokesman for Scotland including Shadow Scottish Secretary (1980–92), Shadow Secretary of State for Social Security and Opposition Chief Whip, being appointed to the position by Tony Blair breaking the tradition of election to the position. Became Secretary of State for Scotland after the 1997 election to steer the party's devolution plans through parliament.

Derek Fatchett (21/1/97)

Labour MP for Leeds Central since 1983. Born in 1945 and educated at Lincoln School, Birmingham University and the LSE (London School of Economics) before lecturing at the University of Leeds in industrial relations. A former local councillor who, shortly after entering Parliament, became a whip and in the 1987 election was a deputy campaigns coordinator under Bryan Gould. He was a spokesman on education (1987–92), trade and industry (1992–4), defence (1994–5) and then foreign affairs. A Minister of State in the Foreign and Commonwealth Office since the 1997 election, with particular emphasis on the Middle East. A former Campaign Group supporter who defected to become a Tribunite in order to pledge allegiance to Kinnock's reforms. Deceased 1999.

John Kenneth Galbraith (via correspondence, December 1995)

Born 1908 in Canada. A world-renowned economist and writer, J. K. Galbraith has been an adviser to a number of American presidents including John F. Kennedy and was a key player in the development of the New Deal. A professor of economics at Harvard University.

George Galloway (20/1/97)

Labour MP for Glasgow, Kelvin since 1987 (the seat being formerly called Glasgow, Hillhead). Born in 1954 in Dundee, he was educated at Harris Academy, Dundee leaving school with four Highers. A former engineering worker, he became an organizer for the Labour Party (1977–83) and then General Secretary for War on Want (1983–7). A formerly TGWU-sponsored MP, pro a united Ireland and a PLO sympathizer, having courted controversy with a meeting held with Saddam Hussein in 1994, and by twinning Dundee with the West Bank town of Nablus. Vice-chair of the PLP Foreign Affairs Committee (1987–91) but more infamous for his nickname 'Gorgeous George' after admitting to dalliances with two women at a conference in Greece in 1985. A left-wing, formerly TGWU-sponsored MP who opposed the purge of Militant.

Mike Gapes (13/11/96)

Labour MP for Ilford South since 1992. Born in 1952 and educated at Buckhurst Hill County High School, Fitzwilliam College, Cambridge and Middlesex Polytechnic gaining a diploma in industrial relations. Before entering Parliament he was an administrative officer in the heath service, a teacher with the VSO and a full-time Labour official starting as a national student organizer before spending 12 years in the international office (being senior international officer, 1988–92). Member of the Foreign Affairs Select Committee since 1992, vice-chair of the PLP Defence Committee, secretary of the All-Party Netherlands Group and vice-chair of the All-Party Committee against Anti-Semitism. His seat has a large Jewish population and he has been a fervent campaigner against racism. A Tribunite who was Co-op sponsored.

Bryan Gould (via correspondence, December 1995)

Born in 1939 and educated at Auckland University and Balliol College Oxford before entering the diplomatic service and working in Brussels. A tutor in Law at Worcester College, Oxford, he then went on to become Labour MP for Southampton Test (1974–9). After working as a presenter and reporter, he re-entered Parliament in 1983 as MP for Dagenham and held numerous front-bench positions: spokesman on trade (1983–6); on economy and party campaigns (1986–7); on Trade and Industry (1987–9); on the environment (1989–92); on national heritage (1992). Ran against John Smith to become Labour leader in 1992 but became increasingly disillusioned with the Labour Party's policy on Europe. Resigned as an MP and became Vice-Chancellor of Waikato University, New Zealand.

Nigel Griffiths (12/11/96)

Labour MP for Edinburgh South since 1987. Born in 1955 and educated Hawick High School, Edinburgh University and Moray House College of Education. Worked as a rights officer for a disabilities group, the TGWU-backed North Edinburgh Action Group, and was active on Edinburgh City Council for seven years (1980–7, where he was chair of housing) before entering Parliament. After becoming an MP, he was an opposition whip (1987–9) and then became opposition spokesperson on consumer affairs. From 1997 to 1998 he was Parliamentary Under-Secretary for Consumer Affairs in the Department of Trade and Industry. A Tribunite who campaigned against the Common Market in the 1970s.

Professor Stephen Haseler (27/6/95)

Professor of Government at the London Guildhall University since 1986. Born in 1942 and attended the LSE, gained a PhD which was subsequently published as *The Gaitskellites*, a cause with which he has been closely identified. Contested the seats of Saffron Walden (1966) and Maldon (1970) for the Labour Party before joining the Greater London Council (1973–7) and being chairman of its General Purposes Committee (1973–5). Co-founder of the SDP in 1981 and, since 1992, chairman of Republic, an anti-monarchy group.

Dr Kim Howells (20/1/97)

Labour MP for Pontypridd since 1989. Born in 1946 and educated at Mountain Ash Grammar School, Hornsey College of Art, Cambridgeshire College of Arts and Technology before finally gaining a PhD at the University of Warwick. Had previously worked as a television and radio writer and presenter and a college lecturer before becoming a research officer with the South Wales NUM (National Union of Mineworkers). Once in Parliament he worked variously as an opposition spokesperson on home and foreign affairs and overseas development before climbing to trade and industry in 1995. In the new Labour government he was Under-Secretary in the Department for Education and Employment responsible for life-long learning (1997–8). In 1998 he moved to the Department of Trade and Industry. A reformed believer in hard left-wing politics, and now a keen advocate of realism.

Martin Jacques (21/1/97)

Former editor of *Marxism Today*, which ceased publication in 1992, now a columnist for *The Sunday Times* and *The Observer*. A revisionist Marxist thinker who contributed to the changing philosophy of the Left. The author of several influential books including *The Politics of Thatcherism*.

Lord Douglas Jay (via correspondence, November 1995)

Former Labour minister under the Wilson governments. Born in 1907 and educated at Winchester College and New College, Oxford. A successful journalist of economics, he worked for several ministries during the Second World War before becoming a personal Assistant to Prime Minister Attlee. Labour MP for Battersea North (1946–74) and Wandsworth, Battersea North (1974–83), he held ministerial office as Economic Secretary to the Treasury (1947–50), Financial Secretary to the Treasury (1950–1) and President of the Board of Trade (1964–7). Ministerial career came to an end primarily because of his anti-European feelings and he became chairman of the Common Market Safeguards Committee (1970–7). Deceased.

Ruth Kelly (22/1/97)

One of the new Labour intake of MPs in 1997 by winning Bolton West. Born in 1968 and educated at Westminster School and Oxford. Previously she had been an economics writer on *The Guardian* (1990–4) and had set-up their 'Seven Wise Women' panel of economists. She had also worked as an economist, Deputy Head of the Inflation Report Division, at the Bank of England.

Roger Liddle (22/5/96)

An adviser to Bill Rodgers in the Wilson–Callaghan government of 1974–9 before going on to be a founder member of the Social Democratic Party (SDP) in 1981. He rejoined the Labour Party and became a special adviser to Tony Blair while being the managing director of Prima Europe, a public policy consultancy. Shortly before the 1997 election he co-authored a book, *The Blair Revolution*, with Peter Mandelson which claimed to be 'an insider account of New Labour's plans for Britain'. In 1997 he became a key full-time adviser to Blair in the Number 10 policy unit.

Martin Linton (20/1/97)

Elected MP for Battersea in 1997. Born in 1944 in Stockholm, Sweden, he was educated at Christ's Hospital and University of Oxford. Before becoming an MP he was a journalist on various newspapers such as *Labour Weekly, The Financial Times, Daily Mail, Daily Star* and, finally, *The Guardian*.

David Lipsey (23/1/97)

A journalist since 1992 and the Political Editor since 1994 of *The Economist*. Born in 1948 and educated at Bryanston School and Magdalen College, Oxford before becoming a research assistant for the General and Municipal Workers Union (1970–2). Special adviser to Anthony Crosland MP (1972–7) in the Department of the Environment (1974–6) and the Foreign Office (1976–7), entering the Prime Minister's Staff at No. 10 Downing Street after Crosland's death. Following this political period he entered journalism working on various titles including *The Sunday Times, The Sunday Correspondent, New Society* and *The Times*.

Calum MacDonald (13/11/96)

Labour MP for the Western Isles, elected in 1987. Born in 1956 in the Hebrides he was educated at Nicholson Institute, Stornoway, Edinburgh University and University of California, Los Angeles (PhD), working as a teaching fellow, in philosophy, at the same institution until becoming an MP. He has been most noticeable, since his election, as a keen advocator of closer Labour–Liberal Democrat ties as co-founder of the LINK group, and a Euro-federalist. In December 1997 he replaced the resigning Malcolm Chisholm as under Secretary at the Scottish Office.

Denis MacShane (21/5/96)

Labour MP for Rotherham after a by-election in 1994. Born in 1948, he was educated at Merton College, Oxford and gained a doctorate from London University. His previous occupations include being a BBC reporter (1969–77), working for the International Metalworkers Federation in Geneva (1980–92) and as a director at the European Policy Institute (1992–4). A firm pro-European, with links to the Blair leadership as demonstrated by his support for the revision of Clause IV, he has written many books including a biography of François Mitterrand.

John McAllion (12/11/96)

Labour MP for Dundee East since 1987. Born in 1948, he was educated at St Augustine's (RC) Secondary School, Glasgow and University of St Andrews. Before entering Parliament he was a teacher. A keen advocate of Scottish politics within the Labour Party by campaigning for a Scottish parliament, he set up Scottish Labour Action (with George Galloway and Willie McKelvey). He was an opposition spokesman on Scotland (1995–6, resigning in protest against Blair's plan to hold a referendum on devolution) and is sceptical of the new Labour project.

Henry McLeish (13/11/96)

Labour MP for Central Fife since 1987. Born in 1948, he was educated at Buckhaven High School and Heriot Watt University before becoming a professional footballer and later a town planner in Dunfermline, as well as a part-time lecturer. His council experience was extensive: Kirkcaldy district councillor (1974–7), Fife councillor (1978–87), being leader of the council (1982–7). After his arrival at Westminster he was soon to reach the frontbench as opposition spokesperson on Scotland (1988–9 and 1992–4), employment (1989–92), transport (1994–6) and social security (1996–7). Since the 1997 election he has been a Minister of State on Home Affairs and Devolution in the Scottish Office. Originally a Tribunite MP who was sponsored by UNISON.

Kevin McNamara (21/5/96)

Labour MP for Kingston upon Hull North (renamed Hull Central, 1974–83) since a by-election in 1966. Born in 1934 and educated St Mary's (RC) College, Crosby and Hull University. Before entering Parliament he was a school master and then a lecturer. During his time as an MP he has been an opposition spokesperson on defence, then Northern Ireland (1987–94) before being replaced by Mo Mowlam and finding himself speaking on the Civil Service. His Irish Republican leanings as a member of the Labour Party Irish Society may not have been to the taste of Tony Blair. A Tribunite who was sponsored by the TGWU.

David Miliband (15/11/96)

Current director of policy at the No. 10 Policy Unit and former Research Fellow at the IPPR, but first came to prominence as Secretary of the Commission on Social Justice. Son of the late Marxist academic Ralph Miliband and brother of special adviser to Gordon Brown, Ed, David was an Oxford graduate and Kennedy Scholar at Harvard. Part of the modernizing left, he has written several publications on the topic, is active in Nexus, a group of academics that communicate through the Internet, but is viewed as 'stronger on ideas than presentation'.

Austin Mitchell (21/5/96)

Labour MP for Great Grimsby since 1983, being MP for Grimsby (1977–83). He won the original seat at the by-election caused by the death of Anthony Crosland. Born in 1934 and educated at Bingley Grammar School, Manchester University and Nuffield College, Oxford, he first became a university lecturer (spending eight years in New Zealand, and then two at Oxford) before working as a television journalist at Yorkshire TV and the BBC (1967–77). He also claims to have spent time as a radio station director and disc jockey. During his time as an MP he has been a PPS (1977–9) to John Fraser (a prices minister), a whip, and a spokesperson for trade and industry (1987–9). Since his sacking by Neil Kinnock from that position, as a result of his part-time Sky television presenter's job, he has been readily available for television and quiz show appearances. A Europhobe right-wing member of the party and former ex-Solidarity group officer, he is sceptical of the new Labour project.

Paul Ormerod (23/1/97)

Formerly a leading economist at the Henley Forecasting Centre and more recently the chairman of the consultancy, Post-Orthodox Economics.

Ted Rowlands (22/5/96)

Labour MP Merthyr Tydfil and Rhymney since 1972, having first entered Parliament as MP for Cardiff North in 1966. Born in 1940 and educated at Rhondda Grammar School, Wirral Grammar School and King's College, London. Briefly lectured in politics before gaining his seat. Once in Parliament he became a junior minister at the Welsh Office by 1969, and in the Labour government of 1974–9 was a Foreign Office minister (with responsibility for Africa) continuing with the job in opposition (1979–80). After this he became opposition spokesperson on energy (1980–7) before taking a position on the Foreign Affairs Select Committee after 1987. A Eurosceptic from a centre-right position.

Mark Seddon (12/11/96)

Editor of Tribune. Successfully stood for election to the constituency section of the Labour Party's NEC in 1998 and 1999.

Dennis Skinner (21/1/97)

Labour MP for Bolsover since 1970. Born in 1932 and educated at Tupton Hall Grammar School and Ruskin College, Oxford. Was a miner, coming from a mining family, before his election to Parliament. The voice of the hard left in the Parliamentary Labour Party, for many years guaranteed a platform because of his position on the NEC (member of the NEC since 1994 and 1978–92, Chair of the Labour Party 1988–9). Member of the Campaign Group, the NUM, the PLP Miners' Group (chair 1975–6, and secretary 1992–4), and the Common

Market Safeguards Committee. He has consistently defended all things of the left and dislikes the term 'new Labour'.

Andrew Smith (13/11/96)

Labour MP for Oxford East since 1987. Born in 1951 and educated at Reading Grammar School and St John's College, Oxford. Was a member relations officer for the Oxford and Swindon Co-operative Society and an Oxford city councillor for the Blackbird Leys estate (1976–87), being chair of planning and of recreation, before gaining his seat. His first parliamentary position was as opposition spokesman on higher and continuing education (1989–92), a position that was complemented by his chair at Oxford Brookes University (1987–93). He then became opposition spokesperson on Treasury affairs (1992–4) before being promoted to Shadow Chief Secretary to the Treasury (1994–6) for his part in the Blair leadership election campaign. His next move was to Shadow Secretary of State for Transport (1996–7) and in the new Labour government became the Minister for Employment and Disability Rights.

Jean-François Vallin (29/1/97)

Former secretary-general of the Party of European Socialists (PES) with a background in the French Socialist Party.

Malcolm Wicks (13/11/96)

A Labour MP since winning Croydon North West in 1992 and then Croydon North in 1997 (a new seat). Born in 1947 and educated at Elizabeth College, Guernsey, North West London Polytechnic and the LSE. Was a social policy analyst and lecturer before he set up the Family Policy Studies Centre and acted as a director. Once in Parliament his first major achievement was the passing of his Private Members' Bill now the Carers' (Recognition and Services) Act 1995 which came into force in April 1996 and provides social services support to family 'carers'. He was Secretary of the PLP Social Security Committee (1992–5) and became opposition spokesperson on social security (1995–7). He maintains a keen interest in social security and the future of the welfare state.

Philip Whitehead (29/1/97)

Labour MEP for Staffordshire East and Derby since 1994. Born in 1937 most of his political experience has come from Westminster, being the MP for Derby North (1970–83) holding the positions of frontbench spokesperson on higher education (1981–3) and the arts (1982–3). He introduced the first successful Police Complaints Bill, the NHS (Family Planning) Act of 1972 and co-sponsored the Children's Act (1975). A member of the Council of Europe (1974–9) and delegate to the Western European Union for five years, he has also been an award-winning television producer. In the European Parliament he is a member of the Environment, Public Health, Consumer Protection Committee and a member of the temporary committee into BSE (1996–7).

Larry Whitty (23/1/97)

Former general secretary of the Labour Party (1985–94) he succeeded in updating the party bureaucracy and placing it on a sound financial keel. Not viewed as reformist enough by Blair because of his failure to support OMOV, so replaced by Tom Sawyer, only to be rescued by John Prescott and placed in charge of liaison with Labour MEPs and its European sister parties.

Tony Wright (12/11/96)

Became Labour MP for Cannock and Burntwood in 1992 before winning Cannock Chase in 1997. Born in 1948 and educated at Kettering Grammar School, LSE, University of Harvard, and Balliol College, Oxford. Became a university lecturer (Reader in Politics, University of Birmingham) specializing in political thought (Cole, Tawney, etc.) and his book *Socialisms: Old and New* reflects this. He is also co-editor of *Political Quarterly* and an executive member of the Fabian Society. He advocates Labour–Liberal Democrat cooperation being a co-founder of LINK. A member of the Public Services Select Committee and enthusiast of the modernizing agenda but claims not to be part of the Blair 'inner circle'.

Appendix 2
Jospin's 'Propositions pour la France' – 1995 Presidential Manifesto

Putting man at the heart of the economy

This involves six priorities:

1   Give true value back to work – the belief being that a better balance between wages and profits is necessary for the economy and it will help on the social level also. Wage earners are promised a more favourable share of revenue.
2   Create jobs – all capacities will be used in the service of employment. Three major programmes will be launched to fulfil this aim:

   (a) the reconstruction of the suburbs and the development of social accommodation;
   (b) the development of services to the people by bringing in state and private money;
   (c) preservation of the landscape and the national heritage, which also means improvement of the environment.

   Emphasis is also given to private enterprise with help to small and medium-sized businesses to obtain credit, and simplified formalities for setting up a business. To ensure the future of French industry and services diversification has to be encouraged through research. The creation of regional techno-logical centres and local development communities, backed by local banks with reduced rate loans to small and medium-sized businesses, will contribute to this.

3   Reduce the working week – to 37 hours in 1997. But with an emphasis placed upon personal freedom to allow for the organization of an indivi-dual's time throughout their lives. The emphasis is placed upon freedom of choice for the individual.
4   Promote social security and protect the most fragile – this will occur through the defence of the European model (with its unifying of an efficient economy) combined with social protection for all. Jospin emphasizes solidarity. There is a guarantee of the right to health for all but with spending more closely monitored, and public hospitals defended (but with management efforts better monitored).
   Pensions are guaranteed and they will also share in the fruits of growth.

Increased child benefit for young families and low-income families, and help from the birth of the first child, only when justified by low income, are promised.

Handicapped people are to be favoured in social policies.

5   Making the tax system more just – while bearing in mind that public deficit reduction is a responsibility. The principles of tax reform are more justice and more efficiency through:

(a)   lower social charges on low pay;
(b)   making income tax clearer and fairer;
(c)   simplifying, clarifying and making more just local taxes;
(d)   with redistribution between rich and poor local communities.

6   Work to put the world economy back in order – strengthening the European Union (through reaffirming a single currency and prolonging the European growth initiative) and a new international monetary system would aid stability. In the meantime a tax on the movement of capital is proposed.

Get ready with the young to enter the twenty-first century

The new society of the next century must be built with the young, an intelligent society but also a fraternal and generous one. There are five objectives to be realized with, and for, the young:

1   Permit the young to be the first actors of the social transformation – the first stage of this is action for employment to enable the young to benefit quickly from it. There are three major employment programmes of which the young will be the principle beneficiaries:

(a)   the renovation of social life in the localities;
(b)   development of services to the people;
(c)   the reconquest of the landscape;

A fourth destined for the young is engagement in humanitarian action.

2   Make schools a priority – and confirm the secular and republican concept of state education. The emphasis in schools should be to construct an education that is useful in professional life.

The fight against social inequality will take place through the encouragement and development of all forms of aid to education and the creation of a veritable social solidarity around schools.

3   Win the battle of intelligence – to prepare for the future individual and collective intelligence is essential, being the challenge and source of wealth in the twenty-first century. The construction of a University of the Twenty-First Century is required. The role of universities is essential but different forms of higher education must be developed. The student social plan will permit all the capable young to have a superior education.

4   Take up the cultural and audio-visual challenge – to allow access to culture for all by bringing the cultural budget to a minimum of 1 per cent of the state budget.

5   Promote sport for all.

Develop the territories and the quality of life by ecology

With three actions which will give concrete improvement to life for the French and France.

1   Put in place a plan to reconquer ecology – 'Green' companies should be developed along with new trade and employment, but any plan should proceed with democratic consultations and with a role for the state in coordination and co-financing.
2   Ensure solidarity in the development of the territories – which means pursuing, clarifying and democratizing decentralization based on a global vision of complementarity. The building up of towns and cities with TGV, telecommunications, research, universities and so on, means that they could rival their European counterparts.
3   Reinvent a policy for our towns – by realizing a right to accommodation and a roof for everyone. Social accommodation could be boosted by an ambitious construction objective and a review of housing attribution.

Wanting Europe for France and for the world

France has responsibilities as regards the international community and its privileged partners. The President of the Republic is responsible for foreign policy and defence. The choice for the future is:

1   Reaffirm the principles of our foreign policy – guided by four principles:

   (a) peace;
   (b) democracy;
   (c) development;
   (d) solidarity.

2   Put Europe at the service of its people – France must remain in the front line of European construction. It is European construction that has assured forty years of peace, stability and growth. A major initiative for the Mediterranean countries to promote peace and security with development and democracy is appropriate. Moves towards a single currency must be made as soon as possible and at the moment of a single currency an initiative should be made on world-wide negotiations to re-establish a stable and balanced international monetary system. Europe should lead the common fight for employment for social cohesion against exclusion. Social legislation should be harmonized to the highest level among all countries.
3   Rethink our defence policy – with Communism and the eastern bloc now gone and the development of regional conflicts, France has to adapt its army structure, equipment and means to the new situation. Nuclear dissuasion is to be maintained as it is the pillar of defence and the guarantee of independence, but the moratorium on nuclear tests will be prolonged.

A new practice of power

Liberty, equality of chances and rights for all – particularly between women and men – the impartiality of the state, secularization, security, a just balance between the interests of the individual and of the collective and national solidarity between generations and territories are the values of the republic, but society suffers a democratic deficit. There needs to be a profound change in the exercise of power, a need to regain the confidence of citizens, a new way of governing to renew the spirit of democracy – so resolute action is based on six objectives:

1   Democratize our institutions – with the conception of a 'citizen president' and the five-year mandate. The role of government and Parliament has to be restored, with government as a place of collective deliberations. The strict limits of the accumulation of mandates will go to a referendum.
2   Guarantee security – a remaining republican ideal. The priorities are the fight for employment, combating drugs, renovation of the localities and the plan for the young.
3   Reinforce the independence of the justice system to service the citizens – citizens want an impartial justice system and responsible magistrates so guarantees about the independence of legal procedures are needed (with political power carrying no weight).
4   Give new confidence to public life – do this by rooting out corruption and letting justice work freely and calmly.
5   Realize equality between women and men.
6   Develop citizenship in everyday life – the development of the associative life should be favoured with the state stabilizing the financial position of citizens.

Appendix 3
The New Clause IV

1   The Labour Party is a democratic socialist party. It believes that by the strength of our common endeavour, we will achieve more than we achieve alone; so as to create: for each of us the means to realize our true potential and for all of us a community in which power, wealth and opportunity are in the hands of the many not the few, where the rights we enjoy reflect the duties we owe, and where we live together, freely, in a spirit of solidarity, tolerance and respect.

2   To these ends we work for:

   – a dynamic economy, serving the public interest, in which the enterprise of the market and the rigour of competition are joined with the forces of partnership and cooperation to produce the wealth the nation needs and the opportunity for all to work and prosper, with a thriving private sector and high quality public services, where those undertakings essential to the common good are either owned by the public or accountable to them;

   – a just society, which judges its strength by the condition of the weak as much as by the strong, provides security against fear, and justice at work; which nurtures family life, promotes equality of opportunity and delivers people from the tyranny of poverty, prejudice and the abuse of power;

   – an open democracy, in which government is held to account by the people; decisions are taken as far as practicable by the communities they affect; and where fundamental human rights are guaranteed; a healthy environment, which we protect, enhance and hold in trust for future generations.

3   Labour is committed to the defence and security of the British people, and to cooperating in European institutions, the United Nations, the Commonwealth and other international bodies to secure peace, freedom, democracy, economic security and environmental protection for all.

4   Labour will work in pursuit of these aims with its affiliated organizations such as trade unions and cooperative societies, and also with voluntary organizations, consumer groups and other representative bodies.

5   On the basis of these principles, Labour seeks the trust of the people to govern.

Appendix 4
A Comparison of Old and New Labour

Tony Blair's most informative compendium of work, *New Britain: My Vision of a Young Country*, brought together a series of articles, speeches and some new narrative. In terms of the debate between Old and New Labour it provided some interesting comparisons.

Old Labour – was explicit about the need for redistribution and placed the improvement of the well-being of its citizens as part of a moral crusade to build the new Jerusalem.

New Labour – 'Social justice, the extension to all of a stake in a fair society, is the partner of economic efficiency and not its enemy.'[1] The link is between the economy and the well-being of citizens; a society has to be fairer in order to achieve economic growth. This link was not recognized by Old Labour. This point is made more explicitly by the following: 'Social cohesion – a society in which there is not gross inequality nor the absence of opportunity for a significant number of citizens is an indisputable part of an efficient economy.'[2]

Old Labour – was confrontational in its industrial wing between workers and managers. The state's role was to instruct the market and to replace it in many cases, and the belief was that the free market could not achieve the desired end result for the party and the country. The trade unions would have a close relationship with a Labour government to ensure that the interests of the workers were maintained.

New Labour – 'On the economy, we should replace the choice between the crude free market and the command economy with a new partnership between government and industry, workers and managers – not to abolish the market, but to make it dynamic and work in the public interest, so that it provides opportunities for all.'[3] The emphasis is placed upon partnership between government and the private sector, with the government working with the private sector.

The role of government in a modern economy is limited but crucial. It should provide a secure low-inflation environment and promote long-term investment; ensure that business has well-educated people to recruit into the workforce; ensure a properly functioning first-class infrastructure; work with business to promote regional development and small and growing firms; seek to open markets for our goods around the word; and create a strong and cohesive society which removes the drag on the economy of social costs like unemployment and related welfare benefits.[4]

The social costs to a country's citizens are not mentioned – the priority of this element was higher under Old Labour. The new role for the trade unions is 'to play a positive role in creating the partnerships at work which can help Britain become a more successful and competitive economy'.[5]

Old Labour – would use the state to intervene directly against the private market if it was deemed necessary and in order protect the poorest elements of society. Equality was a stated aim.

New Labour – 'the public sector must accept its responsibility to act in partnership with the private sector'.[6] Although these responsibilities are not outlined, the inference is clear that it is up to the public sector to prove its worthiness to work with the private sector, rather than the opposite course which was the Old Labour method. New Labour places the 'consumer first', and will ensure a 'competitive market place through regulatory protection'.[7] This emphasis on the consumer infers that those with greater wealth, that carry greater weight as consumers, will be the best protected element in society. The party sees equality as merely 'giving everyone the education that helps them achieve all that they can'.[8]

Appendix 5
Changes in Labour Party Policy Positions[1]

Tax

1992 – top rate of income tax to be 50p in the pound and 'ceiling' on national insurance contributions dropped so that for high earners, income tax and NI combined jumped from 40p to 59p in the pound.
1997 – no increase in the basic or top rates of income tax; long-term objective of new starting rate of 10p.

Child benefit

1992 – child benefit to be increased in value.
1997 – child benefit to be increased in line with prices; possible changes post-16 to ensure higher rates of staying on in education.

Education

1992 – end selection at age 11. Cut numbers in primary school classes to a maximum of 40 within one year and then to 30. Phase out the assisted places scheme with savings redirected to meet 'wider educational needs'.
1997 – any changes in admissions policy of grammar schools to be decided by local parents; 'set' pupils in comprehensive schools; target improvements for primary pupils; cut class sizes to 30 or under for 5, 6 and 7 year olds.

Law and order

1992 – concentration on 'designing out' crime from urban estates; extra resources for bobbies on the beat; promote alternatives to prison for non-violent offenders.
1997 – measures to clamp down on public disorder including 'threatening and disruptive' neighbours; free vote on a hand-gun ban; fast-track punishment for persistent young offenders; more police on the beat.

Employment

1992 – 'swift reduction' in unemployment and 'direct' investment' to create thousands of new jobs.
1997 – 250 000 young unemployed off benefit and into work; the revenue of a one-off windfall levy to fund the programmes; rights and responsibilities; action on long-term unemployed.

Pensions

1992 – basic retirement pension to be increased by £5 a week for a single person and £8 for a married couple; pledge to increase pensions in line with increases in prices or earnings – whichever was the higher.
1997 – retain basic state pension, to be increased at least in line with prices; encourage new partnerships between financial services companies, employers and employees to develop second-tier stakeholder pensions.

Constitution

1992 – House of Lords to be scrapped and replaced by elected second chamber; commitment to immediate creation of Scottish parliament with tax-raising powers and to set up Welsh Assembly within first five years.
1997 – reform of the House of Lords, removing the right of hereditary peers to sit and vote; referendums on Scottish parliament and whether it should have tax-raising powers and a Welsh Assembly; referendum on the electoral system.

Workers' rights

1992 – Charter of Rights for all workers from the first day of employment; right of individuals to be represented by trade union; secondary picketing to be legalized in some circumstances; national minimum wage to be set at £3.40 (half average male earnings).
1997 – a sensibly set national minimum wage; key elements of the 1980s trade union reforms to remain; minimum standards for the individual at work.

Defence

1992 – reduce defence spending to level of European allies; question mark over whether fourth Trident nuclear deterrent submarine would be completed.
1997 – retain Trident; press for multilateral negotiations on the reduction of nuclear weapons; conduct a defence and security review.

Health

1992 – halt the 'privatization' of the health service and return opted-out hospitals and other services to the NHS; make at least £1 bn available for investment over the next two years in preference to cutting income tax.

1997 – save and modernize the NHS; end the internal market directing the savings to patient care; remove the disadvantages of GP 'fundholding'.

Economy and spending

1992 – 'tax and spend' philosophy with commitment to 'strong and continued emphasis on investment for economic strength'; Large investment programmes planned for NHS, education and transport funded partly by not cutting taxes.

1997 – 'save and invest, not tax and spend' with strict rules for borrowing and taxation; over the economic cycle it will only borrow to invest and not to fund current expenditure.

Notes

Introduction

1 W. Merkl, 'After the Golden Age: Is Social Democracy Doomed to Decline?', in J. Maravall (ed.), *Socialist Parties in Europe* (Barcelona, Institut d'Ediciones de la Diputació de Barcelona, 1992), p. 199. He also believes that social democracy will prosper once more when a demand for the regulation of the market develops, cited by R. Cuperus and J. Kandel, 'The Magical Return of Social Democracy – An Introduction', in R. Cuperus and J. Kandel (eds), *European Social Democracy: Transformation in Progress* (Amsterdam, Wiardi Beckman Stichting/Friedrich Ebert Stiftung, 1998), p. 13.

2 W. E. Paterson and A. H. Thomas, *The Future of Social Democracy* (Oxford: Clarendon Press, 1986), p. 3.

3 E. Shaw, 'Towards renewal? The British Labour Party's policy review', *West European Politics*, 16, p. 116.

4 D. Marquand, 'After Socialism', *Political Studies*, 41, p. 52.

5 J. Gray, *After Social Democracy* (London: Demos, 1996), p. 25.

6 *Ibid.*, p. 26.

7 J. Gaffney, 'The Emergence of a Presidential Party', in A. Cole (ed.), *French Political Parties in Transition* (Aldershot: Dartmouth, 1990), p. 63.

8 C. Crouch, 'The Terms of the Neo-Liberal Consensus', *Political Quarterly*, 68(4), p. 352.

9 G. Esping-Andersen, *Politics Against Markets – The Social Democratic Road to Power* (Princeton, NJ: Princeton University Press, 1985), p. 72.

10 *ibid.*, p. 72.

11 I. Budge, D. Robertson and D. Hearl, *A Comparative Analysis of Post-War Election Programmes in Twenty Democracies*, Essex Papers in Politics and Government, 34.

12 A. Ware, *Political Parties and Party Systems* (Oxford: Oxford University Press, 1995), p. 27.

Chapter 1   Diversity and change in models of social democracy

1 A. Fried and R. Sanders (eds), *Socialist Thought: A Documentary History* (Edinburgh: Edinburgh University Press, 1964), p. 3.

2 See P. Gay, *The Dilemma of Democratic Socialism* (New York: Collier Books, 1962).

3 For instance, Crosland claimed that 'society becomes more social-democratic with the passing of the old injustices': *The Future of Socialism* (London: Jonathan Cape, 1956), p. 353.

4 A. Lijphart, *The Politics of Accommodation: Pluralism and Democracy in the Netherlands* (Berkeley: University of California, 1968) recognizes a model of democratic management constructed by the political elites to ensure stability. The leading examples of this model of consociational democracy are the Netherlands, Belgium, Switzerland and Austria.

5   G. Esping-Andersen, *The Three Worlds of Welfare Capitalism* (Oxford: Polity Press, 1990), p. 27.
6   Ibid., p. 27.
7   A. Cole, *François Mitterrand: A Study in Political Leadership* (London: Routledge, 1994), p. 175.
8   For a fuller discussion of these incentives see A. Ware, *Political Parties and Party Systems* (Oxford: Oxford University Press, 1996).
9   See ibid., p. 35.
10 R. Gillespie and T. Gallagher, 'Democracy and Authority in the Socialist Parties of Southern Europe', in T. Gallagher and A. Williams (eds), *Southern European Socialism – Parties, Elections and the Challenge of Government* (Manchester: Manchester University Press, 1989), pp. 179–83.
11 See A. Cole, *François Mitterrand*, for a more detailed description of Mitterrand's tactics.
12 As suggested in R. Gillespie and T. Gallagher, *Democracy and Authority*, pp. 179–83.
13 Proof of early interaction can be seen by the close links between the Spanish PSOE and German SPD – see R. Gillespie, *The Spanish Socialist Party: A History of Factionalism* (Oxford: Clarendon Press, 1989). It is possible to suggest that the characteristics of the Northern model made it impossible for the South to follow, i.e. its lack of strong peak organizations.
14 The modern economic environment is the subject of discussion in many texts such as W. Hutton, *The State We're In* (London: Jonathan Cape, 1995); H. Kitschelt, *The Transformation of European Social Democracy* (Cambridge: Cambridge University Press, 1994); M. O'Brien and C. Wilkes, *The Tragedy of the Market – A Social Experiment in New Zealand* (Palmerstone North, New Zealand: Dunmore Press, 1993); F. Vandenbroucke, *Globalization, Inequality and Social Democracy*, ECPR Joint Sessions in Warwick, March 1998; and P. Ormerod, *The Death of Economics* (London: Faber & Faber, 1994).
15 D. Sassoon, 'Fin-de-siècle Socialism – Some Historical Reflections', in R. Cuperus and J. Kandel (eds), *European Social Democracy: Transformation in Progress* (Amsterdam: Wiardi Beckman Stichting/Friedrich Ebert Stiftung, 1998), picks up on some of the driving forces behind this convergence such as the homogeneity of communications. However, one could also speculate as to the impact of the political and economic movements in the EC on this process.
16 Interview, 23/1/97, Paul Ormerod.
17 This value is recognized by J. Gray, *After Social Democracy* (London: Demos, 1996).
18 For explanations of these electoral cleavages see F. Parkin, *Middle Class Radicalism* (Manchester: Manchester University Press, 1968) for his discussion of middle-class participation; and F. Parkin 'Working Class Conservatives: A Theory of Political Deviance', *British Journal of Sociology*, 18(3), 1967, pp. 278–90.
19 The strains to which the welfare state are now exposed are examined in G. Esping-Andersen, 'After the Golden Age? Welfare State Dilemmas in a Global Economy', in G. Esping-Andersen (ed.), *Welfare States in Transition – National Adaptations in Global Economics* (London: Sage, 1996).

20 D. Marquand, *The Unprincipled Society* (London: Jonathan Cape, 1988), suggests that Keynesian social democracy broke down because of the lack of a notion of the public realm or public good.

21 The importance of the institutional structures of a country are demonstrated by their importance in explaining the class radicalism as is shown by D. Gallie, *Social Inequality and Class Radicalism in France and Britain* (Cambridge: Cambridge University Press, 1983). The role and form of state institutions are examined in K. Dyson, *The State Tradition in Western Europe* (Oxford: Martin Robertson, 1980).

Chapter 2   Theories to explain the 'decline' of social democracy

1 M. O'Brien and C. Wilkes, *The Tragedy of the Market – A Social Experiment in New Zealand* (Palmerstone North, New Zealand: Dunmore Press, 1993), p. 7.

2 For a fuller description of the characteristics of the Fordist model see ibid., pp. 14–16.

3 Ibid., p. 7.

4 For a fuller description of the characteristics of post-Fordism see ibid., pp. 19–21.

5 J. Pontusson, 'Explaining the Decline of European Social Democracy: The Role of Structural Economic Change', *World Politics*, 47(4), p. 496.

6 See I. Crewe 'Labor Force Changes, Working Class Decline and Labour Vote', in F. F. Piven (ed.), *Labor Parties in Postindustrial Societies* (New York: Oxford University Press, 1991).

7 For a full discussion see M. O'Brien and C. Wilkes, *The Tragedy of the Market*, pp. 26–8.

8 During a detailed study of the development of the Left in Western Europe during the twentieth century, D. Sassoon, *One Hundred Years of Socialism – The West European Left in the Twentieth Century* (London: I. B. Tauris, 1996), the author states that the main achievement for the Left during the past one hundred years has been the civilizing of capitalism. But A. Przeworski, *Capitalism and Social Democracy* (Cambridge: Cambridge University Press, 1985), suggests that social democrats have struggled to make capitalism more efficient and humane. According to C. C. Hodge, *The Trammels of Tradition – Social Democracy in Britain, France and Germany* (London: Greenwood Press, 1994), it was the organizational and ideological adaptations made by social democratic parties after the First World War which undermined their effectiveness in later years.

9 A. Butler, *Transformative Politics: The Future of Socialism in Western Europe* (London: Macmillan, 1995), suggests that the postwar boom allowed socialists to evade intellectual challenges. F. W. Scharpf, *Crisis and Choice in European Social Democracy* (Ithaca, NY: Cornell University Press, 1991), contends that social democrats placed excessive faith in Keynesianism in the postwar decades.

10 R. Skidelsky, 'The Decline of Keynesian Politics', in C. Crouch (ed.), *State and Economy in Contemporary Capitalism* (London: Croom Helm, 1979), p. 56.

11   In his book, *The Death of Economics* (London: Faber & Faber, 1994), Ormerod notes a general failure of economics to explain recent events.

12   Under which each country defined its own currency value in terms of the US dollar, with the US maintaining the value of gold.

13   See R. Skidelsky, 'The Decline of Keynesian Politics'.

14   The literature on globalization is very extensive. It is one of the most considered topics because it involves many aspects such as the political, economic, cultural and legal. However, there is a general agreement that the process of globalization is taking place. In addition to those texts cited in the discussion, others which provide insights are: D. Archibugi and D. Held (eds), *Cosmopolitan Democracy: An Agenda for a New World Order* (Oxford: Polity Press, 1995); R. Axtmann (ed.), *Globalization and Europe: Theoretical and Empirical Investigations* (London: Pinter, 1998); R. Cox, 'A Perspective on Globalization', in J. Mittelman (ed.), *Globalization: Critical Reflections* (London: Lynne Reiner, 1996); D. Held, 'Political Community and the Cosmopolitan Order', in D. Held (ed.), *Democracy and the Global Order: From the Modern State to Cosmopolitan Governance* (Oxford: Polity Press, 1995); M. Miyoshi, 'A Borderless World? From Colonialism to Transnationalism and the Decline of the Nation State', *Critical Inquiry*, 19, Summer 1993, pp. 726–51; K. Ohmae, *The Borderless World* (London: Collins, 1990); J. Rosenau, 'Globalization', in J. Rosenau (ed.), *Along the Domestic-Foreign Frontier: Exploring Governance in a Turbulent World* (Cambridge: Cambridge University Press, 1997). A sociological approach to the topic more concerned with cultural studies is adopted by M. Featherstone et al. (eds), *Global Modernities* (London: Sage, 1995), whereas B. Barber, 'Global Democracy or Global Law: Which Came First?', *Indiana Journal of Legal Studies*, 1(1), Fall 1993, pp. 2–23, is more concerned with what he sees as the 'McDonaldization' of the globe, i.e. the spread of universal codes. Hirst and Thompson are the main writers who are in a more revisionist school of thought and look to counter globalization – see 'Globalisation and the Future of the Nation State', *Economy and Society*, 24(3), 1995, pp. 408–42; 'Global Myths and National Policies Renewal', 4(2); and most fully *Globalisation in Question: The International Economy and the Possibilities of Governance* (Oxford: Polity Press, 1996).

15   L. Wilde, *Modern European Socialism* (Cambridge: Dartmouth, 1994), p. 175.

16   M. Campanella, 'The Effects of Globalisation and Turbulence', *Government and Opposition*, 28, p. 192.

17   D. Held and A. McGrew, 'Globalisation and the Liberal Democratic State', *Government and Opposition*, 23, p. 262.

18   Ibid., p. 262.

19   Ibid., p. 263.

20   J. Camilleri and J. Falk, *The End of Sovereignty? The Politics of a Shrinking and Fragmenting World* (London: Edward Elgar, 1992), p. 69.

21   M. Waters, *Globalization* (London: Routledge, 1995), p. 3.

22   P. Jay and P. Kennedy, *The 1996 Analysis Lecture – Globalisation and Its Discontents* (Transcript) (London: BBC Radio Four, 30 May 1996).

23   Ibid.

24   D. Held and A. McGrew, *Globalization and the Liberal Democratic State*, p. 268.

25 E. Luard, *The Globalization of Politics – The Changed Focus of Political Action in the Modern World* (New York: New York University Press, 1990) sees that a global system of economic management is required if the redistribution that is necessary at the global level is to be pursued.

26 In an earlier text, Kennedy examines the global impacts and suggests that it highlights a new agenda of relative competitiveness: *Preparing for the Twenty First Century* (Glasgow: HarperCollins, 1993).

27 P. Jay and P. Kennedy, *The 1996 Analysis Lecture*.

28 The terms of trade is a measure of the balance between imports and exports from countries.

29 His exposition includes an examination of the works by F. Blau and L. Kahn, 'International Differences in Male Wage Inequality: Institutions Versus Market Forces', *Journal of Political Economy*, 104(4), pp. 791–837; D. Corry and G. Holtham *Growth with Stability: Progressive Macroeconomic Policy* (London: IPPR, 1996); A. Glyn and B. Sutcliffe, 'Global but Leaderless: The New Capitalist Order', in R. Miliband (ed.), *The Socialist Register 1992* (London: Merlin Press, 1992); E. Phelps, *Rewarding Work: How to Restore Participation and Self-Support to Free Enterprise* (Cambridge, Mass: Harvard University Press, 1997); R. Rowthorn, 'Centralisation, Employment and Wage Dispersion', *Economic Journal*, 102(412), pp. 506–23; A. Wood *North–South Trade, Employment and Inequality. Changing Fortunes in a Skill-Driven World* (Oxford: Clarendon Press, 1994).

30 But, he notes, these egalitarian employment policies rest on two factors: 'firstly, upon a willingness to redistribute resources from rich (often high-skilled) to poor (often low-skilled) to finance targeted employment policies by means of wage subsidies or public employment schemes, improved education and training, and to remedy unacceptable income inequalities which cannot be eliminated by such policies; secondly, upon a willingness to accept some discipline with regard to the increase of the average wage level in both slack and tight labour markets (and, consequently, the acceptance that the evolution of wage and overall income differentials is a legitimate concern for policy in the framework of that incomes discipline). Principles of reciprocity and efficiency in the implementation of employment programmes and social policies have to underpin the willingness to redistribute.' F. Vandenbroucke, *Globalization, Inequality and Social Democracy: A Survey,* paper presented to the ECPR Conference, 23–28 March 1998, University of Warwick, p. 45.

31 Another form of response to globalization is that suggested by J. Goldsmith in *The Trap* (London: Macmillan, 1994) of protectionism.

32 See J. Gray, *False Dawn: The Delusions of Global Capitalism* (London: Granta Books, 1998) for a full discussion of the role of the nation state.

33 See M. Albert, *Capitalism Versus Capitalism* (London: Whurr, 1993); and C. Hampden-Turner and A. Trompenaars, *The Seven Cultures of Capitalism – Values Systems for Creating Wealth in the United States, Japan, German, France, Britain, Sweden and the Netherlands* (New York: Currency Doubleday, 1993) for full descriptions of the varieties of capitalism.

34 W. Hutton *The State to Come* (London: Vintage, 1997), p. 17.

35 Stakeholder groups can range from employees, suppliers and the wider community. The difficulty lies in deciding which should participate, and how much influence they should wield.

36 J. K. Galbraith, *The New Industrial State* (London: Penguin Books, 1972), p. 76.
37 W. Hutton, 'Stake That Claim', *The Guardian*, 9 January 1996.
38 W. Hutton, *The State We're In* (London: Jonathan Cape, 1995), p. 269.
39 The stakeholder debate is forwarded still further in W. Hutton, *The State to Come*, and G. Kelly, D. Kelly and A. Gamble (eds), *Stakeholder Capitalism* (London: Macmillan, 1997).
40 The large military budget run by the United States during the 1980s acted in a pump-priming Keynesian manner and the Lawson budgets of the late 1980s in Britain, although performed under the name of neoliberalism, also acted in a Keynesian manner.
41 D. Goodhart, *The Reshaping of the German Social Market* (London: IPPR, 1994), p. 52. In this piece he examines the problems facing the German system. Similarly, for an examination of Japan's problems see S. Cockerill and C. Sparks, 'Japan in Crisis', *International Socialism*, Autumn 1996, pp. 27–57.
42 An examination of the debate concerning convergence between the varieties of capitalism is undertaken by H. Perkin, 'The Third Revolution and Stakeholder Capitalism: Convergence or Collapse', *Political Quarterly*, 67(3), pp. 198–208.
43 See S. Thomson, *New Labour and Stakeholding: A Brief Encounter*, Department of Politics and International Relations Working Paper No. 2, University of Aberdeen.
44 F. Fukuyama, *The End of History and the Last Man* (London: Hamish Hamilton, 1992), p. 296.
45 W. Hutton, 'Class that Plays for Keeps – Interview with J. K. Galbraith', *The Guardian,* 23 June 1992.
46 *Ibid.*
47 It is possible to argue that the social democratic parties themselves became contented. This form of inertia is suggested by C. Lemke and G. Marks, 'From Decline to Demise?', in C. Lemke and G. Marks (eds), *The Crisis of Socialism in Europe* (Durham, NC: Duke University Press, 1992) as they claim that social democracy lost its radical nature and became defenders of the status quo. This defensive nature of social democracy is also discussed by D. Sassoon, 'Introduction', in D. Sassoon (ed.), *Looking Left: European Socialism after the Cold War* (London: I. B. Tauris, 1997)
48 I. Budge and D. Farlie, *Explaining and Predicting Elections – Issue Effects and Party Strategies in Twenty-Three* (London: George Allen & Unwin, 1983) p. 50.
49 B. Barry, 'The Continuing Relevance of Socialism', in R. Skidelsky (ed.), *Thatcherism* (London: Chatto & Windus, 1988), p. 145.
50 J. Rentoul, *Me and Mine – The Triumph of the New Individualism?* (London: Unwin Hyman, 1989), p. 19.
51 See I. Crewe, 'The Thatcher Legacy', in A. King (ed.), *Britain at the Polls* (Chatham: Chatham House, 1993), pp. 1–28, and J. Rentoul, *Me and Mine*.
52 B. Crick, *Socialism* (Milton Keynes: Open University Press, 1987), p. 91.
53 Titmuss and Marshall, cited by B. Barry, *The Continuing Relevance*, p. 155.
54 D. Marquand, *The New Reckoning – Capitalism, States and Citizens* (Cambridge: Polity Press, 1997) contains a series of essays and within these the ethos of wartime solidarity is recognized.

55 F. Muller-Rommel, 'Green Parties and Alternative Lists under Cross-National Perspectives', in F. Muller-Rommel (ed.), *New Politics in Western Europe* (Boulder, Colo.: Westview Press, 1989), p. 3.

56 R. Inglehart, *The Silent Revolution* (Princeton, NJ: University Press, 1977), p. 8.

57 F. Muller-Rommel, 'Green Parties and Alternative Lists under Cross-National Perspectives', in F. Muller-Rommel (ed.), *New Politics in Western Europe,* p. 18.

58 J. Gray, *After Social Democracy* (London: Demos, 1996), p. 8.

59 R. Nayar, 'Book Review – The End of History and the Last Man by Francis Fukuyama', *Political Quarterly,* 63, p. 356.

60 S. Wolinetz, 'Party System Change: "The Catch-All Thesis Revisited"', *West European Politics,* 14(1), pp. 113–28.

61 A. Ware, *Political Parties and Party Systems* (Oxford: Oxford University Press, 1996), pp. 326–7.

62 In addition to these points D. Robertson, *A Theory of Party Competition* (London: John Wiley & Sons, 1976) also contends that:

(a) There may exist constraints leading a party not to take up an ideologically expedient position, because to do so is to lose vital resources in voluntary workers or finance, to the point that the potential vote cannot be realized.

(b) There may be situations in which a party cannot credibly take up an ideologically vote-maximizing position.

(c) There may be situations where a party can win an election without taking up such a position.

(d) Individual candidates may find that they cannot hope to win in their constituency by adopting the official party position, or by modifying it within the permitted limit.

(e) Other candidates may benefit from this by being in a constituency that their opponent cannot win. Downs fails to explain the existence of 'safe' seats in elections.

63 For the role of trust in modern politics see M. Wickham-Jones, 'New Labour and Business: The Search for Credibility', in A. Dobson and J. Stanyer (eds), *Contemporary Political Studies 1998,* vol. 2 (Nottingham: PSA, 1998).

64 The decline of the blue-collar working class is charted in A. Przeworski and J. Sprague, *Paper Stones – A History of Electoral Socialism* (Chicago: Chicago University Press, 1986).

65 See the discussion by R. Inglehart, *The Silent Revolution.*

66 The changing nature of patterns in the work environment are also examined in F. F. Piven, 'The Decline of Labor Parties: An Overview', in F. F. Piven (ed.), *Labor Parties in Post-Industrial Societies* (Cambridge: Polity Press, 1991).

67 See D. Denver, *Elections and Voting Behaviour in Britain* (Hemel Hempstead: Harvester Wheatsheaf, 1994) for a fuller discussion of theories of voting behaviour.

68 G. Esping-Andersen, 'Equality and Work in the Post-Industrial Life-Cycle', in D. Miliband (ed.), *Reinventing the Left* (London: Polity Press, 1994), p. 167.

69 See A. Heath et al., *How Britain Votes* (Oxford: Pergamon, 1985).

70 W. Hutton, *The State We're In,* p. 96.

71   H. Kitschelt, *The Transformation of European Social Democracy* (Cambridge: Cambridge University Press, 1994), p. 17.
72   Ibid., p. 21.
73   Ibid., p. 32.
74   According to Kitschelt there are four possible strategies:

   (a)   to pursue a short-term vote-maximizing strategy and adopt a left-libertarian stance when the distribution of voter sentiment is favourable to such appeals;
   (b)   to pursue a short-term vote-maximizing strategy when the party system places a larger number of competitors for social democrats in the centre of the party system rather than at the left-libertarian periphery;
   (c)   to pursue an office-seeking or pivotal strategy which will sacrifice votes and seats, in order to improve their chance of holding a pivotal position in government coalition formation. 'A party is pivotal if no majority coalition can be formed against it';
   (d)   to pursue a long-term vote-seeking strategy of oligopolistic competition which sacrifices votes for the sake of long-term office or vote-maximization by moving toward a more extreme left-libertarian position to remove an opponent. Once the competitor has been eliminated, a moderated stance will regain votes. Ibid., p. 130.

75   See E. Shaw, 'Book Review of Herbert Kitschelt, The Transformation of European Social Democracy', *Party Politics*, 2(3), pp. 421–24.

Chapter 3   The Southern European model of social democracy

1   The development of the Socialist Party in France can be traced in a number of books: N. Nugent and D. Lowe, *The Left in France* (London: Macmillan, 1982); D. S. Bell and B. Criddle, *The French Socialist Party: The Emergence of a Party of Government* (Oxford: Clarendon Press, 1988); D. Pickles, *The Government and Politics of France – Volume One, Institutions and Parties* (London: Methuen, 1972); R. W. *Johnson, The Long March of the French Left* (London: Macmillan, 1981); M. Larkin, *France since the Popular Front: Government and People 1936–1986* (Oxford: Clarendon Press, 1988); S. Williams (ed.), *Socialism in France: From Jaurés to Mitterrand* (London: Pinter Publishers, 1983); S. Hazareesingh, *Political Traditions in Modern France* (Oxford: Oxford University Press, 1994); and J. Gaffney, *The French Left and the Fifth Republic: The Discourses of Communism and Socialism in Contemporary France* (London: Macmillan, 1989).
2   Communist involvement occurred only in terms of support as opposed to direct participation in the government, as they wished to protect their image of transforming the position of the working class.
3   R. W. Johnson, *The Long March of the French Left*, p. 23.
4   A full examination of the Fourth Republic is undertaken in P. Williams, *Crisis and Compromise – Politics in the Fourth Republic* (London: Longman, 1972).

5 The presidentialization of the French party system is examined in B. Criddle, 'France', in A. Ware (ed.), *Political Parties – Electoral Change and Structural Response* (Oxford: Basil Blackwell, 1987); A. Cole 'The Presidential Party and the Fifth Republic', *West European Politics*, 16(2), pp. 49–66; and J. Gaffney 'The Emergence of a Presidential Party: The Socialist Party', in A. Cole (ed.), *French Political Parties in Transition* (Aldershot: Dartmouth, 1990).

6 A detailed study of CERES is undertaken in D. Hanley, *Keeping Left? CERES and the French Socialist Party* (Manchester: Manchester University Press, 1986).

7 The Mitterrand victory is examined in H. Machin and V. Wright, 'Why Mitterrand Won: The French Presidential Elections of April-May 1981', *West European Politics*, 5, pp. 5–35.

8 The change in economic policy is often viewed as the defining moment of the Mitterrand presidency and is examined in more detail in D. Cobham, 'French Macroeconomic Policy under President Mitterrand: An Assessment', *National Westminster Bank Quarterly Review*, February 1984, pp. 41–51; H. Machin and V. Wright (eds), *Economic Policy and Policy-Making under the Mitterrand Presidency 1981–84* (Exeter: Frances Pinter, 1985); and P. Hall, 'The Evolution of Economic Policy under Mitterrand', in G. Ross, S. Hoffmann and S. Malzacher (eds), *The Mitterrand Experiment – Continuity and Change in Modern France* (Oxford: Polity Press, 1987).

9 Cited in A. Knapp, *Gaullism since De Gaulle* (Aldershot: Dartmouth, 1994), p. 402.

10 A. Cole, *François Mitterrand – A Study in Political Leadership* (London: Routledge, 1994), p. 45.

11 G. Ross and J. Jenson, 'France: Triumph and Tragedy', in P. Anderson and P. Camiller (eds), *Mapping the West European Left* (London: Verso, 1994), p. 185.

12 See D. S. Bell and B. Criddle, 'Presidential Dominance Denied', *Parliamentary Affairs*, 39(4), pp. 477–88, for a study of the 1986 parliamentary elections.

13 The 1988 presidential election is examined in J. Gaffney (ed.), *The French Presidential Elections of 1988* (Worchester: Dartmouth, 1989); and Paul Hainsworth, 'The Re-Election of François Mitterrand: The 1988 French Presidential Election', *Parliamentary Affairs*, 41(4), pp. 536–47. The following legislative election is discussed by D. S. Bell and B. Criddle, 'No Majority for the President: The French Legislative Elections of June 1988', *Parliamentary Affairs*, 42(1), pp. 72–83.

14 The record of the Socialist governments can be followed in S. Mazey and M. Newman (eds), *Mitterrand's France* (London: Croom Helm, 1987); D. Manent and H. Machin, 'Two Views of the Mitterrand Presidency (1981–1988)', *Government and Opposition*, 23, pp. 186–209; A. Cole, 'The French Socialist Party in Transition', *Association of Modern and Contemporary France*, 37, pp. 14–23; R. Elgie, 'La Méthode Rocard Existe-T-Elle?', *Association of Modern and Contemporary France*, 39, pp. 11–19; and A. Daley (ed.), *The Mitterrand Era – Policy Alternatives and Political Mobilisation in France* (London: Macmillan, 1996). The most negative assessment of the Mitterrand presidency is provided by J. Laughland, *The Death of Politics – France under*

Mitterrand (London: Michael Joseph, 1994). A useful summary of the events of the 1980s is provided by G. Ross and J. Jenson, 'The Tragedy of the French Left', *New Left Review*, 171, pp. 5–44.

15 A full examination of the role that factions play in the PS is made by A. Cole, 'Factionalism, the French Socialist Party and the Fifth Republic: An Explanation of Intra-Party Divisions', *European Journal of Political Research*, 17, pp. 77–94.

16 D. S. Bell and B. Criddle, 'The French Socialist Party: Presidentialised Factionalism', in D. S. Bell and E. Shaw (eds), *Conflict and Cohesion in Western European Social Democratic Parties* (London: Pinter Publishers, 1994), p. 118.

17 A. Queval, 'Strengths and Weaknesses of the French Socialist Party', in R. Cuperus and J. Kandel (eds), *European Social Democracy: Transformation in Progress* (Amsterdam: Wiardi Beckman Stichting/Friedrich Ebert Stiftung, 1998), argues that generally this openness has provided the PS with an image of democracy which the other parties lack.

18 J. Gaffney, 'The French Socialist Party Conference, Paris, 13–15 December 1991', *Modern and Contemporary France*, 50, p. 11.

19 The nature of the electoral defeats of 1993 are analysed in R. Eatwell, 'The 1993 French Elections', *Political Quarterly*, 64, pp. 462–5; H. Machin, 'How the Socialists Lost the 1993 Elections to the French Parliament', *West European Politics*, 16, pp. 595–606; A. Guyomarch, 'The 1993 Parliamentary Election in France', *Parliamentary Affairs*, 46(4), pp. 605–36; and D. Hanley, 'Socialism Routed', *Modern and Contemporary France*, 1(4), pp. 417–27.

20 A. Cole, 'François Mitterrand', in J. Gaffney (ed.), *The French Presidential Elections of 1988* (Aldershot: Dartmouth, 1989), p. 46.

21 The interplay between the PS and the trade union movement is explained by F. Wilson, *Interest Group Politics in France* (Cambridge: Cambridge University Press, 1987).

22 The 1995 presidential election is examined by D. B. Goldey and A. Knapp, 'The French Presidential Election of 23 April–7 May 1995', *Electoral Studies*, 15(1), pp. 97–109; J. Szarka, 'The Winning of the 1995 French Presidential Election', *West European Politics*, 19(1), pp. 151–67; and J. Gaffney and L. Milne (eds), *French Presidentialism and the Election of 1995* (Aldershot: Ashgate, 1997).

23 D. Carton, P. Jarreau and L. Mauduit, 'Dans cette élection, je porte le rêve face à la resurgence de certaines rêveries Bonapartistes' (interview with Lionel Jospin), *Le Monde*, 21 April 1995.

24 An edited version of Jospin's 1995 presidential campaign manifesto, 'Propositions pour la France', is given in Appendix 2.

25 P. Rousanvallon, 'Jospin et la nouvelle culture politique de la gauche', *Libération*, 4 May 1995.

26 D. S. Bell, 'The French Parti Socialiste', in A. Dobson and J. Stanyer (eds), *Contemporary Political Studies 1998* (Nottingham: PSA, 1998), p. 476.

27 J. Wolfrey, 'What Price Unity? The "Plural Left" in France', in A. Dobson and J. Stanyer (eds), *Contemporary Political Studies 1998* (Nottingham: PSA, 1998), p. 803.

28 M. Noblecourt, 'Une inflexion sur la fiscalité de l'épargne', *Le Monde*, 5 May 1997.

29 M. Noblecourt, 'Changeons d'avenir, changeons de majorité: Nos engagements pour la France', *Le Monde*, 3 May 1997.

30 M. Noblecourt, 'Lionel Jospin invoque Tony Blair pour revigorer la campagne du PS', *Le Monde,* 5 May 1997.
31 *Ibid.*
32 P. Jarreau and M. Noblecourt, 'Lionel Jospin inscrit son programme dans la dureé d'une législature', *Le Monde,* 21 May 1997.
33 L. Mauduit, 'Le PS admet que l'état puisse vendre des participations minoritaires', *Le Monde,* 7 May 1995.
34 L. Jospin, *General Policy Statement by Lionel Jospin, Prime Minister, to the National Assembly,* France Statements, Ambassade de France à Londres, 26 June 1997, p. 9.
35 Ibid., p. 12.
36 Paid to households of two or more children.
37 A. Cole, *French Socialism in Longitudinal Comparative Perspective: Systemic Transformation and Partisan Identity,* paper prepared for the ECPR joint sessions, University of Warwick, 23–28 March 1998.
38 P. Webster, 'Paris Plans Jobs Blitz for Young', *The Guardian,* 31 July 1997.
39 D. MacShane, 'French Disconnection', *Prospect,* July 1997.
40 P. Webster, 'Jospin Cure Hard to Swallow', *The Guardian,* 26 January 1998.
41 'Lionel Jospin, Escape Artist', *The Economist,* 14 February 1998.
42 J. Wolfrey, 'What Price Unity?', p. 804.
43 'Jospin Discovers America', *The Economist,* 27 June 1998.
44 An early evaluation of the Jospin government is undertaken in G. Ross, 'Jospin so far', *French Politics and Society,* 15(3), pp. 9–19.
45 A. L. Pina, 'Shaping the Constitution', in H. Penniman and E. Mujal-León (eds), *Spain at the Polls, 1977, 1979 and 1982: A Study of National Elections* (New York: Duke University Press, 1985), p. 45.
46 R. Gillespie, *The Spanish Socialist Party: A History of Factionalism* (Oxford: Clarendon Press, 1989), p. 300.
47 Ibid., p. 356.
48 Ibid., p. 415.
49 B. Pollack and G. Hunter, 'The Spanish Socialist Workers' Party Foreign and Defence Policy: The External Dimension of Modernisation', in T. Gallagher and A. Williams (eds), *Southern European Socialism – Parties, Elections and the Challenge of Government* (Manchester: Manchester University Press, 1989), p. 98.
50 J. Maravall, 'From Opposition to Government: The Politics and Policies of the PSOE', in J. Maravall et al., *Socialist Parties in Europe* (Barcelona: Institut d'Ediciones de la Diputació de Barcelona, 1992), p. 26.
51 P. Camiller, 'Spain: The Survival of Socialism?', in P. Anderson and P. Camiller (eds), *Mapping the West European Left* (London: Verso, 1994), p. 258.
52 Ibid., p. 263.
53 D. Share, *Dilemmas of Social Democracy: The Spanish Socialist Workers Party in the 1980s* (New York: Greenwood Press, 1989), pp. 142–6.
54 R. Gillespie, 'The Resurgence of Factionalism in the Spanish Socialist Workers Party', in D. S. Bell and E. Shaw (eds), *Conflict and Cohesion in Western European Social Democratic Parties* (London: Pinter Publishers, 1994), p. 55.
55 J. Maravall, *From Opposition to Government,* p. 17.
56 Ibid., p. 19.

57 The PSD appealed on the basis of 'socialist humanism', and in the early years of the new Portuguese state applied to join the Socialist International but were rejected because the PS opposed the move and voted against them joining. Their goals were 'to create a free and democratic socialist system which would transform all sectors of society' (T. Bruneau and A. MacLeod, *Politics in Contemporary Portugal* (Boulder, Colo.: Lynne Reiner Publishers, 1986), pp. 87–8). After rejection at the hands of the Socialist International, the party became very hostile to Marxism and took on a progressively more right-wing agenda by adopting privatization and constitutional revision at a time of democratic consolidation.

58 T. Gallagher, 'The Portuguese Socialist Party: The Pitfalls of Being First', in T. Gallagher and A. Williams (eds), *Southern European Socialism* (Manchester: Manchester University Press, 1989), p. 12. By claiming to stand for 'undogmatic Marxism', Soares was attempting to show radicalism but with a realistic edge.

59 Ibid., p. 14.

60 T. Bruneau and A. MacLeod, *Politics in Contemporary Portugal*, p. 66.

61 T. Gallagher, *The Portuguese Socialist Party*, p. 23.

62 S. Giner, *Southern European Socialism in Transition* (ECPR Joint Sessions in Barcelona, 1985), p. 33.

63 D. Corkill, 'Portugal Votes for Change and Stability: The Election of 1995', *West European Politics*, 19(2), p. 405.

64 Ibid., p. 403.

65 'Aiming for Convergence: Portugal', *The Observer*, 10 August 1997, p. 4.

66 Ibid., p. 4.

67 As is shown in the policies of Carlos Cesar, President of the Autonomous Region of the Azores, in ibid., p. 21.

68 T. Gallagher, *The Portuguese Socialist Party*, p. 35.

69 See M. Spourdalakis, 'PASOK in the 1990s. Structure, Ideology, Political Strategy', in J. Maravall et al., *Socialist Parties in Europe* (Barcelona: Institut d'Ediciones de la Diputació de Barcelona, 1992), p. 160.

70 Ibid., p. 171.

71 C. Lyrintzis, 'PASOK in Power: The Loss of the "Third Road to Socialism"', in T. Gallagher and A. Williams (eds), *Southern European Socialism* (Manchester: Manchester University Press, 1989), p. 40.

72 Which followed on from the 1983 Law for the Socialization of Public Enterprises which made it difficult for them to be held.

73 See M. Spourdalakis, 'PASOK in the 1990s', p. 176.

74 See ibid., p. 176.

75 See ibid., pp. 172–3.

76 J. Petras, 'Greek Socialism: The Patrimonial State Revisited', in J. Kurth and J. Petras (eds), *Mediterranean Paradoxes – The Politics and Social Structure of Southern Europe* (Oxford: Berg, 1993), p. 215.

77 M. Spourdalakis, *The Rise of the Greek Socialist Party* (London: Routledge, 1988), pp. 236–7.

78 C. Lyrintzis, 'PASOK in Power', p. 51.

79 V. Fouskas, 'The Left and the Crisis of the Third Hellenic Republic, 1989–97', in D. Sassoon (ed.), *Looking Left: European Socialism after the Cold War* (London: I. B. Tauris, 1997), p. 65.

80 Ibid., p. 83.
81 Characteristics adopted from A. Cole, *French Socialism in Longitudinal Comparative Perspective.* But in *French Politics and Society* (Hemel Hempstead) Prentice Hall, 1998) Cole provides a fuller explanation. He lists the elements of exceptionalism as including:

- a powerful, unified and indivisible central state, a legacy of the process of nation building;
- a distrust of intermediary institutions and a suspicion of civil society;
- a model of Parisian centralization, producing in comparative terms a homogeneous political and administrative elite;
- a tradition of state intervention (*dirigisme*) in the economic and industrial sphere;
- an ideologically charged political discourse.

M. MacLean, 'Privatisation, Dirigisme, and the Global Economy: An End to French Exceptionalism', *Modern and Contemporary France,* 5(2), pp. 215–28, also undertakes a study of exceptionalism. The historical role of the state in French society and economy is described in P. Hall, *Governing the Economy – The Politics of State Intervention in Britain and France* (Oxford: Polity Press, 1986).
82 T. Gallagher, *The Portuguese Socialist Party,* p. 31.

Chapter 4   The Northern European model of social democracy

1 K. Molin, 'Historical Orientation', in K. Misgeld, K. Molin and K. Åmark (eds), *Creating Social Democracy – A Century of the Social Democratic Labour Party in Sweden* (University Park, Pa: Pennsylvania State University, 1992), p. xxiii.
2 In cooperation until 1936, thereafter as a coalition partner.
3 G. Therborn, 'A Unique Chapter in the History of Democracy: The Social Democrats in Sweden', in K. Misgeld, K. Molin and K. Åmark (eds), *Creating Social Democracy,* p. 15.
4 By the late 1940s earlier general economic policies had developed into the Rehn-Meidner plan, the main elements of this model being: an anti-inflationary economic policy, coupled with counter-cyclical measures in order to guarantee stability; a solidaristic wage policy, according to the principles of equal pay for equal work and a gradual diminishing of wage differentials; and an active labour market policy, ensuring a fast adaptation of supply to demand – J. Otto, 'The Economic Policy Strategies of the Nordic Countries', in H. Keman, H. Palaheimo and P. Whiteley (eds), *Coping with Economic Crisis: Alternative Responses to Economic Recession in Advanced Industrial Societies* (London: Sage Publications, 1987), p. 168.
5 G. Esping-Andersen, 'The Making of a Social Democratic Welfare State', in K. Misgeld, K. Molin and K. Åmark (eds), *Creating Social Democracy,* p. 58.
6 Apart from a brief spell in June–September 1936.

7 The top rate of taxation was reduced from 45 per cent to 20 per cent being paid for by a tax on capital income, an extended scope of value added tax (VAT) and increased housing costs.

8 J. Pontusson, 'Sweden: After the Golden Age', in P. Anderson and P. Camiller, *Mapping the West European Left* (London: Verso, 1994), pp. 35–6.

9 1991 saw the abolition of the collective affiliation of union members to the SAP, at the LO's request. A massive decline in party membership resulted.

10 The reforms being: the introduction of a sixth week of paid holidays, the extension of parental leave insurance from 9 to 15 months, and the expansion of public day care so that every pre-school child above the age of 18 months would be ensured a place. As cited by J. Pontusson, *Sweden: After the Golden Age*, p. 37.

11 J. Fulcher, 'The Social Democratic Model in Sweden: Termination or Restoration?', *Political Quarterly*, 65(2), April–June 1994, p. 208.

12 Ibid., p. 210.

13 That is, to help technological development.

14 Part of the recent decline of social democracy in Sweden could be accounted for by the steady rise in conservatism, as illustrated by their dominance of the 1991–4 government.

15 In the case of nuclear energy, although it was the bourgeois government who used the referendum, it was under the suggestion of the social democrats.

16 This factionalizing is illustrated by the joining of the European Union which was only confirmed in a referendum by 52. 2 per cent, with white-collar workers, private-sector employees and the self-employed all agreeing. Blue-collar union members came out against membership.

17 M. Stigendal, 'The Swedish Model: Renaissance or Retrenchment?', *Renewal*, 3(1), January 1995, p. 21.

18 J. Pontusson, *The Limits of Social Democracy – Investment Politics in Sweden* (Ithaca, NY: Cornell University Press, 1992) adopts a critical examination of investment politics and offers part of the explanation for the Swedish model's collapse as being disagreements between the SAP leadership and the unions' ambitions. So although the relationship between the two groups was close, it was not always united.

19 The failure of the model is tracked by R. Meidner, 'Why Did the Swedish Model Fail?', in R. Miliband and L. Panitch (eds), *Socialist Register 1993* (London: Merlin Press, 1993); J.-E. Lane, 'The Decline of the Swedish Model', *Governance*, 8, pp. 579–90; J. Pontusson, 'At the End of the Third Road: Swedish Social Democracy in Crisis', *Politics and Society*, 20, pp. 305–32; and M. Stigendal, *The Swedish Model*, pp. 14–23.

20 SAP, *The Swedish Social Democratic Party – An Introduction* (Stockholm: SAP, 1996), p. 3.

21 SAP, *Sweden Into the Twenty-First Century* (Stockholm: SAP, 1996), p. 26.

22 Ibid., p. 23.

23 SAP, *The Swedish Social Democratic Party Programme*, p. 11.

24 Ibid., p. 17.

25 They view the EU's role as one of an employment union. Because of the inability of individual countries to affect the economic environment, the

potential role of the EU has increased especially in providing a 'social floor' of minimum rules.

26 A.-M. Lindgren, 'Swedish Social Democracy in Transition', in R. Cuperus and J. Kandel (eds), *European Social Democracy: Transformation in Progress* (Amsterdam: Wiardi Beckman Stichting/Friedrich Ebert Stiftung, 1998), p. 89, states that the party no longer stands for the redistribution of income but the 'redistribution of possibilities'.

27 SAP, *Sweden Into the Twenty-First Century*, p. 8.

28 N. F. Christiansen, 'Denmark: End of an Idyll?', in P. Anderson and P. Camiller (eds), *Mapping the West European Left* (London: Verso, 1994), p. 82.

29 S. M. Lipset, 'No Third Way: A Comparative Perspective on the Left' in Chirot, D. (ed.), *The Crisis and Decline of Leninism and the Decline of the Left: The Revolutions of 1989* (London: University of Washington Press, 1991), p. 192.

30 E. Berntzen, 'Social Democracy in Scandinavia: Questions, Processes, Comparisons', in J. Maravall et al., *Socialist Parties in Europe* (Barcelona: Institut d'Edicions de la Diputació de Barcelona, 1992), p. 107.

31 J. O. Anderrson, 'The Economic Policy Strategies of the Nordic Countries', in H. Keman, H. Palaheimo and P. Whiteley (eds), *Coping with Economic Crisis*, p. 169.

32 The Social Democratic Party of Denmark, *The Social Democratic Party of Denmark, 1871–1990: Achievements and Problems* (Copenhagen: Social Democratic Party of Denmark, 1990), p. 18.

33 G. Esping-Andersen, *Politics Against Markets – The Social Democratic Road to Power* (Princeton, NJ: Princeton University Press, 1985), p. 95.

34 The SF was formed after a split in the Communist Party and it was willing to cooperate with the SD on some socialist reforms.

35 The new parties were aided by the electoral system which lacked a threshold for representation, i.e. one similar to the 5 per cent required in Sweden in order to gain representation in Parliament.

36 Danish Social Democratic Party, *Common Future – Common Goals* (Copenhagen: Danish Social Democratic Party, 1996), p. 4.

37 Ibid., p. 4.

38 Danish Social Democratic Party, *Beyond the Year 2000* (Copenhagen: Danish Social Democratic Party, 1992), p. 6.

39 Danish Social Democratic Party, *Common Future – Common Goals*, p. 5.

40 Ibid., p. 16.

41 Danish Social Democratic Party, *Beyond the Year 2000*, p. 3.

42 Ibid., p. 4.

43 Ibid., p. 5.

44 G. Esping-Andersen, *Politics against Markets*, p. 81.

45 L. Mjøset, Å. Cappelen, J. Fagerberg and B. S. Tranøy, 'Norway: Changing the Model', in P. Anderson and P. Camiller (eds), *Mapping the West European Left* (London: Verso, 1994), pp. 58–60.

46 G. Esping-Andersen, *Politics against Markets*, p. 100.

47 K. Heidar, 'The Norwegian Labour Party: "En Attendant l'Europe"', *West European Politics*, 16, p. 65.

48 L. Mjøset, Å. Cappelen, J. Fagerberg and B. S. Tranøy, 'Norway: Changing the Model', p. 68.

49   That government collapsed because of a failure to agree on the negotiations on the European Economic Area between EFTA and the EC.
50   For a discussion of the changing nature of the state see J. Fagerberg, Å. Cappellen, L. Mjøset and R. Skarstein, 'The Decline of State Capitalism in Norway', *New Left Review*, 181, pp. 60–91.
51   K. Heidar, 'Towards Party Irrelevance? The Decline of Both Conflict and Cohesion in the Norwegian Labour Party', in D. S. Bell and E. Shaw (eds), *Conflict and Cohesion in Western European Social Democratic Parties* (London: Pinter Publishers Ltd., 1994), pp. 107–9.
52   K. Heidar, *The Norwegian Labour Party*, p. 75.
53   My italics.
54   DNA, *Togetherness: A Social Democratic Programme for the 1990s* (Oslo: DNA, 1992), p. 26.
55   DNA, *Co-determination: Statement of Principles and Action Programme* (Oslo: DNA, 1996), p. 64.
56   DNA, *Togetherness*, p. 23.
57   Ibid., p. 12.
58   DNA, *Co-determination*, p. 12.
59   S. Padgett and W. Paterson, 'Germany: Stagnation of the Left', in P. Anderson and P. Camiller (eds), *Mapping the West European Left* (London: Verso, 1994), see this cross-class appeal as a tradition of political Catholicism.
60   Ibid., p. 103.
61   W. Paterson, 'The German Social Democratic Party', in W. Paterson and A. Thomas (eds), *Social Democratic Parties in Western Europe* (London: Croom Helm, 1977), p. 185.
62   See S. Padgett, 'The German Social Democratic Party: Between Old and New Left', in D. S. Bell and E. Shaw (eds), *Conflict and Cohesion in Western European Social Democratic Parties* (London: Pinter Publishers, 1994) for more details on their demands.
63   W. Paterson, 'The German Social Democratic Party', p. 188.
64   S. Padgett, 'The German Social Democratic Party', p. 19.
65   S. Padgett and W. Paterson, 'Germany: Stagnation of the Left', p. 115.
66   S. Padgett, 'The German Social Democratic Party', p. 22.
67   S. Padgett, 'The German Social Democrats: A Redefinition of Social Democracy or Bad Godesberg Mark II', *West European Politics*, 16, pp. 28–9.
68   S. Padgett, 'The German Social Democratic Party', p. 22.
69   SPD, *Work, Innovation and Justice* (Bonn: SPD, 1998), p. 6.
70   Ibid., p. 10.
71   Ibid., p. 23.
72   Ibid., p. 51.
73   I. Traynor, 'Kohl's Rival Masters New Media Politics', *The Guardian*, 4 March 1998.
74   I. Traynor, 'Schröder Heads for the Centre with Pro-EU Tack', *The Guardian*, 3 March 1998.
75   I. Traynor, 'Schröder Says Bonn Is Taking Brakes Off EU Social Policy' *The Guardian*, 11 November 1998.
76   S. Jochem, *The Social Democratic Full-Employment Model in Transition – The Scandinavian Experiences in the 80s and 90s*, paper presented to the ECPR workshop, 23–28 March 1998.

Chapter 5   The British case: the development of New Labour

1   The New Labour project is outlined in a series of pieces by Tony Blair: 'Why Modernisation Matters', *Renewal* 1(4); 'Power for a Purpose', *Renewal* 3(4); *Socialism*, Fabian Society Pamphlet 565 (London: Fabian Society, 1994); and *New Britain: My Vision of a Young Country* (London: Fourth Estate, 1996). Further 'insiders' accounts are provided by P. Mandelson and R. Liddle *The Blair Revolution: Can New Labour Deliver?* (London: Faber & Faber, 1996); G. Brown and T. Wright (eds), *Values, Visions and Voices – An Anthology of Socialism* (Edinburgh: Mainstream Publishing, 1995); R. Layard *What Labour Can Do* (London: Warner Books, 1997); C. Smith, *New Questions for Socialism*, Fabian Society Pamphlet 577 (London: Fabian Society, 1996); G. Radice, *Southern Discomfort,* Fabian Society Pamphlet 555 (London: Fabian Society, 1992); G. Radice and S. Pollard *More Southern Discomfort: A Year On – Taxing and Spending*, Fabian Society Pamphlet 560 (London: Fabian Society, 1993); P. Hain, *Ayes to the Left: A Future for Socialism* (London: Lawrence & Wishart, 1995) who adopts a more libertarian approach; D. Miliband (ed.), *Reinventing the Left* (London: Polity Press, 1994); T. Wright, *Who Dares Wins: New Labour – New Politics,* Fabian Society Pamphlet 579 (London: Fabian Society, 1997); and G. Radice, *What Needs to Change: New Visions for Britain* (London: Harper Collins, 1996).

2   The rise and development of the Labour Party is examined by H. Pelling *A Short History of the Labour Party*, 8th edn. (London: Macmillan, 1985); A. J. Davies, *To Build a New Jerusalem – The Labour Movement from the 1880s to the 1990s* (London: Michael Joseph, 1992); and K. Laybourn, *The Rise of Labour: The British Labour Party, 1890–1979* (London: Edward Arnold, 1988). For more recent developments see P. Seyd 'Tony Blair and New Labour', in A. King (ed.), *New Labour Triumphs: Britain at the Polls* (Chatham: Chatham House, 1998).

3   The ideological development of the Labour Party is described by J. Callaghan, 'The Left: The Ideology of the Labour Party', in L. Tivey and A. Wright (eds), *Party Ideology in Britain* (London: Routledge, 1989); E. Shaw, *The Labour Party since 1945* (Oxford: Blackwell, 1996) and *The Labour Party since 1979: Crisis and Transformation* (London: Routledge, 1994); and G. Foote, *The Labour Party's Political Thought: A History,* 3rd edn. (London: Macmillan, 1997).

4   The categorizations are mainly adopted from E. Shaw, *The Labour Party since 1945*; however, each has been elaborated by the use of additional material.

5   E. Shaw, *The Labour Party since 1945*, p. 3.

6   The revisionist agenda is fully explored by S. Haseler *The Gaitskellites: Revisionism in the British Labour Party, 1951–1964* (London: Macmillan, 1969). But the faults of revisionism were fully recognized by J. P. Mackintosh, 'Has Social Democracy Failed in Britain?', in W. John Morgan (ed.), *Politics and Consensus in Modern Britain – Lectures in Memory of Hugh Gaitskell* (London: Macmillan, 1988).

7   For the definitive account of relations between the Labour Party and the trade union movement see L. Minkin, *The Contentious Alliance: Trade Unions and the Labour Party* (Edinburgh: Edinburgh University Press, 1992).

8 The victory of the Left and its subsequent decline are detailed by P. Seyd, *The Rise and Fall of the Labour Left* (Macmillan, 1987); D. Kogan and M. Kogan, *The Battle for the Labour Party* (Glasgow: Fontana Paperbacks, 1982); D. Kavanagh (ed.), *The Politics of the Labour Party* (London: George Allen & Unwin, 1982); and P. Byrd, 'The Labour Party in Britain' in W. E. Paterson and A. H. Thomas (eds), *The Future of Social Democracy* (Oxford: Clarendon Press, 1986). A more left-wing view of this period is provided by K. Coates, *The Social Democrats: Those Who Went and Those Who Stayed – The Forward March of Labour Halted?* (Nottingham: Spokesman, 1983).

9 The development of Labour's economic policies are followed in N. Thompson, *Political Economy and the Labour Party: The Economics of Democratic Socialism, 1884–1995* (London: UCL Press, 1996); and J. Eatwell, 'The Development of Labour Policy, 1979–1992', in J. Michie (ed.), *The Economic Legacy* (London: Academic Press, 1992).

10 The choice of Labour leaders is examined by P. Stark, *Choosing a Leader: Party Leadership Contests in Britain from Macmillan to Blair* (London: Macmillan, 1996).

11 The problems for the Labour Party, as identified in the early 1980s, are given by P. Whiteley, *The Labour Party in Crisis* (London: Methuen, 1983); A. Mitchell, *Four Years in the Death of the Labour Party* (London: Methuen, 1983); and S. Haseler, *The Tragedy of Labour* (Oxford: Basil Blackwell, 1980). The viewpoint from the 1970s is provided by L. Minkin and P. Seyd, 'The British Labour Party', in W. E. Paterson and A. H. Thomas (eds), *Social Democratic Parties in Western Europe* (London: Croom Helm, 1977).

12 The developments of the 1980s and the Policy Review Process are tackled by C. Hughes and P. Wintour, *Labour Rebuilt: The New Model Party* (London: Fourth Estate, 1990); and M. Smith and J. Spear (eds), *The Changing Labour Party* (London: Routledge, 1992). An interesting insider's account of this period is provided by B. Gould, *Goodbye to All That* (London: Macmillan, 1995).

13 See A. McSmith, *John Smith: A Life 1939–1994* (Reading: Mandarin, 1994).

14 Blair's background and rise in the Labour Party are detailed in two biographies: J. Rentoul, *Tony Blair* (London: Little, Brown, 1995) and J. Sopel, *Tony Blair – The Moderniser* (London: Bantam Books, 1995).

15 A view of the Labour Party as an essentially conservative party in which continuity dominates is considered by D. Marquand, *The Progressive Dilemma* (St Ives: William Heinemann, 1991). This version of events places the failures of the party in the context of an inability to construct an enduring electoral coalition. N. Ellison, 'From Welfare State to Post-Welfare Society', in B. Brivati and T. Bale (eds), *New Labour in Power: Precedents and Prospects* (London: Routledge, 1997) believes that the party entered a collectivist statis which prevented it from fully realizing the need to adapt and move into the 'post-welfare era'. Among those interviewed there appeared to be a split between those from the Left who were wary of these moves while the modernizers embraced it.

16 See T. Jones, *Remaking the Labour Party – From Gaitskell to Blair* (London: Routledge, 1996).

17 G. Radice and S. Pollard, *More Southern Discomfort: A Year On – Taxing and Spending*, Fabian Society Tract 560 (London: Fabian Society, 1993), p. 16.

18 J. Sopel, *Tony Blair*, p. 259.
19 Several of these so-called barons actually urged the executives of their unions to accept the new clause, i.e. Bill Morris and Rodney Bickerstaffe – see Eric Shaw, *The Labour Party since 1945*.
20 Scargill received a standing ovation from only seven constituency and union delegates.
21 Lewis Minkin, *The Labour Party Conference* (Manchester: Manchester University Press, 1980), examines the role of the party conference in great detail and is able to show how their management traditionally operated in the years before the Bennite reforms. The period until the late 1960s was characterized by the close association of the political (parliamentary) leaders and the industrial (trade union) leaderships. To ignore the decisions of conference would have been to take on the trade unions, and this would cause serious divisions within the party. The two leaderships remaining close minimized the danger of a defeat for the parliamentary leadership. Consultations, both formal and informal, i.e. through liaison committees, took place to ensure the support of the union leadership, especially on matters of greatest concern to them. Political leaders often operated through the NEC trade union representatives to attempt to influence their delegations. The power of the trade union leaders, and the influence that they then wielded at conference – 90 per cent of the overall vote as well as votes on members of the NEC, etc. – aided this process. The right-wing block vote, where the main right-wing trade unions voted together to prevent unrepresentative factions from taking over, worked in conjunction with the power of the union leaders over their delegations. Carron's Law, named after the then AEU leader Bill Carron, was based around 'his open arrogation to himself of the right to interpret National Committee policy where he said it was clear' (p. 186). This led to his persistent, but not constant, support for the political leadership of the Labour Party which was of particular use to Hugh Gaitskell. Union delegations did not always vote the way that was demanded by their mandate if they felt that the political leadership was in danger of an embarrassing defeat. Conflicts did occur but they altered in nature between periods of opposition and periods of government – when in opposition fundamental disagreements occurred over public ownership, defence and nuclear weapons but these were soon forgotten once in government in favour of debates concerning economic management, incomes policy and industrial policy.

A breakdown in this association between the two sets of leaders took place as part of the fallout from the first Wilson governments, 1964–70, and with the Tribune MPs making contact with left-wing representatives of trade unions at the 1969 conference. Effective management of conferences, from that point on, became more problematic because the two sets of leaders did not enjoy the close contacts and relationships that they once did. The unions began to vote against the political leadership and this perception of division together with the perceived misuse of the block vote contributed to the electoral defeats that occurred after 1979.
22 Figures taken from Labour Party, *New Labour, New Britain: The Magazine for Labour Party Members,* New Year 1997, p. 5.
23 For a comparison between the stances of Old and New Labour see Appendix 4.

24 E. Shaw, *The Labour Party since 1945*, p. ix.
25 Particular concern was expressed by some about the possibility of growing inequality and unemployment, which may, in turn, lead to resentment among the party's traditional electorate.
26 C. Hay, 'Labour's Thatcherite Revisionism: Playing the "Politics of Catch-Up"', *Political Studies*, 42.
27 Ibid., p. 702.
28 E. Shaw, *New Labour*, paper prepared for Elections, Parties and Public Opinion Conference, Guildhall University, 15–17 September 1995.
29 E. Shaw, *The Labour Party since 1945*, p. 218.
30 *Parliamentary Socialism* was the title of a book by the Marxist intellectual Ralph Miliband in which he examined the nature of Old Labour's relationship to parliament and the state.
31 See *Regeneration* 'So You Want Change? – Interview with Tony Blair', 1, Winter 1994, p. 10, where Blair states 'I would like to see the culture of the party transformed. Meetings are often boring and off-putting. I think many young people cannot see their relevance to any genuine political activity.'
32 Cited in A. Lent, *Ethos in Kinnock's Labour Party*, paper presented to the PSA Annual Conference 1996, p. 4.
33 H. M. Drucker, *Doctrine and Ethos in the Labour Party* (London: George Allen & Unwin, 1979), pp. 12–17.
34 Ibid., p. 21.
35 A. Lent, *Ethos in Kinnock's Labour Party*, p. 6.
36 Ibid., p. 7.
37 Through the various discussions it was possible to note that cooperation is viewed more warmly by the 'modernizers' but that MPs do not convey any sense of unity on electoral reform.
38 Such as Peter Davies, head of Prudential Insurance, who chairs an advisory group on tackling youth and long-term unemployment; Robert Ayling, chairman of British Airways, who has a place on the committee designing the millennium celebrations; and Martin Taylor, chief executive of Barclays Bank, who is heading the taskforce on social security reform.
39 This was also shown to be the case in the Uxbridge by-election where Blair, as Prime Minister, made an unprecedented visit.
40 See P. Seyd and P. Whiteley, *Labour's Grass Roots: The Politics of Party Membership* (Oxford: Clarendon Paperbacks, 1992).
41 A. Ware, 'Activist–Leader Relations and the Structure of Political Parties: "Exchange" Models and Vote-Seeking Behaviour in Parties', *British Journal of Political Science*, 22, pp. 71–92.
42 T. Bale, 'A Symbolic Triumph', *Fabian Review*, 107(3), p. 9.
43 P. Whiteley and P. Seyd, *New Labour – New Grass Roots Party?*, paper presented at the annual PSA Conference, April 1998.
44 By removing much of this power from the National Executive Committee.
45 Of those interviewed, those on the Left were more suspicious of the Blair reforms while the 'modernizers' were very enthusiastic.
46 The revised version of the plans contained very few alterations, with the only one of major significance being the ability to present motions to conference being restored.

47 A. Grice, 'Left Revolts Over Blair's Power Bid', *The Sunday Times*, 12 January 1997.

48 Comprising members of the government and the NEC including the Leader, Deputy Leader, Chair, Vice Chair, Treasurer and equal numbers of NEC members and representatives of the Labour government – the Labour Party, *Labour into Power: A Framework for Partnership* (London: Labour Party, 1997), p. 11. This composition will ensure a Blairite majority.

49 Ibid., p. 14.

50 Labour Coordinating Committee, *New Labour: A Stakeholders' Party – Interim Report of the Labour Party Co-ordinating Committee's Commission on Party Democracy* (London: LCC, 1997), p. 3.

51 D. Fatchett and P. Hain, *A Stakeholder Party* (London: Tribune Pamphlet, 1997), pp. 4/5.

52 *Ibid.*, p. 7.

53 See P. Seyd, 'Tony Blair and New Labour', p. 57.

54 The future of union–party relations is discussed in S. Ludlam, *From Social Contract to Social Partnership*, paper presented to the Political Studies Association Annual Conference 1998.

55 For a fuller exploration of the events surrounding these policy reversals see I. Hargreaves and S. Richards, 'Doomed by the Time the First Edition Came Off the Press', *New Statesman,* 24 October 1997. The role of spin doctors and the modern media machinery is examined in N. Jones, *Soundbites and Spin doctors: How Politicians Manipulate the Media – and Vice Versa* (London: Cassell, 1995). Labour's attitude is set out in more detail in R. Heffernan and J. Stanyer *Strengthening the Centre: The Labour Party, Political Communications and the Enhancement of Leadership Power*, paper presented at the EPOP Conference, September 1996.

56 D. Draper, *Blair's 100 Days* (London: Faber & Faber, 1997), p. 32.

57 Many of the processes and developments under New Labour find much criticism with the Left and these are explored by L. Panitch and C. Leys, *The End of Parliamentary Socialism – From New Left to New Labour* (London: Verso, 1997); M. Barrett Brown and K. Coates, *The Blair Revelation: Deliverance from Whom?* (Nottingham: Spokesman, 1996); P. Anderson and N. Mann, *Safety First – The Making of New Labour* (London: Granta Publications, 1997); R. Blackburn, 'Reflections On Blair's Velvet Revolution', New Left Review, 223; A. Callinicos, 'Betrayal and Discontent: Labour under Blair', International Socialism, Autumn 1996; M. Marqusee, 'New Labour and Its Discontents', *New Left Review*, 224; C. Leys, 'The British Labour Party's Transition from Socialism to Capitalism', in L. Panitch (ed.), *The Socialist Register 1996* (London: Merlin Press, 1996); C. Leys, 'The British Labour Party since 1989', in D. Sassoon (ed.), *Looking Left: European Socialism after the Cold War* (London: I. B. Tauris, 1997); and R. Heffernan and M. Marqusee, *Defeat from the Jaws of Victory: Inside Kinnock's Labour Party* (London: Verso, 1992).

58 Some of these are examined in M. Kenny and M. Smith, *Reforming Clause IV: Tony Blair and the Modernisation of the Labour Party*, paper presented to the Political Studies Association Conference, 1996.

59 A fuller explanation of the theory is given in Chapter 2.

60 These terms are employed by C. Hay, 'Labour's Thatcherite Revisionism'.

61   The political impact of Thatcherism is recognized by R. Heffernan, *Engineering Political Change: 'Thatcherism' and the Reordering of British Politics, 1979–1995*, paper presented to Elections, Parties and Public Opinion Conference, 1995. The electoral impact of Thatcherism is examined in A. T. Russell, R. J. Johnston and C. J. Pattie, 'Thatcher's Children: Explaining the Links Between Age and Political Attitudes', Political Studies, 40, pp. 742–56; and P. Norris, 'Thatcher's Enterprise Society and Electoral Change', *West European Politics*, 13, pp. 63–78. But the paradoxes of Thatcherism and its failures are clearly explored by S. Jenkins, *Accountable to None: The Tory Nationalisation of Britain* (London: Hamish Hamilton, 1995). John Gray goes still further in his criticism in *Beyond the New Right* (Chatham: Routledge, 1993) and in J. Gray and D. Willetts, *Is Conservatism Dead?* (London: Profile Books, 1997).

62   W. Thompson traces the decline of Labourism and an adaptation to quasi-Thatcherite institutions in *The Long Death of British Labourism – Interpreting a Political Culture* (London: Pluto Press, 1993).

63   Earlier policies given as examples by A. Grice, 'What's Left?', *The Sunday Times*, 23 July 1995.

64   See the British Election Panel surveys. More details of these can be found at: http://www. strath. ac. uk/other/CREST/

65   Analysis, *John Kampfner on the Philosophical Heart of New Labour*, BBC Radio Four, 17 December 1995. However, a common line among the 'modernizers' interviewed was the idea of a balance between individual and community.

66   M. Perryman 'Coming up for Air', in M. Perryman (ed.), *The Blair Agenda* (London: Lawrence & Wishart, 1996), p. 4.

67   T. Wright, *Who Dares Wins: New Labour – New Politics*, Fabian Society Pamphlet 579 (London: Fabian Society, 1997), p. 4.

68   Analysis *John Kampfner on the Philosophical Heart of New Labour*.

69   'Roundtable on Britain: After the Landslide' *Prospect* June 1997. There did exist a perception, on the part of the 'modernizers' interviewed, that the association with the public sector hindered the Labour Party. But this was rejected by the Left.

70   New Labour's moral agenda is examined by D. Walker, 'The Moral Agenda', in B. Brivati and T. Bale (eds), *New Labour: Precedents and Prospects* (London: Routledge, 1997).

71   Analysis, *John Kampfner on the Philosophical Heart of New Labour*.

72   Adopting the example of economic policy, the supporters of 'modernization' interviewed tried to maintain that the party had merely adhered to realism but others from the Left perceived caution.

73   But on these issues there has been a lessening of the government's commitment.

74   See R. Heffernan, 'Labour's Transformation: A Staged Process', *Politics*, 18(2), pp. 101–6 for an argument based around the party's continuous development.

75   The 'Labour Into Power' document (London: Labour Party, 1997), p. 6 refers to culture as 'the predominant ethos, atmosphere and attitudes in the party, its major symbols and defining characteristics'.

76   D. Coates, 'Labour Governments: Old Constraints and New Parameters', *New Left Review*, 219, 1996, p. 68.

77 Labour Party, *Parliamentary Labour Party Standing Orders – July 1997* (London: Labour Party, 1997). The onus is, very much, placed on members of the PLP to maintain an adherence to the prearranged policy line. Although an avenue for input for members of the PLP is outlined in the document, the disciplinary procedures are given the greatest emphasis.

It is the duty of Members to conduct themselves at all times in a manner consistent with membership of the Parliamentary Labour Party, and in particular:

(a) to be in regular attendance at the House and to maintain a good division record.
(b) to refrain from personal attacks upon colleagues orally or in writing.
(c) to act in harmony with the policies of the Parliamentary Labour Party.
(d) to do nothing which brings the Party into dispute.

These duties shall not be interpreted in such a way as to stifle democratic debate on policy matters or weaken the spirit of tolerance and respect referred to in Clause 4 of the Labour Party Constitution.

(p. 19)

78 B. Brivati, 'Earthquake or Watershed? Conclusions on New Labour in Power', in B. Brivati and T. Bale (eds), *New Labour in Power: Precedents and Prospects* (London: Routledge, 1997) sees that the New Labour government has absorbed the lessons of the past and of its extended period in opposition and is pushing the executive as the dominant body in British politics, while G. Holtham and R. Hughes, 'The State of Social Democracy in Britain', in R. Cuperus and J. Kandel (eds), *European Social Democracy: Transformation in Progress* (Amsterdam: Wiardi Beckman Stichting/Friedrich Ebert Stiftung, 1998) believe that New Labour's goal is 'efficient government'.

Chapter 6   The failures of 'new' social democracy

1 This implicit consensus was recognized in interviews with leading left-wing MPs.
2 See T. H. Marshall, *Citizenship and Social Class and Other Essays* (Cambridge: Cambridge University Press, 1950).
3 See C. Hay, 'Blaijorism: Towards a One Vision Polity', *Political Quarterly*, 68(4), p. 377.
4 The concept of the 'reflexivity' of markets, as helpfully discussed by George Soros and Anthony Giddens ('Beyond Chaos and Dogma...', *New Statesman*, 31 October 1997), shows that markets are dynamic and interact with the values that people hold. Markets are not, therefore, passive instruments that can be introduced into all sections of social and economic life.
5 See S. Driver and L. Martell, 'Beyond Equality and Liberty: New Labour's Liberal-Conservatism', *Renewal*, 4(3), p. 9.
6 *Ibid.*, p. 14.
7 For a fuller discussion of political participation see R. Dalton, *Citizen Politics: Public Opinion and Political Parties in Advanced Western Democracies*, 2nd edn (Chatham: Chatham House, 1996).

8 Social protection expenditure and receipts are drawn up according to a European system of integrated social protection statistics (ESSPROS). Only current transactions are included in the data. Expenditure is broken down into benefits, administration costs and other current expenditure. Benefits are made up of transfers to households to cover social risks which entail financial costs or loss of income. Eurostat, *Social Protection and Expenditure and Receipts 1980–1991* (Luxembourg: Office for Official Publications of the European Community, 1993), p. 3.

9 The Gini coefficient is defined as half of the arithmetic average of the absolute differences between all pairs of incomes, the total then being normalized on mean income so that if incomes are distributed completely equally, the coefficient will be zero. See N. Barr, *The Economics of the Welfare State* (London: Weidenfeld & Nicolson, 1993), p. 155.

10 D1 to D9 refer to the upper earnings limits of, respectively, the first and ninth deciles of employees ranked in order of their earnings from lowest to highest, i.e. 10 per cent of employees earn less than the D1 earnings limit and 90 per cent less than the D9 earnings limit. D8 and D5 are defined similarly and, thus, D5 corresponds to the median earnings. See OECD, *Employment Outlook*, July 1996.

11 People not in the labour force. 'They are neither employed nor unemployed. Apart from retired and disabled people they include young people still in education and people working without earning an income, whether they do housework or charity work': *Eurostat Yearbook 1996* (Luxembourg: Office for Official Publications of the European Community, 1996), p. 496. The definition is often widened to include those who are unemployed but are not eligible for welfare benefits.

12 The periods of rule for parties other than social democrats were for France 1986–8 and 1993–8, Greece 1989–93 and Sweden 1991–4.

13 An examination of the impact of this event on the fortunes of the Conservative Party is given in D. Sanders, 'Economic Performance, Management Competence and the Outcome of the Next General Election', *Political Studies*, 44 (2), pp. 203–31.

14 P. Norris, 'Anatomy of a Labour Victory', *Parliamentary Affairs*, 50(4), p. 509.

15 *Ibid.*, p. 516.

16 *Ibid.*, p. 524.

17 D. Marquand, 'After the Euphoria: The Dilemmas of New Labour', *Political Quarterly*, 68(4), p. 337.

18 P. Kellner, 'Why the Tories Were Trounced', *Parliamentary Affairs*, 50(4), p. 623.

19 D. Denver, 'The Results: How Britain Voted', in A. Geddes and J. Tongue (eds), *Labour's Landslide: The British General Election 1997* (Manchester: Manchester University Press, 1997), p. 19.

20 R. Rose, 'The New Labour Government: On the Crest of a Wave', *Parliamentary Affairs*, 50(4), p. 754.

21 The best summaries of developments in the two parties are: for the Australian Labor Party, see P. Beilharz, *Transforming Labor – Tradition and the Labor Decade in Australia* (Cambridge: Cambridge University Press, 1994) and P. Kelly, *The End of Certainty – Power, Politics and Business in Australia* (Victoria, Australia: Allen & Unwin, 1994); for the New Zealand Labour Party, see M. Holland and

J. Boston (eds), *The Fourth Labour Government – Politics and Policy in New Zealand* (Auckland: Oxford University Press, 1990). A comparative study is provided by F. Castles, R. Gerritsen and J. Vowels (eds), *The Great Experiment: Labour Parties and Public Policy Transformation in Australia and New Zealand* (St Leonards, Australia: Allen & Unwin, 1996).

22 For a discussion of the relative merits of the experiments in each country see F. Castles, R. Gerritsen and J. Vowels, 'Conclusion: The Great Experiment in Perspective', in F. Castles, R. Gerritsen and J. Vowels (eds), *The Great Experiment*.

23 See Ibid., pp. 212–13.

24 The development of the Accord process is traced in G. Singleton, *The Accord and the Australian Labour Movement* (Carlton, Victoria: Melbourne University Press, 1990).

25 C. Johnson, 'Shaping the Social: Keating's Integration of Social and Economic Policy', *Just Policy*, 5, p. 9.

26 B. Frankel, 'Beyond Labourism and Socialism: How the Australian Labor Party Developed the Model of "New Labour"', *New Left Review*, 221, p. 9.

27 See J. Pilger, 'The End of the Keating Myth' *New Statesman and Society*, 8 March 1996; and J. Wiseman, 'A Kinder Road to Hell? Labor and the Politics of Progressive Competitiveness in Australia', in L. Panitch (ed.), *The Socialist Register 1996* (London: Merlin Press, 1996).

Chapter 7 Conclusion

1 Cited from J. Lloyd, 'In the Steps of Tony Benn', *New Statesman*, 5 December 1997.

2 The best example of this being G. Soros, *The Crisis of Global Capitalism* (London: Little, Brown, 1998).

3 See Chapter 2 for a discussion of the varieties of capitalism.

4 I. Crewe, 'The Thatcher Legacy', in A. King (ed.), *Britain at the Polls 1992* (Chatham: Chatham House, 1993), p. 21.

5 Ibid., p. 22.

6 Ibid., p. 22.

7 The Hutton theory is described in Chapter 2.

8 E. J. Dionne, *They Only Look Dead – Why Progressives Will Dominate the Next Century* (New York: Simon & Schuster, 1996), p. 12.

9 Ibid., p. 15.

10 Ibid., p. 67.

11 Ibid., p. 86.

12 W. Hutton, *The State We're In* (London: Jonathan Cape, 1995), p. 14.

13 R. Reich, 'The Dangers of Moving to the Mushy Middle', *The Observer*, 27 April 1997.

14 Such an approach was advocated during the interviews conducted.

15 Suggestions for movement by government were given by several interviewees, such as splitting the Public Sector Borrowing Requirement into current and capital accounts so that investment can be made in the capital side without being defined as 'borrowing'.

16 C. Leadbeater, 'Gordon and the Green Budget', *New Statesman*, 28 November 1997.

17　C. Daniel, 'A World Beyond Hire and Fire', *New Statesman,* 17 October 1997.
18　R. Haveman, 'Equity with Employment', *Renewal,* 5(3/4), p. 35. Other moves towards 'progressive' economic policies are outlined in D. Corry and G. Holtham, *Growth with Stability: Progressive Macroeconomic Policy* (London: IPPR, 1995); D. Corry, 'Living with Capitalism: The Macroeconomic Policy Alternatives', *Renewal,* 2(1), pp. 47–60; and J. Grieve Smith, *Full Employment in the 1990s* (London: IPPR, 1992).
19　The need for a new collective narrative is recognized by J. Krieger, 'Class, Consumption, and Collectivism: Perspectives on the Labour Party and Electoral Competition in Britain', in F. F. Piven (ed.), *Labor Parties in Post-Industrial Societies* (Cambridge: Polity Press, 1991).
20　On which there is no conclusive evidence.
21　C. Crouch and D. Marquand, 'Reinventing Collective Action', in C. Crouch and D. Marquand (eds), *Reinventing Collective Action – From the Global to the Local* (Oxford: Blackwell Publishers, 1995), p. 15.
22　A. Giddens, 'Beyond Left and Right', *The Observer,* 13 September 1998 suggests that to ensure positive reform of the welfare state and benefits 'the guideline is investment in human capital wherever possible, rather than the direct provision of economic maintenance' to ensure the effective management of risk. Far from developing a new ideological approach, I. Traynor and D. Walker, 'Pretty in Pink', *The Guardian,* 15 September 1998, suggest that the social democratic parties in government are guided purely by pragmatism.
23　The realization that trust brings economic and social benefits has even been recognized by the arch market enthusiast Francis Fukuyama, *Trust: The Social Virtues and the Creation of Prosperity* (London: Hamish Hamilton, 1995).
24　Empowerment should occur in education, child-care provision, the decent provision of housing, full participation in the labour force, and their participation in the running of elements of business.
25　The decommodification of labour has been worked for for over a century.
26　Social democrats have not transformed the EU into a people's Europe; it is, instead, a process driven by economics and a single market which reflect Thatcherite objectives. This is the primary argument in D. Sassoon, *Social Democracy at the Heart of Europe* (London: IPPR, 1996).
27　There is an extensive literature on the concept of citizenship but useful starting points are T. H. Marshall, *Citizenship and Social Class* (Cambridge: Cambridge University Press, 1950) and R. Bendix, *Nation Building and Citizenship: Studies of Our Changing Social Order* (New York: New York University Press, 1964). For a socialist perspective see R. Plant, *Citizenship, Rights and Socialism* (London: Fabian Society, 1988). More generally, see the works of Rainer Baubock and Michael Walzer.
28　P. Hirst and G. Thompson, *Globalisation in Question – The International Economy and the Possibilities of Governance* (Oxford: Polity Press, 1996), p. 3.
　　There are five levels at which these forms of governance operate:

　　1)　governance through agreement between the major nation states, particularly the G3 (Europe, Japan, and North America), to stabilise the exchange rates, to co-ordinate fiscal and monetary policies, and to co-operate in limiting speculative short-term financial transactions.

2) governance through a speculative number of states creating international regulatory agencies for some specific dimensions of economic activity, such as the World Trade Organisation (WTO) to police the GATT settlement, or possible authorities to police foreign direct investment and common standards.

3) governance of large economic areas by trade and investment blocs such as the EU or NAFTA. Both are large enough to pursue social and environmental objectives in a way that a medium-sized nation state may not be able to do independently, enforcing high standards in labour market policies or forms of social protection. The blocs are big enough markets in themselves to stand against global pressures if they so choose.

4) governance through national-level policies that balance co-operation and competition between firms and the major social interests, producing quasi-voluntary economic co-ordination and assistance in providing key inputs such as research and development, the regulation of industrial finance, international marketing, information and export guarantees, training etc., thereby enhancing national economic performance and promoting industries located in the national territory.

5) governance through regional-level policies of providing collective services to industrial districts, augmenting their international competitiveness and providing a measure of protection against external shocks. (pp. 121–2)

29 Progressive Policy Institute, *The New Progressive Declaration: A Political Philosophy for the Information Age* (Washington, DC: PPI, 1996), p. i.
30 Ibid., pp. 3/4.
31 Ibid., pp. 13–15.
32 SPD Party Congress, *Key Motion I 44*.
33 Ibid.
34 M. Walker, 'Community Spirit', *The Guardian*, 13 March 1995.
35 A. Etzioni, *The Spirit of Community: Rights, Responsibilities and the Communitarian Agenda* (London: Fontana Press, 1995), p. ix.
36 Although D. Bell, *Communitarianism and Its Critics* (Oxford: Clarendon Press, 1993) does identify three levels of community – communities of place, memory and psychology.
37 See S. Holmes, *The Anatomy of Antiliberalism* (Cambridge, Mass.: Harvard University Press, 1993).
38 For a fuller discussion of Labour's embrace of communitarianism see S. Driver and L. Martell, *New Labour's Communitarians*, paper presented to the EPOP Conference, University of Sheffield, 13–15 September 1996.
39 K. Raes, 'The Socio-Cultural Factor – Postmodernism, Individualism and Multi-culturalism as Challenges for Social Democracy', in R. Cuperus and J. Kandel (eds), *European Social Democracy: Transformation in Progress* (Amsterdam: Wiardi Beckman Stichting/Friedrich Ebert Stiftung, 1998), p. 298, suggests that notions of 'community' and of 'community based on a shared conception of the good' are ambiguous.
40 C. Woollard, *Beyond Ideology? The Changing Conception of Citizenship in the Ideology of the Labour Party and the PCI-PDS(-DS)*, paper presented at the ECPR, Warwick, 23–28 March 1998, p. 14.

41 A. Giddens, *The Third Way – The Renewal of Social Democracy* (Cambridge: Polity Press, 1998), p. 26.
42 In an earlier text, Giddens considered that the relevance of the Left–Right divide as a guide to politics was being diluted by two movements. Firstly, Left parties used to be considered 'radical' and Right parties as 'conservative'; however, there has been a rearticulation so that the parties are no longer closely tied to these values. Secondly, 'emancipatory politics' has given way to 'life politics'. By this Giddens means that concerns about economic rights and equality have given way to concerns about identity, quality of life, the private sphere and civil society. The Left–Right divide is, therefore, being outdated by this shift to 'life politics'. See A. Giddens, *Beyond Left and Right* (London: Polity Press, 1994).
43 The theory of 'stakeholding' is developed in Chapter 2.
44 T. Blair, *The Third Way – New Politics for the New Century*, Fabian Society Pamphlet 588 (London: Fabian Society, 1998), p. 7.
45 A. Giddens, *The Third Way*, p. 100.
46 Ibid., p. 69.
47 The positive effect that the increased use of democracy can play is described in T. Blackstone et al., *Next Left: An Agenda for the 1990s* (London: IPPR, 1992).

Appendix 4   A comparison of Old and New Labour

1 T. Blair, *New Britain: My Vision of a Young Country* (London: Fourth Estate, 1996), p. x.
2 Ibid., p. 116.
3 Ibid., p. 32.
4 Ibid., p. 110.
5 Ibid., p. 134.
6 Ibid., p. 85.
7 Ibid., p. 102.
8 Ibid., p. 173.

Appendix 5   Changes in labour party policy positions

1 Sources: M. White, 'Hard Sell On the Road to Downing Street', *The Guardian*, 5 July 1996; A. McSmith, 'Changes to Labour Party Policies since May 1992', *The Observer*, 30 June 1996; and Labour Party, *New Labour: Because Britain Deserves Better* (London: Labour Party, 1997).

Bibliography

Primary sources

Blair, T. (1995–8) Various speeches, including *Speech to the NewsCorp Leadership*, 17 July 1995, Hayman Island, Australia.
Beazley, K. (1996) *Employment Industrial Relations and Labor in Opposition*, 18 July.
Beazley, K. (1996) *Address to the NSW ALP Conference*, 5 October.
Beazley, K. (1997) *Transcript of Speech at ALP Dinner, Newcastle*, 11 April.
Beazley, K. (1997) *Address to the Australian Institute of Company Directors*, 23 May.
Beazley, K. (1998) *Plan for the Nation. Jobs. Security. Opportunity*. Melbourne: ALP.
DNA (1992) *Togetherness: A Social Democratic Programme for the 1990s*. Oslo: DNA.
DNA (1996) *Co-determination: Statement of Principles and Action Programme*. Oslo: DNA.
International Centre of the Swedish Labour Movement (1982) *The Swedish Labour Movement*. Stockholm: AIC.
Jospin, L. (1997) *General Policy Statement by Lionel Jospin, Prime Minister, to the National Assembly – France Statements, 26 June*. London: Ambassade de France à Londres.
Jospin, L. (1997) *Meeting of French Ambassadors, Speech by M. Lionel Jospin, Prime Minister – France Statements, 5 September*. London: Ambassade de France à Londres.

Labour Party (British – all publications London: Labour Party):
A Fresh Start for Britain – Labour's Strategy for Britain in the Modern World, 1996.
A New Economic Future for Britain, 1995.
Access to Justice (Conference 1995), 1995.
Access to Justice – A Consultation Paper on Labour's Proposals for Improving the Justice System, 1995.
Aiming Higher – Labour's Plans for Reform of the 14–19+ Curriculum, 1996.
Britain Will Win, 1987.
Building Prosperity – Flexibility, Efficiency and Fairness at Work, 1996.
Charter for Employees, 1994.
Consensus for Change – Labour's Transport Strategy in the Twenty-First Century, 1996.
Democratic Socialist Aims and Values, 1988.
Design for the 90s, 1991.
Excellence for Everyone – Labour's Crusade to Raise Standards, 1996.
Families in Focus – A Consultation Document, 1995.
Financing Infrastructure Investment – Promoting a Partnership Between Public and Private Finance – Gordon Brown, Robin Cook and John Prescott, 1994.
Getting Welfare to Work, 1996.
Going Private – The Growth of Private Sector Health Care under the Tories, 1994.
Health 2000 – The Health and Wealth of the Nation in the Twenty-First Century, 1994.

In Trust for Tomorrow – Report of the Labour Party Policy Commission on the Environment, 1994.

Jobs and Social Justice – Labour's Response to the Green Paper on European Social Policy: Options for the Union, 1994.

Labour in Government – Delivering Our Contract to the People, 1997.

Labour Into Power: A Framework for Partnership, 1997.

Labour Means Action on Crime, 1994.

Labour Party News, January 1995.

Labour Party News, July/August 1995.

Labour Party/Trade Union Links – Interim Report on the Review Group and Questionnaire, 1993.

Learn as You Earn – Labour's Plans for a Skills Revolution, 1996.

Lifelong Learning, 1996.

Looking to the Future, 1990.

Making Britain's Future, 1993.

Manifesto, 1992.

Modernising Britain's Schools, 1992.

New Labour – New Life in Britain, 1996.

New Labour, New Britain: The Magazine for Labour Party Members, New Year 1997.

New Labour: Because Britain Deserves Better – Manifesto, 1997.

Opening Doors to a Learning Society, 1994.

Parliamentary Labour Party – Standing Orders, July 1997.

Partners Against Crime: Labour's New Approach to Tackling Crime and Creating Safer Communities, 1994.

Partnership in Power, 1997.

Renewing Democracy, Rebuilding Communities (Conference 1995), 1995.

Renewing Democracy, Rebuilding Communities, 1995.

Renewing the NHS, 1995.

Report of the National Policy Forum, London 8–9th May 1993, 1993.

Report on the Working Party on Electoral Systems, 1993 – Summary Version, 1993.

Safer Communities, Safer Britain, 1995.

Signposts for the Sixties, 1961.

Tackling Tax Abuses – Tackling Unemployment, 1994.

Taking the Temperature, 1993.

The Future of the European Union, 1995.

The Maples Report, 1995.

The New Hope for Britain, 1983.

The Next Generation: A New Agenda for Labour's Young Members Policy Briefing, 1993.

Time for Decision: Election Manifesto 1966, 1966.

TUC–Labour Party Liaison Committee: Economic Policy and the Cost of Living, 1973.

Vision for Growth – A New Industrial Strategy for Britain, 1996.

Winning for Britain: Labour's Strategy for Industrial Success, 1994.

Parti Socialiste (1996) *Vendredi – Convention Nationale*, 5 April.

Parti Socialiste (1997) *Elections législatives 1997 – Augmentaire Europe*.

Parti Socialiste (1997) *Lionel Jospin Letter to Oskar Lafontaine*, 23 April.

Parti Socialiste, *Positions sur la C.I. G.*, n.d.

Parti Socialiste, *Communiqué du Parti socialiste*, n.d.

Parti Socialiste (1997) *L'hebdo des socialistes*, 13 June.

Parti Socialiste (1997) *L'hebdo des socialistes*, 20 June.

PES (1995) *Good Environment Gives Good Jobs*. Brussels: PES.

PSOE *Cien Medidas De Gobierno*. Madrid: PSOE, n.d.

PSOE *33 Congreso. Resoluciones*. Madrid: PSOE, n.d.

PSOE (1993) *Ques Es El PSOE*. Madrid: PSOE.

PSOE (1994) *Estatutoes Federales*. Madrid: PSOE.

PSOE (1995) *Manifiesto Autonomico 1995. Un Proyecto Comartido*. Madrid: PSOE.

PSOE (1996) *Programa Electoral. Elecciones Generales 1996*. Madrid: PSOE.

SAP (1990) *The Swedish Social Democratic Party Programme*. Stockholm: SAP

SAP (1994) *Democracy Without Frontiers – Security and Solidarity for the Twenty First Century*. Stockholm: SAP.

SAP (1996a) *The Swedish Social Democratic Party – An Introduction*. Stockholm: SAP.

SAP (1996b) *Sweden into the Twenty First Century*. Stockholm: SAP.

SAP (1998) *Election Manifesto*. Stockholm: SAP.

Scharping, R. (1994) *Challenges and Choices: The SPD Agenda for Political and Economic Change in Germany*. Speech, 12 April.

Short, Co (1995) *NEC Supplementary Report on Leeds North East*, 3 October.

Social Democratic Party of Denmark *A Social Democratic Vision – The Danish Model*. Copenhagen: Social Democratic Party of Denmark, n.d.

Social Democratic Party of Denmark (1990) *The Social Democratic Party of Denmark, 1871–1990: Achievements and Problems*. Copenhagen: Social Democratic Party of Denmark.

Social Democratic Party of Denmark (1992) *Beyond the Year 2000*. Copenhagen: Social Democratic Party of Denmark.

Social Democratic Party of Denmark (1996) *Common Future – Common Goals*. Copenhagen: Social Democratic Party of Denmark.

Socialist International (1996) *XX Congress of the Socialist International – Draft Declaration, Agenda Point One: The World Economy*.

SPD (1959) *Bad Godesberg Programme*. Bonn: SPD.

SPD (1989) *Basic Policy Programme*. Bonn: SPD.

SPD (1994) *Government Programme*. Bonn: SPD.

SPD (1995) *Motion No. 2 – Economic, Employment and Financial Policies: Jobs for Germany*. Resolution passed at the National Party Conference in Mannheim.

SPD (1997) *Key Motion EU 26 On Our Perspective*. Motion at National Party Conference in Hanover.

SPD (1997) *Key Motion I44 on Innovations for Germany*. Motion at National Party Conference in Hanover.

SPD (1997) *Summary of Key Motion I159 on the Information Society*. Motion at National Party Conference in Hanover.

SPD (1997) *Key Motion A1 on Foreign, Security and Development Policies*. Motion at National Party Conference in Hanover.

SPD (1998) *Work, Innovation and Justice – SPD Manifesto for the 1998 General Election*.

Trades Union Congress (1996) *Your Stake at Work: TUC Proposals for a Stakeholding Economy*. London: TUC.

Secondary sources

Texts

Addison, P. (1987) 'The Road from 1945', in P. Hennessy and A. Seldon (eds), *Ruling Performance*. Oxford: Basil Blackwell.

Albert, Michel (1993) *Capitalism against Capitalism*. London: Whurr.

Alcock, P. (1992) 'The Labour Party and the Welfare State', in M. Smith and J. Spear (eds), *The Changing Labour Party*. London: Routledge.

Åmark, K. (1992) 'Social Democracy and the Trade Union Movement: Solidarity and the Politics of Self-Interest' and 'Afterword: Swedish Social Democracy on a Historical Threshold', in K. Misgeld, K. Molin and K. Åmark (eds), *Creating Social Democracy – A Century of the Social Democratic Labour Party in Sweden*. University Park, Pa.: Pennsylvania University Press.

Ambler, J. S. (1985) 'French Socialism in Comparative Perspective', in J. S. Ambler (ed.), *The French Socialist Experiment*. Philadelphia: ISHI.

Anderson, P. (1992) *A Zone of Engagement*. London: Verso.

Anderson, P. (1994) 'Introduction', in P. Anderson and P. Camiller (eds), *Mapping the West European Left*. London: Verso.

Anderson, P. and Camiller, P. (eds), (1994) *Mapping the West European Left*. London: Verso.

Anderson, P. and Mann, N. (1997) *Safety First: The Making of New Labour*. London: Granta Publications.

Andersson, J. O. (1987) 'The Economic Policy Strategies of the Nordic Countries', in H. Keman, H. Paloheimo and P. Whiteley (eds), *Coping with Economic Crisis – Alternative Responses to Economic Recession in Advanced Industrial Societies*. London: Sage Publications.

Archibugi, D. and Held, D. (eds), (1995) *Cosmopolitan Democracy: An Agenda for a New World Order*. Oxford: Polity Press.

Arseneau, T. (1990) 'A Bill of Rights', in M. Holland and J. Boston (eds), *The Fourth Labour Government – Parties and Policy in New Zealand*. Auckland: Oxford University Press.

Arter, D. (1994) '"The War of the Roses": Conflict and Cohesion in the Swedish Social Democratic Party', in D. Bell and E. Shaw (eds), *Conflict and Cohesion in Western European Social Democratic Parties*. London: Pinter Publishers.

Atkinson, A. B. (1995) *Incomes and the Welfare State: Essays on Britain and Europe*. Cambridge: Cambridge University Press.

Atkinson, V. and Spear, J. (1992) 'The Labour Party and Women: Policies and Practices', in M. Smith and J. Spear (eds), *The Changing Labour Party*. London: Routledge.

Axtmann, R. (ed.), (1998) *Globalization and Europe: Theoretical and Empirical Investigations*. London: Pinter.

Backhouse, R. (1985) *A History of Modern Economic Analysis*. Oxford: Basil Blackwell.

Barr, N. (1993) *The Economics of the Welfare State*. London: Weidenfeld & Nicolson.

Barratt Brown, M. and Coates, K. (1996) *The Blair Revelation: Deliverance for Whom?* Nottingham: Spokesman.

Barry, B. (1988) 'The Continuing Relevance of Socialism', in R. Skidelsky (ed.), *Thatcherism*. London: Chatto & Windus.

Barry, B. (1996) 'Does Society Exist? The Case for Socialism', in P. King (ed.), *Socialism and the Common Good: New Fabian Essays*. London: Frank Cass.

Baslé, M. A. (1989) 'Economics and Economists in France', in J. Howorth and G. Ross (eds), *Contemporary France, Volume Three*. London: Frances Pinter.

Beilharz, P. (1992) *Labour's Utopias: Bolshevism, Fabianism and Social Democracy*. London: Routledge.

Beilharz, P. (1994) *Transforming Labor: Labour Tradition and the Labour Decade in Australia*. Cambridge: Cambridge University Press.

Bell, D. S. (1989) 'A Hunger for Power: Jacques Chirac', in J. Gaffney (ed.), *The French Presidential Elections of 1988*. Aldershot: Dartmouth.

Bell, D. (1993) *Communitarianism and Its Critics*. Oxford: Clarendon.

Bell, D. S. (1998) 'The French Parti Socialiste', in A. Dobson and J. Stanyer (eds), *Contemporary Political Studies 1998*. Nottingham: PSA.

Bell, D. S. and Criddle, B. (1988) *The French Socialist Party: The Emergence of a Party of Government*. Oxford: Clarendon Press.

Bell, D. S. and Criddle, B. (1994) 'The French Socialist Party: Presidentialised Factionalism', in D. S. Bell and E. Shaw (eds), *Conflict and Cohesion in Western European Social Democratic Parties*. London: Pinter Publishers.

Bell, D. S. and Shaw, E. (1994) 'Introduction' and 'Conclusion', in D. Bell and E. Shaw (eds), *Conflict and Cohesion in Western European Social Democratic Parties*. London: Pinter Publishers.

Bendix, R. (1964) *Nation Building and Citizenship: Studies of Our Changing Social Order*. New York: New York University Press.

Benn, T. (1985) *Arguments for Socialism*. Reading: Penguin Books.

Benn, T., Fraser, M., Marquand, D. and Butler, D. (1987) 'British Politics, 1945–1987: Four Perspectives', in P. Hennessy and A. Seldon (eds), *Ruling Performance*. Oxford: Basil Blackwell.

Benton, R. (1990) 'Biculturalism in Education: Policy and Practice under the Fourth Labour Government', in M. Holland and J. Boston (eds), *The Fourth Labour Government – Parties and Policy in New Zealand*. Auckland: Oxford University Press.

Berger, S. (1985) 'The Socialists and the Patronat: The Dilemmas of Coexistence in a Mixed Economy', in H. Machin and V. Wright (eds), *Economic Policy and Policy-Making under the Mitterrand Presidency 1981–84*. Exeter: Frances Pinter.

Bergström, W. (1992) 'Party Program and Economic Policy: The Social Democrats in Government', in K. Misgeld, K. Molin and K. Åmark (eds), *Creating Social Democracy – A Century of the Social Democratic Labour Party in Sweden*. University Park, Pa.: Pennsylvania University Press.

Berntzen, E. (1991) 'Democratic Socialism in Spain, Portugal and Greece', in L. Karvonen and J. Sunberg (eds), *Social Democracy in Transition*. Aldershot: Dartmouth.

Berntzen, E. (1992) 'Social Democracy in Scandinavia: Questions, Processes, Comparisons', in J. Maravall et al., *Socialist Parties in Europe*. Barcelona: Institut d'Ediciones de la Diputació De Barcelona.

Bing, I. and Carey, K. (1987) 'John Rawls and American Liberalism', in A. Kilmarnock (ed.), *The Radical Challenge: The Response of Social Democracy*. Worcester: André Deutsch.

Blackburn, R. (1991) 'Preface', in R. Blackburn (ed.), *After the Fall*. London: Verso.

Blackstone, T., Cornford, J., Hewitt, P. and Miliband, D. (1992) *Next Left: An Agenda for the 1990s*. London: IPPR.

Blair, T. (1994) *Socialism*, Fabian Society Pamphlet 565. London: Fabian Society.

Blair, T. (1995) *Let Us Face the Future: The 1945 Anniversary Lecture*, Fabian Society Pamphlet **571**. London: Fabian Society.

Blair, T. (1996a) 'Introduction: My Vision for Britain', in G. Radice (ed.), *What Needs to Change: New Visions for Britain*. London: HarperCollins.

Blair, T. (1996b) *New Britain: My Vision of a Young Country*. London: Fourth Estate.

Blair, T. (1998) *The Third Way – New Politics for the New Century*, Fabian Society Pamphlet 588. London: Fabian Society.

Bootle, R. (1997) *The Death of Inflation*. London: Nicholas Brealey Publishing.

Bosanquet, N. (1987) 'Challenging the New Right', in A. Kilmarnock (ed.), *The Radical Challenge: The Response of Social Democracy*. Worcester: André Deutsch.

Boston, J. (1990) 'The Cabinet and Policy-Making under the Fourth Labour Government', in M. Holland and J. Boston (eds), *The Fourth Labour Government – Parties and Policy in New Zealand*. Auckland: Oxford University Press.

Boswell, J. (1993) 'Catholicism, Christian Democrats and "Reformed Capitalism"', in C. Crouch and D. Marquand (eds), *Ethics and Markets*. Oxford: Blackwell Publishers.

Bray, M. and Neilson, D. (1996) 'Industrial Relations Reform and the Relative Autonomy of the State', in F. Castles, R. Gerritsen and J. Vowels (eds), *The Great Experiment: Labour Parties and Public Policy Transformation in Australia and New Zealand*. St Leonards, Australia: Allen & Unwin.

Brivati, B. (1998) 'Earthquake or Watershed? Conclusions on New Labour in Power', in B. Brivati and T. Bale (eds), *New Labour in Power: Precedents and Prospects*. London: Routledge.

Brown, G. (1994) 'The Politics of Potential: A New Agenda for Labour', in D. Miliband (ed.), *Reinventing the Left*. London: Polity Press.

Brown, G. and Wright, T. (eds), (1995) *Values, Visions and Voices: An Anthology of Socialism*. Edinburgh: Mainstream Publishing.

Bruneau, T. C. and Macleod, A. (1986) *Politics in Contemporary Portugal: Parties and the Consolidation of Democracy*. Boulder, Colo.: Lynne Rienner Publishers.

Budge, I. and Farlie, D. (1977) *Voting and Party Competition: A Theoretical Critique and Synthesis Applied to Surveys from Ten Democracies*. London: John Wiley & Sons.

Budge, I. and Farlie, D. (1983a) *Explaining and Predicting Elections: Issue Effects and Party Strategies in Twenty-Three Democracies*. London: George Allen & Unwin.

Budge, I. and Farlie, D. (1983b) 'Party Competition – Selective Emphasis Or Direct Confrontation? An Alternative View with Data', in H. Daalder and P. Mair (eds), *Western European Party Systems – Continuity and Change*. London: Sage.

Budge, I. and Laver, M. (1992) *Party Policy and Government Coalitions*. London: Macmillan.

Budge, I. and Robertson, D. (1985) 'Do Parties Differ? Comparative Discriminant and Factor Analysis', in I. Budge, D. Robertson and D. Hearl (eds), *Ideology, Strategy and Party Change: Spatial Analyses of Post-War Election Programmes in Nineteen Democracies*. Cambridge: Cambridge University Press.

Budge, I., Robertson, D. and Hearl, D. (1986) *A Comparative Analysis of Post-War Election Programmes in Twenty Democracies*, Essex Papers in Politics and Government 34.

Bush, G. (1990) 'The Historic Reorganisation of Local Government', in M. Holland and J. Boston (eds), *The Fourth Labour Government – Parties and Policy in New Zealand*. Auckland: Oxford University Press.

Butler, A. (1995) *Transformative Politics: The Future of Socialism in Western Europe*. London: Macmillan.

Butler, D. and Kavanagh, D. (1992) *The British General Election of 1992*. London: Macmillan.

Butler, D. and Kavanagh, D. (1997) *The British General Election of 1997*. London: Macmillan.

Byrd, P. (1986) 'The Labour Party in Britain', in W. Paterson and A. Thomas (eds), *The Future of Social Democracy*. Oxford: Clarendon Press.

Byrne, P. (1989) 'Great Britain: The "Green Party"', in F. Muller-Rommel (ed.), *New Politics in Western Europe*. Boulder, Colo.: Westview Press.

Callaghan, J. (1989) 'The Left: The Ideology of the Labour Party', in L. Tivey and A. Wright (eds), *Party Ideology in Britain*. London: Routledge.

Callaghan, J. (1990) *Socialism in Britain since 1884*. Oxford: Basil Blackwell.

Callinicos, A. (1991) *The Revenge of History*. Cambridge: Polity Press.

Cameron, D. (1996) 'Exchange Rate Politics in France, 1981–83: The Regime Defining Choices of the Mitterrand Presidency', in A. Daley (ed.), *The Mitterrand Era – Policy Alternatives and Political Mobilisation in France*. London: Macmillan.

Camiller, P. (1994) 'Spain: The Survival of Socialism', in P. Anderson and P. Camiller (eds), *Mapping the West European Left*. London: Verso.

Camilleri, J. and Falk, J. (1992) *The End of Sovereignty? The Politics of a Shrinking and Fragmenting World*. London: Edward Elgar.

Carter, N. (1992) 'The Greening of Labour', in M. Smith and J. Spear (eds), *The Changing Labour Party*. London: Routledge.

Castles, F. and Shirley, I. (1996) 'Labour and Social Policy: Gravediggers or Refurbishers of the Welfare State', in F. Castles, R. Gerritsen and J. Vowels (eds), *The Great Experiment: Labour Parties and Public Policy Transformation in Australia and New Zealand*. St Leonards, Australia: Allen & Unwin.

Castles, F., Gerritsen, R. and Vowels, J. (1996) 'Introduction: Setting the Scene for Economic and Political Change' and 'Conclusion: The Great Experiment in Perspective', in F. Castles, R. Gerritsen and J. Vowels (eds), *The Great Experiment: Labour Parties and Public Policy Transformation in Australia and New Zealand*. St Leonards, Australia: Allen & Unwin.

Cerny, P. (1983) 'Economic Policy: Crisis Management, Structural Reform and Socialist Politics', in S. Williams (ed.), *Socialism in France: From Jaurés to Mitterrand*. London: Frances Pinter.

Cerny, P. (1988) 'Modernisation and the Fifth Republic', in J. Gaffney (ed.), *France and Modernisation*. Aldershot: Gower.

Chilcote, R. H. (1993) 'Portugal: From Popular Power to Bourgeois Democracy', in J. Kurth and J. Petras (eds), *Mediterranean Paradoxes – The Politics and Social Structure of Southern Europe*. Oxford: Berg.

Christiansen, N. F. (1994) 'Denmark: End of an Idyll?', in P. Anderson and P. Camiller (eds), *Mapping the West European Left*. London: Verso.

Clarke, P. (1996) 'The Keynesian Consensus and Its Enemies – The Argument over Macro-Economic Policy in Britain since the Second World War', in D. Marquand and A. Seldon (eds), *The Ideas that Shaped Post-War Britain*. London: Fontana Press.

Clifford, P. and Heath, A. (1994) 'The Election Campaign', in A. Heath, R. Jowell and J. Curtice (eds), *Labour's Last Chance? The 1992 Election and Beyond*. Cambridge: Dartmouth Publishing.

Coates, D. (1980) *Labour in Power? A Study of the Labour Government 1974–1979*. Suffolk: Longman.

Coates, K. (1983) *The Social Democrats: Those Who Went and Those Who Stayed – The Forward March of Labour Halted?* Nottingham: Spokesman.

Cole, A. (1989) 'François Mitterrand: From Republican Contender to President of all the French' and 'La France Unie? François Mitterrand', in J. Gaffney (ed.), *The French Presidential Elections of 1988*. Aldershot: Dartmouth.

Cole, A. (1990) 'The Evolution of the Party System, 1974–90', in A. Cole (ed.), *French Political Parties in Transition*. Aldershot: Dartmouth.

Cole, A. (1994) *François Mitterrand: A Study in Political Leadership*. London: Routledge.

Cole, A. (1998) *French Society and Politics*. Hemel Hempstead: Prentice Hall.

Commission of the European Communities (1995) *Basic Statistics of the European Community*. Luxembourg: Office for Official Publications of the European Commission.

Commission of the European Community (1996) *A Social Portrait of Europe*. Luxembourg: Office for Official Publications of the European Commission.

Cooper, Y. (1996) '1997', in G. Radice (ed.), *What Needs to Change: New Visions for Britain*. London: HarperCollins.

Coopey, R., Fielding, S. and Tiratsoo, N. (1993) *The Wilson Governments, 1964–1970*. Exeter: Pinter Publishers.

Cornford, J. and Hewitt, P. (1994) 'Dos and Don'ts for Social Democrats', in D. Miliband (ed.), *Reinventing the Left*. London: Polity Press.

Corry, D. and Holtham, G. (1995) *Growth with Stability: Progressive Macro-Economic Policy*. London: IPPR.

Cowling, K. and Sugden, R. (1994) *Beyond Capitalism: Towards a New World Economic Order*. London: Pinter Publishers.

Cox, R. (1996) 'A Perspective on Globalization', in J. Mittelman (ed.), *Globalization: Critical Reflections*. London: Lynne Reiner.

Craig, F. W. S. (ed.), (1989) *British Electoral Facts, 1832–1987*, 5th edn. Aldershot: Dartmouth.

Crewe, I. (1994) 'Electoral Behaviour', in D. Kavanagh and A. Seldon (eds), *The Major Effect*. London: Macmillan.

Crick, B. (1987) *Socialism*. Milton Keynes: Open University Press.

Criddle, B. (1977) 'The French Parti Socialiste', in W. Paterson and A. Thomas (eds), *Social Democratic Parties in Western Europe*. London: Croom Helm.

Criddle, B. (1987) 'France', in A. Ware (ed.), *Political Parties – Electoral Change and Structural Response*. Oxford: Basil Blackwell.

Criddle, B. (1997) 'MPs and Candidates', in D. Butler and D. Kavanagh, *The British General Election of 1997*. London: Macmillan.

Crewe, I. (1991) 'Labor Force Changes, Working Class Decline, and the Labour Vote: Social and Electoral Trends in Post-War Britain', in F. F. Piven (ed.), *Labor Parties in Post-Industrial Societies*. Cambridge: Polity Press.

Crewe, I. (1993) 'The Thatcher Legacy', in A. King (ed.), *Britain at the Polls 1992* Chatham: Chatham House.

Crewe, I. (1994) 'Essex Man Has Not Been Converted', in M. Linton (ed.), *Whatever Next?* London: Guardian/Samizdat Production.

Crewe, I. and King, A. (1994) 'Did Major Win? Did Kinnock Lose?', in A. Heath, R. Jowell and J. Curtice (eds), *Labour's Last Chance? The 1992 Election and Beyond*. Cambridge: Dartmouth Publishing.

Crosland, A. (1957) *The Future of Socialism*. London: Jonathan Cape.

Crosland, A. (1975) *Social Democracy in Europe*, Fabian Society Tract 438. London: Fabian Society.

Crosland, A. (1988) 'The British Economy in 1965', in W. John Morgan (ed.), *Politics and Consensus in Modern Britain – Lectures in Memory of Hugh Gaitskell*. London: Macmillan.

Crouch, C. (1993) 'Co-operation and Competition in an Industrialised Economy, the Case of Germany', in C. Crouch and D. Marquand (eds), *Ethics and Markets*. Oxford: Blackwell Publishers.

Crouch, C. and Marquand, D. (1995) 'Reinventing Collective Action', in C. Crouch and D. Marquand (eds), *Reinventing Collective Action – From the Global to the Local*. Oxford: Blackwell Publishers.

Cuperus, R. and Kandel, J. (1998) 'The Magical Return of Social Democracy – An Introduction', in R. Cuperus and J. Kandel (eds), *European Social Democracy: Transformation in Progress*. Amsterdam: Wiardi Beckman Stichting/Friedrich Ebert Stiftung.

Curran, J. (ed.) (1984) *The Future of the Left*. Oxford: Polity Press.

Curtice, J. and Semetko, H. (1994) 'Does It Matter What the Papers Say?', in A. Heath, R. Jowell and J. Curtice (eds), *Labour's Last Chance? The 1992 Election and Beyond*. Cambridge: Dartmouth Publishing.

Dahrendorf, R. (1979) *Life Chances: Approaches to Social and Political Theory*. London: Weidenfeld & Nicolson.

Dahrendorf, R. (1988) *The Modern Social Conflict*. London: Weidenfeld & Nicolson.

Daley, A. (1996) 'François Mitterrand, the Left and Political Mobilisation in France', in A. Daley (ed.), *The Mitterrand Era – Policy Alternatives and Political Mobilisation in France*. London: Macmillan.

Dalton, R. (1996) *Citizen Politics: Public Opinion and Political Parties in Advanced Western Democracies,* 2nd edn. Chatham: Chatham House.

Davey, K. (1996) 'The Impermanence of New Labour', in M. Perryman (ed.), *The Blair Agenda*. London: Lawrence & Wishart.

Davies, A. (1992) *To Build a New Jerusalem: The Labour Movement from the 1880s to the 1990s*. London: Michael Joseph.

Denemark, D. (1990) 'Social Democracy and the Politics of Crisis in New Zealand, Britain and Sweden', in M. Holland and J. Boston (eds), *The Fourth Labour Government – Parties and Policy in New Zealand*. Auckland: Oxford University Press.

Denver, D. (1994) *Elections and Voting Behaviour in Britain* Hemel Hempstead: Harvester Wheatsheaf.

Denver, D. (1997) 'The Results: How Britain Voted', in A. Geddes and J. Tonge (eds), *Labour's Landslide: The British General Election 1997*. Manchester: Manchester University Press.

Denver, D. (1998) 'The Government That Could Do No Right', in A. King (ed.), *New Labour Triumphs: Britain at the Polls*. Chatham, NJ: Chatham House.

De Winter, L. (1992) 'Socialist Parties in Belgium', in J. Maravall et al., *Socialist Parties in Europe*. Barcelona: Institut d'Ediciones de la Diputació de Barcelona.

Dionne Jr, E. J. (1996) *They Only Look Dead – Why Progressives Will Dominate the Next Political Era*. New York: Simon & Schuster.

Dore, R. (1993) 'What Makes the Japanese Different?', in C. Crouch and D. Marquand (eds), *Ethics and Markets*. Oxford: Blackwell Publishers.

Downs, A. (1957) *An Economic Theory of Democracy*. New York: Harper & Bros.

Draper, D. (1997) *Blair's 100. Days* London: Faber & Faber.

Driver, S. and Martell, L. (1998) *New Labour: Politics after Thatcherism*. Cambridge: Polity Press.

Drower, G. (1994) *Kinnock*. London: Woodham Ferrers.

Drucker, H. M. (1979) *Doctrine and Ethos in the Labour Party*. London: George Allen & Unwin.

Duncan, G. (1989) *The Australian Labor Party: A Model for Others?*, Fabian Society Tract 535. London: Fabian Society.

Dunleavy, P. and O' Leary, B. (1987) *Theories of the State,* 5th edn. London: Macmillan.

Dyson, K. (1980) *The State Tradition in Western Europe*. Oxford: Martin Robertson.

Easton, B. and Gerritsen, R. (1996) 'Economic Reform: Parallels and Divergences', in F. Castles, R. Gerritsen and J. Vowels (eds), *The Great Experiment: Labour Parties and Public Policy Transformation in Australia and New Zealand*. St Leonards, Australia: Allen & Unwin.

Eatwell, J. (1992) 'The Development of Labour Policy, 1979–1992', in J. Michie (ed.), *The Economic Legacy*. London: Academic Press.

Eley, G. (1992) 'Reviewing the Socialist Tradition', in C. Lemke and G. Marks (eds), *The Crisis of Socialism in Europe*. Durham, NC: Duke University Press.

Elliott, G. (1993) *Labourism and the English Genius: The Strange Death of Labour England?* London: Verso.

Ellison, N. (1997) 'From Welfare State to Post-Welfare Society? Labour's Social Policy in Historical and Contemporary Perspective', in B. Brivati and T. Bale (eds), *New Labour in Power: Precedents and Prospects*. London: Routledge.

Emmet, D. (1987) 'The Moral Roots of Social Democracy', in A. Kilmarnock (ed.), *The Radical Challenge: The Response of Social Democracy*. Worcester: André Deutsch.

Esping-Andersen, G. (1985) *Politics Against Markets – The Social Democratic Road to Power*. Princeton, NJ: Princeton University Press.

Esping-Andersen, G. (1990) *The Three Worlds of Welfare Capitalism*. Oxford: Polity Press.

Esping-Andersen, G. (1991) 'Post-Industrial Cleavage Structures: A Comparison of Evolving Patterns of Social Stratification in Germany, Sweden and the United States', in F. F. Piven (ed.), *Labor Parties in Post-Industrial Societies*. Cambridge: Polity Press.

Esping-Andersen, G. (1992) 'The Making of a Social Democratic Welfare State', in K. Misgeld, K. Molin and K. Åmark (eds), *Creating Social Democracy – A*

Century of the Social Democratic Labour Party in Sweden. University Park, Pa.: Pennsylvania University Press.

Esping-Andersen, G. (1994) 'Equality and Work in the Post-Industrial Life-Cycle', in D. Miliband (ed.), *Reinventing the Left.* London: Polity Press.

Esping-Andersen, G. (1996) 'After the Golden Age? Welfare State Dilemmas in a Global Economy', in G. Esping-Andersen (ed.), *Welfare States in Transition – National Adaptations in Global Economics.* London: Sage.

Etzioni, A. (1988) *The Moral Dimension – Toward a New Economics.* New York: Free Press.

Etzioni, A. (1995) *The Spirit of Community: Rights, Responsibilities and the Communitarian Agenda.* London: Fontana.

Etzioni, A. (ed.) (1995) *Rights and the Common Good: The Communitarian Perspective.* New York: St. Martin's Press.

Etzioni, A. (1997) 'The Parenting Deficit', in G. Mulgan (ed.), *Life after Politics: New Thinking for the Twenty-First Century.* London: Fontana.

Eurobarometer (various issues) *Public Opinion in the European Union.* Luxembourg: Office for Official Publications of the European Commission.

Eurostat (1993) *Social Protection Expenditure and Receipts 1980–1991.* Luxembourg: Office for Official Publications of the European Commission.

Eurostat (1996) *Yearbook.* Luxembourg: Office for Official Publications of the European Commission.

Fabra, P. (1985) 'Banking Policy under the Socialists', in H. Machin and V. Wright (eds), *Economic Policy and Policy-Making under the Mitterrand Presidency 1981–84.* Exeter: Frances Pinter.

Fajardic, R. (1983) 'The French Socialist Party Today', in S. Williams (ed.), *Socialism in France: From Jaurés to Mitterrand.* London: Frances Pinter.

Fatchett, D. and Hain, (1997) P. *A Stakeholder Party.* London: A Tribune Pamphlet.

Faux, J. (1994) 'Does America Have the Answer?', in S. Pollard (ed.), *Jobs and Growth: The International Perspective.* London: Fabian Society.

Featherstone, K. (1989) 'Socialist Parties in Southern Europe and the Enlarged European Community', in T. Gallagher and A. M. Williams (eds), *Southern European Socialism – Parties, Elections and the Challenge of Government.* Manchester: Manchester University Press.

Featherstone, K. (1990) 'Political Parties and Democratic Consolidation in Greece', in G. Pridham (ed.), *Securing Democracy: Political Parties and Democratic Consolidation in Southern Europe.* London: Routledge.

Featherstone, M. et al. (eds) (1995) *Global Modernities.* London: Sage.

Field, F. (1996) 'Reforming the Welfare State', in G. Radice (ed.), *What Needs to Change: New Visions for Britain.* London: HarperCollins.

Fielding, S. (1997) *The Labour Party: 'Socialism' and Society since 1951.* Manchester: Manchester University Press.

Finkelstein, D. (1987) 'Revisionists without a Cause', in A. Kilmarnock (ed.), *The Radical Challenge: The Response of Social Democracy.* Worcester: André Deutsch.

Fisera, V. C. (1983) 'The French New Left and the Left-Wing Regime', in S. Williams (ed.), *Socialism in France: From Jaurés to Mitterrand.* London: Frances Pinter.

Fishman, N. (1996) 'Modernisation, Moderation and the Labour Tradition', in M. Perryman (ed.), *The Blair Agenda.* London: Lawrence & Wishart.

Foote, G. (1997) *The Labour Party's Political Thought: A History, 3rd edn*. London: Macmillan.

Forbes, I. (1986) 'Introduction' and 'Conclusion', in I. Forbes (ed.), *Market Socialism: Whose Choice?* Fabian Society Tract 516. London: Fabian Society.

Fouskas, V. (1997) 'The Left and the Crisis of the Third Hellenic Republic, 1989–1997', in D. Sassoon (ed.), *Looking Left – European Socialism after the Cold War*. London: I. B. Tauris.

Frears, J. (1991) *Parties and Voters in France*. London: Hurst & Company.

Fried, A. and Sanders, R. (eds), (1964) *Socialist Thought: A Documentary History*. Edinburgh: Edinburgh University Press.

Fukuyama, F. (1992) *The End of History and the Last Man*. London: Hamish Hamilton.

Fukuyama, F. (1995) *Trust: The Social Virtues and the Creation of Prosperity*. London: Hamish Hamilton.

Gaffney, J. (1988) 'Introduction: French Political Culture and Modernisation', in J. Gaffney (ed.), *France and Modernisation*. Aldershot: Gower.

Gaffney, J. (ed.) (1989a) *The French Presidential Elections of 1988*. Aldershot: Dartmouth.

Gaffney, J. (1989b) *The French Left and the Fifth Republic: The Discourses of Communism and Socialism in Contemporary France*. London: Macmillan.

Gaffney, J. (1990) 'The Emergence of a Presidential Party: The Socialist Party', in A. Cole (ed.), *French Political Parties in Transition*. Aldershot: Dartmouth.

Galbraith, J. K. (1967) *The New Industrial State*. London: Penguin Books.

Galbraith, J. K. (1992) *The Culture of Contentment*. London: Sinclair-Stevenson.

Gallagher, T. (1989) 'The Portuguese Socialist Party: The Pitfalls of Being First', in T. Gallagher and A. M. Williams (eds), *Southern European Socialism – Parties, Elections and the Challenge of Government*. Manchester: Manchester University Press.

Gallagher, T. and Williams, A. M. (1989) 'Introduction' and 'Southern European Socialism in the 1990s', in T. Gallagher and A. M. Williams (eds), *Southern European Socialism – Parties, Elections and the Challenge of Government*. Manchester: Manchester University Press.

Gallie, D. (1983) *Social Inequality and Class Radicalism in France and Britain*. Cambridge: Cambridge University Press.

Gallie, D. (1985) 'Les Lois Auroux: The Reform of French Industrial Relations?', in H. Machin and V. Wright (eds), *Economic Policy and Policy-Making under the Mitterrand Presidency 1981–84*. Exeter: Frances Pinter.

Gallup (1997) *Political and Economic Index*. London: Gallup (various issues).

Gamble, A. (1988) *The Free Economy and the Strong State: The Politics of Thatcherism*. London: Macmillan.

Gamble, A. (1992) 'The Labour Party and Economic Management', in M. Smith and J. Spear (eds), *The Changing Labour Party*. London: Routledge.

Gamble, A. (1996) 'The Legacy of Thatcherism', in M. Perryman (ed.), *The Blair Agenda*. London: Lawrence & Wishart.

Gay, P. (1962) *The Dilemma of Democratic Socialism*. New York: Collier Books.

Giddens, A. (1994a) 'Brave New World: The New Context of Politics', in D. Miliband (ed.), *Reinventing the Left*. London: Polity Press.

Giddens, A. (1994b) *Beyond Left and Right – The Future of Radical Politics*. Cambridge: Polity Press.

Giddens, A. (1998) *The Third Way – The Renewal of Social Democracy.* Cambridge: Polity Press.

Gillespie, E. and Schellhas, B. (1994) *Contract with America – The Bold Plan by Rep. Newt Gingrich, Rep. Dick Armey and the House Republicans to Change the Nation.* New York: Times Books.

Gillespie, R. (1989a) *The Spanish Socialist Party: A History of Factionalism.* Oxford: Clarendon Press.

Gillespie, R. (1989b) 'Spanish Socialism in the 1980s', in T. Gallagher and A. M. Williams (eds), *Southern European Socialism – Parties, Elections and the Challenge of Government.* Manchester: Manchester University Press.

Gillespie, R. (1990) 'Regime Consolidation in Spain: Party, State and Society', in G. Pridham (ed.), *Securing Democracy: Political Parties and Democratic Consolidation in Southern Europe.* London: Routledge.

Gillespie, R. (1992) *Socialist Programmatic Renewal in Spain,* PAIS Papers, Working Paper 104. Warwick: Department of Politics and International Studies, University of Warwick.

Gillespie, R. (1994) 'The Resurgence of Factionalism in the Spanish Socialist Workers' Party', in D. S. Bell and E. Shaw (eds), *Conflict and Cohesion in Western European Social Democratic Parties.* London: Pinter Publishers.

Gillespie, G. and Gallagher, T. (1989) 'Democracy and Authority in the Socialist Parties of Southern Europe', in T. Gallagher and A. M. Williams (eds), *Southern European Socialism – Parties, Elections and the Challenge of Government.* Manchester: Manchester University Press.

Gladdish, K. (1990) 'Portugal: an Open Verdict', in G. Pridham (ed.), *Securing Democracy: Political Parties and Democratic Consolidation in Southern Europe.* London: Routledge.

Glyn, A. and Sutcliffe, B. (1992) 'Global But Leaderless: The New Capitalist Order', in R. Miliband (ed.), *The Socialist Register 1992.* London: Merlin Press.

Goldsmith, J. (1994) *The Trap.* London: Macmillan.

Goldthorpe, J., Lockwood, D., Bechhoffer, F. and Platt, J. (1969) *The Affluent Worker in the Class Structure.* London: Cambridge University Press.

Goodhart, D. (1994a) *The Reshaping of the German Social Market.* London: IPPR.

Goodhart, D. (1994b) 'Reforming British Employers', in M. Linton (ed.), *Whatever Next?* London: Guardian/Samizdat Production.

Goodwin, B. (1989) *Using Political Ideas,* 2nd edn. Chichester: John Wiley & Sons.

Gould, B. (1995) *Goodbye to All That.* London: Macmillan.

Gould, B., Mills, J. and Stewart, S. (1979) *The Politics of Monetarism,* Fabian Tract 462. London: Fabian Society.

Grace, G. (1990) 'Labour and Education: The Crisis and Settlements of Education Policy', in M. Holland and J. Boston (eds), *The Fourth Labour Government – Parties and Policy in New Zealand.* Auckland: Oxford University Press.

Graham, A. (1994) 'Did Keynesianism Work?', in S. Pollard (ed.), *Jobs and Growth: The International Perspective.* London: Fabian Society.

Gray, J. (1993) *Beyond the New Right.* London: Routledge.

Gray, J. (1996) *After Social Democracy – Politics, Capitalism and the Common Life.* London: Demos.

Gray, J. (1998) *False Dawn: The Delusions of Global Capitalism.* London: Granta Books.

Gray, J. and Willetts, D. (1997) *Is Conservatism Dead?* London: Profile Books.

Green, D. (1985) 'Comment', in H. Machin and V. Wright (eds), *Economic Policy and Policy-Making under the Mitterrand Presidency 1981–84*. Exeter: Frances Pinter.

Grosser, A. (1966) 'France: Nothing But Opposition', in R. Dahl (ed.), *Political Oppositions in Western Democracies*. New Haven, Conn.: Yale University Press.

Groux, G. (1989) 'French Industrial Relations: From Crisis to Today', in J. Howorth and G. Ross (eds), *Contemporary France, Volume Three*. London: Frances Pinter.

Groux, G. and Mouriaux, R. (1996) 'The Dilemma of Unions without Members', in A. Daley (ed.), *The Mitterrand Era – Policy Alternatives and Political Mobilisation in France*. London: Macmillan.

Grunberg, G. (1985) 'France', in I. Crewe and D. Denver (eds), *Electoral Change in Western Democracies – Patterns and Sources of Electoral Volatility*. London: Croom Helm.

Habermas, J. (1991) 'What Does Socialism Mean Today? The Revolutions of Recuperation and the Need for New Thinking', in R. Blackburn (ed.), *After the Fall*. London: Verso.

Hain, P. (1995) *Ayes to the Left: A Future for Socialism*. London: Lawrence & Wishart.

Halimi, S. (1996) 'Less Exceptionalism than Meets the Eye', in A. Daley (ed.), *The Mitterrand Era – Policy Alternatives and Political Mobilisation in France*. London: Macmillan.

Hall, P. (1986) *Governing the Economy – The Politics of State Intervention in Britain and France*. Oxford: Polity Press.

Hall, P. (1987) 'The Evolution of Economic Policy under Mitterrand', in G. Ross, S. Hoffman and S. Malzacher (eds), *The Mitterrand Experiment – Continuity and Change in Modern France*. Oxford: Polity Press.

Hall, S. (1988) *The Hard Road to Renewal: Thatcherism and the Crisis of the Left*. London: Verso.

Halliday, F. (1991) 'The Ends of Cold War' and 'A Reply to Edward Thompson', in R. Blackburn (ed.), *After the Fall*. London: Verso.

Hamilton, M. B. (1989) *Democratic Socialism in Britain and Sweden*. London: Macmillan.

Hampden-Turner, C. and Trompenaars, A. (1993) *The Seven Cultures of Capitalism – Value Systems for Creating Wealth in the United States, Japan, Germany, France, Britain, Sweden, and the Netherlands*. New York: Currency Doubleday.

Hampden-Turner, C. (1997) 'Masters of the Infinite Game', in G. Mulgan (ed.), *Life after Politics: New Thinking for the Twenty-First Century*. London: Fontana Books.

Hampshire, S. (1974) 'Epilogue', in L. Kolakowski and S. Hampshire (eds), *The Socialist Idea: A Reappraisal*. London: Wiedenfeld & Nicolson.

Handy, C. (1988) *The Empty Raincoat: Making Sense of the Future*. London: Hutchinson.

Handy, C. (1995) *Beyond Certainty: The Changing Worlds of Organisations*. London: Hutchinson.

Handy, C. (1996) 'People and Change', in G. Radice (ed.), *What Needs to Change: New Visions for Britain*. London: HarperCollins.

Hanley, D. (1983) '"Les Variables de Solferino" or Thoughts on Steering the Socialist Economy: An Analysis of the Economic Discourse of the French Parti Socialiste', in S. Williams (ed.), *Socialism in France: From Jaurés to Mitterrand*. London: Frances Pinter.

Hanley, D. (1986) *Keeping Left? CERES and the French Socialist Party*. Manchester: Manchester University Press.

Hanley, D. (1987) 'The Parti Socialiste: Socialist Synthesis or Ambiguous Compromise?', in S. Mazey and M. Newman (eds), *Mitterrand's France*. London: Croom Helm.

Hanley, D. (1989) 'Waiting for the President: The Political Year in Retrospect, September 1987–August 1988', in J. Howorth and G. Ross (eds), *Contemporary France, Volume Three*. London: Frances Pinter.

Harrison, M. (1993) 'The President, Cultural Projects and Broadcasting Policy', in J. Hayward (ed.), *De Gaulle to Mitterrand – Presidential Power in France*. London: Hurst & Co.

Haseler, S. (1969) *The Gaitskellites: Revisionism in the British Labour Party, 1951–64*. London: Macmillan.

Haseler, S. (1980) *The Tragedy of Labour*. Oxford: Basil Blackwell.

Haseler, S. and Gyford, J. (1971), *Social Democracy: Beyond Revisionism*, Fabian Research Series **292**. London: Fabian Society.

Hattersley, R. (1987) *Choose Freedom*. Reading: Penguin Books.

Hay, C. (1997) 'No Left Turn? What to Expect from New Labour in Power', in J. Stanyer and G. Stoker (eds), *Contemporary Political Studies, Volume One*. Nottingham: PSA.

Hay, C. (1998) 'Labouring under False Pretences? The Revision of Policy in the "Modernisation" of the British Labour Party' in A. Dobson and J. Stanyer (eds), *Contemporary Political Studies 1998*. Nottingham: PSA.

Hayward, J. (1985) 'Comment', in H. Machin and V. Wright (eds), *Economic Policy and Policy-Making under the Mitterrand Presidency 1981–84*. Exeter: Frances Pinter.

Hazareesingh, S. (1994) *Political Traditions in Modern France*. Oxford: Oxford University Press.

Healey, D. (1989) *The Time of My Life*. London: Michael Joseph.

Heath, A. and Jowell, R. (1994) 'Labour's Policy Review', in A. Heath, R. Jowell and J. Curtice (eds), *Labour's Last Chance? The 1992 Election and Beyond*. Cambridge: Dartmouth Publishing.

Heath, A., Jowell, R. and Curtice, J. (1994) 'Can Labour Win?', in A. Heath, R. Jowell and J. Curtice (eds), *Labour's Last Chance? The 1992 Election and Beyond*. Cambridge: Dartmouth Publishing.

Heath, A. et al. (1985) *How Britain Votes*. Oxford: Pergamon Press.

Heffernan, R. and Marqusee, M. (1992) *Defeat from the Jaws of Victory: Inside Kinnock's Labour Party*. London: Verso.

Heider, K. (1977) 'The Norwegian Labour Party: Social Democracy in a Periphery of Europe', in W. Paterson and A. Thomas (eds), *Social Democratic Parties in Western Europe*. London: Croom Helm.

Heider, K. (1994) 'Towards Party Irrelevance? The Decline of Both Conflict and Cohesion in the Norwegian Labour Party', in D. Bell and E. Shaw (eds), *Conflict and Cohesion in Western European Social Democratic Parties*. London: Pinter Publishers.

Held, D. (1993) 'Democracy and Globalisation', in A. Barnett, C. Ellis and P. Hirst (eds), *Debating the Constitution: New Perspectives on Constitutional Reform*. Cambridge: Polity Press.

Held, D. (1994) 'Inequalities of Power, Problems of Democracy', in D. Miliband (ed.), *Reinventing the Left*. London: Polity Press.

Held, D. (1995) 'Political Community and the Cosmopolitan Order', in D. Held (ed.), *Democracy and the Global Order: From the Modern State to Cosmopolitan Governance*. Oxford: Polity Press.

Hennessy, P. (1987) 'The Attlee Governments, 1945–51', in P. Hennessy and A. Seldon (eds), *Ruling Performance* Oxford: Basil Blackwell.

Hennessy, P. (1992) *Never Again: Britain 1945–1951*. London: Jonathan Cape.

Hennessy, P. (1996) 'The Prospects for a Labour Government', in G. Radice (ed.), *What Needs to Change: New Visions for Britain*. London: HarperCollins.

Hewitt, P. (1996) 'Family and Work', in G. Radice (ed.), *What Needs to Change: New Visions for Britain*. London: HarperCollins.

Hincker, F. (1983) 'The Communist Party and the Government of the Left in France', in S. Williams (ed.), *Socialism in France: From Jaurés to Mitterrand*. London: Frances Pinter.

Hincker, F. (1997) 'The French Socialists: Towards Post-Republican Values?', in D. Sassoon (ed.), *Looking Left – European Socialism after the Cold War*. London: I. B. Tauris.

Hines, C. and Lang, T. (1995) '*Employment and the Culture of Insecurity: Time to Protect Is Jobs?*', *Employment Policy Institute Economic Report*, 9(5).

Hirschman, A. (1982) *Shifting Influences: Private Interest and Public Action*. Oxford: Martin Robertson.

Hirst, P. and Thompson, G. (1996) *Globalisation in Question – The International Economy and the Possibilities of Governance*. Oxford: Polity Press.

Hobsbawm, E. (1994) *Age of Extremes – The Short Twentieth Century 1914–1991*. London: Michael Joseph.

Hodge, C. C. (1994) *The Trammels of Tradition – Social Democracy in Britain, France and Germany*. London: Greenwood Press.

Hoffman, S. (1987) 'Conclusion', in G. Ross, S. Hoffman and S. Malzacher (eds), *The Mitterrand Experiment – Continuity and Change in Modern France*. Oxford: Polity Press.

Holland, M. (1990) 'Engineering Electoral Success: Electoral Reform and Voting Behaviour under the Fourth Labour Government', in M. Holland and J. Boston (eds), *The Fourth Labour Government – Parties and Policy in New Zealand*. Auckland: Oxford University Press.

Holland, M. and Boston, J. (1990) 'Introduction', in M. Holland and J. Boston (eds), *The Fourth Labour Government – Parties and Policy in New Zealand*. Auckland: Oxford University Press.

Holland, S. (1975) *The Socialist Challenge*. London: Quartet.

Holmberg, S. and Weibull, L. (1992) *Perspektiv På Kriven – Samhälle Opinion Massmedia 9*. Göteborgs: Göteborgs Universitet.

Holmes, M. (1985) *The Labour Government, 1974–79 – Political Aims and Economic Reality*. London: Macmillan

Holmes, P. (1985) 'Comment', in H. Machin and V. Wright (eds), *Economic Policy and Policy-Making under the Mitterrand Presidency 1981–84*. Exeter: Frances Pinter.

Holmes, P. and Estrin, S. (1988) 'Planning for Modernisation', in J. Gaffney (ed.), *France and Modernisation*. Aldershot: Gower.

Holmes, S. (1993) *The Anatomy of Antiliberalism*. Cambridge, Mass.: Harvard University Press.

Holmstedt, M. and Schou, T-L. (1987) 'Scandinavian Setting', in I. Budge, D. Robertson and D. Hearl (eds), *Ideology, Strategy and Party Change: Spatial Analyses of Post-War Election Programmes in Nineteen Democracies*. Cambridge: Cambridge University Press.

Holtham, G. and Hughes, R. (1998) 'The State of Social Democracy in Britain', in R. Cuperus and J. Kandel (eds), *European Social Democracy: Transformation in Progress*. Amsterdam: Wiardi Beckman Stichting/Friedrich Ebert Stiftung.

Howell, C. (1996) 'French Socialism and the Transformation of Industrial Relations since 1981', in A. Daley (ed.), *The Mitterrand Era — Policy Alternatives and Political Mobilisation in France*. London: Macmillan.

Howorth, J. and Ross, G. (1989) 'Introduction', in J. Howorth and G. Ross (eds), *Contemporary France, Volume Three*. London: Frances Pinter.

Hughes, C. and Wintour, P. (1990) *Labour Rebuilt – The New Model Party*. London: Fourth Estate.

Hutton, W. (1993a) 'Evicting the Rentier State', in A. Barnett, C. Ellis and P. Hirst (eds), *Debating the Constitution: New Perspectives On Constitutional Reform* Cambridge: Polity Press.

Hutton, W. (1993b) 'Wither Global Capitalism', in C. Crouch and D. Marquand (eds), *Ethics and Markets*. Oxford: Blackwell Publishers.

Hutton, W. (1994a) 'Comment: The Social Market in a Global Context', in D. Miliband (ed.), *Reinventing the Left*. London: Polity Press.

Hutton, W. (1994b) 'Full Employment in a Free Society', in S. Pollard (ed.), *Jobs and Growth: The International Perspective*. London: Fabian Society.

Hutton, W. (1995) *The State We're In*. London: Jonathan Cape.

Hutton, W. (1996) 'The Stakeholder Society', in D. Marquand and A. Seldon (eds), *The Ideas That Shaped Post-War Britain*. London: Fontana Press.

Hutton, W. (1997) *The State to Come*. London: Vintage.

Inglehart, R. (1977) *The Silent Revolution*. Princeton, NJ: Princeton University Press.

Institute for Public Policy Research (1994) *Commission On Social Justice. Social Justice: Strategies for National Renewal. The Report of the Commission on Social Justice*. London: IPPR.

Involvement and Participation Association (1996) *European Works Councils – A Guide to Effective Consultation* London: IPA.

Jacobs, F. (1989) *Western European Political Parties*. Harlow: Longman.

Jaravsch, K. H. (1992) 'Towards a Post Socialist Politics?', in C. Lemke and G. Marks (eds), *The Crisis of Socialism in Europe*. Durham, NC: Duke University Press.

Jay, D. (1980) *Change and Fortune: A Political Record*. London: Hutchinson.

Jenkins, S. (1995) *Accountable to None – The Tory Nationalisation of Britain*. London: Hamish Hamilton.

Johnson, R. W. (1981) *The Long March of the French Left*. London: Macmillan.

Johnston, D. (1983) 'Introduction', in S. Williams (ed.), *Socialism in France: From Jaurés to Mitterrand*. London: Frances Pinter.

Johnston, R., Pattie, C. and Fieldhouse, E. (1994) 'The Geography of Voting and Representation', in A. Heath, R. Jowell, and J. Curtice (eds), *Labour's Last Chance? The 1992 Election and Beyond.* Cambridge: Dartmouth Publishing.

Jones, G. (1989) 'Business as Usual: The Employers', in J. Gaffney (ed.), *The French Presidential Elections of 1988.* Aldershot: Dartmouth.

Jones, N. (1995) *Soundbites and Spindoctors: How Politicians Manipulate the Media – and Vice Versa.* London: Cassell.

Jones, T. (1996) *Remaking the Labour Party – From Gaitskell to Blair.* London: Routledge.

Jungar, A-C. (1991) 'Italian Socialism: A Century of Trial and Error', in L. Karvonen and J. Sunberg (eds), *Social Democracy in Transition.* Aldershot: Dartmouth.

Karvonen, L. and Sunberg, J. (1991) 'Introduction: Social Democracy Old and New', in L. Karvonen and J. Sunberg (eds), *Social Democracy in Transition.* Aldershot: Dartmouth.

Kavanagh, D. (1982) *The Politics of the Labour Party.* London: George Allen & Unwin.

Kavanagh, D. (1994) 'Opposition', in D. Kavanagh and A. Seldon (eds), *The Major Effect.* London: Macmillan.

Kay, J. (1995) *Foundations of Corporate Success.* Oxford: Oxford University Press.

Keat, R. (1993) 'The Moral Boundaries of the Market', in C. Crouch and D. Marquand (eds), *Ethics and Markets.* Oxford: Blackwell Publishers.

Keating, M. (1985) 'Comment', in H. Machin and V. Wright (eds), *Economic Policy and Policy-Making under the Mitterrand Presidency 1981–84.* Exeter: Frances Pinter.

Keegan, W. (1992) *The Spectre of Capitalism – The Future of the World Economy after the Fall of Communism.* London: Radius.

Kelly, G., Kelly, D. and Gamble, A. (1997) *Stakeholder Capitalism.* London: Macmillan.

Kelly, P. (1994) *The End of Certainty – Power, Politics and Business in Australia.* Victoria, Australia: Allen and Unwin.

Keman, H. and Van Dijk, T. (1987) 'Political Strategies to Overcome the Crisis: Policy Formation and Economic Performance in Seventeen Capitalist Democracies' in H. Keman, H. Paloheimo and P. Whiteley (eds), *Coping with Economic Crisis – Alternative Responses to Economic Recession in Advanced Industrial Societies.* London: Sage Publications.

Kennedy, P. (1993) *Preparing for the Twenty-First Century.* Glasgow: HarperCollins.

Kennedy, P. (1997) 'The PSOE: Modernisation and the Welfare State', in D. Sassoon (ed.), *Looking Left – European Socialism after the Cold War.* London: I. B. Tauris.

Kesselman, M. (1996) 'French Labour Confronts Technological Change: Reform that Never Was?', in A. Daley (ed.), *The Mitterrand Era – Policy Alternatives and Political Mobilisation in France.* London: Macmillan.

Kessous, N. (1998) 'Cohabitation – Act III', in A. Dobson and J. Stanyer (eds), *Contemporary Political Studies 1998.* Nottingham: PSA.

Kettle, M. (1994) 'It Ain't a Playground for the Educated', in M. Linton (ed.), *Whatever Next?* London: Guardian/Samizdat Production.

King, A. (1998) 'Why Labour Won – At Last', in A. King (ed.), *New Labour Triumphs: Britain at the Polls.* New Jersey: Chatham House.

King, P. (1996) 'Introduction' and 'Labour: A Choice of Constituency', in P. King (ed.), *Socialism and the Common Good: New Fabian Essays.* London: Frank Cass.

Kingdom, J. (1992) *No Such Thing as Society? Individualism and Community*. Milton Keynes: Open University Press.

Kirchheimer, O. (1990) 'The Catch-All Party', in P. Mair (ed.), *The West European Party System*. Oxford: Oxford University Press.

Kitschelt, H. (1992) 'The Socialist Discourse and Party Strategy in West European Democracies', in C. Lemke and G. Marks (eds), *The Crisis of Socialism in Europe*. Durham, NC: Duke University Press.

Kitschelt, H. (1994) *The Transformation of European Social Democracy*. Cambridge: Cambridge University Press.

Klingemann, H.-D. (1987) 'Electoral Programmes in West Germany 1949–1980: Explorations in the Nature of Political Controversy', in I. Budge, D. Robertson and D. Hearl (eds), *Ideology, Strategy and Party Change: Spatial Analyses of Post-War Election Programmes in Nineteen Democracies*. Cambridge: Cambridge University Press.

Klingemann, H.-D., Hofferbert, R. and Budge, I. (1994) *Parties, Policies and Democracy*. Boulder, Colo.: Westview Press.

Knapp, A. (1994) *Gaullism since De Gaulle*. Aldershot: Dartmouth.

Koelble, T. A. (1991) *The Left Unravelled*. Durham, NC: Duke University Press.

Kogan, D. and Kogan, M. (1982) *The Battle for the Labour Party*. Glasgow: Fontana Paperbacks.

Kolakowski, L. (1974) 'Introduction', in L. Kolakowski and S. Hampshire (eds), *The Socialist Idea: A Reappraisal*. London: Wiedenfeld & Nicolson.

Koopman-Boyden, P. G. (1990) 'Social Policy: Has There Been One?', in M. Holland and J. Boston (eds), *The Fourth Labour Government – Parties and Policy in New Zealand*. Auckland: Oxford University Press.

Kornhauser, W. (1959) *The Politics of Mass Society*. London: Routledge & Kegan Paul.

Krieger, J. (1991) 'Class, Consumption, and Collectivism: Perspectives On the Labour Party and Electoral Competition in Britain', in F. F. Piven (ed.), *Labor Parties in Post-Industrial Societies*. Cambridge: Polity Press.

Labour Coordinating Committee (1997) *New Labour: A Stakeholder's Party – Interim Report of the Labour Party Co-ordinating Committees' Commission on Party Democracy*. London: LCC.

Lansley, S. (1994) *After the Gold Rush – The Trouble with Affluence: 'Consumer Capitalism' and the Way Forward*. London: Century Books.

Larkin, M. (1988) *France since the Popular Front: Government and People 1936–1986*. Oxford: Clarendon Press.

Laughland, J. (1994) *The Death of Politics – France under Mitterrand*. London: Michael Joseph.

Layard, R. (1997) *What Labour Can Do*. London: Warner Books.

Laybourn, K. (1988) *The Rise of Labour: The British Labour Party 1890–1979*. London: Edward Arnold.

Leadbeater, C. and Mulgan, G. (1997) 'The End of Unemployment: Bringing Work to Life', in G. Mulgan (ed.), *Life after Politics: New Thinking for the Twenty-First Century*. London: Fontana Books.

Leadbeater, C. and Mulgan, G. (1997) 'Lean Democracy and the Leadership Vacuum', in G. Mulgan (ed.), *Life after Politics: New Thinking for the Twenty-First Century*. London: Fontana Books.

Lees, C. (1998) 'Germany: The Social Democratic Compromise', in A. Dobson and J. Stanyer (eds), *Contemporary Political Studies 1998*. Nottingham: PSA.

Le Grand, J. and Estrin, S. (1989) 'Market Socialism', in J. Le Grand and S. Estrin (eds), *Market Socialism*. Oxford: Clarendon Press.

Lemke, C. and Marks, G. (1992) 'From Decline to Demise?', in C. Lemke and G. Marks (eds), *The Crisis of Socialism in Europe*. Durham, NC: Duke University Press.

Letwin, S. R. (1992) *The Anatomy of Thatcherism*. Glasgow: Fontana.

Leys, C. (1996) 'The British Labour Party's Transition from Socialism to Capitalism', in L. Panitch (ed.), *The Socialist Register 1996*. London: Merlin Press.

Leys, C. (1997) 'The British Labour Party since 1989', in D. Sassoon (ed.), *Looking Left – European Socialism after the Cold War*. London: I. B. Tauris.

Liebert, U. (1990) 'From Polarisation to Pluralism: Regional-Nationalist Parties in the Process of Democratic Consolidation in Post-Franco Spain', in G. Pridham (ed.), *Securing Democracy: Political Parties and Democratic Consolidation in Southern Europe*. London: Routledge.

Lijphart, A. (1968) *The Politics of Accommodation: Pluralism and Democracy in the Netherlands*. Berkeley: University of California.

Lindgren, A.-M. (1998) 'Swedish Social Democracy in Transition', in R. Cuperus and J. Kandel (eds), *European Social Democracy: Transformation in Progress*. Amsterdam: Wiardi Beckman Stichting/Friedrich Ebert Stiftung.

Lindstron, U. (1991) 'From Cadres to Citizens to Clients: Toward a Theory of the Electoral Coalitions of Social Democracy', in L. Karvonen and J. Sunberg (eds), *Social Democracy in Transition*. Aldershot: Dartmouth.

Linz, J. (1978) 'Crisis, Breakdown and Reequilibrium', in J. Linz and A. Stepan (eds), *The Breakdown of Democratic Regimes*. Baltimore, MD: Johns Hopkins University Press.

Linz, J. and Stepan, A. (1978) 'Preface' in J. Linz and A. Stepan (eds), *The Breakdown of Democratic Regimes*. Baltimore, MD: Johns Hopkins University Press.

Lipset, S. M. (1983) *Political Man*. London: Heinemann.

Lipset, S. M. (1991) 'No Third Way: A Comparative Perspective on the Left', in D. Chirot (ed.), *The Crisis of Leninism and the Decline of the Left – The Revolutions of 1989*. London: University of Washington Press.

Lipsey, D. (1996) 'Taxing and Spending', in G. Radice (ed.), *What Needs to Change: New Visions for Britain*. London: HarperCollins.

Luard, E. (1990) *The Globalization of Politics – The Changed Focus of Political Action in the Modern World*. New York: New York University Press.

Lyrintzis, C (1989) 'PASOK in Power: The Loss of the "Third Road to Socialism"', in T. Gallagher and A. M. Williams (eds), *Southern European Socialism – Parties, Elections and the Challenge of Government*. Manchester: Manchester University Press.

McCormick, J. (1985) 'Apprenticeship for Governing: An Assessment of French Socialism in Power', in H. Machin and V. Wright (eds), *Economic Policy and Policy-Making under the Mitterrand Presidency 1981–84*. Exeter: Frances Pinter.

MacEaggart, F. (1994) 'Wooing Back the Middle Class', in M. Linton (ed.), *Whatever Next?* London: Guardian/Samizdat Production.

MacFarlane, L. (1996) 'Socialism and Common Ownership: An Historical Perspective', in P. King (ed.), *Socialism and the Common Good: New Fabian Essays*. London: Frank Cass.

Machin, H. (1994) 'Changing Patterns of Party Competition' and 'Political Leadership', in P. A. Hall, J. Hayward and H. Machin (eds), *Developments in French Politics*. London: Macmillan.

Machin, H. and Wright, V. (1985) 'Preface' and 'Economic Policy under the Mitterrand Presidency, 1981–1984: An Introduction', in H. Machin and V. Wright (eds), *Economic Policy and Policy-Making under the Mitterrand Presidency 1981–84*. Exeter: Frances Pinter.

Mackie, T. H. (1990) 'Appendix', in D. Urwin and W. Paterson (eds), *Politics in Western Europe Today*. London: Longman.

Mackintosh, J. P. (1988) 'Has Social Democracy Failed in Britain?', in W. John Morgan (ed.), *Politics and Consensus in Modern Britain – Lectures in Memory of Hugh Gaitskell*. London: Macmillan.

McSmith, A. (1994) *John Smith: A Life 1938–1994*. Reading: Mandarin.

Mair, P. (1994) 'Britain: Labour and Electoral Reform', in P. Anderson and P. Camiller (eds), *Mapping the West European Left*. London: Verso.

Mandelson, P. (1997) *Labour's Next Steps: Tackling Social Exclusion*, Fabian Society Pamphlet 581. London: Fabian Society.

Mandelson, P. and Liddle, R. (1996) *The Blair Revolution: Can New Labour Deliver?* London: Faber & Faber.

Maravall, J. (1985) 'The Socialist Alternative: The Policies and Electorate of the PSOE', in H. Penniman and E. Mujal-Leó (eds), *Spain at the Polls 1977, 1979 and 1982: A Study of National Elections*. New York: Duke University Press.

Maravall, J. (1992) 'From Opposition to Government: The Politics and Policies of the PSOE', in J. Maravall et al., *Socialist Parties in Europe*. Barcelona: Institut d'Ediciones de la Diputació de Barcelona.

Maravall, J. et al. (1992) *Socialist Parties in Europe*. Barcelona: Institut d'Ediciones de la Diputació de Barcelona.

Markovits, A. S. and Gorski, P. S. (1993) *The German Left: Red, Green and Beyond*. Cambridge: Polity Press.

Marquand, D. (1987) 'Phoenix from the Ashes', in A. Kilmarnock (ed.), *The Radical Challenge: The Response of Social Democracy*. Worcester: André Deutsch.

Marquand, D. (1988a) 'The Paradoxes of Thatcherism', in R. Skidelsky (ed.), *Thatcherism*. London: Chatto & Windus.

Marquand, D. (1988b) *The Unprincipled Society*. London: Jonathan Cape.

Marquand, D. (1991) *The Progressive Dilemma*. St Ives: William Heinemann.

Marquand, D. (1994) 'Reinventing Federalism: Europe and the Left', in D. Miliband (ed.), *Reinventing the Left*. London: Polity Press.

Marquand, D. (1996a) 'Community and the Left', in G. Radice (ed.), *What Needs to Change: New Visions for Britain*. London: HarperCollins.

Marquand, D. (1996b) 'Moralists and Hedonists', in D. Marquand and A. Seldon (eds), *The Ideas that Shaped Post-War Britain*. London: Fontana Press.

Marquand, D. (1997) *The New Reckoning: Capitalism, States and Citizens*. Oxford: Polity Press.

Marr, A. (1995) *Ruling Britannia – The Failure and Future of British Democracy*. London: Michael Joseph.

Marshall, T. H. (1950) *Citizenship and Social Class and Other Essays*. Cambridge: Cambridge University Press.

Martin, J. (1990) 'Remaking the State Services', in M. Holland and J. Boston (eds), *The Fourth Labour Government – Parties and Policy in New Zealand*. Auckland: Oxford University Press.

Mazey, S. (1987) 'Introduction', in S. Mazey and M. Newman (eds), *Mitterrand's France*. London: Croom Helm.

Meidner, R. (1993) 'Why Did the Swedish Model Fail?', in R. Miliband and L. Panitch (eds), *Socialist Register 1993*. London: Merlin Press.

Mendras, H. and Cole, A. (1991) *Social Change in Modern France*. Cambridge: Cambridge University Press.

Mény, Y. (1985) 'Local Authorities and Economic Policy', in H. Machin and V. Wright (eds), *Economic Policy and Policy-Making under the Mitterrand Presidency 1981–84*. Exeter: Frances Pinter.

Merkel, W. (1992) 'After the Golden Age: Is Social Democracy Doomed to Decline', in J. Maravall et al., *Socialist Parties in Europe*. Barcelona: Institut d'Ediciones de la Diputació de Barcelona.

Meyer, T. (1997) 'The Transformation of German Social Democracy', in D. Sassoon (ed.), *Looking Left – European Socialism after the Cold War*. London: I. B. Tauris.

Miliband, D. (1993) 'The New Politics of Economics', in C. Crouch and D. Marquand (eds), *Ethics and Markets*. Oxford: Blackwell Publishers.

Miliband, D. (1994) 'Introduction', in D. Miliband (ed.), *Reinventing the Left*. London: Polity Press.

Miliband, R. (1991) 'Reflections on the Crisis of Communist Regimes', in R. Blackburn (ed.), *After the Fall*. London: Verso.

Miller, D. and Estrin, S. (1986) 'Market Socialism: A Policy for Socialists', in I. Forbes (ed.), *Market Socialism: Whose Choice?*, Fabian Society Tract 516. London: Fabian Society.

Milner, H. (1989) *Sweden: Social Democracy in Practice*. Oxford: Oxford University Press.

Milner, H. (1994) *Social Democracy and Rational Choice: The Scandinavian and Rational Choice*. London: Routledge.

Milner, S. (1989) 'Guardians of the Republican Tradition? The Trade Unions', in J. Gaffney (ed.), *The French Presidential Elections of 1988*. Aldershot: Dartmouth.

Minkin, L. (1980) *The Labour Party Conference – A Study in the Politics of Intra-Party Democracy*. Manchester: Manchester University Press.

Minkin, L. (1992) *The Contentious Alliance: Trade Unions and the Labour Party*. Edinburgh: Edinburgh University Press.

Minkin, L. and Seyd, P. (1977) 'The British Labour Party', in W. Paterson and A. Thomas (eds), *Social Democratic Parties in Western Europe*. London: Croom Helm.

Misgeld, K., Molin, K. and Åmark, K. (1992) 'Introduction', in K. Misgeld, K. Molin and K. Åmark (eds), *Creating Social Democracy – A Century of the Social Democratic Labour Party in Sweden*. University Park, Pa.: Pennsylvania University Press.

Missirol, A. (1992) 'The SPD. Portrait of a Party', in J. Maravall et al., *Socialist Parties in Europe*. Barcelona: Institut d'Ediciones de la Diputació de Barcelona.

Mitchell, A. (1983) *Four Years in the Death of the Labour Party*. London: Methuen.

Mjøset, L., Cappelen, Å., Fagerberg, J. and Tranøy, B. S. (1994) 'Norway: Changing the Model', in P. Anderson and P. Camiller (eds), *Mapping the West European Left*. London: Verso.

Moene, K. O. and Wallerstein, M. (1993) 'What's Wrong with Social Democracy?', in R. Bardhan and J. Roemer (eds), *Market Socialism – The Current Debate*. Oxford: Oxford University Press.

Molin, K. (1992) 'Historical Orientation', in K. Misgeld, K. Molin and K. Åmark (eds), *Creating Social Democracy – A Century of the Social Democratic Labour Party in Sweden*. University Park, Pa.: Pennsylvania University Press.

Morgan, K. O. (1984) *Labour in Power, 1945–51*. Oxford: Clarendon Press.

Morgan, R. (1987) 'Continental Social Democracy', in A. Kilmarnock (ed.), *The Radical Challenge: The Response of Social Democracy*. Worcester: André Deutsch.

Morvan, Y. (1985) 'Industrial Policy', in H. Machin and V. Wright (eds), *Economic Policy and Policy-Making under the Mitterrand Presidency 1981–84*. Exeter: Frances Pinter.

Muet, P.-A. (1985) 'Economic Management and the International Environment, 1981–1983', in H. Machin and V. Wright (eds), *Economic Policy and Policy-Making under the Mitterrand Presidency 1981–84*. Exeter: Frances Pinter.

Mujal-León, E. (1985) 'Spanish Politics: Between the Old Regime and the New Majority', in H. Penniman and E. Mujal-León (eds), *Spain at the Polls 1977, 1979 and 1982: A Study of National Elections*. New York: Duke University Press.

Mulgan, G. (1993a) 'Reticulated Organisations: The Birth and Death of the Mixed Economy', in C. Crouch and D. Marquand (eds), *Ethics and Markets*. Oxford: Blackwell Publishers.

Mulgan, G. (1993b) 'The Constitution of the Economy in an Age of Human Capital', in A. Barnett, C. Ellis and P. Hirst (eds), *Debating the Constitution: New Perspectives on Constitutional Reform*. Cambridge: Polity Press.

Mulgan, G. (1996) 'Democracy as Self Government', in G. Radice (ed.), *What Needs to Change: New Visions for Britain*. London: HarperCollins.

Mulgan, G. and Murray, R. (1997) 'Reconnecting Taxation', in G. Mulgan (ed.), *Life after Politics: New Thinking for the Twenty-First Century*. London: Fontana Books.

Mulgan, R. (1990) 'The Changing Electoral Mandate', in M. Holland and J. Boston (eds), the *Fourth Labour Government – Politics and Policy in New Zealand*. Auckland: Oxford University Press.

Muller-Rommel, F. (1989) 'Green Parties and Alternative Lists under Cross-National Perspectives', in F. Muller-Rommel (ed.), *New Politics in Western Europe*. Boulder, Colo.: Westview Press.

Newman, M. (1987) 'The Balance Sheet', in S. Mazey and M. Newman (eds), *Mitterrand's France*. London: Croom Helm.

Norman, D. (1993) 'Trade Unions and New Management Techniques', in C. Crouch and D. Marquand (eds), *Ethics and Markets*. Oxford: Blackwell Publishers.

Norris, P. (1994) 'Labour Factionalism and Extremism', in A. Heath, R. Jowell and J. Curtice (eds), *Labour's Last Chance? The 1992 Election and Beyond*. Cambridge: Dartmouth Publishing.

Northcutt, W. (1992) *Mitterrand – A Political Biography*. New York: Holmes & Meiner.

Nugent, N. and Lowe, D. (1982) *The Left in France*. London: Macmillan.

O'Brien, M. and Wilkes, C. (1993) *The Tragedy of the Market – A Social Experiment in New Zealand*. Palmerston North, New Zealand: Dunmore Press.

OECD (various issues) *Economic Outlook*. Paris: OECD.

OECD (1996) *Employment Outlook July 1996*. Paris: OECD.

Offe, C. (1991) 'Smooth Consolidation in the West German Welfare State: Structural Change, Fiscal Policies and Populist Politics', in F. F. Piven (ed.), *Labor Parties in Post-Industrial Societies*. Cambridge: Polity Press.

Ohmae, K. (1990) *The Borderless World*. London: Collins.

Ormerod, P. (1994) *The Death of Economics*. London: Faber & Faber.

Ozenda, M. and Strauss-Kahn, D. (1985) 'French Planning: Decline or Renewal?', in H. Machin and V. Wright (eds), *Economic Policy and Policy-Making under the Mitterrand Presidency 1981–84*. Exeter: Frances Pinter.

Padgett, S. (1994) 'The German Social Democratic Party: Between Old and New Left', in D. S. Bell and E. Shaw (eds), *Conflict and Cohesion in Western European Social Democratic Parties*. London: Pinter Publishers.

Padgett, S. and Paterson, W. (1991) *A History of Social Democracy in Post-War Europe*. London: Longman.

Padgett, S. and Paterson, W. (1994) 'Germany: Stagnation of the Left', in P. Anderson and P. Camiller (eds), *Mapping the West European Left*. London: Verso.

Panitch, L. and Leys, C. (1997) *The End of Parliamentary Socialism – From New Left to New Labour*. London: Verso.

Parekh, B. (1975) *The Concept of Socialism*. Guildford: Croom Helm.

Parkin, F. (1968) *Middle Class Radicalism*. Manchester: Manchester University Press.

Pasquino, G. (1990) 'Party Elites and Democratic Consolidation: Cross-National Comparison of Southern European Experience', in G. Pridham (ed.), *Securing Democracy: Political Parties and Democratic Consolidation in Southern Europe*. London: Routledge.

Paterson, W. E. (1977) 'The German Social Democratic Party', in W. E. Paterson and A. Thomas (eds), *Social Democratic Parties in Western Europe*. London: Croom Helm.

Paterson, W. E. and Campbell, I. (1974) *Social Democracy in Post-War Europe*. London: Macmillan.

Paterson, W. E. and Thomas, A. H. (1986) *The Future of Social Democracy*. Oxford: Clarendon Press.

Pelling, H. (1984) *The Labour Governments, 1945–51*. London: Macmillan.

Pelling, H. (1985) *A Short History of the Labour Party*, 8th edn. London: Macmillan.

Perryman, M. (1996) 'Introduction: Coming up for Air', in M. Perryman (ed.), *The Blair Agenda*. London: Lawrence & Wishart.

Petit, P. (1988) 'The Economy and Modernisation', in J. Gaffney (ed.), *France and Modernisation*. Aldershot: Gower.

Petras, J. (1993) 'Spanish Socialism: The Politics of Neoliberalism', in J. Kurth and J. Petras (eds), *Mediterranean Paradoxes – The Politics and Social Structure of Southern Europe*. Oxford: Berg.

Petras, J., Raptis, E. and Sarafopoulos, S. (1993) 'Greek Socialism: The Patrimonial State Revisited', in J. Kurth and J. Petras (eds), *Mediterranean Paradoxes – The Politics and Social Structure of Southern Europe*. Oxford: Berg.

Pétry, F. (1987) 'France 1958–1981: The Strategy of Joint Government Platforms', in I. Budge, D. Robertson and D. Hearl (eds), *Ideology, Strategy and Party Change: Spatial Analyses of Post-War Election Programmes in Nineteen Democracies*. Cambridge: Cambridge University Press.

Pickles, D. (1972) *The Government and Politics of France – Volume One: Institutions and Parties*. London: Methuen.

Pierson, C. (1991) *Beyond the Welfare State*. Oxford: Polity Press.

Pimlott, B. (1988) 'The Making of Consensus', in L. M. Smith (ed.), *The Making of Britain – Echoes of Greatness*. London: Macmillan.

Pimlott, B. (1993) *Harold Wilson*. London: HarperCollins.

Pimlott, B. (1994) 'In the Steps of Stafford Cripps', in M. Linton (ed.), *Whatever Next?* London: Guardian/Samizdat Production.

Pina, A. L. (1985) 'Shaping the Constitution', in H. Penniman and E. Mujal-León (eds), *Spain at the Polls 1977, 1979 and 1982: A Study of National Elections*. New York: Duke University Press.

Piven, F. F. (1991) 'The Decline of Labor Parties: An Overview', in F. F. Piven (ed.), *Labor Parties in Post-Industrial Societies*. Cambridge: Polity Press.

Piven F. F. (1994) 'Comment: Imperatives and Social Reform', in D. Miliband (ed.), *Reinventing the Left* London: Polity Press.

Plant, R. (1988) *Citizenship, Rights and Socialism*. London: Fabian Society.

Plant, R. (1996) 'Social Democracy', in D. Marquand and A. Seldon (eds), *The Ideas that Shaped Post-War Britain*. London: Fontana Press.

Poguntke, T. (1989) 'The "New Politics Dimension" in European Green Parties', in F. Muller-Rommel (ed.), *New Politics in Western Europe*. Boulder, Colo.: Westview Press

Pollack, B. and Hunter, G. (1989) 'The Spanish Socialist Workers' Party Foreign and Defence Policy: The External Dimension of Modernisation', in T. Gallagher and A. M. Williams (eds), *Southern European Socialism – Parties, Elections and the Challenge of Government*. Manchester: Manchester University Press.

Pollard, S. (1994) 'The Only Real Issue', in S. Pollard (ed.), *Jobs and Growth: The International Perspective*. London: Fabian Society.

Ponting, C. (1989) *Breach of Promise: Labour in Power 1964–1970*. St Ives: Penguin Books.

Pontusson, J. (1992) *The Limits of Social Democracy – Investment Politics in Sweden*. Ithaca, NY: Cornell University Press.

Pontusson, J. (1994) 'Sweden: After the Golden Age', in P. Anderson and P. Camiller (eds), *Mapping the West European Left*. London: Verso.

Power, M. (1997) 'The Audit Explosion', in G. Mulgan (ed.), *Life after Politics: New Thinking for the Twenty-First Century*. London: Fontana Books.

Pridham, G. (1989) 'Southern European Socialists and the State: Consolidation of Party Rule or Consolidation of Democracy', in T. Gallagher and A. M. Williams (eds), *Southern European Socialism – Parties, Elections and the Challenge of Government*. Manchester: Manchester University Press.

Pridham, G. (1990) 'Southern European Democracies on the Road to Consolidation: A Comparative Assessment of the Role of Political Parties', in G. Pridham (ed.), *Securing Democracy: Political Parties and Democratic Consolidation in Southern Europe*. London: Routledge.

Progressive Foundation (1996) *The New Progressive Declaration. A Political Philosophy for the Information Age, July 1996*. Washington, DC: Progressive Foundation.

Przeworski, A. (1985) *Capitalism and Social Democracy*. Cambridge: Cambridge University Press.

Przeworski, A. and Sprague, J. (1986) *Paper Stones – A History of Electoral Socialism*. Chicago: Chicago University Press.

Puttnam, D. (1996) 'The Creative Imagination', in G. Radice (ed.), *What Needs to Change: New Visions for Britain*. London: HarperCollins.

Queval, A. (1998) 'Strengths and Weaknesses of the French Socialist Party', in R. Cuperus and J. Kandel (eds), *European Social Democracy: Transformation in Progress*. Amsterdam: Wiardi Beckman Stichting/Friedrich Ebert Stiftung.

Radice, G. (1992) *Southern Discomfort,* Fabian Society Tract 555. London: Fabian Society.

Radice, G. (1996) '1964' and 'Conclusion: The New Agenda', in G. Radice (ed.), *What Needs to Change: New Visions for Britain*. London: HarperCollins.

Radice, G. and Pollard, S. (1993) *More Southern Discomfort: A Year On – Taxing and Spending*, Fabian Society Tract 560. London: Fabian Society.

Raes, K. (1998) 'The Socio-Cultural Factor – Postmodernism, Individualism and Multi-culturalism as Challenges for Social Democracy', in R. Cuperus and J. Kandel (eds), *European Social Democracy: Transformation in Progress*. Amsterdam: Wiardi Beckman Stichting/Friedrich Ebert Stiftung.

Raymond, G. (1989) 'His Master's Voice? André Lajoinie', in J. Gaffney (ed.), *The French Presidential Elections of 1988*. Aldershot: Dartmouth.

Reader, K. (1983) '"Que Reste-t-Il de Nos Amours?" Intellectuals and the Left in Post 1968 France', in S. Williams (ed.), *Socialism in France: From Jaurés to Mitterrand*. London: Frances Pinter.

Rentoul, J. (1989) *Me and Mine – The Triumph of the New Individualism?* London: Unwin Hyman.

Rentoul, J. (1995) *Tony Blair*. London: Little, Brown.

Reynolds, F. (1996) 'Environment for All', in G. Radice (ed.), *What Needs to Change: New Visions for Britain*. London: HarperCollins.

Reynolds, S. (1988) 'The French Ministry of Women's Rights 1981–86: Modernisation or Marginalisation?', in J. Gaffney (ed.), *France and Modernisation*. Aldershot: Gower.

Rhodes, M. (1988) 'Industry and Modernisation: An Overview', in J. Gaffney (ed.), *France and Modernisation*. Aldershot: Gower.

Richter, M. (1964) *The Politics of Conscience: T. H. Green and His Age*. London: Weidenfeld & Nicolson.

Robertson, D. (1976) *A Theory of Party Competition*. London: John Wiley & Sons.

Robertson, D. (1987) 'Britain, Australia, New Zealand and the United States 1946–1981, an Initial Comparative Analysis', in I. Budge, D. Robertson and D. Hearl (eds), *Ideology, Strategy and Party Change: Spatial Analyses of Post-War Election Programmes in Nineteen Democracies*. Cambridge: Cambridge University Press.

Rocard, M. (1994) 'Social Solidarity in a Mixed Economy', in D. Miliband (ed.), *Reinventing the Left* London: Polity Press.

Roemer, J. E. (1994) *A Future for Socialism*. London: Verso.

Rosamond, B. (1992) 'The Labour Party, Trade Unions and Industrial Relations', in M. Smith and J. Spear (eds), *The Changing Labour Party*. London: Routledge.

Rosenau, J. (1997) 'Globalization', in J. Rosenau (ed.), *Along the Domestic–Foreign Frontier: Exploring Governance in a Turbulent World*. Cambridge: Cambridge University Press.

Ross, G. (1987) 'Introduction', in G. Ross, S. Hoffman, and S. Malzacher (eds), *The Mitterrand Experiment – Continuity and Change in Modern France*. Oxford: Polity Press.

Ross, G. (1991) 'The Changing Face of Popular Power in France', in F. F. Piven (ed.), *Labor Parties in Post-Industrial Societies*. Cambridge: Polity Press.

Ross, G. (1996) 'The Limits of Political Economy: Mitterrand and the Crisis of the French Left', in A. Daley (ed.), *The Mitterrand Era – Policy Alternatives and Political Mobilisation in France*. London: Macmillan.

Ross, G. and Jenson, J. (1994) 'France: Triumph and Tragedy', in P. Anderson and P. Camiller (eds), *Mapping the West European Left*. London: Verso.

Rude, C. (1990) 'Politics and Markets: The Role of the State in the New Zealand Economy', in M. Holland and J. Boston (eds), *The Fourth Labour Government – Parties and Policy in New Zealand*. Auckland: Oxford University Press.

Sainsbury, D. (1996) 'A Competitive Economy', in G. Radice (ed.), *What Needs to Change: New Visions for Britain*. London: HarperCollins.

Sanders, D. (1999) 'The New Electoral Battleground', in A. King (ed.), *New Labour Triumphs: Britain at the Polls 1997*. Chatham: Chatham House.

Sassoon, A. S. (1996) 'Beyond Pessimism of the Intellect: Agendas for Social Justice and Change', in M. Perryman (ed.), *The Blair Agenda*. London: Lawrence & Wishart.

Sassoon, D. (1996a) *One Hundred Years of Socialism – The West European Left in the Twentieth Century*. London: I. B. Tauris.

Sassoon, D. (1996b) *Social Democracy at the Heart of Europe*. London: IPPR.

Sassoon, D. (1997) 'Introduction', in D. Sassoon (ed.), *Looking Left – European Socialism after the Cold War*. London: I. B. Tauris.

Sassoon, D. (1998) 'Fin-de-siècle Socialism – Some Historical Reflections', in R. Cuperus and J. Kandel (eds), *European Social Democracy: Transformation in Progress*. Amsterdam: Wiardi Beckman Stichting/Friedrich Ebert Stiftung.

Savasand, L. and Lindstrom, U. (1996) 'Scandinavian Political Parties and the European Union', in J. Gaffney (ed.), *Political Parties in the European Union*. London: Routledge.

Scase, R. (1977a) *Social Democracy in Capitalist Society*. London: Croom Helm.

Scase, R. (1977b) 'Social Democracy in Sweden', in W. Paterson and A. Thomas (eds), *Social Democratic Parties in Western Europe*. London: Croom Helm.

Scharpf, F. W. (1991) *Crisis and Choice in European Social Democracy*. Ithaca, NY: Cornell University Press.

Schmidt, V. (1996) 'An End to French Economic Exceptionalism? The Transformation of Business under Mitterrand', in A. Daley (ed.), *The Mitterrand Era – Policy Alternatives and Political Mobilisation in France*. London: Macmillan.

Seldon, A. (1996) 'Ideas Are Not Enough', in D. Marquand and A. Seldon (eds), *The Ideas that Shaped Post-War Britain*. London: Fontana.

Selle, P. (1991) 'The Idea of Equality and Security in Nordic Social Democracy', in L. Karvonen and J. Sunberg (eds), *Social Democracy in Transition*. Aldershot: Dartmouth.

Semetko, H., Scammell, M. and Nossiter, T. (1994) *Labour's Last Chance? The 1992 Election and Beyond*. Aldershot: Dartmouth.

Seyd, P. (1987) *The Rise and Fall of the Labour Left*. London: Macmillan.

Seyd, P. (1992) 'Party Renewal: The British Labour Party', in J. Maravall et al., *Socialist Parties in Europe*. Barcelona: Institut d'Ediciones de la Diputació de Barcelona.

Seyd, P. (1998) 'Tony Blair and New Labour', in A. King (ed.), *New Labour Triumphs: Britain at the Polls*. Chatham, NJ: Chatham House.

Seyd, P. and Whiteley, P. (1992a) *Labour's Grass Roots: The Politics of Party Membership*. Oxford: Clarendon Paperbacks.

Seyd, P. and Whiteley, P. (1992b) 'Labour's Renewal Strategy', in M. Smith and J. Spear (eds), *The Changing Labour Party*. London: Routledge.

Sferza, S. (1996) 'The Stifling Advantages of Organisational Formats: Factionalism and the French Socialist Party', in A. Daley (ed.), *The Mitterrand Era – Policy Alternatives and Political Mobilisation in France*. London: Macmillan.

Sferza, S. and Lewis, S. (1989) 'The Second Mitterrand Experiment: Charisma and the Possibilities of Partisan Renewal', in J. Howorth and G. Ross (eds), *Contemporary France, Volume Three*. London: Frances Pinter.

Share, D. (1989) *Dilemmas of Social Democracy: The Spanish Socialist Workers' Party in the 1980s*. New York: Greenwood Press.

Sharp, A. (1990) 'The Problems of Maori Affairs, 1984–89', in M. Holland and J. Boston (eds), *The Fourth Labour Government – Parties and Policy in New Zealand*. Auckland: Oxford University Press.

Shaw, E. (1988) *Discipline and Discord in the Labour Party*. Manchester: Manchester University Press.

Shaw, E. (1994a) *The Labour Party since 1979 – Crisis and Transformation*. London: Routledge.

Shaw, E. (1994b) 'Conflict and Cohesion in the British Labour Party', in D. Bell and E. Shaw (eds), *Conflict and Cohesion in Western European Social Democratic Parties*. London: Pinter Publishers.

Shaw, E. (1996a) *The Labour Party since 1945*. Oxford: Blackwell.

Shore, P. (1993) *Leading the Left*. London: Weidenfeld & Nicolson.

Singer, D. (1988) *Is Socialism Doomed?* New York: Oxford University Press.

Singleton, G. (1990) *The Accord and the Australian Labour Movement*. Carlton, Victoria: Melbourne University Press.

Skidelsky, R. (1979) 'The Decline of Keynesian Politics', in C. Crouch (ed.), *State and Economy in Contemporary Capitalism*. London: Croom Helm.

Skidelsky, R. (1987) 'Keynes's Political Legacy', in A. Kilmarnock (ed.), *The Radical Challenge: The Response of Social Democracy*. Worcester: André Deutsch.

Skidelsky, R. (1989) 'Keynes and the State', in D. Helm (ed.), *The Economic Borders of the State*. Oxford: Oxford University Press.

Skidelsky, R. (1996) 'The Fall of Keynesianism: A Historian's View', in D. Marquand and A. Seldon (eds), *The Ideas that Shaped Post-War Britain*. London: Fontana Press.

Smith, C. (1996) *New Questions for Socialism*, Fabian Society Pamphlet 577. London: Fabian Society.

Smith, G. (1990) 'Stages of European Development: Electoral Change and System Adaptation', in D. Urwin and W. Paterson (eds), *Politics in Western Europe Today*. London: Longman.

Smith, G. (1992) 'The New Party System', in G. Smith, W. Paterson, P. Merkl and S. Padgett (eds), *Developments in German Politics* London: Verso.

Smith, J. and McLean, I. (1994) 'The Poll Tax and the Electoral Register', in A. Heath, R. Jowell and J. Curtice (eds), *Labour's Last Chance? The 1992 Election and Beyond*. Cambridge: Dartmouth Publishing.

Smith, J. G. (1992) *Full Employment in the 1990s*. London: IPPR.

Smith, M. (1992) 'The Labour Party in Opposition', 'A Return to Revisionism? The Labour Party's Policy Review' and 'Continuity and Change in Labour Party Policy', in M. Smith and J. Spear (eds), *The Changing Labour Party*. London: Routledge.

Smyth, G. (1996) '"The Centre of My Political Life": Tony Blair's Sedgefield', in M. Perryman (ed.), *The Blair Agenda*. London: Lawrence & Wishart.

Spear, J. (1992) 'The Labour Party and Foreign Policy', in M. Smith and J. Spear (eds), *The Changing Labour Party*. London: Routledge.

Sopel, J. (1995) *Tony Blair – The Moderniser*. London: Bantam Books.

Soros, G. (1998) *The Crisis of Global Capitalism*. London: Little, Brown.

Soskice, D. (1985) 'Comment', in H. Machin and V. Wright (eds), *Economic Policy and Policy-Making under the Mitterrand Presidency 1981–84*. Exeter: Frances Pinter.

Spellar, J. (1994) 'Who Needs Pacts When Labour Can Win Kent?', in M. Linton (ed.), *Whatever Next?* London: Guardian/Samizdat Production

Spourdalakis, M. (1988) *The Rise of the Greek Socialist Party*. London: Routledge.

Spourdalakis, M. (1992) 'PASOK in the 1990s. Structure, Ideology, Political Strategy', in J. Maravall et al., *Socialist Parties in Europe*. Barcelona: Institut d'Ediciones de la Diputació de Barcelona.

Stark, P. (1996) *Choosing a Leader: Party Leadership Contests in Britain from Macmillan to Blair*. London: Macmillan.

Stevens, A. (1992) *The Government and Politics of France*. London: Macmillan.

Stoffaës, C. (1985) 'The Nationalisations 1981–1984: An Initial Assessment', in H. Machin and V. Wright (eds), Economic Policy and Policy-Making under the Mitterrand Presidency 1981–84. Exeter: Frances Pinter.

Sully, M. A. (1977) 'The Socialist Party of Austria', in W. Paterson and A. Thomas (eds), *Social Democratic Parties in Western Europe*. London: Croom Helm.

Summers, M. (1996) 'Only Connect: Towards a New Democratic Settlement', in M. Perryman (ed.), *The Blair Agenda*. London: Lawrence & Wishart.

Taylor, R. (1996) 'Democracy in the Workplace', in G. Radice (ed.), *What Needs to Change: New Visions for Britain*. London: HarperCollins.

Therborn, G. (1991) 'Swedish Social Democracy and the Transition from Industrial to Post-Industrial Politics', in F. F. Piven (ed.), *Labor Parties in Post-Industrial Societies*. Cambridge: Polity Press.

Therborn, G. (1991) 'Vorsprung Durch Rethink', in R. Blackburn (ed.), *After the Fall*. London: Verso.

Therborn, G. (1992) 'A Unique Chapter in the History of Democracy: The Social Democrats in Sweden', in K. Misgeld, K. Molin and K. Åmark (eds), *Creating Social Democracy – A Century of the Social Democratic Labour Party in Sweden*. University Park, Pa.: Pennsylvania University Press.

Thomas, A. (1977) 'Social Democracy in Denmark', in W. Paterson and A. Thomas (eds), *Social Democratic Parties in Western Europe*. London: Croom Helm.

Thompson, E. (1991) 'The Ends of Cold War: A Rejoinder', in R. Blackburn (ed.), *After the Fall*. London: Verso.

Thompson, N. (1996) *Political Economy and the Labour Party: The Economics of Democratic Socialism, 1884–1995*. London: UCL Press.

Thompson, W. (1993) *The Long Death of British Labourism – Interpreting a Political Culture*. London: Pluto Press.

Thomson, S. (1998) *New Labour and Stakeholding: A Brief Encounter,* Department of Politics and International Relations Working Paper No. 2. Aberdeen: University of Aberdeen.

Tilton, T. (1990) *The Political Theory of Swedish Social Democracy.* Oxford: Clarendon Press.

Tindale, S. (1996) 'A People's Europe', in G. Radice (ed.), *What Needs to Change: New Visions for Britain.* London: HarperCollins.

Trumpbour, J. (1993) 'Preface: Southern Europe Past and Present', in J. Kurth and J. Petras (eds), *Mediterranean Paradoxes – The Politics and Social Structure of Southern Europe.* Oxford: Berg.

Verney, S. (1990) 'To Be or Not to Be Within the European Community: The Party Debate and Democratic Consolidation in Greece', in G. Pridham (ed.), *Securing Democracy: Political Parties and Democratic Consolidation in Southern Europe.* London: Routledge.

Volkens, A. (1994) *Dataset CMP94. Programmatic Profiles of Political Parties in 27 Countries, 1945–1992.* Berlin: W2B.

Walden, B. (1997) *Walden On Labour Leaders.* London: BBC Education.

Walker, D. (1987) 'The First Wilson Governments, 1964–70', in P. Hennessy and A. Seldon (eds), *Ruling Performance.* Oxford: Basil Blackwell.

Walker, D. (1997) 'The Moral Agenda', in B. Brivati and T. Bale (eds), *New Labour: Precedents and Prospects.* London: Routledge.

Waller, M. et al. (eds), (1994) *Social Democracy in a Post-Communist Europe.* Ilford: Frank Cass.

Ware, A. (1996) *Political Parties and Party Systems.* Oxford: Oxford University Press.

Waters, M. (1995) *Globalization.* London: Routledge.

Whitehead, P. (1987) 'The Labour Governments, 1974–79', in P. Hennessy and A. Seldon (eds), *Ruling Performance.* Oxford: Basil Blackwell.

Whiteley, P. (1983) *The Labour Party in Crisis.* London: Methuen.

Whiteley, P. (1987) 'The Monetarist Experiments in the United States and the United Kingdom: Policy Responses to Stagflation', in H. Keman, H. Paloheimo and P. Whiteley (eds), *Coping with Economic Crisis – Alternative Responses to Economic Recession in Advanced Industrial Societies.* London: Sage Publications.

Whitwell, J. L. (1990) ' The Rogernomics Monetarist Experiment', in M. Holland and J. Boston (eds), *The Fourth Labour Government – Parties and Policy in New Zealand.* Auckland: Oxford University Press.

Wickham-Jones, M. (1998) 'New Labour and Business: The Search for Credibility', in A. Dobson and J. Stanyer (eds), *Contemporary Political Studies 1998.* Nottingham: PSA.

Wilde, L. (1994) *Modern European Socialism.* Cambridge: Dartmouth Publishing Company.

Wilkinson, H. (1996) 'The Making of a Young Country', in M. Perryman (ed.), *The Blair Agenda.* London: Lawrence & Wishart.

Wilkinson, H (1997) 'No Turning Back – Generations and the Genderquake', in G. Mulgan (ed.), *Life after Politics: New Thinking for the Twenty-First Century.* London: Fontana Books.

Wilkinson, H. and Mulgan, G. (1997) 'Freedom's Children and the Rise of Generational Politics', in G. Mulgan (ed.), *Life after Politics: New Thinking for the Twenty-First Century.* London: Fontana Books.

Williams, A. (1989) 'Socialist Economic Policies: Never off the Drawing Board?', in T. Gallagher and A. M. Williams (eds), *Southern European Socialism – Parties, Elections and the Challenge of Government*. Manchester: Manchester University Press.

Williams, M. (1990) ' The Political Economy of Privatisation', in M. Holland and J. Boston (eds), *The Fourth Labour Government – Parties and Policy in New Zealand*. Auckland: Oxford University Press.

Williams, P. M. (1972) *Crisis and Compromise – Politics in the Fourth Republic*. London: Longman Paperback.

Williams, S. (ed.), (1983) *Socialism in France: From Jaurés to Mitterrand*. London: Pinter Publishers.

Wilson, F. L. (1985) 'Trade Unions and Economic Policy', in H. Machin and V. Wright (eds), *Economic Policy and Policy-Making under the Mitterrand Presidency 1981–84*. Exeter: Frances Pinter.

Wilson, F. L. (1987) *Interest Group Politics in France*. Cambridge: Cambridge University Press.

Wilson, H. (1971) *The Labour Government, 1964–1970: A Personal Record*. London: Weidenfeld & Nicolson.

Wilson, H. (1976) *Final Term: The Labour Government, 1974–1976*. London: Weidenfeld & Nicolson.

Winter, D. (1986) 'Socialism, Markets and Market Socialism', in I. Forbes (ed.), *Market Socialism: Whose Choice?*, Fabian Society Tract 516. London: Fabian Society.

Winter, D. (1996) 'Is Collectivism Essential?', in P. King (ed.), *Socialism and the Common Good: New Fabian Essays*. London: Frank Cass.

Wiseman, J. (1996) 'A Kinder Road to Hell? Labor and the Politics of Progressive Competitiveness in Australia', in L. Panitch (ed.), *The Socialist Register 1996*. London: Merlin Press.

Wolfrey, J. (1998) 'What Price Unity? The "Plural Left" in Office', in A. Dobson and J. Stanyer (eds), *Contemporary Political Studies 1998*. Nottingham: PSA.

Wood, A. (1994) *North–South Trade, Employment and Inequality: Changing Fortunes in a Skill-Driven World*. Oxford: Clarendon Press.

Wörland, I. (1991) 'The Electoral Decline of Social Democracy: Is There a Geographical Factor?', in L. Karvonen and J. Sunberg (eds), *Social Democracy in Transition*. Aldershot: Dartmouth.

Wright, T. (1994) 'Building a New Hegemony', in M. Linton (ed.), *Whatever Next?* London: Guardian/Samizdat Production.

Wright, T. (1996) *Socialisms – Old and New*. London: Routledge.

Wright, T. (1997) *Who Dares Wins: New Labour – New Politics*, Fabian Society Pamphlet 579. London: Fabian Society.

Wright, V. (1993) 'The President and the Prime Minister: Subordination, Conflict Symbiosis or Reciprocal Parasitism?', in J. Hayward (ed.), *De Gaulle to Mitterrand – Presidential Power in France*. London: Hurst & Co.

Ziegler, P. (1993) *Wilson*. London: Weidenfeld & Nicolson.

Articles

Albert, M. and Gonenc, R. (1996) 'The Future of Rhenish Capitalism', *The Political* Quarterly, 67(3), pp. 184–93.

Altmann, D. (1988) 'The Paradox of Australian Labor's Success', *Socialist Review*, 18(1), pp. 119–28.

Bale, T. (1994) 'A Symbolic Triumph', *Fabian Review*, 107(3), p. 9.

Barber, B. (1993) 'Global Democracy or Global Law: Which Came First?', *Indiana Journal of Legal Studies*, 1(1), pp. 2–23.

Beer, S. (1997) 'Britain after Blair', *Political Quarterly*, 68(4), pp. 317–24.

Bell, D. (1988a) 'The End of Ideology Revisited (Part One)', *Government and Opposition*, 23, pp. 131–50.

Bell, D. (1988b) 'The End of Ideology Revisited (Part Two)', *Government and Opposition*, 23, pp. 321–31.

Bell, D. S. and Criddle, B. (1983) 'The French Municipal Elections of March 1983', *Parliamentary Affairs*, 36(3), pp. 248–357.

Bell, D. S. and Criddle, B. (1986a) 'Mortal Allies: The French Left in the Eighties', *Parliamentary Affairs*, 39(4), pp. 449–62.

Bell, D. S. and Criddle, B. (1986b) 'Presidential Dominance Denied: The French Parliamentary Elections of 1986', *Parliamentary Affairs*, 39(4), pp. 477–88.

Bell, D. S. and Criddle, B. (1989) 'No Majority for the President: The French Legislative Elections of June 1988', *Parliamentary Affairs*, 42(1), pp. 72–83.

Blackburn, R. (1997) 'Reflections on Blair's Velvet Revolution', *New Left Review*, 223, pp. 3–16.

Blair, T. (1993) 'Why Modernisation Matters', *Renewal*, 1(4), pp. 4–11.

Blair, T. (1995) 'Power for a Purpose', *Renewal*, 3(4), pp. 11–16.

Blau, F. and Kahn, L. (1996) 'International Differences in Male Wage Inequality: Institutions versus Market Forces', *Journal of Political Economy*, 104(4), pp. 791–837.

Blyth, M. (1997) 'Moving the Political Boundaries: Redefining the Boundaries of State Action', *Political Quarterly*, 68(3), pp. 231–40.

Boston, J. and Jackson, K. (1988) 'The New Zealand General Election of 1987', *Electoral Studies*, 7(1), pp. 70–5.

Bowd, G. (1965) 'France: La Fracture Sociale', *New Left Review*, 212, pp. 94–100.

Budge, I. and Farlie, D. (1978) 'The Potentiality of Dimensional Analyses for Explaining Voting and Party Competition (1)', *European Journal of Political Research*, 6, pp. 203–31.

Bull, M. (1993) 'The Crisis of European Socialism: Searching for a (Really) Big Idea', *West European Politics*, 16(3), pp. 413–23.

Burkitt, B. and Whyman, P. (1995) 'Lessons from Sweden: Full Employment and the Evolution of Keynesian Political Economy', *Renewal*, 3(1), pp. 24–36.

Callinicos, A. (1996) 'Betrayal and Discontent: Labour under Blair', *International Socialism*, 72, pp. 3–25.

Camilleri, J. (1986) 'After Social Democracy', *Arena*, 77, pp. 48–73.

Campanella, M. L. (1993) 'The Effects of Globalisation and Turbulence', *Government and Opposition*, 28, pp. 190–205.

Clogg, R. (1982) 'The Greek Elections of 1981', *Electoral Studies*, 1, pp. 95–9.

Coates, D. (1996) 'Labour Governments: Old Constraints and New Parameters', *New Left Review*, 219, pp. 62–77.

Cobham, D. (1984) 'French Macro-Economic Policy under President Mitterrand: An Assessment', *National Westminster Bank Quarterly Review*, February, pp. 41–51.

Cockerill, S. and Sparks, C. (1996) 'Japan in Crisis', *International Socialism*, 72, pp. 27–57.

Cole, A. (1989a) 'The French Socialist Party in Transition', *Association of Modern and Contemporary France*, 37, pp. 14–23.

Cole, A. (1989b) 'Factionalism, the French Socialist Party and the Fifth Republic: An Explanation of Intra-Party Divisions', *European Journal of Political Research*, 17, pp. 77–94.

Cole, A. (1993) 'The Presidential Party and the Fifth Republic', *West European Politics*, 16(2), pp. 49–66.

Cole, A. (1994) 'Studying Political Leadership: The Case of François Mitterrand', *Political Studies*, 42, pp. 453–468.

Corkill, D. (1996) 'Portugal Votes for Change and Stability: The Election of 1995', *West European Politics*, 19(2), pp. 403–9.

Corry, D. (1994) 'Living with Capitalism: The Macro-Economic Policy Alternatives', *Renewal*, 2(1), pp. 47–60.

Crick, B. (1997) 'Still Missing: a Public Philosophy?', *Political Quarterly*, 68(4), pp. 344–51.

Crouch, C. (1997) 'The Terms of the Neo-Liberal Consensus', *Political Quarterly*, 68(4), pp. 352–60.

Dahrendorf, R. (1996) 'On the Dahrendorf Report', *Political Quarterly*, 67(3), pp. 194–7.

Debnam, G. (1992) 'Conflict and Reform in the New Zealand Labour Party, 1984–1992', *Political Science*, 44(2), pp. 42–59.

Demos (1994) 'Open Letter to Tony Blair', 27 September 1994.

Devine, F. (1994) 'Class Politics and the Labour Party', *Renewal*, 2(4), pp. 21–31.

Driver, S. and Martell, L. (1996) 'Beyond Equality and Liberty: New Labour's Liberal-Conservatism', *Renewal*, 4(3), pp. 8–16.

Dunn, J. (1993) 'The Heritage and Future of the European Left', *Economy and Society*, 22(4), pp. 516–24.

Eatwell, R. (1993) 'The 1993 French Elections', *Political Quarterly*, 64, pp. 462–5.

Ebeling, R. M. (1993) 'Liberalism and Collectivism in the Twentieth Century', *Political Studies*, 41, pp. 66–77.

Elgie, R. (1991a) 'La Methode Rocard Existe-t-Elle?', *Association of Modern and Contemporary France*, 39, pp. 11–19.

Elgie, R. and Griggs, S. (1991) 'A Quoi Sert Le PS? The Influence of the Parti Socialiste on Public Policy since 1981', *Association of Modern and Contemporary France*, 39, pp. 20–9.

Fagerberg, J., Cappellen, Å., Mjøset, L. and Skarstein, R. (1990) 'The Decline of State Capitalism in Norway', *New Left Review*, 181, pp. 60–91.

Field, W. H. (1994) 'Electoral Volatility and the Structure of Competition: A Reassessment of Voting Patterns in Britain, 1959–1992', *West European Politics*, 17(4), pp. 149–65.

Frank, A. G. (1990) 'Revolution in Eastern Europe: Lessons for Democratic Social Movements (and Socialists?)', *Third World Quarterly*, 12(2), pp. 36–52.

Frankel, B. (1997) 'Beyond Labourism and Socialism: How the Australian Labor Party Developed the Model of "New Labour"', *New Left Review*, 221, pp. 3–33.

Frears, J. (1988) 'The 1988 French Presidential Election', *Government and Opposition*, 23(3), pp. 276–89.

Fulcher, J. (1994) 'The Social Democratic Model in Sweden: Termination and Restoration?', *Political Quarterly*, 65(2), pp. 203–13.

Gaffney, J. (1988) 'French Socialism and the Fifth Republic', *West European Politics*, 11, pp. 42–56.

Gaffney, J. (1992) 'The French Socialist Party Conference, Paris, 13–15 December 1991', *Modern and Contemporary France*, 50, pp. 10–18.

Gamble, A. and Kelly, G. (1996a) 'Stakeholder Capitalism and One Nation Socialism', *Renewal*, 4(1), pp. 23–32.

Gamble, A. and Kelly, G. (1996b) 'The New Politics of Ownership', *New Left Review*, 220, pp. 62–97.

Gillespie, R. (1993) 'A Programme for Social Democratic Revival?', *West European Politics*, 16, pp. 174–8.

Glyn, A. (1995) 'Social Democracy and Full Employment', *New Left Review*, 211, pp. 33–55.

Goldey, D. and Knapp, A. (1982) 'Time for a Change: The French Elections of 1981 – I. The Presidency', *Electoral Studies*, 1, pp. 3–42.

Goldey, D. and Knapp, A. (1982) 'Time for a Change: The French Elections of 1981 – II. The National Assembly Elections', *Electoral Studies*, 1, pp. 169–94.

Goldey, D. and Knapp, A. (1996) 'The French Presidential Election of 23 April–7 May 1995', *Electoral Studies*, 15(1), pp. 97–109.

Goldey, D. and Johnson, R. (1988) 'The French Presidential Election of 24 April–8 May and the General Election of 5–12 June 1988', *Electoral Studies*, 7(3), pp. 195–223.

Goodhart, D. (1995) 'Germany: Social Democracy and Social Market', *Renewal*, 3(1), pp. 7–14.

Gould, B. (1994) 'Review of "More Southern Discomfort" by Giles Radice and Stephen Pollard', *Renewal*, 2(1), pp. 99.

Grant, C. (1993) 'The Cul-De-Sac of the French Left', *Renewal*, 1(3), pp. 43–9.

Gregory, R. and Keeney, R. L. (1994) 'Creating Policy Alternatives Using Stakeholder Values', *Management Science*, 40(8), pp. 1035–48.

Guyomarch, A. (1993) 'The 1993 Parliamentary Election in France', *Parliamentary Affairs*, 46(4), pp. 605–36.

Hainsworth, P. (1988) 'The Re-Election of François Mitterrand: The 1988 French Presidential Election', *Parliamentary Affairs*, 41(4), pp. 536–47.

Halliday, F. (1992) 'An Encounter with Fukuyama', *New Left Review*, 193, pp. 89–95.

Hanley, D. (1993) 'Socialism Routed', *Modern and Contemporary France*, 1(4), pp. 417–27.

Hanley, D. (1996) 'The Search Goes On: The Socialists' Identity Crisis', *Modern and Contemporary France*, 4(4), pp. 507–9.

Harman, C. (1993) 'Where Is Capitalism Going?', *International Socialism*, 58(2), pp. 3–57.

Haveman, R. (1997) 'Equity with Employment', *Renewal*, 5(3/4), pp. 30–42.

Hay, C. (1994) 'Labour's Thatcherite Revisionism: Playing the "Politics of Catch-Up"', *Political Studies*, 42, pp. 700–7.

Hay, C. (1997) '*Blaijorism: Towards a One-Vision Polity?*', *Political Quarterly*, 68(4), pp. 372–8.

Heffernan, R. (1998) 'Labour's Transformation: A Staged Process with No Single Point of Origin', *Politics*, 18(2), pp. 101–6.

Heidar, K. (1993) 'The Norwegian Labour Party: "En Attendant l'Europe"', *West European Politics*, 16, pp. 62–77.

Held, D. and McGrew, A. (1993) 'Globalisation and the Liberal Democratic State', *Government and Opposition*, 23, pp. 261–88.

Hewlett, N. (1992) 'Some Thoughts in the New Stage in French Politics', *Modern and Contemporary France*, 48, pp. 22–32.

Hird, C. (1996) 'Building Societies: Stakeholding in Practice under Threat', *New Left Review*, 218, pp. 40–52.

Hirst, P and Thompson, G. (1995) 'Globalisation and the Future of the Nation State', *Economy and Society*, 24(3), pp. 408–42.

Hirst, P. and Thompson, G. (1996) 'Global Myths and National Policies', *Renewal*, 4(2), pp. 57–65.

Hobsbawm, E. (1992) 'The Crisis of Today's Ideologies', *New Left Review*, 192, pp. 55–64.

Hodges, M. and Woolcock, S. (1993) 'Atlantic Capitalism versus Rhine Capitalism in the European Community', *West European Politics*, 16(3), pp. 329–44.

Hutton, W. (1993) 'Seizing the Moment: Constitutional Change and the Modernising of Labour', *Renewal*, 1(3), pp. 50–4.

Inglehart, R. (1981) 'Post-Materialism in an Environment of Insecurity', *American Political Science Review*, 75, pp. 880–900.

Jackson, K. and Bean, C. (1982) 'The 1981 New Zealand General Election – The Problems and Effects of Third Party Intrusion', *Electoral Studies*, 1, pp. 374–80.

Jenson, J. and Ross, G. (1988) 'On the Roller Coaster: The French Left 1945–88', *New Left Review*, 171, pp. 5–44.

Johnson, C. (1991) 'Labor Governments 1891–1991: Then and Now', *Current Affairs Bulletin*.

Johnson, C. (1996) 'Shaping the Social: Keating's Integration of Social and Economic Policy', *Just Policy*, 5, pp. 9–16.

Kellner, P. (1997) 'Why the Tories Were Trounced', *Parliamentary Affairs*, 50(4), pp. 616–30.

Keman, H. (1993) 'Theoretical Approaches to Social Democracy', *Journal of Theoretical Politics*, 5, pp. 291–316.

Kenny, M. and Smith, M. J. (1997) '(Mis)understanding Blair', *Political Quarterly*, 68(3), pp. 220–30.

Kettle, M. (1996) 'The Blair Revolution: Can New Labour Deliver? R. Liddle and P. Mandelson – Review', *Renewal*, 4(2), pp. 94–7.

Kinnock, N. (1994) 'Reforming the Labour Party', Contemporary Record, *Journal of Contemporary British History*, 8(3).

Lane, J.-E. (1995) 'The Decline of the Swedish Model', *Governance*, 8, pp. 579–90.

Lane, M. (1997) 'Equality, Security, Justice and Freedom: On the Core Values of the Centre-Left', *Renewal*, 5(3/4), pp. 24–9.

Lawson, N. (1993) 'All Together Now? Community and Socialism in the Search for a New Philosophy of Governance', *Renewal*, 1(2), pp. 43–54.

Lent, A. (1997) 'Labour's Transformation: Searching for the Point of Origin', *Politics*, 17(1), pp. 9–15.

Levine, S. and Roberts, N. S. (1994) 'The New Zealand General Election and Electoral Referendum of 1993', *Political Science*, 46(1), pp. 40–69.

Levy, D. A. and Machin, H. (1986) 'How Fabius Lost: The French Elections of 1986', *Government and Opposition*, 21, pp. 269–85.

Leys, C. (1995) 'A Radical Agenda for Britain', New Left Review, 212, pp. 3–12.

Lovecy, J. (1991) '"Une Majorité à Géométrie Variable": Government, Parliament and the Parties June 1988–June 1990', *Association of Modern and Contemporary France*, 39, pp. 49–62.

Lucas, B. (1996) 'Labour, Unions and Stakeholding in Australia', *Renewal*, 4(2), pp. 28–36.

Lucio, M. M. and Weston, S. (1994) 'The Denial of Politics and the New Industrial Relations', *Renewal*, 2(1), pp. 74–80.

McAllister, I. (1991) 'Party Adaptation and Factionalism within the Australian Party System', *American Journal of Political Science*, 35(1), pp. 206–27.

MacDonald, C. and Arnold-Forster, J. (1995) *Working Together*, LINC Pamphlet 1.

Machin, H. (1982) 'The "Third Ballot" of 1981: The French Legislative Elections of 14 and 21 June', *West European Politics*, 5, pp. 94–7.

Machin, H. (1989) 'Stages and Dynamics in the Evolution of the French Party System', *West European Politics*, 12(4), pp. 59–81.

Machin, H. (1993) 'How the Socialists Lost the 1993 Elections to the French Parliament', *West European Politics*, 16, pp. 595–606.

Machin, H. and Wright, V. (1982) 'Why Mitterrand Won: The French Presidential Elections of April–May 1981', *West European Politics*, 5, pp. 5–35.

MacLean, M. (1997) 'Privatisation, Dirigisme, and the Global Economy: An End to French Exceptionalism'. Modern and Contemporary France **5(2)**, pp. 215–28.

Maley, M. and Green, P. (1988) 'The Australian Election General Election of 1987', *Electoral Studies*, 7(1), pp. 67–9.

Manent, P. and Machin, H. (1988) 'Two Views of the Mitterrand Presidency (1981–88)', *Government and Opposition*, 23, pp. 186–209.

Marquand, D. (1987) 'Beyond Social Democracy', *Political Quarterly*, 58, pp. 243–53.

Marquand, D. (1993) 'After Socialism', *Political Studies*, 41, pp. 43–56.

Marquand, D. (1997) 'After Euphoria: The Dilemmas of New Labour', *Political Quarterly*, 68(4), pp. 335–8.

Marquand, D. and Wright, T. (1996) 'Commentary: The Pimpernel of British Politics', Political Quarterly, 67(3), pp. 181–3.

Marqusee, M. (1997) 'New Labour and Its Discontents', *New Left Review*, 224, pp. 127–42.

Meidner, R. (1995) 'The Limits of Social Democracy: Investment Politics in Sweden (Review)', *Economic and Industrial Democracy*, 16(3), pp. 457–60.

Miliband, D. (1994) 'From Welfare to Wealthfare', *Renewal*, 2(1), pp. 87–90.

Miliband, R. (1992) 'Fukuyama and the Socialist Alternative', *New Left Review*, 193, pp. 108–13.

Miliband, R. (1994) 'The Plausibility of Socialism', *New Left Review*, 206, pp. 3–14.

Militant (1996) 'Worldwide: The Challenge of Globalisation', Discussion Paper.

Milner, H. (1996) 'The Welfare State As Rational Choice: Social Democracy in a Post-Socialist World', *Scandinavian Political Studies*, 19(2), pp. 151–66.

Milner, S. (1988) 'Trade Unions and Change. A Review Article', *Modern and Contemporary France*, 32, pp. 23–6.

Minogue, K. (1993) 'Ideology and the Collapse of Communism', *Political Studies*, 41, pp. 4–20.

Miyoshi, M. (1993) 'A Borderless World? From Colonialism to Transnationalism and the Decline of the Nation State', *Critical Inquiry*, 19, pp. 726–51.

Mouzelis, N. (1993) 'The Balance Sheet of the Left', *New Left Review*, 200, pp. 182–5.

Murray, C. (1986) 'No, Welfare Isn't Really the Problem', *Public Interest*, 84, pp. 3–11.

Murray, C. (1987) 'Poverty and Welfare: Another Look', *Public Interest*, 89, pp. 3–19.

Murray, C. (1990) 'The British Underclass', *Public Interest*, 99, pp. 4–28.

Murray, C. (1994) 'Welfare and the Family: The US Experience', *Journal of Labor Economics*, 11(1), pp. S224–S262.

Nayar, R. (1992) 'Book Review – The End of History and the Last Man by Francis Fukuyama', *Political Quarterly*, 63, pp. 236–359.

Norris, P. (1990) 'Thatcher's Enterprise Society and Electoral Change', *West European Politics*, 13, pp. 63–78.

Norris, P. (1997) 'Anatomy of a Labour Landslide', *Parliamentary Affairs*, 50(4), pp. 509–32.

Northcutt, W. (1991) 'François Mitterrand and the Political Use of Symbols: the Construction of a Centrist Republic', *French Historical Studies*, 17(1), pp. 141–58.

Olsen, G. M. (1996) 'Re-Modelling Sweden: The Rise and Demise of the Compromise in a Global Economy', *Social Problems*, 43(1), pp. 1–20.

O'Sullivan, N. (1993) 'Political Integration, the Limited State and the Philosophy of Post Modernism', *Political Studies*, 41, pp. 21–42.

Padgett, S. (1993) 'The German Social Democrats: A Redefinition of Social Democracy Or Bad Godesberg Mark II?', *West European Politics*, 16, pp. 20–38.

Parkin, F. (1967) 'Working Class Conservatives: A Theory of Political Deviance', *British Journal of Sociology*, 18(3), pp. 278–90.

Paterson, W. (1993) 'Reprogramming Democratic Socialism', *West European Politics*, 16, pp. 1–4.

Pennetier, J.-M. (1997) 'A "New Deal" in Europe? Reflections On the French Socialists' Victory', *Renewal*, 5(3/4), pp. 131–8.

Perkin, H. (1996) 'The Third Revolution and Stakeholder Capitalism: Convergence Or Collapse', *Political Quarterly*, 67(3), pp. 198–208.

Pierson, C. (1995) 'From Words to Deeds: Labour and the Just Society', *Renewal*, 3(1), pp. 45–55.

Pimlott, B. (1997) 'New Labour, New Era?', *Political Quarterly*, 68(4), pp. 325–34.

Pontusson, J. (1992) 'At the End of the Third Road: Swedish Social Democracy in Crisis', *Politics and Society*, 20, pp. 305–32.

Pontusson, J. (1995) 'Explaining the Decline of European Social Democracy – The Role of Structural Economic Change', *World Politics*, 147(4), pp. 495–533.

Rose, R. (1997) 'The New Labour Government: On the Crest of a Wave', *Parliamentary Affairs*, 50(4), p. 750–756.

Ross, G. (1997) 'Jospin So Far', *Politics and Society*, 15(3), pp. 9–19.

Ross, G. and Jenson, J. (1988) 'The Tragedy of the French Left', *New Left Review*, 171, pp. 5–44.

Rowthorn, R. (1992) 'Centralisation, Employment and Wage Dispersion', *Economic Journal,* 102(412), pp. 506–23.

Rubinstein, D. (1997) 'How New Is New Labour?', *Political Quarterly,* 68(4), pp. 339–43.

Russell, A. T., Johnston, R. J. and Pattie, C. J. (1992) 'Thatcher's Children: Explaining the Links Between Age and Political Attitudes', *Political Studies,* 40, pp. 742–56.

Russell, C. (1996) 'New Labour: Old Tory Writ Large', *New Left Review,* 219, pp. 78–88.

Rustin, M. (1992) 'No Exit from Capitalism?', *New Left Review,* 193, pp. 96–107.

Sanders, D. (1996) 'Economic Performance, Management Competence and the Outcome of the Next General Election', *Political Studies,* 44(2), pp. 203–31.

Shaw, E. (1993) 'Towards Renewal? The British Labour Party's Policy Review', *West European Politics,* 16, pp. 112–32.

Shaw, E. (1996) 'Book Review – Herbert Kitschelt, the Transformation of European Social Democracy', *Party Politics,* 2(3), pp. 421–4.

Shields, J. G. (1997) 'Europe's Other Landslide: The French National Assembly Elections of May–June 1997', *The Political Quarterly,* 68(4), pp. 412–24.

Skinner, P. and Nevin, B. (1995) 'Communitiarians: New Left Or Moralising Right'. *Fabian Review,* 107(1), pp. 9–11.

Smith, M. (1994) 'Understanding "The Politics of Catch-Up": The Modernisation of the Labour Party', *Political Studies,* 42, pp. 708–15.

Smith, W. Rand (1996) 'Topical Items: The View from America: Candidates and Parties in the 1995 French Presidential Election – A Conference Roundtable Held at the APSA Meeting', *Modern and Contemporary France,* 4(2), pp. 209–19.

Stigendal, M. (1995) 'The Swedish Model: Renaissance Or Retrenchment?', *Renewal,* 3(1), pp. 14–23.

Szarka, J. (1996) 'The Winning of the 1995 French Presidential Election', *West European Politics,* 19(1), pp. 151–67.

Szarka, J. (1997) 'Snatching Defeat from the Jaws of Victory: The French Parliamentary Elections of 25 May and 1 June 1997', *West European Politics,* 20(4), pp. 192–9.

Taylor, A. (1993) 'Trade Unions and the Politics of Social Democratic Renewal', *West European Politics,* 16, pp. 133–53.

Temple, N. (1994) 'The Crisis of Politics and the Democratic Left's Alternative', *Renewal,* 2(1), pp. 81–6.

Therborn, G. (1992) 'The Life and Times of Socialism', *New Left Review,* 194, pp. 17–32.

Thompson, N. (1996) 'Supply Side Socialism: The Political Economy of New Labour', *New Left Review,* 216, pp. 37–54.

Thompson, P. (1994) 'Introduction to the Future of Trade Unions', *Renewal,* 2(1), pp. 61–3.

Thompson, P. (1996) 'Stakeholding As State Strategy', *Renewal,* 4(2), pp. 3–10.

Thompson, P. (1997) 'A Third Way?', *Renewal,* 5(3/4), pp. 5–10.

Thorburn, H. G. (1968) 'Towards a Simplified Party System in France', *Canadian Journal of Political Science,* 1, pp. 204–16.

Valen, H. (1982) 'Norway: The 1981 Election Confirms Trend to the Right', *Electoral Studies,* 1, pp. 243–50.

Verheugen, G. (1994) 'German Social Democracy Before a Decisive Election Year', *Renewal,* 2(1), pp. 40–6.

Ware, A. (1992) 'Activist–Leader Relations and the Structure of Political Parties: "Exchange" Models and Vote-Seeking Behaviour in Parties', *British Journal of Political Science*, 22, pp. 71–92.

Williamson, J. (1996) 'The Road to Stakeholding', *Political Quarterly*, 67(3), pp. 209–17.

Wolinetz, S. (1991) 'Party System Change: "The Catch-All Thesis Revisited"', *West European Politics*, 14(1), pp. 113–28.

Wright, T. (1994) 'What New Politics?', *Renewal*, 2(2), pp. 75–81.

In addition to the above various issues of *Electoral Studies* and the *European Journal of Political Research* were used to obtain election statistics.

Newspapers

Barnett, A. (1998) 'The Party's Over for Tony Donations', *The Observer*, 1 February.

Baxter, S. (1995) 'Blair's Quest for the Grail of Power', *The Observer*, 16 July.

Beavis, S. (1997) 'French Lessons for the UK', *The Guardian*, 28 April.

Blair, T. (1995) 'The Flavour of Success', *The Guardian*, 6 July.

Blair, T. (1995) 'Left with No Option', *The Guardian*, 27 July.

Blair, T. (1995) 'True Story of the Wilderness Years', *The Observer*, 17 December.

Blair, T. (1996) 'Tomorrow's Socialism', *The Guardian*, 19 September.

Blair, T. (1998) 'Europe's Left-of-Centre Parties Have Discovered the "Third Way"', *The Independent*, 7 April.

Blair, T. (1998) 'In Britain Today, Millions Are Still Trapped in a Cash Economy; Vulnerable, Extorted, Prey to Loan Sharks in Britain Today, That Is Not Acceptable', *The Observer*, 31 May.

Brown, D. (1997) 'Man of the People Faces a More Polite Question Time', *The Guardian*, 14 June.

Brown, G. (1996) 'In the Real World', *The Guardian*, 2 August.

Brown, G. (1997) 'Why Labour Is Still Loyal to the Poor', *The Guardian*, 2 August.

Buckby, S. and Lawson, N. (1998) 'Third Way? No Way, Tony', *New Statesman*, 13 March.

Campbell, B. (1995) 'Grandaddy of the Backlash', *The Guardian*, 1 April.

Carton, D. (1995) 'Le Candidat Socialiste: Déjá Prépare le Second Tour', *Le Monde*, 22 April.

Carton, D. (1995) 'Renouver la Politique pour Amener plus de Françaises et de Français Á Participer Á "La Vie Publique" (interview with Lionel Jospin)', *Le Monde*, 6 May.

Carton, D., Jarreau, P. and Mauduit, L. (1995) 'Dans Cette Election, Je Porte le Rêve Face Á la Resurgence de Certaines Rêveries Bonapartistes (interview with Lionel Jospin), *Le Monde*, 21 April.

Coyle, D. and Brown, C. (1997) 'Brown's Radical Budget', *The Independent*, June 27.

Daniel, C. (1996) 'New Labour, New Networks', *New Statesman*, 27 September.

The Economist (1985) 'New Paths for Socialism', 21 December.

The Economist (1995) 'Jospin, the Surprise to Beat', 29 April.

The Economist (1996) 'Stakeholder Capitalism', 10 February.

The Economist (1996) 'Blair on the Constitution', 14 September.

The Economist (1997) 'The French Election', 24 May.
The Economist (1997) 'France Still Trapped', 5 July.
The Economist (1997) 'Lionel Jospin, équilibriste', 26 July.
The Economist (1997) 'Remodelling Scandinavia', 23 August.
The Economist (1997) 'Nobody Won', 20 September.
The Economist (1997) 'The Vision Thing', 27 September.
The Economist (1998) 'Lionel Jospin, Escape Artist', 14 February.
The Economist (1998) 'The Centre Held', 21 March.
The Economist (1998) 'The Strangest Tory Ever Sold', 2 May.
The Economist (1998) 'Jospin Discovers America', 27 June.
Elliott, L. (1997) 'In Place of Fear of Ethical Socialism', *The Guardian*, 13 January.
Elliott, L. (1998) 'Norway Keeps the Faith', *The Guardian*, 6 April.
Elliott, M. (1994) 'What's Left?', *Newsweek*, 10 October.
Etzioni, A. (1995) 'Common Values', *New Statesman*, 12 May.
Fukuyama, F. (1990) 'Forget Iraq – History Is Dead', *The Guardian*, 7 September.
Fukuyama, F. (1990) 'The World Against a Family', *The Guardian*, 12 September.
Galbraith, J. K. (1990) 'The Price of World Peace', *The Guardian*, 8 September.
Galbraith, J. K. (1991) 'The Call of Arms and the Poor Man', *The Guardian*, 27 March.
Galbraith, J. K. (1992) 'Shifting Gear, Not Direction', *The Guardian*, 25 November.
Galbraith, J. K. (1995) 'To Have and Not Have', *The Observer*, 29 October.
Giddens, A. (1995) 'What's He Up To?', *New Statesman and Society*, 24 February.
Giddens, A. (1998) 'Beyond Left and Right', *The Observer*, 13 September.
Gooch, A. (1998) 'Outsider's Surprise Win Splits Spain's Socialists', *The Guardian*, 27 April.
Gray, J. (1994) 'Setting Course for the Left', *The Guardian*, 20 June.
Gray, J. (1994) 'Into the Abyss?', *The Sunday Times*, 30 October.
Gray, J. (1994) 'Suicide of the Leviathan', *The Guardian*, 7 November.
Gray, J. (1995) 'Hollowing Out the Core', *The Guardian*, 8 March.
Gray, J. (1995) 'Casualties of the Carousel', *The Guardian*, 27 April.
Gray, J. (1995) 'Bite of the New Right', *The Guardian*, 23 October.
Gray, J. (1996) 'Putting Britain Together Again', *The Guardian*, 29 January.
Gray, J. (1996) 'What Liberalism Cannot Do', *New Statesman*, 20 September.
Gray, J. (1997) 'The Discreet Demise of the Bourgeoisie', *The Guardian*, 29 March.
Gray, J. (1997) 'Dangerous Games', *The Guardian*, 17 April.
Gray, J. (1998) 'Globalisation – The Dark Side', *New Statesman*, 13 March.
Grice, A. (1995) 'What's Left?', *The Sunday Times*, 23 July.
Grice, A. (1996) 'Has Stakeholding Shrunk to a Slogan?', *The Sunday Times*, 21 January.
Grice, A. (1996) 'The End of Socialism – Interview with Tony Blair', *The Sunday Times*, 1 September.
Grice, A. (1997) 'Left Revolts Over Blair's Power Bid', *The Sunday Times*, 12 January.
Hargreaves, I. and Richards, S. (1996) 'Interview with Tony Blair', *New Statesman*, 5 July.
Hargreaves, I., and Richards, S. (1997) 'Doomed by the Time the First Edition Came Off the Press', *New Statesman*, 24 October.

Hattersley, R. (1996) 'Balance of Power', *The Guardian*, 25 July.

Hattersley, R. (1996) 'The Silent Socialists', *The Guardian*, 4 September.

Hattersley, R. (1996) 'Back to the Future', *The Guardian*, 28 September.

Hattersley, R. (1998) 'Blair Finally Gets Some Opposition', *The Observer*, 3 May.

Helm, S. (1997) 'Lionel Jospin and Tony Blair Are Staunch Socialists... How Can They Stand So Far Apart?', *The Independent*, 7 June.

Hooper, J. (1997) 'Lisbon Talk-Alike Sets An Example for Blair', *The Guardian*, 24 January.

Hugill, B. (1996) 'Asia's High Economies Earn Their Stripes', *The Observer*, 7 January.

Hutton, W. (1992) 'Class That Plays for Keeps – Interview with J. K. Galbraith', *The Guardian*, 23 June.

Hutton, W. (1993) 'Labour Must Seize the Moment', *The Guardian*, 4 January.

Hutton, W. (1993) 'Running for the Lifeboats', *The Guardian*, 10 February.

Hutton, W. (1993) 'Keynes Is Overdue for a Comeback', *The Guardian*, 31 August.

Hutton, W. (1994) 'Monetarist Mantra Has Lost Its Magic', *The Guardian*, 12 September.

Hutton, W. (1995) 'Minimum Wage Can Return Maximum Rewards', *The Guardian*, 17 July.

Hutton, W. (1996) 'Stake That Claim', *The Guardian*, 9 January.

Hutton, W. (1996) 'Left with No Illusions', *Prospect*, March.

Hutton, W. (1997) 'Equality Is a Casualty of the Drive for Power', *The Observer*, 26 January.

Hutton, W. (1997) 'Lack of Welfare State Causes Poverty', *The Observer*, 21 December.

Hutton, W. and Kay, J. (1996) 'Only Working Together Will Save the Economy', *The Observer*, 13 October.

Jacques, M. (1996) 'His Project for the Party Is a Triumph, But What About His Project for the Country?', *The Guardian*, 26 September.

Jacques, M. and Hall, S. (1997) 'The Great Moving Centre Show', *New Statesman*, 21 November.

Jacques, M. and Hall, S. (1997) 'Les Enfants de Marx et de Coca-Cola', *New Statesman*, 28 November.

Jacques, M. and Hall, S. (1997) 'Cultural Revolutions', *New Statesman*, 5 December.

Jarreau, P. and Noblecourt, M. (1997) 'Lionel Jospin Inscrit Son Programme dans la Dureé d'Une Législature', *Le Monde*, 21 May.

Jenkins, S. (1997) 'To Thatcher, a Son', *The Times*, 1 October.

Kay, J. (1996) 'The Good Market', *Prospect*, May.

Kellner, P. (1997) 'Keynesianism Is Dead', *New Statesman*, 28 February.

Kellner, P. (1997) 'More Equal Than Others', *New Statesman*, 17 October.

Laurence, B. and Keegan, W. (1998) 'Galbraith on Crashes, Japan and Walking Sticks', *The Observer*, 21 June.

Leadbeater, C. (1996) 'What's the Big Idea?', *The Observer*, 4 August.

Leadbeater, C. (1997) 'Gordon and the Green Budget', *New Statesman*, 28 November.

Leadbeater, C. and Mulgan, G. (1996) 'Stakeholding: Nice Idea, Shame About the Reality', *The Observer*, 6 October.

Lloyd, J. (1997) 'More Equal Than Ever', *New Statesman*, 24 January.

Lloyd, J. (1997) 'So Speaks the Prophet of New Capitalism: "The UK Has a Chance to Chart a Different Path: Neither the Zero-Sum Game of Europe, Nor America's Cruelties"', *New Statesman*, 14 November.

Lloyd, J. (1997) 'In the Steps of Tony Benn', *New Statesman*, 5 December.

MacAskill, E. (1998) 'Stuff That Envelope, Say the Activists', *The Guardian*, 23 June.

MacShane, D. (1997) 'French Disconnection', *Prospect*, July.

McSmith, A. (1996) 'Changes to the Labour Party Policies since May 1992', *The Observer*, 30 June.

McSmith, A. (1998) 'Third Way? Which Way?', *The Observer*, 10 May.

Maguire, K. (1998) 'The Full Tony – Interview with Tony Blair', *The Scottish Mirror*, 20 March.

Mann, N. (1994) 'Blair Faces Row Over Timetable for Clause Four Revision', *New Statesman and Society*, 9 December.

Marquand, D. (1992) 'Labour and the Implications of Post-Socialism', *The Guardian*, 23 June.

Marquand, D. (1993) 'Labour's New Model Party', *The Guardian*, 26 May.

Marquand, D. (1995) 'Vision Wanted', *The Guardian*, 18 September.

Marquand, D. (1996) 'A Stake Through the Heart of Old Simplicities', *The Independent*, 15 January.

Marquand, D. (1996) 'How Radical Is Tony Blair?', *Parliament*, March.

Marquand, D. (1996) 'Victorian Values, Modern Strife', *The Guardian*, 28 October.

Marquand, D. (1997) 'The Real Choice Here', *The Guardian*, 27 March.

Marquand, D. (1997) 'Blair's Split Personality', *The Guardian*, 16 July.

Marquand, D. (1998) 'The Blair Paradox', *Prospect*, May.

Marquand, D. and Wright, T. (1995) 'Engaging the Eggheads', *The Guardian*, 11 December.

Mauduit, L. (1995) 'Le PS Admet L'Etat Puisse Vendre des Participations Minoritaires', *Le Monde*, 7 May.

Mulgan, G. (1996) 'What's Left in the Heart of the Left?', *The Observer*, 21 July.

Mulgan, G. (1997) 'On the Brink of a Real Society', *The Guardian*, 1 February.

Murray, C. (1994) 'White America's Deadly Seducer', *The Observer*, 23 October.

Murray, C. (1997) 'Freedom Like You Never Knew', *The Sunday Times*, 2 February.

Noblecourt, M. (1997) 'Une Inflexion sur la Fiscalité de L'Épargne', *Le Monde*, 5 May.

Noblecourt, M. (1997) 'Changeons D'Avenir, Changeons De Majorité: Nos Engagements pour la France', *Le Monde*, 3 May.

Noblecourt, M. (1997) 'Lionel Jospin Invoque Tony Blair pour Revigorer la Campagne Du PS', *Le Monde*, 5 May.

The Observer (1997) 'Aiming for Convergence: Portugal', 10 August.

Pilger, J. (1996) 'The End of the Keating Myth', *New Statesman and Society*, 8 March.

Prospect (1997) 'Roundtable On Britain: After the Landslide', June.

Regeneration (1994) 'So You Want Change? Interview with Tony Blair', Issue 1, Winter.

Reich, R. (1997) 'The Dangers of Moving to the Mushy Middle', *The Observer*, 27 April.

Richards, S. (1997) 'The Inner Circle Is Broken', *New Statesman*, 21 November.

Rousanvallon, P. (1995) 'Jospin et la Nouvelle Culture Politique de la Gauche', *Libération*, 4 May.

Rustin, M. (1996) 'The Clintonising of New Labour', *The Guardian*, 18 November.

Ryan, L. (1990) 'Has Socialism Failed?', *Living Marxism*, April 1990.

Sassoon, D. (1996) 'Riformisti... Renovadores... Les Nouveaux Realistes ... New Labour ...', *The Observer*, 24 November.

Sassoon, D. (1997) 'Don't Misread Jospin', *New Statesman*, 25 April.

Seabrook, J. (1996) 'Not a Lot to Smile About', *New Statesman*, 19 January.

Seyd, P. and Whiteley, P. (1994) 'Red in Tooth and Clause', *New Statesman and Society*, 9 December.

Simpson, J. (1996) 'Verbal Remedies', *The Guardian*, 3 June.

Soros, G. and Giddens, A. (1997) 'Beyond Chaos and Dogma', *New Statesman*, 31 October.

Soskice, D. (1996) 'The State We're In', *Prospect*, April.

Thomas, R. (1997) 'Britain Hailed as Model for German Revival', *The Guardian*, 20 August.

The Times (1997) 'Leader', 2 June.

Traynor, I. (1998) 'Schröder Heads for the Centre with Pro-EU Tack', *The Guardian*, 3 March.

Traynor, I. (1998) 'Kohl's Rival Masters New Media Politics', *The Guardian*, 4 March.

Traynor, I. (1998) 'Jobs, Jobs, Jobs, Says Schröder', *The Guardian*, 18 April.

Traynor, I. (1998) 'Schröder Says Bonn Is Taking Brakes Off EU Social Policy', *The Guardian*, 11 November.

Traynor, I. and Walker, D. (1998) 'Pretty in Pink', *The Guardian*, 15 September.

Tribune (1996) *Conference Facts*, 4 October.

Veltroni, W. (1997) 'Right to Be Left', *The Guardian*, 28 February.

Walker, M. (1995) 'Community Spirit', *The Guardian*, 13 March.

Webb, B. (1996) 'The Big Idea?', *New Statesman*, 29 March.

Webster, P. (1994) 'Socialists Strive for Unity as They Look to Elections', *The Guardian*, 19 November.

Webster, P. (1995) 'Victorious Jospin to Take High Moral Road in Poll', *The Guardian*, 6 February.

Webster, P. (1995) 'Balladur Pull-Out Bolsters Chirac', *The Guardian*, 24 April.

Webster, P. (1995) 'Rivals Rally to Chirac', *The Guardian*, 1 May.

Webster, P. (1997) 'Paris Plans Jobs Blitz for Young', *The Guardian*, 31 July.

Webster, P. (1998) 'Le Pen's Extremists Gain and Gaullists Lose in Regional Polls', *The Guardian*, 17 March.

Webster, P. (1998) 'French Left Takes Rightwing Bastions', *Guardian Weekly*, 22 March.

White, M. (1995) 'Blair Acts to Head Off Rebels', *The Guardian*, 2 October.

White, M. (1996) 'Hard Sell On the Road to Downing Street', *The Guardian*, 5 July.

White, M. (1996) 'Question for All British Voters: Is Tony Blair a Liberal?', *The Guardian*, 1996.

Whiteley, P. (1997) 'Flirting with Marginals', *The Guardian*, 24 February.

Whiteley, P. and Seyd, P. (1998) 'Blair's Armchair Supporters', *The Guardian*, 7 April.

Wilkinson, R. (1998) 'Why Inequality Is Bad for You', *Marxism Today*, November/December.

Wintour, P. (1995) 'Scargill Threat to Leave after Clause IV Rebuff', *The Guardian*, 4 October.
Wintour, P. (1995) 'How the Party Fixed the Show', *The Guardian*, 7 October.
Wintour, P. (1997) 'The Death of Tax and Spend', *The Observer*, 26 January.
Wintour, P. (1997) 'Tony – Spend the Money. Interview with Tony Blair', *The Observer*, 23 November.
Wintour, P. and Adonis, A. (1996) 'Tony Blair: Why I Won't Tax and Spend', *The Observer*, 29 September.
Wright, T. (1995) 'Old Labour Up in Smoke', *The Guardian*, 29 May.
Wright, T. and Marquand, D. (1995) 'Come the Revolution', *The Guardian*, 23 October.

In addition to the above articles regular reference was made to *The Guardian, The Times, The Sunday Times, Daily Telegraph, The Independent, The Observer, The Financial Times, The Economist, Prospect* and *The New Statesman*.

Audio tapes

Benn, T. (1994) *The Benn Tapes*. BBC Radio Collection.

Broadcasts

Analysis (1995) *John Kampfner on the Philosophical Heart of New Labour*. BBC Radio Four, 17 December.
Analysis (1995) *Peter Jay and Paul Kennedy – Globalization and Its Discontents: The 1996 Analysis Lecture*. BBC Radio Four Transcript, 30 May.
Hutton, W. (1996) *Broke? False Economy*. October Films, Broadcast on Channel Four (Programme One, 4 June; Programme Two, 11 June; Programme Three, 18 June).

Unpublished papers

Bell, D. S. (1998) *Social Democratic Modernisation and the Jospin Government in France: Closing the Parenthesis?* ECPR Joint Sessions Warwick, March.
Clarke, H. D., Stewart, M. C. and Whiteley, P. (1996) *New Models for New Labour: The Political Economy of Labour Party Support Since 1992*. EPOP Conference, Sheffield 13–15 September.
Cole, A. (1998) *French Socialism in Longitudinal Comparative Perspective: Systemic Transformation and Partisan Identity*. ECPR Joint Sessions, Warwick, March.
Driver, S. and Martell, L. (1996) *New Labour's Communitarianisms*. Paper presented to EPOP Conference, Sheffield, 13–15 September.
Ersson, S. (1998) *Does Social Democracy Have An Impact On Public Policies and Socio-Economic Outcomes Any More? A Study of Social Democracy in Western Europe from the Mid-1970s to the Mid-1990s*. ECPR Joint Sessions, Warwick, March.
Fielding, S. (1997) *Assessing Kitschelt: The British Labour Party*. Political Studies Association Conference, Ulster, 8–10 April.
Geyer, R. (1997) *Assessing Kitschelt's the Transformation of European Social Democracy: The Case of Norway*. Political Studies Association Conference, Ulster, 8–10 April.

Grosvenor, P. (1998) *Corporate Governance and Social Cohesion in British Economic Debate: The Stakeholder Analysis*. WPSA Conference, Los Angeles, 19–21 March.

Heffernan, R. (1995) *Engineering Political Change: Thatcherism and the Reordering of British Politics, 1979–1995*. Paper Prepared for the Election, Parties and Opinion Polls Conference, London: 15–17 September.

Heffernan, R. and Stanyer, J. (1996) *Strengthening the Centre: The Labour Party, Political Communications and the Enhancement of Leadership Power*. EPOP Conference, Sheffield, 13–15 September.

Heise, A. (1997) *The British and German Models of Labour Market Regulation Compared*. Paper Prepared for Manchester International Centre for Labour Studies.

Henig, S. (1997) *Labour's Target Seats Strategy*. EPOP Conference, Essex, 26–28 September.

Jahn, D. and Henn, M. (1998) *Programmatic Adjustment of Social Democratic Labor Parties in Sweden, Germany and Great Britain*. ECPR Joint Sessions, Warwick, March.

Jochem, S. (1998) *The Social Democratic Full-Employment Model in Transition – The Scandinavian Experiences in the 80s and 90s*. ECPR Joint Sessions, Warwick, March.

Kenny, M. and Smith, M. J. (1996) *Reforming Clause IV: Tony Blair and the Modernisation of the Labour Party*. Political Studies Association Conference, Glasgow.

King, D. and Wickham-Jones, M. (1998) *Training Without the State? British Social Democracy, New Labour and Labour Markets*. ECPR Joint Sessions, Warwick, March.

Ladner, A. (1998) *Success and Metamorphosis of the Swiss Social Democratic Party*. ECPR Joint Sessions, Warwick, March.

Lent, A. (1996) *Ethos in Kinnock's Labour Party*. Paper presented to the PSA Annual Conference.

Ludlam, S. (1998) *From Social Contract to Social Partnership: Can New Labour + New Unionism = New Labourism?* Political Studies Association Conference, Keele, 7–9 April.

Marlière, D. (1997) *Assessing Kitschelt's the Transformation of European Social Democracy: The Case of France*. Political Studies Association Conference, Ulster, 8–10 April.

Millard, F. (1998) *Social Democrats and Welfare State Retrenchment: Pensions Reform in the Visegrad States*. ECPR Joint Sessions, Warwick, March.

Milner, H. (1998) *Social Democracy in the 21st Century? Prospects for the Sustainable Welfare State*. ECPR Joint Sessions, Warwick, March.

Pennings, P. (1998) *Social Democracy between Planning and Market. A Comparative Exploration of Recent Trends and Variations in the OECD*. ECPR Joint Sessions, Warwick, March.

Perkin, H. (1996) Presentation to Stakeholding Conference, University of Sheffield, March 1996.

Rhodes, M. (1997) *Globalisation, Labour Markets and Welfare States: A Future of 'Competitive Corporatism'?* Paper prepared for Manchester International Centre for Labour Studies.

Sanchez de Dios, M. (1998) *The Spanish Welfare State Under the PSOE Government* (1982–1996). ECPR Joint Sessions, Warwick, March.

Seyd, P. and Whiteley, P. (1997) *Labour's Grassroots Campaign in 1997*. Paper presented to Elections, Parties and Public Opinion Conference, Essex University, 26–28 September.

Shaw, E. (1995) *New Labour*. Paper prepared for Elections, Parties and Public Opinion Conference, Guildhall University, 15–17 September.

Shaw, E. (1996) *The Death of Social Democracy? The Left and the Politics of High Finance*. EPOP Conference, Sheffield, 13–15 September.

Shaw, E. (1998) *'Safe in Our Hands': The Blair Government and the Future of the Welfare State*. ECPR Joint Sessions, Warwick, March.

Taylor, G. (1994) *The Labour Party Policy Review: A Strategy for Renewal*. Unpublished PhD thesis, Essex University.

Vandenbroucke, F. (1998) *Globalization, Inequality and Social Democracy*. ECPR Joint Sessions, Warwick, March.

Whiteley, P. and Seyd, P. (1995) *The Dynamics of Party Activism in Britain*. EPOP Conference, London, 15–17 September.

Whiteley, P. and Seyd, P. (1997) *Labour's Grassroots Campaign in 1997*. EPOP Conference, Essex, 26–28 September.

Whiteley, P. and Seyd, P. (1998) *New Labour – New Grass Roots Party?* Paper presented at the annual meeting of the Political Studies Association, University of Keele, April.

Woollard, C. (1998) *Beyond Ideology? The Changing Conception of Citizenship in the Ideology of the Labour Party and the PCI-PDS(-DS)*. ECPR Joint Sessions, Warwick, March.

Websites

Australian Labour Party – http://www. alp. org. au/

CREST homepage – http://www. strath. ac. uk/other/CREST/

New Zealand Labour Party – http://labour. org. nz/

Nexus homepage – http://www. netnexus. org/

Translation of Jospin's 'Propositions pour la France' – http://mosique. oleane. com/elysee/engtxt/candidats/jospin/programme/

Weekly updates from the Democratic Leadership Council – WEBMASTER@LIST. DLNPPI. ORG

Index